Restoration and Revolution in Britain

British Studies Series

General Editor JEREMY BLACK

Published

Alan Booth **The British Economy in the Twentieth Century**
John Charmley **A History of Conservative Politics, 1900–1996**
David Childs **Britain since 1939** Second Edition
John Davis **A History of Britain, 1885–1939**
Gary S. De Krey **Restoration and Revolution in Britain: A Political History of the Era of Charles II and the Glorious Revolution**
David Eastwood **Government and Community in the English Provinces, 1700–1870**
Philip Edwards **The Making of the Modern English State, 1460–1660**
W. H. Fraser **A History of British Trade Unionism, 1700–1988**
John Garrard **Democratisation in Britain Elites, Civil Society and Reform since 1800**
Brian Hill **The Early Parties and Politics in Britain, 1688–1832**
Katrina Honeyman **Women, Gender and Industrialisation in England, 1700–1870**
Kevin Jeffreys **Retreat from New Jerusalem: British Politics, 1951–1964**
T. A. Jenkins **The Liberal Ascendancy, 1830–1886**
David Loades **Power In Tudor England**
Ian Machin **The Rise Of Democracy in Britain, 1830–1918**
Alan I. Macinnes **The British Revolution, 1629–1660**
Alexander Murdoch **British History, 1660–1832: National Identity And Local Culture**
Anthony Musson and W. M. Ormrod **The Evolution of English Justice: Law, Politics and Society in the Fourteenth Century**
Murray G. H. Pittock **Inventing and Resisting Britain: Cultural Identities in Britain and Ireland, 1685–1789**
Nick Smart **The National Government, 1931–40**
Howard Temperley **Britain and America since Independence**
Andrew Thorpe **A History of The British Labour Party** Second Edition

---

British Studies Series
Series Standing Order
ISBN 0-333-71691-4 hardcover
ISBN 0-333-69332-9 paperback
(*outside North America only*)

You can receive future titles in this series as they are published by placing a standing order. Please contact your bookseller or, in case of difficulty, write to us at the address below with your name and address, the title of the series and the ISBN quoted above.

Customer Services Department, Macmillan Distribution Ltd
Houndmills, Basingstoke, Hampshire RG21 6XS, England

Restoration and Revolution in Britain

A Political History of the Era of Charles II and the Glorious Revolution

Gary S. De Krey

First published 2007 by
PALGRAVE MACMILLAN
Houndmills, Basingstoke, Hampshire RG21 6XS and
175 Fifth Avenue, New York, N.Y. 10010
Companies and representatives throughout the world

PALGRAVE MACMILLAN is the global academic imprint of the Palgrave Macmillan division of St. Martin's Press, LLC and of Palgrave Macmillan Ltd. Macmillan® is a registered trademark in the United States, United Kingdom and other countries. Palgrave is a registered trademark in the European Union and other countries.

ISBN-13: 978–0–333–65103–2   hardback
ISBN-10: 0–333–65103–0   hardback
ISBN-13: 978–0–333–65104–9   paperback
ISBN-10: 0–333–65104–9   paperback

This book is printed on paper suitable for recycling and made from fully managed and sustained forest sources. Logging, pulping and manufacturing processes are expected to conform to the environmental regulations of the country of origin.

A catalogue record for this book is available from the British Library.

A catalog record for this book is available from the Library of Congress.

10   9   8   7   6   5   4   3   2   1
16   15   14   13   12   11   10   09   08   07

Printed and bound in China

For Will
son, student, friend

Contents

Preface and Acknowledgements

I have written this book in my overlapping capacities as scholar, teacher, and student of British history in the early modern period. More so than most of my previous work, this book has cast me in the role of a student; and I have written it primarily for other students, non-specialist readers, and teachers. My interests as a student took me especially into the late Stuart histories of Ireland and Scotland, about which I learned much in the course of my writing and expect to learn still more.

I hope this book will be useful as a general introduction to the period. It was never intended as a scholarly monograph. I have aimed more to produce a work informed by the most recent historical writing than one that necessarily breaks new ground itself. My own previous scholarship is evident in my treatment of some matters; and the book reflects 30 years of immersion in the sources for English political history from the 1650s to the 1710s. In treating topics about which I have not previously written, I have, however, more often turned for guidance to the work of others than to new research of my own.

As a teacher of a course about the Restoration, I am particularly aware of the need for a suitable text about this period that is written for students from different national backgrounds and with different degrees of preparation. I hope this book will work for many. I have tried to produce a readable narrative of the politics of Britain in the era of Charles II and the Glorious Revolution. In the first and last chapters I have departed from the narrative framework in order to place the political patterns and problems of the period in broader seventeenth- and eighteenth-century contexts. I have also tried to keep the needs of teachers and students of English literature in mind, and I have assumed as expansive a definition of politics as possible. Parliamentary politics are central to the book; but I have sought to take the reader into other political venues extending from the court to the streets. I have also attempted to explain the bearing of religion upon politics at every stage along the way. For the sake of clarity, I have generally modernized the spelling, punctuation, and capitalization of quotations from seventeenth-century sources. I have also sought to avoid cluttering the text with the names of too many people of secondary importance.

I have drawn upon the scholarship of many colleagues in the field; and I have profited enormously from their work. I have confined my acknowledgement of this indebtedness to the notes and have generally avoided interrupting the narrative with scholarly digressions. My perspectives have been shaped, challenged, and transformed by too many other scholars for me to attempt to name them all individually. I would, nevertheless, like to acknowledge the influence of a few historians who persuaded me, in one way or another, that I might have a vocation as a writer and teacher of history. Lawrence Stone and W. Frank Craven, among my Princeton graduate instructors, were exemplars of the craft of historical writing and interpretation. Lois Schwoerer and Henry Horwitz, senior colleagues in the field of late Stuart English history, have been particularly supportive of my research and professional development. As a teacher at my own undergraduate institution, I have appreciated the encouragement of my former teachers, current colleagues, and retired friends. Students in my 2006 Restoration seminar read through the first draft of the book and provided much useful feedback. Melinda Zook, David Scott, and Robert Bucholz gave helpful critiques of all or parts of the typescript. Finally, I need to thank the series editor, Jeremy Black, for suggesting long ago that I take on this book; and I want to thank the publishing staff for their patience in waiting for the typescript while I completed other projects.

This book is dedicated to one student whose personal growth and intellectual development have been awesome to observe.

Gary De Krey
St. Olaf College

Map 1 *Restoration England: Counties and Towns*   xi

County Abbreviations

Beds	Bedfordshire	Hants	Hampshire	Mdx	Middlesex	Som	Somerset
Berks	Berkshire	Herefs	Herefordshire	Mon	Monmouthshire	Staffs	Staffordshire
Bucks	Buckinghamshire	Herts	Hertfordshire	Northants	Northamptonshire	Warks	Warwickshire
Cambs	Cambridgeshire	Hunts	Huntingdonshire	Northumb	Northumberland	Westmld	Westmorland
Cumb	Cumberland	Lancs	Lancashire	Notts	Nottinghamshire	Wilts	Wiltshire
Derbys	Derbyshire	Leics	Leicestershire	Oxon	Oxfordshire	Worcs	Worcestershire
Gloucs	Gloucestershire	Lincs	Lincolnshire	Salop	Shropshire		

Map 2 *Restoration Scotland: Shires and Major Burghs* xii

ORKNEY

CAITHNESS

SUTHERLAND

ROSS

AND

CROMARTY

NAIRN   MORAY   BANFF

Inverness   ABERDEEN

INVERNESS   Aberdeen

KINCARDINE

Fort William   ANGUS

PERTH   Dundee

Perth   FIFE   St Andrews

CLACKMANNAN   KINROSS

ARGYLL   Stirling   Dunfermline

DUMBARTON   STIRLING

Dumbarton   WEST   EAST

RENFREW   LOTHIAN   LOTHIAN

Glasgow   Edinburgh   MIDLOTHIAN

Hamilton   BERWICK   Berwick

LANARK

PEEBLES   SELKIRK

Ayr   ROXBURGH

AYR   DUMFRIES

• Major burghs   Dumfries

WIGTOWN   KIRKCUDBRIGHT

0   50   Newcastle

Carlisle

Miles   ENGLAND

Map 3 *Restoration Ireland: Counties and Major Towns*   xiii

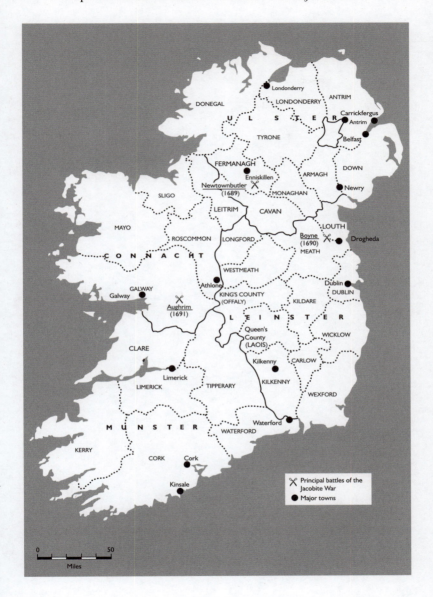

DONEGAL

Londonderry

LONDONDERRY

ANTRIM

U L S T E R

Carrickfergus

Antrim

TYRONE

Belfast

FERMANAGH

DOWN

Enniskillen

ARMAGH

Newtownbutler
(1689)

MONAGHAN

Newry

SLIGO

LEITRIM

CAVAN

MAYO

LOUTH

ROSCOMMON

LONGFORD

Boyne
(1690)

Drogheda

MEATH

C O N N A C H T

WESTMEATH

GALWAY

Athlone

Dublin

Galway

KING'S COUNTY
(OFFALY)

DUBLIN

KILDARE

Aughrim
(1691)

L E I N S T E R

Queen's
County
(LAOIS)

WICKLOW

CLARE

Kilkenny

CARLOW

LIMERICK

Limerick

TIPPERARY

KILKENNY

WEXFORD

M U N S T E R

Waterford

WATERFORD

KERRY

CORK

Cork

Kinsale

Principal battles of the
Jacobite War

Major towns

0   50

Miles

1 Revolution and Restoration, 1658–65

He had a good understanding, was well acquainted with the state of affairs both at home and abroad.... His apprehension was quick, and his imagination and memory good, which ... made him an everlasting talker. His compass of knowledge was very considerable, for he understood physic and chemistry, mechanics and navigation well, and the architecture of a ship. ... But what was the ruin of his reign, and of all his affairs, was his giving himself up to a mad range of pleasures from the very first.

Gilbert Burnet (1724)[1]

Introduction: State and Reformation, 1603–53

In 1658, few observers would have predicted that the impoverished and exiled son of Charles I would soon reclaim the rule of England, Scotland, and Ireland. His father had been executed as a tyrant in England in 1649. The regicide had followed civil wars that claimed almost 200,000 lives in the three kingdoms. In England, the wars pitted Charles I's Anglican royalist supporters against the Long Parliament chosen in 1640, or at least against that part of the Long Parliament that took up arms against the crown and remained in session until a coup by its own New Model Army in 1648. The army and the extreme puritan members of the House of Commons who survived the army's purge of moderates – a few score MPs otherwise known as the Rump – then carried out a revolution in the institutions of English government. The Stuart monarchy had been abolished. So had aristocracy, the House of Lords, and episcopacy (or government by diocesan bishops) in the established national church. The English state was re-established as the Commonwealth, which was, in theory, a republican form of government.

In Scotland, the Presbyterians were aghast at what was happening in England. They dominated the northern kingdom; and they

1

had, in two national covenants of 1638 and 1643, pledged themselves to free their church from the government of bishops. Their spokesmen in the Scots parliament had trimmed the prerogatives of the crown in the early 1640s, but Scottish Presbyterians were still largely committed to a Stuart dynasty that had ruled in Scotland for centuries before it had inherited the English throne. In Ireland, Charles I's death brought a greater degree of unity to an uneasy alliance of Irish Catholic rebels and English royalists against the parliamentary puritans concentrated in Dublin and in the north. The Catholic rebels there hoped to undo the Irish Reformation.

A zealous minority of puritan hard-liners in the army and parliament carried out the 1649 revolution in England. The English Presbyterians, who had hitherto dominated the puritan movement as well as the Long Parliament, opposed them, as did Charles I's original Anglican royalist supporters. The revolution was clearly unacceptable to many, then; and the Commonwealth began as a precarious regime anchored to the large standing army that had imposed it. Yet nothing was inevitable, by 1658, about the restoration of Charles Stuart, as the son of Charles I was known to his English adversaries. In the decade between 1649 and 1658, the puritan general Oliver Cromwell had eliminated many of the handicaps of the republican regime. He had subdued the New Model Army, the English republicans and democratic Levellers, the growing number of separatist religious sects (the Baptists and Quakers among them), the Irish Catholics, and the Scottish Presbyterians. Furthermore, after 1653, the revolution had given way, under Cromwell's guidance, to the Protectorate, a new and seemingly more durable institutional settlement of British political and religious life. As lord protector, Cromwell worked to reconcile the landed social elite to a regime that was increasingly less republican; and he maintained a state church acceptable to a broad spectrum of Protestants.

Cromwell can be interpreted as a consolidator of the revolution, then, and as a precursor of the French Bonaparte. But could he have succeeded in institutionalizing a new political and religious order for Britain? We can never know for certain. Cromwell died in 1658 before completing his work, and his efforts at settlement were quickly overwhelmed thereafter by political tensions he had only partially contained. He had nevertheless achieved a measure of success in dealing with the limitations of the Stuart state that had undermined Charles I and would also impinge upon the rule of Charles II.

What were these enduring limitations upon state authority in early modern Britain? The early modern kingdoms of England and Scotland, as well as the dependent kingdom of Ireland, were by their very nature fragile creations, quite unlike the durable, bureaucratic nation states that developed in Europe a few centuries later. They were tied together through a shared monarchy, but the Stuart kings lacked many of the financial, administrative, and military resources necessary for effective, centralized rule. Moreover, the survival of medieval parliamentary bodies in each kingdom reflected the strong desire of landed aristocrats and gentry to play a strong role in the central affairs of their kingdoms, just as they did in their counties and shires. Conflict between monarchs and local grandees in parliaments was by no means inevitable; and many recent historians have been reluctant to see the civil and military disturbances of the 1640s as outgrowths of previous constitutional quarreling.[2] Nevertheless, in England, such conflict had occurred with some regularity after 1603, when the Scottish Stuart king James VI, father of Charles I, succeeded Elizabeth I as James I of England. Events in Ireland and Scotland were also critical in the breakdown of order in Britain in the 1640s; but the disintegration of the English state in civil war between supporters of the crown and of parliament was the primary precipitant of the general collapse of royal government and of revolution.

The principal weaknesses of the English royal state were its inadequate finances, disagreements among Protestants within the established state church, and the inability of the monarchy to raise adequate military forces. James I and Charles I had too little money for a number of reasons. Their Tudor predecessors had alienated much of the land that once belonged to the monarchy; but landed income had always been the principal source of royal revenue, together with old feudal fees and the collection of customs duties on trade. James also inherited Elizabeth's debts and made matters worse by spending more than he took in on himself and his favourite courtiers. Still, the assumptions of the landed families who dominated parliament contributed as much as James's extravagance to his financial embarrassment. MPs expected the crown to live off its own resources, except under extraordinary circumstances. Even when extraordinary circumstances developed, however, parliamentary sessions could break down over the subject of additional taxation. County gentry in the House of Commons were stingy about agreeing to more taxes upon landed property because those taxes fell primarily upon themselves and their neighbours.

The English monarchy was, therefore, cash poor compared to continental states such as France and Spain. It could not afford an elaborate centralized administrative structure of government, and it relied upon the same local landed families that dominated parliament to administer their counties as unpaid justices of the peace (JPs). After 1629, Charles I sought to remedy the crown's financial liabilities without summoning parliament or relying upon parliamentary taxes. He revived lapsed feudal sources of royal revenue, and he converted one of them into an annual tax. In doing so, he provoked a reaction among many taxpayers, who refused, in increasing numbers, to pay it. They thought the king was violating a fundamental rule of English constitutional practice, namely, that the consent of subjects' representatives in parliament was necessary for any tax. By 1640, the crown was broke.

If the nobles and gentry who dominated the English parliament had trusted James and Charles, tensions about funding the royal state might have been more easily resolved. But many in parliament and many in the counties did not trust their kings. The principal source of distrust was religion. Ever since Elizabeth I's Protestant religious settlement of 1559, the clerical and lay leadership of the established Church of England had been divided between 'Anglicans' who were comfortable with a royally governed, Episcopalian, and highly liturgical church and other Protestants who were not. The chief alternate model for those who disliked the state church was John Calvin's Geneva. Their contemporary opponents generally called such people puritans, as have most historians; but those who looked to Geneva often loathed the puritan label. They thought of themselves as Reformed Protestants because they generally shared Calvin's Reformed theology of predestination; and like Calvin, they believed lay people should be actively involved with the clergy in administering the church. Referring to these people as Reformed Protestants places their religious posture in a broader European context better than the more insular puritan label.[3] It also emphasizes their commitment to the further reformation of the Church of England.

By the reign of Charles I, Reformed Protestants in the Church of England were increasingly troubled by the state of the church. They disliked the abandonment of predestination and the renewed emphasis upon liturgical ceremony encouraged by some of the bishops, especially by William Laud, who became the Archbishop of Canterbury in 1633. They read Laud's ceremonialism as a retrograde step in the English Reformation because it also elevated the authority of the clergy over the laity, obscuring the classical Protestant emphasis upon the priesthood of all believers. They disliked the Court of High Commission, which harassed puritan critics of the church leadership and operated under the authority of the king as supreme governor of the church. Indeed, puritans saw in Laud's programme a style of 'popery' that might eventually lead the kingdom back to Roman Catholicism. Moreover, since the bishops were the agents and appointees of the monarchy in governing the church, Laud's critics associated this entire development with Charles I, who had married a Catholic princess of France and had perhaps fallen under Catholic influence. The Long Parliament of 1640 was full of MPs not only determined to reverse Laud's programme but also eager to remodel the Church of England along the lines of continental Reformed churches. In 1643 they entered into a Solemn League and Covenant with the Scots Presbyterians in which they promised to do exactly that.

Increasing disagreements about funding the monarchy and about religion might have been contained but for the crown's third weakness in governing the English state. Alone among the major kingdoms of Europe, the English monarchy had never been able to afford a standing army. The English navy had been a significant force since the reign of Henry VIII, but the crown could afford soldiers only with financial support from parliament and only for limited times and objectives. The kingdom's primary means of defence, in addition to the navy, were the county militias, which could theoretically draw upon most able-bodied men. The county militias were, however, local forces rather than national ones. Moreover, although the crown chose the lieutenancy commissioners who managed the militias, the commissioners were largely chosen from the same lords and country grandees who dominated parliament and local government.

After 1618, the military weaknesses of the English state were even more apparent. In that year a general European war broke out that would become known as the Thirty Years' War. It initially pitted Protestant states and principalities against Catholic rulers headed by the Holy Roman Emperor. The chief early victim of the warfare was the Reformed Protestant elector of the Palatinate, who was also briefly a king of Bohemia, and who was James I's son-in-law. For a decade after 1618, the Protestant Reformation on the continent appeared to be in jeopardy. The English monarchy initially took no part in the conflict, however, despite a widespread desire among those of Reformed perspectives that England should come to the defence of European Protestantism. Only in 1624, just before Charles I succeeded his father, did the crown and parliament agree upon funding a land army for continental use. Unfortunately, they then disagreed about how much funding was required, about how the funding was to be raised, about how the army was to be quartered, and about who should command it. Charles's newly raised troops cost much and were frittered away in ill-planned descents upon France and Spain. England failed entirely to contribute to the defence of Protestantism; and many landed gentry were disinclined to trust Charles with further military resources. When the extension of Laud's ceremonialism into the Scottish church in 1637 provoked a Presbyterian rebellion, Charles was therefore without adequate military means to suppress it. Moreover, when Charles and the Long Parliament turned to a military resolution of their differences in 1642, both sides had to raise armies from scratch.

The English state was not alone in Europe in suffering from financial and military weaknesses. England was not unusual in experiencing sharp internal religious differences, and neither was the assertiveness of the English parliament exceptional. Rather, what was exceptional was how the operation of these factors had regularly produced internal divisions and external weaknesses. After 1640 they combined, with other factors, to produce civil war and revolution. Several continental states also exhibited internal breakdowns of varying extents in the middle of the seventeenth century; but no major continental state experienced collapse on the scale of that suffered by England.[4] As the English state divided against itself, moreover, the difficulties of Stuart rule in Scotland and Ireland were also exposed. Charles I's negotiations with the great Scottish lords and their Irish Catholic counterparts demonstrated the extent to which government in both kingdoms had always rested upon trade-offs between the crown and regional magnates, mostly Protestant in Scotland, but still heavily Catholic in much of Ireland.

This collapse of order was what Cromwell sought to address, even before the republic of 1649–53 demonstrated its inability to forge a framework of government likely to endure. Although Cromwell's rule in Britain is often treated as a continuation of the unsettlement that engulfed the three kingdoms in the 1640s, Cromwell consciously sought to overcome the weaknesses of British governing structures and to place the revolutionary state on a firmer basis. Settlement was his programme before it was Charles II's, and he addressed many of the political fault-lines that had repeatedly shaken Stuart government.

Settlement and Revolution, 1653–60

In England, Cromwell had, by 1658, established a central regime that republicans thought looked suspiciously like the one they had overthrown in 1649. Many of the five and a half million people of England and Wales were beginning to believe that disorder was a thing of the past, and most welcomed Cromwell's efforts at settlement and stability. Three parliaments sat in the five years after Cromwell seized power from the purged Rump of the Long Parliament. Historians have customarily emphasized the troubles that erupted between Cromwell and each of these bodies, but the fact that he sought to govern with the assistance of men sent from the localities is just as notable. So is his serious consideration, in 1657, of accepting the crown. Although Cromwell declined to become king, he worked with anti-republican parliamentarians to recreate as much as possible of the traditional royal framework of government. A new upper house of some 40-odd lords joined the elected House of Commons in Oliver's final parliament. He also named his eldest son, the Hampshire gentleman Richard Cromwell, as his successor, thereby affirming the ancient principle of hereditary rule.

Many of the governing institutions of Cromwell's Protectorate were also derived from or re-fashioned from those of the pre-1649 monarchy. A Privy Council appointed by the lord protector, subject to parliamentary confirmation, functioned in much the same way as the old royal council of the same name. The two chief royal law courts of England, King's Bench and Common Pleas, also continued to function, the former renamed Upper Bench. Judges travelled their twice-annual circuits in the counties as part of a largely unchanged structure of local government. County administration remained largely in the hands of JPs who met regularly in quarter sessions to try minor offences. Local commissioners superintended the collection of property taxes, as before; and county sheriffs acted as intermediaries between their counties and the regime. These offices were, moreover, increasingly in the hands of the same landed families that had dominated affairs before the outbreak of civil war. The republican regime had removed royalist, Presbyterian, and moderate gentry from local administration after 1649, or they had removed themselves, giving way to lesser squires, merchants, lawyers, and others of middling means. By 1658, however, Cromwell was achieving some success in coaxing the more substantial gentry back into the ranks of county government. Still, many new men, who had first contributed to country government after 1649, were also active. Similarly, in the towns, many of them incorporated boroughs with seats in the House of Commons, new men and old governors worked together in local magistracies.[5]

More change had occurred in the government of souls in England; but religious settlement was also being achieved by 1658. The Long Parliament had eliminated diocesan bishops and the liturgical *Book of Common Prayer*, and voluntary congregations outside the national order of parish churches had been accepted after 1649. The old puritan movement within the church had divided in the 1640s, but many of its original goals had been achieved. The Westminster confession of faith, a Reformed Protestant statement drawn up by a puritan clerical conference in 1646, more or less guided the church. The Cromwellian church was supported by most Presbyterians, who would have liked to tie it together better through elected synods and assemblies of laity and clergy. It was accepted, with various degrees of resentment, by many former Anglican clergy and laity, who remained attached to church governance by bishops. It also included many Independents, who saw the national church merely as an association of self-governing and voluntary congregations. The clergy of this Reformed Protestant establishment may have differed about some things; but many of them nevertheless identified with predestination as an explanation for justification by faith alone and preferred preaching to ceremony. The clergy sought, in good puritan fashion, to reduce idleness and drunkenness and to draw village and town populations away from the traditional community calendar of games, ales, and revels on holidays. Such godly reformation was probably as successful in producing popular resentment as in altering manners, however; and some parish traditionalists looked for inspiration to expelled Anglican clergy hostile to the new religious order.

The most apparent threat to the state church in 1658 did not come, however, from clerical or popular upholders of the pre-civil war Episcopal order. It instead came from those Protestant sects that sought freedom of religious expression outside the state church and that were uncomfortable with its privileges, especially with its collection of tithes for the maintenance of the clergy. These sectarians or separatists included some Independents who preferred complete congregational autonomy to any national establishment. They also included the Quakers and the Baptists. The Quakers, or Friends as they called themselves, were the charismatics of their day: they thought all people should be free to pursue the inner light of the Holy Spirit, and they objected to any established ministry. The Baptists, some of whom accepted predestination and some of whom did not, saw adult baptism as marking the entrance of Christians into the true church, which they conceived of as voluntary congregations of the faithful, rather than as a national church order.[6]

Political and religious settlement was a more difficult challenge in Scotland and Ireland. Each kingdom had been subdued by English republican arms and forcibly united under a common British government for the first time ever. Still, the English governors of Scotland and Ireland worked with cooperative Scottish and Irish nobles and landowners to achieve stability in each land.

Most of the Scots population, which was probably still less than a million, resided in the shires of the agricultural Lowlands, adjacent to northern England. The outlying Highlands (and Islands) were distinguished by their Gaelic culture, distinctive clan organization, and residual Roman Catholic presence. Charles II had briefly reigned in Scotland after his father's execution; but he had fled to France after Cromwell's subjugation of the Lowlands in 1650–1 and his own military defeat by the puritan general. An English conquest of the Highlands had followed, in 1654–5, after General George Monck and his forces crushed a royalist clan rebellion. The government of the Protectorate focused its energies upon institutionalizing the new union, which provided the Scots with their own representatives in the British parliaments that met under Cromwell. As commander of the army in Scotland, Monck remained the critical figure there, but central administration was placed in the hands of a Council for Scotland, and shire gentry or lairds were preferred for local administration. English officers and civilians filled many places; but the judiciary was largely in Scottish hands, and the regime hoped to attract the landowners of Scotland back into shire government as sheriffs and justices, as in England. Many great nobles had suffered the loss of lands, influence, and feudal perquisites for their royalism; but the Stuart attachments of many smaller property owners were overlooked.

The Scottish church, or kirk, was bitterly divided, as it had been ever since James I restored diocesan bishops to what had previously been a Presbyterian structure. Presbyterians had worked together to throw off the bishops, to maintain church government by presbyteries of clergy and elected laity, and to deprive the crown of the power to undo this reformation. In the wake of the execution of Charles I and of the failure of Charles II, the Scottish Presbyterians had, however, like the English puritans, divided into hostile camps. The Resolutioners, a moderate, majority faction, were prepared to accept a measure of the customary state supervision of the church. The intractable Protesters, on the other hand, sought to maintain the independence of the church and of its clergy from state control. The new Scottish government imposed by Cromwell dispensed with the church's unruly general assembly after 1653 but sought reconciliation with both Resolutioners and Protesters. It enjoyed more success with the former, whose more pronounced royalist posture in the early 1650s also inclined them to support the authority of the Protectorate.[7]

Ireland had been treated more severely in the aftermath of the English revolution of 1649. The English had dominated the island since the twelfth century, and the monarchs of England had ruled it as a separate, dependent kingdom since the reign of Henry VIII. The Irish Protestants, who had dominated Irish governing structures since the Reformation, made up about 20 per cent of the population of somewhat less than two million. They were largely of English and Scots extraction. They generally regarded Irish Catholics as lost in 'popery and superstition' and as deserving punishment for their 1641 assault upon the Protestant minority, which had coincided with the beginnings of civil troubles in England and Scotland. Several thousand Protestants had then died in Ireland, and many had been driven from their properties, as a confederacy of 'Old English' Catholics, whose families had long been in the country, and Irish royalists came to dominate much of the island.

Cromwell himself had superintended the reprisals against Irish Catholics and royalists, beginning in 1649: his English army slaughtered the Irish enemies of Protestant rule by the thousands. Indeed, his treatment of Irish Catholics was as draconian as the treatment of the Bohemian Protestants by the Catholic Emperor Ferdinand II at the beginning of the Thirty Years' War. Cromwell's Irish agenda was to advance the plantation of a Protestant and English Israel in this Gaelic Canaan. The lands of most Catholic landowners, both Irish and 'Old English', were expropriated for the benefit of new settlers, army veterans, and English parliamentary creditors. In one of the greatest upheavals in Irish social history, half the land in the kingdom changed hands within a few years. Catholic landowners who could prove their innocence of rebellion were compensated with small land holdings to the west of the River Shannon. The Catholic ecclesiastical structure that had continued to operate for a century, despite its legal proscription since the establishment of Protestantism in Elizabeth's reign, was disrupted. Most Catholic bishops, priests, and monastics were expelled. Catholic merchants and traders were banned from the Irish towns.

Despite the arrival of some new settlers, the Protestant hosts whom Cromwell envisaged as the key to transforming Ireland never arrived, however. The chief result of expropriating the Catholic elite was to establish the rule of the existing Protestant English landowners, despite their pervasive royalism in the 1640s. Many of them acquired additional lands taken from Catholics and originally granted to English army veterans and creditors, and they took the seats allotted to Ireland in Cromwell's all-British parliaments. By 1657, Henry Cromwell, second son of the lord protector, and by then Lord Deputy of Ireland, was working hand in hand with the old Protestant leaders to achieve normalcy and dominance for Irish Protestants. A broadly defined Reformed Protestant state church and Protestant JPs completed the subjection of Irish Catholics as aliens in their own land.[8]

Cromwell was, in these ways, bringing order to the entire British Isles by 1658; and, in so doing, he had also addressed the traditional weaknesses of the English state. Following in the footsteps of both the Long Parliament and the republican Rump, his regime taxed property and trade on a scale unheard of before 1640. The protector tried to overcome the religious divisions of his country-men through a religious settlement that brought Protestants of different perspectives into the same church and by tolerating sec-tarian congregations outside the establishment. A standing army of over 40,000 men – a force of which the Stuart kings could only have dreamed – maintained domestic order as well as the union of Scotland and Ireland with England. Finally, while the republi-can regime of 1649–53 had contributed little to the international advancement of Protestantism in its commercial war against the Protestant Dutch, Cromwell launched a great patriotic war against Spain in 1655, finally bringing British Protestant might to bear against continental Catholicism.

Nevertheless, Cromwell had not achieved full settlement, and the regime still had an air of improvisation. The weaknesses of the Stuart regime had been addressed, but they had not been over-come. Many who paid the heavy taxes of the Protectorate resented them and quarrelled with the legitimacy of the protector and of the parliaments who levied them. The union remained relatively unpopular in both Scotland and Ireland. Anglicans and sectarians remained hostile to the state church in England, while Catholics, Episcopalians, and some Presbyterians rejected the new religious orders of Ireland and Scotland. Many English country gentry were as suspicious of the New Model Army and its assertive republican officers as they were of Cromwell's taxes. Indeed, within the army, sectarian and republican officers and soldiers were disturbed by the protector's adoption of monarchical forms of rule: Cromwell kept the army under control primarily through his forceful person-ality and his commitment to religious reformation. Furthermore, despite the conquest of Jamaica, Cromwell's Protestant war was a disappointment: its chief result was the disruption of the English trade it was intended to advance. While Cromwell laboured to advance settlement and Protestantism, Charles Stuart nevertheless floundered abroad. He was able neither to stage a major insurrec-tion against Cromwell nor to secure significant support from the kings of France and Spain or the princes of Germany.

The protector's unexpected death in September 1658 altered the political calculus entirely, however. It was the first of several factors that quickly returned England to a state of unsettlement and civil war. Cromwell's death stimulated the energies of Baptists, Quakers, and other sectarians who sought to advance religious freedom at

the expense of the church establishment and who often also preferred republicanism in the state. Similarly, it removed from the
army the one person who could restrain officers and soldiers from
meddling in civil affairs. Renewed sectarian attacks on the church
establishment, a restless army, and an exorbitant level of taxation
eventually generated a demand, from all social ranks and from all
parts of the country, for a better settlement. Many came to prefer
a settlement along the lines of the 'ancient constitution' of government by king and parliament. Those who sought to govern after
Cromwell merely stimulated a great fear that the role of parliament
in government, the national Protestant church, and social order
would never be secured without a king. Indeed, they succeeded in
persuading the country that the alternatives to a Stuart restoration
were military rule, sectarian excess, and endless taxation. Charles II
would be restored more through the force of public opinion than
through the force of arms. His restoration represented a repudiation of the means the Interregnum regimes had adopted to overcome the traditional weaknesses of the English state.[9]

Scholars and students alike have shaken their heads trying
to make sense of the bewildering sequence of events between
Cromwell's death in 1658 and Charles's recall to England in 1660.
The essential question of these 18 months was that of who would
rule. The failure of successive answers to the question worked
in Charles's favour. The 'sober party' of moderates who had fur-
thered Oliver's settlement hoped that the mild Richard Cromwell
could be instrumental 'in the healing of the land'.[10] Richard recip-
rocated by calling a parliament in which the House of Commons
was elected from the pre-1649 borough and county constituencies.
Political moderates and supporters of the Cromwellian church
establishment held the upper hand in the large and freely elected
parliament that assembled in January 1659, much to the unease of
republicans and sectarians.

Concerned junior army officers quickly responded with secretive London gatherings on behalf of the 'good old cause' of 'civil
and spiritual liberties' now imperilled by 'all manner of tyranny
and oppression'.[11] They looked for leadership to republicans in
the House of Commons, like Sir Henry Vane, and to Richard's
kinsmen among the army generals. In April 1659, the generals deposed Richard, who lived happily ever after in obscurity,
and dismissed his parliament. In May, the generals summoned

the surviving members of the Rump of the Long Parliament to Westminster. The army and the Rump received numerous expressions of support from the voluntary congregations of separatists, and the Rump responded by inserting sectarians into the lieutenancy commissions responsible for the county militias. Government was again in the hands of those who had executed Charles I, abolished the House of Lords, and established the republic. Revolution had triumphed over settlement, though the triumph would prove short-lived.

For the remainder of 1659, the army sought first to rule with the Rump, then to rule without it, and finally to rule with it again. None of these answers to the question of who should govern received sufficient public support, however; and none of them lasted as long as Richard and his parliament. The revival of the Commonwealth was accompanied by a revival of republican and sectarian writing. John Milton, James Harrington, and Sir Henry Vane were the most accomplished of the republican theorists to appear again in print. Yet their contributions to the republican cause were ambiguous reminders of how far short of republican ideals the Rump, the remnant of a parliament elected almost a generation earlier, actually fell. Quarrelling within the Rump about a new framework for republican civil government, as well as quarrelling between the Rump and the army leaders, was interrupted in August 1659 by an anti-republican rising of disaffected Presbyterians, royalists, and moderates in Cheshire. Col John Lambert, who put down the rebellion, ended the political quarrelling as well. In October, Lambert also put down the Rump and transferred power to a Committee of Safety more to the army's liking.

Unfortunately for the colonels and the generals, the Committee of Safety was little to the liking of anybody else. Dispersed by force, Rump MPs organized resistance to the army in several counties. In London, apprentices attacked soldiers, whose presence was necessary to collect taxes; and the city government eventually rejected the legitimacy of any form of the restored Commonwealth. Legal processes ground to a halt as well: several judges of the chief law courts refused to act, even before the dispersal of the Rump. In Scotland, General Monck demanded the restoration of parliament in the form of the Rump and made preparations to move his forces south.

By the time Monck and his troops entered England in January 1660, the Rump was back at Westminster. The army re-accepted it in a desperate effort to impede the movement of opinion throughout the country in favour of another freely elected parliament or of a restoration of those Presbyterian and moderate members of the Long Parliament that had been purged in 1648. Opinion nevertheless turned against both the army and the Rump and in favour of a real parliament. 'Parliaments are the constitution fundamental of the nation,' thundered one pamphlet writer, while London apprentices affirmed that 'the interest which every man hath in the legislative power of the nation' was 'the grand and essential privilege' of the 'free people of England'.[12] As the number of manifestoes and tracts demanding a free or full parliament swelled, tax proceeds evaporated, leaving the regime as financially paralysed as Charles I had been in 1640.

What county elites throughout the country and the aroused citizens of London wanted, then, was a restoration of parliament rather than a restoration of monarchy per se. But Charles's increasingly active English agents hoped to turn the movement for parliament into a movement for king-and-parliament. In this they succeeded, largely because of General Monck. A strong supporter of parliamentary government and of the public ministry of the established church, Monck judged the Rump incapable of securing either. After arriving in London, he aligned himself with the opponents of the revived Commonwealth. The general's insistence that purged MPs of the Long Parliament should be readmitted touched off spontaneous popular celebrations that were highlighted by the roasting of beef rumps. The news of Monck's decision 'ran like wild fire', according to one London diarist, who soon observed 'bonfires very thick in every street, and bells ringing in every church and the greatest acclamations of joy that could possibly be expressed, and many drunk for joy'.[13]

The night of the 'roasting of the Rump' was a celebration of the recovery of settlement from the revolutionary forces that had disrupted it ten months earlier. But how the demand for settlement would be answered was as yet unclear. The restored Long Parliament was the same body that had waged war against Charles I and sought to abridge his authority. It might have restored Richard Cromwell, and it might have named Monck himself lord protector. But a great fear about the possibly violent intentions of the sects and republicans, stimulated by the country's descent into near anarchy, was now driving opinion in a royalist direction.

'Everybody now drink[s] the king's health,' recorded Samuel Pepys in London on 6 March, and royalist propaganda was by then circulating freely.[14] The widespread demand for a free parliament could also be answered only through a new election of MPs, as many in the Long Parliament recognized. They therefore quickly adopted a provisional and 'Presbyterian' settlement and retired from the scene. They placed county militias back in the hands of landed county leaders. They reaffirmed the Solemn League and Covenant, the agreement under which the English and the Scots had sought together to impose limited monarchy, parliament, and a Reformed church on Charles I. With Monck in London to maintain order, the Long Parliament deferred the question of who would rule to its successor. It dissolved itself after providing for a new parliamentary election.

As electors throughout England chose their MPs, two events ended all doubt that the ensuing Convention – so called because, as a parliament, it met without royal sanction – would summon Charles from his exile in the Netherlands. The first of these was Charles's Declaration of Breda, issued on 4 April 1660. Charles assured his future subjects that he had the same regard for their 'just, ancient and fundamental rights' as for his own, and he offered both a generous pardon and liberty for conscience, each subject to parliamentary confirmation.[15] The second event that assisted Charles was a last-ditch republican revolt against the emerging settlement. Led by the diehard Col Lambert, the revolt failed, but it confirmed the conviction of Reformed Protestants and Episcopal royalists alike that security could be found only in the king.

Few republicans were chosen for seats in the Convention, which was elected from the customary constituencies, the counties and those incorporated towns or boroughs with parliamentary representation. Most members were elected from the 200 boroughs rather than from the 50 counties of England and Wales, but many towns preferred wealthy and influential county landowners as their MPs. The 548 members of the House of Commons were almost evenly divided between those whose families had supported parliament in the 1640s and those who had supported the crown. Three-quarters of the members who had never sat in a parliament were Episcopalian royalists ready to return diocesan bishops to the church; but overall, Reformed Protestants of different persuasions were perhaps as numerous as Anglicans. The Convention met on 25 April 1660. Within a week, the old nobility had taken their place in the House of Lords; and the Convention had voted to restore government by king, lords, and commons. Charles II arrived in London on his 30th birthday, 29 May, amid unparalleled scenes of popular approval. His cavalcade required seven hours to pass through London streets clogged by residents and sightseers. 'I stood in the Strand, and beheld it, and blessed God,' wrote John Evelyn; 'And all this without one drop of blood. ... It was the Lord's doing ... for such a Restoration was never seen in ... history ... nor so joyful a day ... in this nation.'[16]

Charles II

What kind of a man was this Stuart prince who had so unexpect-edly and so miraculously, at least to his contemporaries, reclaimed the rule of his kingdoms? At six foot two, Charles towered over his contemporaries in an age in which few European males stood above five and a half feet. In many other ways, he was also a larger-than-life figure. Bred to rule, Charles had a remarkable ability to awe and to inspire those who came into contact with him, from dispirited royalist gentry to mutinous English seamen and ordinary peasants. He was not well educated by the classical standards of Renaissance humanism. Nevertheless, he possessed a lively intel-ligence. He quickly grasped the core of a problem, and this skill was arguably of greater importance in a monarch than a bookish education. Witty, flirtatious, and an 'everlasting talker', Charles was also capable of resolve. He possessed an iron determination, and necessity had encouraged an opportunistic streak in his personality. Since his mid-teens, Charles had also acted in military capacities, commanding men in arms and plotting strategies to aid his father in the west of England, for instance. Above all, he was a man of strong feelings, a person given to extremes. Charles pur-sued his private and public goals relentlessly, but he was sometimes frustrated by his inability to moderate his passions.

Many stories about Charles's early adulthood could serve to illus-trate these characteristics. Two stand out for what they foreshadow about Charles's wily risk-taking, as monarch, on behalf of major objectives and about his repeated recoveries from political missteps. The first of these stories is the tale of the 1651 battle of Worcester and of Charles's ensuing dramatic escape to France, which achieved mythic status as a 'royal miracle' during the Restoration. When Charles briefly ruled in Scotland in 1650–1, he had been frustrated at every juncture by obdurate Presbyterians. By August 1651, the occupation of major Scottish cities and fortresses by Cromwell and his invading English army might have suggested a quick retreat, on Charles's part, to the safety of France. Instead, Charles seized the initiative, crossed the English border with a force of 12,000 men, and called upon English royalists to come to his assistance. Penetrating as far as Worcester, he prepared to take a stand against a much larger army with which Cromwell quickly surrounded the city. The battle was a rout. Charles nevertheless demonstrated much courage and resourcefulness, frequently exposing himself to danger, and show-ing, according to royalist writers 'so much steadiness of mind and undaunted courage … that had not God … wonderfully preserved his sacred person, he must … have perished'.[17]

Charles escaped the carnage that followed and the executioner's axe that took the life of one of his principal commanders. For five weeks, with a price on his head as a 'malicious and dangerous traitor', he followed a circuitous route to Shoreham and to a ship bound for France. Disguised as a 'country fellow' and as a servant, with his hair close cropped, he travelled by night and sheltered by day. Frequently recognized, he always secured protection, despite the printed proc-lamations in circulation against him. In one encounter with repub-lican soldiers, he boldly rode through their midst, in disguise, as the best means of disarming any suspicions. On another occasion, as a doubtful blacksmith re-shod his horse, he gained the man's trust by assuring him 'that rogue Charles Stuart … deserved to be hanged more than all the rest for bringing in the Scots'. When his hosts and companions despaired for their safety, he roused them with his cheerfulness and pluck until at last 'it pleased the divine wisdom and goodness' to deliver him from his enemies and to France.[18]

Charles was lucky, both in 1650–1 and throughout his life. Luck is insufficient to explain his successes, however. He often prevailed against his enemies because he was astute, crafty, and more skilful – traits that were much in evidence on the road from Worcester to France. Charles also had a good understanding of circumstance and frequently outwitted his opponents through novel and risky strategies. A few decades later, in 1679, for instance, Charles's back was against the wall once more, in the most serious political crisis of his reign. The Country opposition (soon known as the Whigs), who commanded the House of Commons and public opinion, demanded that a Protestant succession take precedence over the claims of James, Duke of York, Charles's brother and heir. James's conversion to Roman Catholicism had aroused the opposition and divided the nation. As in 1651, Charles rode boldly into the ranks of his enemies and divided their counsels by taking some of them onto the Privy Council. Then, three times in 1679–81, he prorogued parliaments that challenged the hereditary succession, eventually driving his opponents to aggressive behaviour and language that strengthened his loyalist allies, the Anglican Tories. Public opinion turned back in Charles's direction, as the crown hammered home the point that the opposition was likely to revive the unsettlement of the 1640s. Charles had been lucky again. Nonetheless, Charles had also played a strong political hand of his own: the comeback king of his age, he could prevail in a jam through his own political artistry.

A second story about Charles in exile that prefigures important characteristics of Charles as a ruler is that of his brief relationship with Lucy Walter. Lucy was a Welsh gentlewoman of modest means but other endowments whom Charles impregnated in 1648, in the Netherlands, when they were both teenagers. She had already had an affair with Algernon Sidney, a parliamentary military officer and future republican political theorist, and she had high hopes for her relationship with the Stuart heir. Indeed, Walter was soon the mother of Charles's first son, later created the Duke of Monmouth and destined to become one of his father's most troublesome subjects. Lucy's relationship with Charles lasted only a year or two, however. In 1651 another royalist gentlewoman took her place, bearing Charles a daughter. Other mistresses quickly succeeded in Paris and Bruges, but Lucy Walter continued to bother Charles with demands for money and recognition until her untimely death in 1658.[19]

What is interesting here for the study of Restoration politics is the pattern Charles initiated in wooing alternate lovers in rapid succession. Royal mistresses were commonplace in the seventeenth century, of course; but Charles was uncommon in pursuing multiple mistresses, both serially and simultaneously. Charles's restoration coincided, for instance, with the beginning of his relationship with Barbara Villiers Palmer, the nineteen-year-old wife of an obscure Catholic gentleman. After Charles married Catherine of Braganza, daughter of the king of Portugal, in 1662, the extravagant, imperious Barbara dominated his court rather than the pious, infertile Catherine. Over the next decade, Charles provided Mrs Palmer with titles of nobility, a royal palace, and hundreds of thousands of pounds. Lady Castlemaine, as she became, provided Charles with five children in return.

By the late 1660s, however, Castlemaine's aging star was losing its lustre within a constellation of royal mistresses, the exact composition of which has sometimes baffled historians. A new favourite emerged in the teenage actress Eleanor (Nell) Gwyn. Described by the diarist Samuel Pepys as 'a bold merry slut',[20] Nell had learned the colourful language with which she entertained the king in a Drury Lane brothel. As a social underling, however, Nell was forced to share Charles's affections with an aristocratic French rival, Louise de Kéroualle, who took Barbara's place as Charles's leading lady. Created Duchess of Portsmouth, Louise would become a symbol of English resentment about French and Catholic influences at court. Indeed, Gwyn would once charm an angry anti-Catholic crowd, which had mistaken her for Portsmouth, by proudly informing them that she was the '*Protestant* whore'. For the next 15 years, Nell and Portsmouth would exchange insults as they took their turns with Charles. In 1677, the rhythm of their antagonism was disrupted, however, by the arrival of yet a third favourite. Hortense de Mancini, the Duchesse du Mazarin, was niece to the great Cardinal Mazarin who had ruled France during the minority of Louis XIV.[21]

By the time of his death in 1685, Charles had acknowledged a dozen illegitimate children by these and other mistresses; and he had acquired the nickname 'Old Rowley', after one of his best breeding stallions. More than Charles's reputation was damaged, however, by a royal household so disorderly that it bore comparison to a stable. In the patriarchal political theory that was pointedly revived after 1660 by Church of England propagandists, the king's authority, derived from God, was also that of a 'father over many families'. The authority of fathers and the authority of kings were understood as the same. Just as a father naturally exercised authority over the wife, children, and servants who made up his household, so the king's duties were those of a father writ large. The king exercised 'an universal fatherly care of his people' wrote one advocate of patriarchal theory, while another noted that 'a household is a kind of little common-wealth, and a common-wealth a great household'.[22] Patriarchalism was, above all, intended to maintain natural order among the competing demands of individuals in the household and in the commonwealth. Without it, God's intended order for human-kind would collapse. For that reason, any rebellion against the king in the commonwealth or against the father in the household was also sinful rebellion against God.

Yet Charles II's personal behaviour clearly strained patriarchal theory to the breaking point. His household was a harem. His wife's conjugal claims were ignored, while Charles romped from bed to bed. His children by adultery were legion. His personal life was a sexual analogue to the political anarchy that royalists found in the collapse of monarchy in the 1640s. Charles had been restored so that the natural order of governance might be recovered and his people might have 'an honest and peaceable life' under him. But if Charles's kingdoms were great households, his own household was not fit for imitation. A mere three years after Charles's 'happy restoration', Samuel Pepys had reason to reflect 'upon the unhappy posture of things at this time'. Pepys found the root of the trouble in the disorder of the king's household. 'My Lady Castlemaine rules him,' he lamented in language suggesting an inversion of the conventional subordination of women to men.[23]

If that fundamental convention could be undermined, then why not others? In Charles's England, ordinary men and women mocked their monarch openly: one Londoner claimed that the king kept 'nothing but whores' and was 'a scourge to the nation'.[24] In Charles's household, the eldest son, the Duke of Monmouth, intrigued against his father to obtain his political inheritance. Indeed, some Whigs sought legitimacy for Monmouth by claiming that Charles had actually married Lucy Walter. Furthermore, in the great political crisis about the succession with which Charles's reign climaxed, the divisions of the kingdom reflected the disorder of the royal household. The Whig and Tory parties became focussed on the rival claims to the throne of Charles's son and of his brother. Charles would need all the skills he possessed to govern his kingdoms, for his personal behaviour bred disrespect and opposition inimical to the order he sought to maintain. Indeed, his dissolute habits exacerbated the weaknesses of the English state that were restored with him.

Charles and Settlement, 1660–1

The question of *who* would rule in England was decisively answered when the Convention restored Charles. The question of *how* Charles would rule any of his kingdoms remained undetermined. Moreover, those who rejoiced at Charles's return rejoiced for a variety of incompatible reasons: settlement meant different things to different people in each of his kingdoms. Charles worked to satisfy as many interests as possible, or at least to satisfy all those who had actively contributed to his restoration. In England, as he set up his Privy Council, he sought to balance royalists and Anglicans with old parliamentarians and Presbyterians. Sir Edward Hyde, who had been his lord chancellor in exile, retained that office. Of the two offices of secretary of state, one went to a royalist exile; the other went to a Presbyterian. The Treasury went to a royalist courtier. The Exchequer went to Sir Anthony Ashley Cooper, a political survivor who had sat in all the parliaments of the Protectorate. General Monck, now promoted to the peerage as the Duke of Albermarle, became captain-general of the army. Charles's brother James, Duke of York, was named lord high admiral of the navy. The central common law courts were re-established under the direction of judges who had served the Commonwealth and the Protectorate, with a few surviving royalist judges thrown in for good measure.

Appointments for Scotland and Ireland followed somewhat different patterns, reflecting the divergent circumstances of those kingdoms. Determined to rule his domains separately, Charles abandoned the Cromwellian union of the 1650s. Scotland and Ireland reverted to their pre-Interregnum political institutions. Charles was more worried about the problem of political contagions in one kingdom spreading into the others than he was about the problem of coordinating his rule in multiple kingdoms. Keeping his kingdoms separate from one another seemed the safest approach.

In Scotland, power was returned to royalist nobles and lairds, including the Presbyterian Resolutioners who had backed Charles's rule in 1650–1. Charles's most important appointments included John Maitland, Earl of Lauderdale, as secretary of state and John Middleton, Earl of Middleton, as his commissioner to parliament. A former supporter of the Presbyterian covenants, Lauderdale had befriended Charles after the execution of his father and shared Charles's desire for a broad settlement that would accommodate many interests. Lauderdale would wield effective power in the kingdom for much of the next two decades; but Middleton, who was close to Hyde, and an opponent of Presbyterianism, was at first dominant. Charles also provided some offices to the Protesters, the more outspoken Covenanters, who had sought to maintain the autonomy of the Scottish kirk.

Despite the suggestion of balance, the political pendulum in Scotland had, however, swung against those who had been most adamant about the covenants or who had become too strongly identified with the Interregnum government. As Scotland was re-established as a separate kingdom, it was re-established under the authority of its great lords, who, whatever their attitudes toward Charles I, had come to see the restoration of Stuart authority as the best means of maintaining their own. On the whole, Charles's appointments to office in Scotland were drawn from a roster of the country's leading magnates, some of whom still headed significant clientage networks. The 60 Scottish peers would soon resume their place in the customary unicameral Scots parliament of some 200 members. There they dominated the 60-odd commissioners of the shires (mostly lairds), the like number of burgh commissioners, and the dozen bishops who sat as a clerical estate.[25]

In Ireland, Charles favoured the ascendant Protestant interest of old families and new settlers that had gained property and influence in the 1650s. They had worked for settlement with Henry Cromwell, had supported a broad Protestant church, and had been threatened by the collapse of the Protectorate in 1659. Most of them had been anxious about the revival of the English republic, the agitation of the sects, and the Rump's replacement of the Cromwellian government in Ireland with one of its own devising. Led by such magnates as Roger Boyle, Lord Broghill, Protestant leaders acted to restore settlement to Ireland while England was still in uproar. They toppled the republican regime at Dublin in December 1659; and they gravitated towards a Stuart restoration ahead of the Long Parliament by summoning a Convention chosen, like previous Irish parliaments, from the kingdom's counties and boroughs.

Charles responded to these circumstances by creating an Irish government headed by supportive Irish Protestants and English Presbyterians. Albermarle (Monck) became a figurehead lord lieutenant, while Broghill (now the Earl of Orrery) became one of the resident lords justices charged with the actual administration of the kingdom. Conspicuously absent from this initial royal settlement of Ireland was James Butler, Duke of Ormond, titular head of the English nobility in Ireland, once Charles I's lord lieutenant, and a long-time friend of Charles II. Ormond's earlier promises to Irish Catholics on behalf of Charles I and his strong Episcopalian attachments made him an impolitic choice for Irish administration in 1660. But the revival of Anglicanism in England and the political collapse of Presbyterianism in 1661 would soon turn his deficiencies into assets. Becoming lord lieutenant again in 1662, Ormond would administer Ireland for much of the rest of Charles's reign in the traditional vice-regal style, with little reliance on the weak Irish parliament.[26]

The success of Charles's settlement in England required as much attention to policy as to personnel. He was determined to exercise his full authority as monarch, while also respecting the limitations upon kingship that the Long Parliament had adopted in 1641 and that his father had then accepted. Prerogative courts that operated under royal authority, like the Star Chamber, were gone forever, as were non-parliamentary taxation and feudal revenues the crown had once collected. On the other hand, Charles retained control of his own ministers and latitude in calling, proroguing, and dissolving parliament, although the 1641 Triennial Act did permit parliament to assemble without royal summons after an interval of three years. He also possessed the initiative in foreign affairs, which he exercised immediately by concluding the war with Spain left over from Cromwell's day. Still, a broadly based settlement would require compromises over a variety of important issues in church and state. Fortunately, Charles hoped to rule as a king of moderation, compromising where he could and reaching out to most subjects, despite their divergent political and religious views.[27] In seeking to rule through judicious compromises, he was joined by Sir Edward Hyde, the principal parliamentary architect of settlement in England and the dominant figure in British politics in the early Restoration.

Vastly experienced, and vastly aware of his experience, Hyde rubbed many of his contemporaries the wrong way. His relationship with Charles was often prickly: he acted as a micro-managing parent, first to a king in exile, and then to a king in power who was prone to teenager-like bursts of impulsivity. Hyde has been unfairly caricatured as an intolerant and punitive churchman; but he did take both his Episcopalian faith and his moral propriety seriously, unlike Charles and most of the court. His stern moral code also led him into occasional overreactions, like his response to his daughter Anne's announcement, shortly after the restoration, that she was pregnant and that the king's brother, James, was the father. Hyde's relationship with the royal family was jeopardized by Anne's claim that James had promised to wed her, for royal marriage to a commoner was almost unthinkable. Putting his king above his daughter, whom he thought guilty of royal entrapment, Hyde proposed that 'an act of parliament should be immediately passed for the cutting off her head'. This solution proved unnecessary when James embraced Anne as his wife and Hyde was given a baronage, which ended the awkwardness about Anne's lowly status. The marriage also proved fortunate, producing two subsequent Stuart queens in Mary II and her sister Anne.

Hyde's critics claimed, however, that he had merely used his daughter to increase his hold upon power and to pass the crown to his own progeny. In fact, as his parliamentary solution to the pregnancy crisis suggests, Hyde took his stand upon statute law, even above the closest family relationships. He sought to erect the institutions of restored royal government upon respect for English law and custom and upon veneration for the traditional or 'ancient' constitution, of which law was the anchor. As a member of the Long Parliament, he had acted in 1640–1 to restrain Charles I's government from what he saw as its abuse of the law. Turning royalist thereafter, he did so again to protect legal customs and institutions from further trespass, this time by parliament itself. The law was his constant frame of reference. Having seen both king and parliament act contrary to it, he was determined to prevent either from doing so again. He sought to navigate king and parliament between the opposite shoals of French-style absolutism and what he saw as the parliamentary tyranny that had climaxed in the Rump.[28]

In the two 1660 sessions of the Convention Parliament, Charles and Hyde found many members willing to work for balanced, moderate solutions in church and state. The roughly equal numbers of Reformed Protestants and Anglicans in the House of Commons suggested that moderation was the best policy. In the restored House of Lords, older Presbyterian peers had lost the initiative to younger Anglican royalists; but the Presbyterians remained a strong interest. Moreover, Anglican royalism was weakened in the Lords by the absence of the bishops, who had been expelled by act of parliament in 1642. [29]

At the government's urging, parliament quickly adopted a bill of Indemnity and Oblivion that provided full pardon to all who had committed 'crimes' against Charles or his father, with only 33 exceptions. The exceptions were largely members of the judicial court that had condemned Charles I to death; but even many of them escaped the most severe punishment. Ten regicides were publicly executed almost immediately, and a few others, including Sir Henry Vane, followed in 1662. But other leading republicans fled abroad, chiefly to the Netherlands and Switzerland. The tombs of the parliamentary and republican notables at Westminster Abbey were emptied, and the remains of Cromwell and others were ritually desecrated and hanged. Still, virtually all those who had commanded men in arms against Charles I, who had sat in irregular parliaments, and who had held positions of responsibility in the Interregnum governments were exonerated and preserved 'in their lives, liberties, [and] estates'.[30] Charles was also moved to such generosity by his insecurity. The restored royal regime was attempting to function in kingdoms full of rich, powerful, and influential men who had worked to restrain or to destroy monarchy. The king recognized in his former enemies some of his most politically gifted subjects. Their full acquiescence in a moderate settlement could prove invaluable in assuring its success.

If Charles needed his predecessors' support, he would also have liked some of their army. Nothing was less feasible than retaining a sizable army, however, given the association of the New Model soldiery with excessive taxation in the minds of so many country gentry. The Convention Parliament paid off most of the remaining Commonwealth soldiers with short-term taxes, and it established a level of continuing taxation that was less onerous than that of the Interregnum regimes. Part of the navy was also retired. Charles was left with a 'guard' that averaged less than 4000 troops. After 1661 these forces also garrisoned the foreign possessions of Tangiers and Bombay, which were acquired as Catherine of Braganza's dowry.[31] This was clearly an army that scarcely altered the customary military weakness of the English crown. Instead, the county militias, again under the control of the natural governors of rural society, resumed their customary places. At the same time, the countryside filled with disbanded soldiers who retained their arms, their republican memories, and their potential to cause disorder.

Taxation had produced more trouble between parliament and the monarchy before 1640 than any other issue, and Charles had an even greater need for parliamentary revenues at the beginning of his reign than previous kings. He had accumulated debts in exile. He had inherited his father's debt, and parliament had deprived the crown of some customary feudal revenues in 1641. Attempting to resolve an issue that had proved so divisive in the past, the Convention determined that the crown required a peacetime or ordinary revenue of £1.2 million a year. To provide it, parliament raised the customs rates on goods entering the country, voted them for life, and added a direct tax on the purchase of alcoholic beverages. Had these taxes provided the anticipated revenue, Charles might have had sufficient funds to conduct a frugal government in the style of Elizabeth I; but Charles would rule without Elizabeth's restraint. The Convention was also unduly optimistic in its calculation that these taxes would produce the necessary £1.2 million a year. Customs receipts were kept short by the depression in foreign trade that had begun during Cromwell's war against Spain; and the failure of parliament to assume any responsibility for the crown's accumulated debt compounded the problem. Despite the Convention's good intentions, taxation would remain a source of trouble between parliament and the crown for much of Charles's reign. Yet the very fact that the Convention agreed that most of the crown's ordinary revenue must be supplied by parliament, rather than coming from its own lands and old feudal revenues, was in itself a milestone. Indeed, it was another sign that Charles was not alone in 1660 in attempting to heal the divisions of the past.[32]

Sorting out the proper ownership of lands that had been confiscated or sold under duress during the civil wars and the Interregnum was an equally troublesome issue for the Convention and for thousands of landed and tenant families. The crown, the church, and many ardent cavaliers had lost land, while some parliamentary gentry, merchants, lawyers, and tenants had enlarged their holdings. More land had changed hands than at any time since the dissolution of the monasteries in the reign of Henry VIII. The Convention restored all royal lands to the king. It also supported the return to the church of both lands and tithes that had passed into lay hands. Charles reached out to those who now lost property to the crown by privileging such individuals in the provision of new leases, establishing a pattern that also prevailed with church properties. Many dispossessed from crown and church lands were actually able to recoup the cost of their former purchases from continuing profits as lessees. Others received compensation from a royal commission.

Such healing endeavours in the land settlement irritated royalist gentry who had experienced losses. Families who had suffered confiscations since the 1640s for their attachment to the crown or for their failure to pay republican fines and taxes could only turn to the courts for the return of their properties, and many did. Royalist gentry who had actually sold land to pay punitive fines and taxes were left without such legal recourse, however, for voluntary sales were generally held to be good at law. Little wonder that given Charles's efforts to bring former parliamentarians into government and to indemnify their estates, some frustrated cavaliers claimed the king 'had passed an act of oblivion for his friends, and of indemnity for his enemies'.[33] In the end, however, many royalists recovered their properties by one means or another. Despite some redistribution of properties between 1640 and 1660, the landed order of the Restoration was largely the same order that had divided over the political issues of the 1640s.

If resolving issues about property was difficult for Charles and the Convention, resolving the most divisive issue of all – religion – proved impossible. Both Charles and Hyde favoured a healing settlement in religion, but they were simply unable to overcome the mutual distrust of Episcopal and Presbyterian clergy. Quick and decisive action by the king and parliament might have provided a moderate settlement acceptable to Anglicans and Presbyterians alike. The presence of influential and moderate Presbyterians such as Arthur Annesley (subsequently Earl of Anglesey) on the Privy Council sustained Presbyterian hopes. But the suspiciousness of some Anglican clergy for Presbyterians, who had promoted the abolition of episcopacy in the 1640s, as well as the suspiciousness of some Presbyterian clergy for Anglicans, made quick action impossible. So did confusion about who should take the initiative in settling the church. Restored to the monarchy, Charles was also thereby restored as supreme governor of the Church of England. He was expected to govern the church with the advice of parliament and with the assistance of the clergy. Yet the precise roles of parliament and of the clergy in managing church affairs had been a source of disagreement ever since the Elizabethan Reformation.

Moreover, just as land had changed hands during the civil wars and the Interregnum, so had the places or livings of many parish clergy. Hundreds of surviving Episcopal clergy who had been ejected since the late 1640s and replaced by puritan or Reformed incumbents now demanded their places back. They often had the support of local royalist landowners. After some sparring between Anglican and Presbyterian MPs, the Convention deferred consideration of the nature of the church settlement to the king and a conference of clergymen chosen by him. The Convention limited its own efforts to the question of disputed parish livings. An Act for Settling Ministers was intended as another compromise, but Anglican parish patrons and leaders employed it to begin a purge of puritan parish clergy for the sake of sequestered Anglicans. Among those who now lost their livings was Richard Baxter, a leading Presbyterian clerical spokesman.

No one doubted that the conference of Anglican and Presbyterian clergy that met at Hyde's Worcester House residence in London in September 1660 would endorse the re-establishment of episcopacy. Moderate Anglicans had revived earlier proposals for a 'reduced' episcopacy. Presbyterians agreed to an arrangement in which bishops would administer their dioceses with the assistance of the more substantial clergy. The conferees also agreed upon the need for alterations to the *Book of Common Prayer* to make it more acceptable to Presbyterians. Charles proclaimed his acceptance of these proposals as an interim church settlement in the Worcester House Declaration of October 1660, and revisions in the prayer book were delegated to a clerical synod. The declaration made no mention, however, of liberty of conscience for those Protestants who could not accept either moderated episcopacy or a revised liturgy. In the meantime, Charles began appointing bishops for the 18 dioceses of the old church structure that lacked them at the time of his restoration. (A few surviving bishops had returned to their places.) These appointments were consistent with the moderate character of the declaration and with Charles's healing principles. Three leading Presbyterians, including Richard Baxter, were offered bishoprics. Few of the new bishops could be identified with the ceremonialism of the church of Charles I and Archbishop Laud. [34]

These promising developments masked much continuing suspiciousness and uncertainty, however. Many Anglican gentry and some Presbyterian clergy were less willing to compromise than the Worcester House divines. Baxter and his fellow Presbyterian nominees declined their appointments as bishops. They preferred not to accept the office until its new design had been established by parliament, but they thereby also deprived themselves of an important platform from which to promote Protestant union. Furthermore, the ouster of puritan incumbents in favour of Anglicans was but one sign of an accelerating Anglican recovery at the local level. This recovery was driven by royalist gentry and clergy determined to restore the old Episcopalian Church of England without concessions. Cathedral chapters were re-establishing themselves throughout the country, and many parishes readopted the *Book of Common Prayer* on their own. Frightened by the rising Anglican tide and by their loss of momentum, Presbyterians in the Convention attempted a parliamentary enactment of the Worcester House Declaration in November, losing in the Commons on a vote of 183 to 157. This effort was opposed both by the court and by some Independents, who feared the king and the Presbyterians were abandoning liberty of conscience for the sake of a comprehensive state church, at their expense.

'So there was an end of that bill,' wrote Andrew Marvell, poet and MP, who been a teller for it, 'and for those excellent things therein.'[35] Charles's opposition to a parliamentary adoption of his own declaration has always been difficult to explain. Although he was careful to work with Presbyterians, the king did not particularly care for their religious scruples, and he suspected their political principles as well. Moreover, he preferred that church settlement should come through his initiative as supreme governor rather than through that of parliament. The best chance for a moderate parliamentary settlement of religion had been lost in the Commons – lost not by much, but lost nevertheless. Lasting settlement would not, in fact, ever really come to the Church of England in the Restoration, despite numerous efforts to impose it, both by the crown and by parliament.

Charles dissolved the Convention at the end of December 1660, ending the first parliamentary effort at settlement, one that was guided in part by his intention to rule as a reconciler of different interests. Despite its failure to resolve the religious issue, and its other errors and omissions, the Convention had actually accomplished much. It had restored government by king, lords, and commons. Charles governed without any restrictions on his prerogative beyond those agreed to by his father in 1641. The Convention had also confirmed the judicial proceedings of the country's courts between 1642 and 1660, with the exception of enforced land sales. The New Model Army was gone; and although the crown was left again without much of a military, most of the kingdom was relieved to see the soldiers go. The Convention had abandoned the old notion that the king should live off his own revenue, an attitude that had much troubled the relationships between recent monarchs and their parliaments. Charles's monarchy was instead funded, if inadequately, by parliament. The Convention had not achieved settlement in all matters, but it had nevertheless come closer to that goal than any parliament since the 1640s. The settlement that had, in the end, eluded the Cromwellian Protectorate appeared to be on the verge of realization, and the popularity of the restored monarchy compensated for military and financial weaknesses that had not yet really become apparent. Despite the persistence of old religious divisions, further discussions between Presbyterians and Anglicans had already been arranged. Unfortunately, however, the healing principles of 1660 were about to be abandoned in all three kingdoms. The royalist settlement that followed would conflate settlement with revenge, reopening many of the political and religious wounds that had produced civil war and revolution in the 1640s.

The Royalist Settlements in England, Scotland, and Ireland, 1661–5

Elections to the new English parliament in March and April 1661 produced a House of Commons that was remarkably different from that of the Convention. Scores of MPs who had been active before 1660 were gone, and men who were entirely new to parliament took their places. One-third of the MPs in the Convention had sat in Richard Cromwell's parliament, and one quarter had sat in the Long Parliament; but only 12 per cent of the MPs chosen in 1661 had also been members of one of those bodies. Anglican and Reformed MPs had balanced each other in the Convention. In the new parliament, Anglicans outnumbered non-Anglican MPs of all persuasions by at least four to one. The proportion of MPs who held civil or military offices under the crown was doubled; the proportion of lawyers halved. Over half of the new MPs or their families had been strongly identified with cavalier royalism during the Interregnum. The new Commons was more royalist than Charles himself; and unlike Charles, many members had not forgiven their enemies.[36]

If this was a parliament of cavaliers, it was also a parliament of the revived Anglican Church. Its early years are principally notable for its re-establishment of an exclusive, coercive, and uncompromising Episcopalian order. Historians have, however, been too quick to assume the inevitability of this Anglican triumph, just as the extraordinary duration of the parliament chosen in 1661 (until 1678) has provided an aura of solidity to its settlement of church and state. In fact, both the magnitude of the royalist triumph of 1661 and the intolerant religious settlements of 1661–5 in England, Scotland, and Ireland require explanation. These Episcopalian settlements developed from political and religious reactions against the revolutionary experiences of the previous decades, and they were only as strong as those reactions. The Restoration would soon provide other political and religious traumas against which to react. The result was an unstable polity in which religious settlements devised in the reactions of 1659–61 would prove incapable of settling new fears.

Two factors, chiefly, produced a rout for Puritanism in the selection of English MPs in 1661. The first of these was the ongoing revival of Anglican structures and sentiment at the parish, county, and diocesan level. This development was stimulated by the return to their livings of hundreds of dispossessed Episcopal clergy and by Charles's appointment of new bishops. But the chief promoters of the Episcopalian recovery at the local level were probably not the Anglican clergy but rather the royalist gentry, who were crowding back, as JPs, onto the county commissions charged with the maintenance of local order. They were often in an uncompromising mood. The royalist gentry were determined to re-establish the autonomy they had enjoyed in county affairs before the fiscal and military intrusions of the Long Parliament and the Interregnum authorities. They similarly intended to regain the influence in local religious matters they had enjoyed before the puritan alterations to the church in the 1640s and 1650s. Indeed, they sought to marginalize all who had been visible proponents of reformation against Episcopalian structures. In this goal they had willing support from many electors and ordinary people, who had also grown tired of reformation and yearned for a return to 'normalcy'. In sum, what Anglican gentry and electors wanted in 1661 was to re-establish by law the same church that had been established before 1641.[37]

A second cause of the Anglican royalist triumph of 1661 was the continuing fear of sectarianism. Presbyterians had fanned the fear of the sects in 1659–60 as they sought to topple the revived Commonwealth; but anxiety about the sects had not ceased with the restoration of Charles II. Instead, as Presbyterians joined the sects in publicly expressing criticism of an unmodified Episcopal church, they opened themselves to charges that they were no better than the Baptists and the Quakers. When the sectarian Thomas Venner and a few dozen armed London followers proclaimed the reign of King Jesus in place of that of King Charles, in January 1661, they lost their heads; but the Presbyterians lost their credibility. Venner's Rising suggested to many Anglican gentry and electors that the loose ends of the country's religious settlement needed to be tied up immediately. In their eyes, protracted negotiations between Episcopalian and Presbyterian spokesmen were only delaying settlement, encouraging sectarian truculence, and jeopardizing civil, social, and religious order. When London Presbyterian, Independent, and Baptist electors successfully shut out Episcopal candidates in the choice for London's Commons' places in 1661, they further stimulated the Anglican reaction in other constituencies. City Reformed leaders compounded their errors, in country eyes, by sending out letters to influence the selection of MPs elsewhere. Too many country gentry and electors feared that London puritans might unsettle the regime, as they had in the early 1640s, before the Restoration was even completed. They selected their MPs accordingly.[38]

The early sessions of the Cavalier Parliament were devoted to matters other than religion; but the re-establishment of the Church of England was its primary accomplishment. Neither Charles nor Hyde, created Earl of Clarendon in 1661, was able to divert the Commons from requiring clerical conformity to a largely unaltered pre-revolutionary Church of England or from criminalizing Protestant worship outside the parish order. Instead, a faction of Anglican royalist parliamentarians pushed through a set of measures that undermined Charles's efforts to establish a broad, comprehensive state church. Indeed, Charles was even opposed by some within his government. Deadlock over changes to the prayer book between Presbyterian and Episcopal clergy, apparent at the synod called for by the Worcester House Declaration, strengthened the Anglican perception that Presbyterians were really enemies of church settlement. In response, the Commons ordered the public burning, throughout the realm, of the Solemn League and Covenant, which many Presbyterians had sworn to uphold, with a Reformed church, in 1643. Parliament also re-seated the bishops in the House of Lords and proceeded with an Act of Uniformity. The intent of the latter was to drive from the restored church all clergy who would not accept the Anglican liturgy and ceremonies in their entirety, who would not denounce the Solemn League and Covenant, or who would not renounce resistance to the monarch under all circumstances.

Charles sought unsuccessfully to dodge this parliamentary bullet. Ironically, he now confronted what his father had confronted in 1641–2: a House of Commons determined to impose its own church settlement upon the crown. The MPs' insistence that the pre-revolutionary church be re-established by law was, in fact, a demand that it be re-established by their law, and that the king act as supreme governor in a manner defined by them. Clarendon and others floated initiatives to soften the bill, for the sake of comprehending Presbyterians; but these efforts failed, even though some of the bishops were interested in them. Talk of a royal suspension of the act, or of providing dispensations under the prerogative to some clergy unable to conform in all respects did not cease after it took effect on 24 August or St. Bartholomew's Day 1662.

Over 900 parish clergy who could not comply with the provisions of the Uniformity Act left their pulpits after 'black' Bartholomew's Day. They joined another 700 who had already lost their places to returning Anglican incumbents or to new ones. Something approaching one-fifth of all the parishes in England thereby experienced a clerical turnover within two years. The departing clergy, who became dissenters or nonconformists, were often among the best preachers and most experienced pastors in the church. London and its environs were particularly hard hit, as dozens of urban pastors were silenced. The provisions of the act were also applied to Oxford and Cambridge, cleansing the universities of masters and fellows who would not comply, and restricting the granting of degrees to those who would. It was similarly imposed upon teachers throughout the kingdom. Presbyterians and Independents could take some comfort from a royal Declaration of Indulgence, issued in December 1662, which reiterated Charles's hope of securing toleration from parliament for those of 'tender consciences'. A bill to permit religious worship outside the Church of England was, in fact, promoted in 1663 by the Earl of Bristol, a Roman Catholic courtier, and by his protégé Sir Henry Bennet, recently appointed secretary of state. But this effort at toleration was a casualty of fears that it would promote Catholicism and of almost universal Anglican condemnation. The Cavalier Parliament would not budge from its determination to bind the crown to its own version of a church established by law.[39]

Although some puritan clergy remained in the church by complying with the Act of Uniformity, the act achieved a significant ecclesiastical purge of non-Anglicans. The Corporation Act of 1661 produced a similar elimination of Presbyterian and Independent laity from positions of responsibility in town government. The leadership of the boroughs had been repeatedly purged and massaged during the Interregnum. Now Anglican royalists took their turn at controlling the towns, which one Anglican peer described to Charles as 'the common seminaries of faction, sedition, and rebellion', because of their large puritan and sectarian populations.[40] The Corporation Act provided for the inspection of borough officers by local commissioners, who were generally drawn from the ranks of the royalist gentry. The commissioners were to dismiss any office holders who failed to take an oath of allegiance to the king, to disavow resistance under all circumstances, or to repudiate the Solemn League and Covenant. Office holders chosen after the initial inspection were required to qualify according to the same terms.

Perhaps one-third of all borough officers were removed or retired voluntarily under the terms of the Corporation Act. As was the case with the Uniformity Act, the Corporation Act was particularly devastating for Presbyterians, some of whom had recently ousted sectarians from borough leadership in order to bring about settlement. In fact, as opponents suggested at the time, the Corporation Act proved 'a remedy far worse than any disease it pretend[ed] to cure'. At the local level, it divided borough leaders who had cooperated in Charles's restoration into politically privileged Anglicans and politically proscribed non-Anglicans. But the wealth and social standing of the aggrieved 'outs' frequently matched that of the favoured 'ins'. As time passed, an increasing proportion of them contested with Anglicans by qualifying for office or by evading the terms of the act. Indeed, far from settling the boroughs, the Corporation Act guaranteed that faction would remain alive and well in the towns of England.[41]

The Anglican royalist leadership of the Cavalier Parliament also sought to enforce the religious conformity of the laity through penal legislation directed against non-Anglican worship. A law of 1662 prohibited the religious meeting of Quakers and others who refused to take oaths, upon pain of fines, imprisonment, or transportation to the colonies. A more general Conventicle Act, adopted in 1664, applied the same penalties to all non-Anglicans caught worshipping outside the church. Its very adoption was a sign, however, that many sought to do so. The Restoration Church of England was also re-established with its diocesan courts, which, in addition to adjudicating about wills, tithes, and marriages, could employ excommunication (with accompanying civil penalties) against laity who refused to conform. As the punitive church code took effect, republican exiles in the Netherlands were joined by new arrivals who preferred Dutch toleration to cavalier coercion.

Still, the Restoration church was not entirely the church of Archbishop Laud. Few of its bishops subscribed to Laud's anti-Calvinist theology, and the controversial Court of High Commission, which had been employed against recalcitrant clergy, was not restored. The episcopate included a number of moderate bishops who were interested in comprehension and who maintained communication with the nonconformist clergy. Furthermore, the church retained some conformist divines of Reformed perspectives and many Reformed laity: the Herefordshire MP Sir Edward Harley, for instance, attended parish services but also prayed and worshipped separately with friends among the expelled clergy. The ejections and exclusions of the early 1660s nevertheless fundamentally altered the character of the established church. The old internal tension between Puritanism and Episcopal authority had now been formally externalized. Having shorn itself of so many puritan clergy, the Restoration Church of England was, in fact, in search of a new identity. It would eventually redefine its Anglican identity by claiming a unique place between Roman Catholicism and Reformed, puritan tradition, or – to use its own rhetoric – between the pitfalls of popery and fanaticism. Whether it would enjoy more success than Laud in silencing Reformed and sectarian Protestantism remained to be seen, however.[42]

The official expulsion of non-Episcopal Protestantism from the Church of England, which was unexpected by many contemporaries, was accompanied by an even more astonishing subordination of the Kirk of Scotland to Episcopal authority. Scottish Presbyterianism became the victim of its own previous successes and of the bitter division between Resolutioners and Protesters. Both factions were swept aside by Scottish nobles determined to regain their customary political ascendancy from the clergy and the covenants that had dominated Scottish affairs since 1637. The crown's initial gestures to the Protesters proved short-lived. Efforts of the Protester clergy to remind Charles of his covenantal obligations prompted their silencing, while their chief political leader, Archibald Campbell, Marquis of Argyll, was tried and executed for treason. The Resolutioner clergy, on the other hand, hoped their moderate past would gain them control of the kirk; but they were instead marginalized by their own political mistakes and by the anti-clericalism of the royalist nobility. Charles and Clarendon promoted an Episcopalian settlement, believing that Presbyterianism was incompatible with royal authority over the Scottish church and state. They also probably hoped, at least at the beginning, to combine Episcopal and Presbyterian polity in some manner acceptable to most of the clergy and laity.

The Earl of Middleton and his allies directed the Scottish parliament that met in 1661. The revival of the lords of the articles, the legislative steering body that had traditionally prepared the articles or bills for consideration by the estates, was one sign that parliament would release the king and his commissioner from the shackles imposed upon Charles I some 20 years earlier. The commissioner and the lords of the articles had often dominated the proceedings of the Scottish estates in the past, given that their generally short sessions and relatively simple procedures rarely produced as much debate as in the English parliament. The estates quickly confirmed the crown's traditional governing prerogatives, overturning measures of the early 1640s that had trimmed the monarchy's free hand in summoning parliament, selecting ministers, and controlling the military. Indeed, in contrast to England, where the parliamentary limitations on royal authority of 1640–1 held good, in Scotland, a Rescissory Act annulled the legislation of all Scottish parliaments since 1633, which were deemed irregular bodies. The estates' adoption of the Rescissory Act confirmed that the crown was paramount in Scottish government. Nevertheless, as in England, this reaffirmation of royal authority was not supported with an adequate financial provision. Charles was given a lifetime Scottish income of £40,000 p.a. (by English measure), derived from customs and an excise on liquor. These levies fell short of expectations, however, requiring the crown to negotiate with the estates for additional revenues later in the reign and also leaving it only able to maintain a Scottish army of little more than 1000 men. As in England, shire militias dominated by nobles and lairds supplemented these meagre forces.

In church matters, the Scottish parliament proceeded in an even more uncompromising fashion than the Cavalier Parliament in England. The Rescissory Act jeopardized Presbyterianism by removing its legal foundations, while another act concerning religion and church government assigned the king authority to settle the kirk in a manner 'most suitable to monarchical government'.[43] These acts provoked significant opposition in parliament and clerical protests from a number of local presbyteries. They clearly subordinated the Scottish church to secular authority in a manner inconsistent with recent practice, but they did not require an irrevocable break with the Presbyterian past. In London, Middleton's rival the Earl of Lauderdale, and James Sharp, the chief clerical spokesman for the Resolutioners, initially hoped that the Worcester House Declaration might establish a model for episcopacy in both kingdoms that would be acceptable to Scottish Presbyterians.

When Charles announced the restoration of episcopacy to Scotland, Sharp was offered a bishopric, which he accepted. With the backing of Lauderdale, Sharp also attempted to persuade several leading Resolutioner clergy to accept sees. Following the example of their English Presbyterian counterparts, however, all other leading Resolutioners refused to consider Episcopal appointments, throwing the selection of bishops back into the hands of the anti-Presbyterian Middleton. The result was a

Scottish episcopate of relatively obscure, subservient, and zealous royalists, with the exception of Sharp, who became Archbishop of St. Andrews. Middleton also pushed measures through parliament in 1662 that settled the Scottish bishops in a manner more similar to that of the English bishops than to their Episcopal predecessors in the pre-revolutionary Scottish church. The bishops were restored to parliament, and the church courts were placed under their authority. Presbyteries and synods were also to operate under the supervision of the bishops, but the general assembly, the central Presbyterian structure of the national church, was discarded. All ministers who had been elected to places since 1649 were required to obtain confirmation from the lay patrons of their livings and from their bishops. Worship outside the church establishment was forbidden, and an oath renouncing the covenants was required of office holders.

Determined to enforce this settlement, Middleton and the Scottish Privy Council began, in autumn 1662, to deprive ministers who had failed to secure Episcopal confirmation, who refused to recognize the crown's superintendence of the church, or who were otherwise defiant. The Scottish church suffered a clerical turnover that was proportionately more significant than that of England. The 270 deprived clergy were over one quarter of the kingdom's total; but they were concentrated in the more heavily populated area to the south of the River Tay, where over half the clergy were deprived. The proportion in the shires of the Southwest reached two-thirds: only 20 of some 170 incumbents in the synods of Glasgow and Ayr and of Galloway conformed. Gilbert Burnet, the contemporary historian and future bishop, undoubtedly exaggerated when he described the new Episcopalian curates who took their places as men of 'little learning, less piety, and no manner of discretion'.[44] Burnet may nevertheless have captured the perceptions of many laity who found the Restoration Church of Scotland unsettling rather than settling.

The policy of repressing ardent Presbyterians survived Middleton's political demise in 1663. His scheme to except his rival, Lauderdale, from a Scottish Indemnity Act then led instead to his own loss of Charles's confidence. As Lauderdale succeeded to the fallen Middleton's dominance, he came under pressure from the new Scottish bishops to proceed rigorously against deprived ministers. Many of them remained in the neighbourhoods of their former parishes, contrary to law; and some of them and their lay followers soon initiated worship outside the established church. Lauderdale did not hesitate to enforce the new settlement: although he had supported comprehension of Presbyterians, he also supported religious uniformity. A Conventicle Act adopted in 1663 imposed fines on those who absented themselves from parish worship and equated separate worship with treason. The significant clerical losses experienced by the church, as well as the hostility of many laity to the new Episcopal clergy, made enforcement of the Conventicle Act problematic, however. For his part, Archbishop Sharp hoped for reconciliation with his former brethren; and the Scottish episcopate gave no thought to restoring English liturgical importations that had produced uproar in the northern kingdom in 1637.[45]

In Ireland, as in England and Scotland, initial thoughts of re-establishing the church in a broad manner that would comprehend Presbyterians gave way to an exclusively Episcopalian church settlement. Episcopalian advocates in the Irish Convention outmanoeuvred their Presbyterian counterparts, persuading both Charles and anxious Protestant landowners that the old church order was the best guarantee of Irish stability. Largely on the recommendations of Ormond, Charles appointed a dozen new Irish bishops in the summer of 1660, adding to several who had survived the civil wars and the Interregnum. The Irish episcopate included a few token bishops with Calvinist leanings and the brother of the Earl of Orrery; but it was generally more characterized by the uncompromising outlook of its new primate and its numerous sufferers for Episcopal practice. The bishops quickly ejected most of the Protestant clergy of Ulster, where Presbyterians made up some 40 per cent of the population of the three counties facing Scotland (Antrim, Londonderry, and Down). Active persecution of non-Episcopal Protestants was nevertheless restrained in the early 1660s, despite votes by the new Irish parliament chosen in 1661 to ban conventicles and to anathematize the Solemn League and Covenant. Reformed and sectarian Protestants simply made up too large a proportion of the non-Catholic population; and Orrery, as one of the resident lord justices, was a proponent of Protestant accommodation. The restored Church of Ireland could probably command the loyalty of well less than half of Ireland's 300,000 Protestants. The anti-nonconformist Uniformity Act desired by the Irish bishops had to wait until 1666.[46]

The persecution of some Irish Protestants by other Irish Protestants also seemed unwise, given their common fear of the Roman Catholic majority. Protestantism had certainly grown during the Interregnum immigrations, but Catholics still comprised four-fifths of the population. Outside the towns and cities, Protestants were a tiny ruling elite within a Catholic society, politically ascendant to be sure, but heavily outnumbered. The major issue of the early Irish Restoration was, in fact, not the re-settlement of the Protestant church but rather whether Irish Catholics would recover their lands and their priests. After a decade of disaster, Irish Catholics hoped for relief from Charles II, who had followed Ormond's 1649 promise of toleration with his own religious reassurances.

Charles plunged into Irish affairs with a November 1660 declaration confirming the Cromwellian land grants in principle. He also made provision, however, for the relief of 'innocent papists', who had been unjustly treated as rebels, and of Protestant royalists, who had also lost land. This formula proved acceptable to the Irish parliament of 1661, from which Catholics were almost entirely absent, because Protestant leaders expected few Catholics would prove innocent. They were understandably horrified when a new court for adjudicating conflicting land claims proved remarkably sympathetic to dispossessed Roman Catholics. The court had been established under the 1662 parliamentary Act of Settlement, and like the act itself, the court's English judges were expected to confirm most Protestant titles. Instead, its awards to over 500 Catholic families in the single year of its statutory existence doubled the proportion of land owned by Catholics. Such awards generally came at the expense of Cromwellian Protestant grantees who were supposed to receive compensatory lands from the crown.

The claims court's decisions enraged Irish MPs, who threatened to block them; and they embarrassed Charles, who backed his court, but who lacked the landed resources in Ireland that were necessary to support redistributions on this scale. Ironically, the Irish Protestant landowners who had turned to a Stuart restoration to protect their land and interests from the disorders of 1659 now felt threatened by the very monarch they had restored. Not until 1665 was a solution found in the Act of Explanation, which Ormond pushed through parliament against considerable resistance. It required that Cromwellian grantees return about one third of their land to the crown so that Charles might better

compensate those Protestants who had lost land to Catholics. Well
might one observer suggest that 'the lands of Ireland' had become
'a mere scramble'.[47]

In the meantime, after initial difficulties with the Irish parliament
about finances, Charles also secured a permanent Irish revenue
from an excise and a tax on hearths. This income funded an army of
some 7500, which was thought sufficient to police the country and
to protect Protestants. Thereafter, Charles had little further interest
in or use for the Irish MPs. The body that met in 1661–2 (and again
in 1665–6) was only the fourth Irish parliament of the century; and
no parliament would sit again in Ireland during Charles's reign.
The Restoration did little to enhance the Dublin parliament as part
of the kingdom's ordinary governing structures, which were instead
dominated by the crown's lord lieutenant. Poynings's Law, the early
Tudor stipulation requiring the prior approval of the English Privy
Council for all Irish legislation, was untouched by the settlement,
leaving the Irish MPs with little legislative initiative. Yet the Irish Restoration remained a problematic settlement for the crown, which
found that its Irish revenues failed to cover its Irish costs.

Many Irish subjects remained unhappy as well. Thousands of
Catholics whose land claims had not been reviewed during the
short window allowed by the Act of Settlement remained dispossessed. Even after Charles's redistributions, little more than a fifth
of Irish land was in Catholic hands, compared to some 60 per cent
before Cromwell's time. Catholics in the towns were also subjected
to Reformation-era statutes intended to keep them out of offices
and out of trades. They did at least have their clergy back, albeit
on the old surreptitious terms. (Protestant MPs attempted to bar
the Catholic bishops and priests by law in 1661; but the crown
opposed the measure.) Many Protestants were also aggrieved,
especially landowners deprived of property for 'innocent papists'
or for other Protestants. The bishops of the Church of Ireland
felt insecure and were scarcely able to make their presence felt
in many parts of the land. Non-Episcopal Protestants resented
the new church establishment that they believed subordinated
the advance of reformation to the maintenance of order. All
Protestants, including the dominant Episcopalian interest, feared
another Catholic rebellion on the scale of 1641. These complaints
could not, however, obscure the hegemony in Irish politics and
society that Protestants had re-secured in the Restoration.

Once Episcopalian structures had been re-established in the Protestant churches of the three kingdoms, many royalists and church leaders treated them as the bedrock of settlement. In fact, they were nothing of the sort. Instead, these exclusive Episcopalian settlements guaranteed that religion would be as much a source of political division and unsettlement in the reign of Charles II as it had been in the reign of Charles I. The religious settlements healed few old wounds, and they opened many new ones. Episcopacy had been re-established in each realm by driving from the church all those clergy who took their theological and historical ties to the continental Calvinist Reformation most seriously. Those clergy nevertheless had strong followings among some gentry, among the trading populations of London and of many English provincial towns, and in such regions as the West Country, Lowland Scotland, and Ulster. In all three kingdoms, these exclusive church settlements weakened the Restoration: dissenters defied efforts by the state to impose religious uniformity and increasingly saw the new church establishments as riddled with 'popery'. Reformed and sectarian Protestants who could not conform also found themselves formally proscribed from local office holding. Some of them nevertheless managed to participate in local politics despite such proscription, often becoming a factional nucleus for opposition to royalist elites. Little evidence suggests that Anglicans, for their part, found any real security in the coercive religious structures they established in Charles's kingdoms in the early 1660s. Far from strengthening royal government, the religious settlements complicated Charles's political tasks considerably.

Settlement, Security, and Trade, 1661–5

The quest for settlement and security by the Anglican royalist gentry in the English Cavalier Parliament was not restricted to the sphere of religion. MPs were also determined to protect their settlement, and their social and political supremacy, from the popular forces that had erupted in the 1640s. Under a series of additional acts, the people were to relearn their subordinate status and to leave weighty matters to their superiors. A 1661 act against tumultuous petitioning, for instance, was directed against politically hyperactive apprentices, articulate townsmen, and other unruly social inferiors. It outlawed the presentation of petitions to the king or to parliament by more than ten people together; and it forbade public petitions with more than 20 signatures, unless they had the approval of three JPs or a grand jury. Similarly, the 1662 Licensing Act was directed against the free press that had produced over 20,000 printed books, sermons, and pamphlets over the previous two decades. Unlicensed publications continued to appear, despite the vigilance of press licenser Sir Roger L'Estrange. Nevertheless, the heady exchange of printed ideas before 1660 was largely replaced, after 1662, by a much reduced stream of official and clerical commendations of public order, moderation, and respect for social governors. The authority of masters and fathers over their households was also affirmed by a royal proclamation of 1662 that encouraged them to instruct apprentices and dependents in the rationales for divine right and patriarchy.[48] People not settled in households found their mobility restrained by a 1662 addition to the poor laws. This new Act of Settlement was intended to reinforce the authority of local JPs over the disposition of 'rogues, vagabonds, [and] idle and disorderly persons'. It was directed especially against poor 'masterless men' who wandered the roads in search of employment and were thought to have contributed to the unrest of the previous decades.

But the MPs who sought, through these means, to preserve the security of their settlement from threats from below were also creating, through their coercive religious legislation, the very body of disfranchised and alienated subjects most likely to reject it. The thousands of borough office holders and clergy who had been displaced by the Corporation Act and the Uniformity Act were but the tip of a new political iceberg of disfranchised religious dissenters. Historians have generally underestimated the size of the English nonconformist population by drawing upon the Anglican church's own subsequent, self-interested surveys of it. Dissenting spokesmen claimed 20 per cent or more of the population.[49] Their assertions are not unreasonable, especially for London and the heavily populated Southeast of England. Neither is such an estimate improbable in the transitional early years of the Restoration. Many then dissented from the methods of the Episcopal settlement, even while outwardly conforming, wholly or partially, to the national religious order. Others moved ambiguously back and forth between parish worship and support for the expelled clergy.

The implementation of the new religious settlement in England was messy for both church and state. The bishops were under no illusions about the difficulties of achieving religious uniformity. Presbyterians, who were the most likely to conform outwardly, were also embittered by the defection of some of their leaders and shocked to find themselves redefined by Anglicans as sectarians. True to their origins as voluntary churches, Independent congregations were better prepared to meet in defiance of law. Many Baptists and Quakers courted persecution and imprisonment by defying the statutes intended to prevent their worship. Indeed, harassment and incarceration by the authorities often strengthened their resolve. Imprisoned throughout the 1660s, for instance, John Bunyan maintained ties with other sectarian teachers and with his Bedford meeting; and he illegally printed several anti-Anglican works culminating in *The Pilgrim's Progress*.

JPs and borough magistrates singled out Quakers for particular attention. The Friends' refusal to pay tithes or to show customary marks of deference to social superiors were seen as provocative challenges to the Restoration order. So was their rejection of legal oaths and of ordained ministry, as well as the remarkable visibility of Quaker women, which grated against the kingdom's patriarchal social ethos. Seven hundred Quakers were apprehended in London and Bristol in the wake of Thomas Venner's 1661 rising, for example; and another 500 were taken as far away as Yorkshire. This reaction was really a sign of the governing class's fear of the sects and of social disorder, however, for not a single one of Venner's few dozen followers was actually a Quaker. A few years later, in 1664–5, over 90 per cent of the urban London convictions under the Conventicle Act were of Quakers. [50]

Most Quakers now professed the 'peace principle' and declined to employ force in their self-defence, but other sectarians were less restrained. Baptist and Independent meetings were sprinkled with former New Model officers and soldiers, some of whom remained true to their republican past and dreamed of recovering it. Their republicanism was generally an amalgam of political and religious ideas, with the latter often more pronounced; and their unhappiness with the Restoration sometimes did take militant form. Yet the extent of republicanism was always exaggerated by those in authority, who manipulated memories of former republican excesses to maintain attachment to the restored church and state.

Restoration republicans are of interest primarily for their ideas rather than for their numbers; and some of the most interesting republican thinkers, such as Algernon Sidney, were safely abroad in the early 1660s.

Given both the size and the defiant spirit of much of the nonconformist population, the Restoration regime was quick to establish an extensive system of domestic surveillance. Spying, rather than a standing army, became the regime's first-line defence against internal resistance. Convinced that the spirit of unsettlement lurked in secretive dissenting meetings, in fleeting republican conversations, and in hidden printing presses, Charles II's secretaries of state presided over an extensive intelligence-gathering apparatus. The Post Office existed as much to provide the government with opportunities to pry into the letters of those suspected of disloyalty as to convey private communications. Charles's agents infiltrated dissenting meetings, and the 'turning' of suspected incendiaries into informants became a particular art of Restoration government. The counsels of English republicans in the Netherlands were similarly infiltrated. The regime's Dutch spies included the remarkable Aphra Behn, whose subsequent plays reflect her disdain for the political heirs of Puritanism.[51]

Could the crown have reconciled disaffected dissenters and diehard republicans if it had abandoned coercion for the toleration Charles had promised in 1660? An effort to do precisely that produced the first significant political dust-up in the Cavalier Parliament, when the Earl of Bristol and Secretary of State Sir Henry Bennet talked Charles into his 1662 Declaration of Indulgence. They sought also to turn the declaration into a statute in the 1663 parliamentary session. A recent convert to Catholicism, Bristol was working with Lady Castlemaine, and with Lord Ashley and the Duke of Buckingham, each of whom consistently supported both the comprehension of moderate dissenters in the church and the toleration of sectarians. The ambitious Bennet, who would soon develop his own following in the Commons, promoted toleration primarily in order to weaken Clarendon. Not incidentally, Bennet's and Bristol's toleration initiative coincided with a decline in the chancellor's popularity, as well as in that of Charles himself, which they hoped to ride into power. Public perceptions of the government had been damaged by rumours about luxurious and licentious behaviour at court and by a continuing sluggishness in the country's overseas trade.

Speculation about ministerial corruption was fed by the failure of new taxes, including an unpopular assessment on householders, according to the number of their hearths, to solve the regime's financial issues. 'The bishops get all, the courtiers spend all, the citizens pay for all, the king neglects all, and the devils take all' was one London street refrain of 1662.[52]

Clarendon had his own reservations about religious coercion, of course; but when he was challenged by Bristol and Bennet, he stuck with his Episcopalian allies. Recognizing failure, Bennet trimmed his sails to tack another day. Bristol, on the other hand, offered impeachment articles against Clarendon in the House of Lords, citing all the sources of public disillusionment with him and with the regime. This effort guaranteed Bristol's disgrace rather than that of the chancellor. Still, Clarendon never again recovered the mastery of government or the influence over Charles that he had once enjoyed.

In any case, the discovery of two rebellious conspiracies in 1663 soon gave Clarendon and militant Anglicans further justification for the coercion of all those hostile to the Restoration settlements in church and state. The first of these was an Irish plot that tied dissenting Dublin malcontents to the disaffected in Ulster. The Irish conspirators hoped to seize Ormond, to reverse the recent land redistributions to Catholics, and to resettle the Church of Ireland on a broad Protestant basis. As many as eight Irish MPs may have been involved in the Dublin Plot, as was Col Thomas Blood, the dissenting adventurer better known for his subsequent attempt to heist the crown jewels. Scattered risings in the north of England in 1663 were more serious and involved dissenters of all persuasions in several counties and some in London. The ringleaders had established contacts with disaffected elements in Ulster and Scotland as well as with republican exiles in the Netherlands. They produced a manifesto that condemned the court for its waste and licentiousness, the regime for its economic and fiscal failures, and the Anglican establishment for its declension from the continental pattern of Reformed church order. By the time these risings came off in October, however, the government had called out the militias of three northern counties. They joined elements of the royal army under the Duke of Buckingham, producing a force that quickly routed their disorganized foes. Twenty-four conspirators were eventually executed – twice as many as the republican martyrs at the beginning of the reign. Others fled to the Netherlands, where they joined the growing community of English republican and clerical exiles.[53]

Although these conspiracies and risings were fiascos, plotting and rebellion against the Restoration settlements in the three kingdoms would prove endemic. Moreover, the collapse of the initial plots failed completely to steady Anglican nerves. The northern rebels inadvertently drove the Conventicle Act through the English parliament in 1664 with the greatest of ease, and Anglican magistrates redoubled their efforts against dissenting meetings. Toleration was dead for the time being. So was the 1641 Triennial Act, which guaranteed a parliament at least once in every three years, whether summoned by the king or not. A new Triennial Act of 1664, justified in part by the rebels' supposed misconstruction of its predecessor, eliminated this major abridgement of the royal prerogative. It still specified that no more than three years should pass between parliaments, but it left the initiative in calling them to the crown. Yet another effect of the Northern rebellion was to redirect Anglican attention from the domestic underground of conspiratorial dissenters to the foreign refuge of all plotters and 'fanatics'. Anglican royalists soon became persuaded that only an external war against the Netherlands, the chief continental breeding ground of republicanism, and the bulwark of Calvinist Protestantism, would secure the regime from internal threats.

The second Anglo-Dutch War (in the sequence that began under the Commonwealth) has often been treated as a war promoted by London merchants. Their complaints against the unfair trading practices of their Dutch rivals in India, the Americas, and Africa are said to have propelled a sympathetic regime into hostilities. The war was, in fact, about trade: the English ambassador at The Hague believed the Dutch aspired to a 'universal dominion of the seas' and hoped to become 'absolute sole masters of the gold and also of the Negro trade', to the ruin of the English plantations. The Dutch were the pre-eminent colonial and trading power of the Protestant world, with colonies in North America (especially New Netherland, at the mouth of the Hudson River), the West Indies, South America, and South Africa. The Dutch East India Company had long overtaken the Portuguese in the European import of silks and spices from India and Southeast Asia. The Dutch had also come to dominate both the Caribbean sugar trade and the supply of African slaves necessary for sugar production there. For 50 years, they had benefited from their possession of the largest mercantile marine in Europe, which also gave them command of the carrying trade to many parts of Europe.

When Charles was restored to the rule of his kingdoms, he was also restored to the management of a rival English colonial and commercial empire that seemed to have great potential, if only the Dutch could be pushed out of the way. Charles's American possessions included the New England colonies, founded by puritans and separatists, and the Chesapeake colonies of Virginia and Maryland, the latter a proprietary colony of the Catholic Calvert family. They also included several West Indian plantations, especially Barbados and Jamaica, recently taken from Spain by Cromwell. Trade with these colonies was largely in the hands of individual merchants, while chartered companies of merchants and investors carried on other long-distance trades. These large-scale commercial entities included the joint stock East India Company, the Royal Adventurers into Africa, and the Levant Company, which traded to the Middle East. The English colonial domain was nevertheless still in its infancy, and it was challenged by French competition as well as by that of the Dutch. Settlement in the North American colonies remained scattered, for instance, with fewer than 60,000 colonists altogether.[54] Colonial economies were only beginning to develop, and the New Englanders had hitherto accepted little direction from England.

The growth of English overseas trade, especially of its colonial trade, would accelerate noticeable during the Restoration. This development can be attributed in part to the Convention Parliament's endorsement of the protective colonial and commercial policies of the detested English republic. The Commonwealth's 1651 Navigation Act had been designed to preserve the English colonial trade for English merchants, and the republic's war of 1652–4 against Holland had been intended to enforce the provisions of the Navigation Act upon Dutch traders. The new Navigation Act of 1660, which followed the Commonwealth's anti-Dutch model, limited trade with the colonies to English, Irish, and colonial ships. It restricted the import of the principal colonial commodities – especially sugar and tobacco – to English and Irish ports, from which they might be re-exported to Europe. (As foreigners, Scots merchants were placed as much outside the system as the Dutch.) European goods shipped to the colonies were also required to pass first through English ports, where they were subject to English customs duties. A further act of the Cavalier Parliament in 1663 restricted the purchases of colonial subjects to English goods or goods first shipped through England. The primary purpose of these acts was to ensure that England dominated the carrying trade to and from its own colonies. They were also designed to stimulate the construction of English shipping and to ensure that London and other English ports developed as commercial centres for the distribution of colonial goods at home and abroad.

In time, the new colonial system would accomplish these objectives, and the English would overtake their Dutch and French trading rivals. Anglican royalists of the 1660s could not foresee these results, however. Instead, they feared the Dutch and saw Dutch aspirations to trading hegemony as part of a broader effort for the political mastery of Europe. Cavalier royalists were driven to fury by the prosperity of a nation that was founded in rebellion, hostile to monarchy, and praised by dissenters and rebels for its practice of toleration. Indeed, Anglican royalists took the nation to war in 1665 to preserve their settlement against an antithetical foreign regime that offered safe haven to men who would destroy the monarchy again, given half the chance, or so the risings of 1663 had seemingly demonstrated. Comparisons of England's quarrel with the Dutch to ancient Rome's wars against Carthage suggested this was a contest between people with different values and cultures. Exaggerated tales of barbarous Dutch massacres of Englishmen in the East were circulated to drive home the point. Should England falter, royalists feared a dissenting political resurgence in alliance with the Dutch. Should England prevail, the government hoped for a restoration of the House of Orange, intermarried with the Stuarts, to its former quasi-monarchical role in the Dutch government. For his part, Charles was happy to don the bright armour of a warrior king in order to overcome mounting public distaste for his personal behaviour and expenditures.[55]

A resolution of the Commons in 1664 condemning Dutch obstructions of English trade was based upon evidence solicited from London merchants by a committee headed by Thomas Clifford, an associate of Secretary Bennet. The fears of the East India Company that war would ensure the 'complete ruin' of their trade, by opening it to Dutch depredation, were ignored in favour of the

dutiful complaints against the Dutch of the largely cavalier investors in the Royal Adventurers into Africa. Throughout 1664, leading royalists and some ministers stroked public and parliamentary
opinion in favour of hostilities; and provocative English gestures,
including an occupation of New Amsterdam, the chief town of New
Netherland, brought war closer. (Placed under the proprietorship
of the Duke of York, New Amsterdam became New York, to the
satisfaction of English settlers on Long Island.) In November 1664,
an aroused Commons that had been well prepared by its ministerial members offered an unprecedented £2.5 million to fund naval
actions that were clearly intended against the Dutch.

Clarendon stood aloof from this 'immoderate desire' for war,
fearing that its expenses and its uncertainties might unduly stress
the still recently settled governments of Charles's kingdoms.[56]
Despite Clarendon's misgivings, England was on a reasonable footing for war, however. The government's ordinary revenues were
improving with an actual recovery of overseas trade, whatever the
lamentations against the Dutch; and Charles had retained significant naval forces in 1660. The English merchant marine provided
the government with additional maritime resources that could be
hired, especially in light of the windfall of new assessments authorized by parliament. When belligerence was formally proclaimed
in March 1665, the government was readying a fleet of over 100
ships and 16,000 men. Samuel Pepys, clerk to the naval board, was
bursting with pride when it set out at the end of April, with the
Duke of York commanding one of its three squadrons. The English
encountered the best fleet ever assembled by the Dutch off Lowestoft, in the North Sea, in early June. Pepys was soon celebrating
so great a victory as was 'never known in the world'.[57] Twenty-six
Dutch vessels were sunk or destroyed with the loss of 8000 men.
The Dutch admiral was killed; his flagship exploded. Control of
the North Atlantic had passed to Charles.

As news of the victory off Lowestoft spread throughout England,
it was greeted with public celebrations reminiscent of the great victory over Spain in 1588. The Dutch offered terms, eager to offload
their unprofitable Manhattan enterprise in order to protect their
superior trading position in the East. But Charles's government was
not prepared to exchange an obscure outpost already in hand for the
greater Asian trade it desired to acquire at Dutch expense. Expectations of a crushing victory would soon be disappointed, however: the

war's opening battle proved to be its highpoint for England. A late summer attack upon the Dutch East India fleet, which had taken refuge in the Danish-Norwegian port of Bergen, was bungled. Moreover, within a few months, the social and political circumstances of the war were drastically altered. Even as the fleet had set out in April, Pepys recorded 'great fears of the sickness here in the city'. Charles's subjects were about to confront the worst biological scourge of early modern Europe. The plague had again been carried from the Middle East to the Netherlands and to London along the very trading routes over which the war was being fought. The greatest epidemiological catastrophe since the Black Death was beginning. In its train would come extraordinary military, economic, fiscal, and psychological strains that would test the durability of the Restoration settlements in Charles's kingdoms. Little consolation would be found in the fact that the plague first struck the Dutch.[58]

2 Court and Kingdoms, 1665–72

The Court ... was full of gambling, allied pleasures, and everything else that the taste of a prince naturally addicted to such tender amusements could suggest by way of luxury and smartness. The beauties wished to charm and the men tried to please; all sought to set themselves off to the best advantage. Some danced, others put on airs and dressed magnificently, some were wits, others prodigious lovers, and a few were faithful.

Anthony Hamilton, Count Gramont (1714)[1]

Introduction: Three Kingdoms

Charles II was a British monarch, but he was not the monarch of a British state. The political history of Britain in the Restoration is a fragmented history because Charles governed not one kingdom, but multiple kingdoms, each with its own institutions, history, and traditions. He ruled a variety of peoples and cultures on the 'British Isles' who would, for the most part, slowly be integrated over the next few centuries into a single state and 'nationality'. That process could not have been predicted in 1660, however. Even the Welsh, a submerged Celtic people who had been incorporated into the legal and institutional realm of England under the early Tudors, retained much of their own language and cultural identity. The Scots, divided between Lowland and Highland cultures, had firmly rejected the last form of English hegemony in the Cromwellian union. The Gaelic and Catholic Irish were already joining the Welsh as a submerged culture. Losing their lands and their political voices to English and Scots settlers, they would nevertheless more stoutly resist the process of Anglicization that produced modern Britain. The British problem of multiple monarchies was not unique in seventeenth-century Europe, to be sure: state formation in Spain, Austria, and Denmark-Norway also developed around

53

such structures. The British monarchy was nevertheless unusual among the major European states in its combination of limitations upon regal power with the problem of coordinating government in three different realms.[2]

The English kingdom was the dominant kingdom of the 'British Archipelago'. England's population was over twice that of Scotland and Ireland combined. Its trade and productivity surpassed that of the 'outlying' kingdoms by an even greater ratio. England alone was so far involved in the European quest for an empire of colonies and trade: the Scots were excluded from the English colonial sphere after 1660, as were the Irish, by an English act of 1671 that many Irish merchants nevertheless got around. Governed by royal surrogates, and rarely visited by their monarchs, Scotland and Ireland were each 'satellite' kingdoms, despite Scotland's greater autonomy from English intervention. Yet Charles II and his ministers needed to coordinate policy in all three kingdoms rather than focusing single-mindedly upon England. They could never forget that the civil wars that had toppled Charles I had also been British wars, wars initiated in Scotland before they embroiled England, and wars that reached their climax in Ireland. English security required the effective governance of the other kingdoms, especially in wartime.

Each British kingdom possessed a parliament; but that similarity masked a variety of political differences that can be as confusing to students as they were to contemporaries. The English parliament was singular in its size, in the orderliness of its internal functions, and in the concern of county gentry, borough freemen, and even yeomen farmers about its proceedings. In contrast, the parliamentary electorates of Scottish shires and burghs were but a fraction of their larger English counterparts. Contemporaries and historians alike have suggested that Charles was a more autocratic ruler in Scotland than in England. The parliamentary acts of the Scottish Restoration had reversed the shackles previously imposed upon Charles I, whereas the English Restoration had preserved several of the Long Parliament's abridgements of the royal prerogative. Dominated by the nobility, and tightly managed by the lords of the articles, the Scottish estates proved a rubber stamp for most of Charles's reign, agreeing to whatever legislation the government set out. Similarly, although the Irish parliament looked like its English namesake, its competence was limited by Poynings's law;

and it was a body with which only the English and Scottish minorities identified.

The central administration of England was equally unusual within the British context. However small the English government may have been by continental standards, it dwarfed the smaller establishments of Edinburgh and Dublin Castle. Moreover, between the infrequent parliamentary sessions in Scotland and Ireland, the Duke of Lauderdale and the Earl of Ormond governed those realms, respectively, with little local restraint and were largely accountable only to the king. The privy councils over which Lauderdale and Ormond presided were but federations of landed grandees tied to them and to the king himself through grants of offices and favours. The temptations for aggrandizement faced by the Scottish secretary and by the Irish lord lieutenant were considerable; and their success in dominating rivals was a sign of the extent to which Charles relied upon them for the administration of his outlying and unfamiliar realms. Lauderdale's place on the English council and Ormond's influence in the English government did, at least, assist in integrating the administration of multiple polities.

Coordinating policy among the three kingdoms was complicated by these structural differences and by the difficulty of communication by land and by sea. Warfare was especially challenging to the effective coordination of rule, as the strains of the Anglo-Dutch conflict of 1665–7 demonstrated. Despite the initial generosity of the English parliament in funding the war, the conflict quickly compromised the crown's financial position. Hostilities disrupted trade, and customs receipts plummeted. Military expenses mounted, and the war widened to Charles's disadvantage when Louis XIV of France entered on the Dutch side. The Scots and the Irish also found themselves at war through little initiative of their own. Charles and his English ministers more or less made foreign policy for all three realms. In the satellite kingdoms, as well as in England, the war compounded the difficulties of under-funded regimes. Charles genuinely feared Dutch intervention in Scotland, where many subjects were disturbed about the wartime disruption of their economy for the benefit of an English commercial empire from which they were excluded. Lauderdale sought to turn this dissatisfaction to political advantage by developing a plan for complementing the Anglo-Scottish union of crowns with a union of parliaments. Nothing came of his proposal for greater political integration now, but its serious consideration in both kingdoms was a sign of how the war had stressed the ties that bound Scotland and England together. In Ireland, Ormond was replaced a few years after the war, although his departure proved temporary. He had stumbled in his management of the Irish army and of the kingdom's revenues. Thereafter, Irish affairs were more closely monitored from Westminster.

The common British issue that was most significantly highlighted by the war, however, was the problem of religious division. In each of his three kingdoms, Charles had accepted a punitive Episcopalian religious settlement. This uniform church framework was imposed by religious minorities in Scotland and Ireland, however; and it was imposed upon large puritan and sectarian minorities in England as well. But the war that Anglican courtiers had promoted to destroy republicanism soon destroyed the Episcopalian triumph instead. In each of Charles's kingdoms, a distinctive and militant Protestant nonconformist culture began to emerge in the years during and after the war. In England, the puritan movement that had fragmented during the civil wars of the 1640s re-congealed somewhat under the banner of liberty for conscience. Protestants of Reformed background in the three kingdoms also came to identify as strongly with each other's prospects as their Episcopal persecutors identified with each other's church establishments. These were portentous developments that would trouble the Stuart kingdoms for the remainder of the Restoration.

From its conception, the war also undermined the idea that the security of the state could be erected upon the coercion of non-Episcopal Protestants. Charles had never liked persecution, and it seemed an especially unpromising way to ensure the wartime loyalty of any of his subjects. In England, the Anglo-Dutch conflict soon produced a parliamentary opposition that was offended not just by the management of the war but also by the persecution of Protestants. Clarendon became the war's principal political victim, and the coercive Anglican settlement that Clarendon had accepted was challenged as well. The chancellor gave way to a committee of ministers who agreed on little, and who schemed against each other; but they did at least agree that a policy of religious accommodation was more likely than persecution to keep Charles's realms quiet. To the north, the Scottish kingdom was shaken by a wartime rebellion of some of those still attached to covenant principles. The rebellion quickly collapsed, but so did Episcopalian self-confidence, as well as Lauderdale's commitment to persecution. The Scottish secretary moved, after the war, towards the accommodation of moderate Presbyterians, and a similar policy was eventually adopted in Ireland. In all three kingdoms, then, Charles and his ministers returned, after the war, to the more conciliatory religious spirit of 1660. They moved in this direction in response to the circumstances of each kingdom. Yet Charles's rule of multiple kingdoms as much encouraged uniformity in the new religious policy of accommodation, as it had inclined him in the Episcopalian direction in 1660–1. Religious policy proved to be a three-kingdoms policy, because the same divisions among Protestants ran through each of Charles's domains.

The Culture of the Court

One other institution that increasingly entered into this complicated three-kingdoms political calculus after 1665 was Charles's court. The court was potentially a powerful unifying institution for the British realms. Since Charles and his Stuart predecessors had one court rather than three, it was a British institution by definition. Indeed, it was the most important British political institution, other than the monarchy itself; and it was the only path to real power outside the English parliament. Charles's court was the patronage centre of all three kingdoms. Dominated by the English, it was nevertheless the one political venue where Scots and Irish office holders and office seekers regularly mingled with their English counterparts in pursuing their interests and access to the king.

If the court provided the crown with important integrative political possibilities, it also provided Charles with a stage upon which to display and to dramatize important political messages. Although remarkable for his 'common touch' and casual ways, Charles also well understood the importance of ceremony in enhancing his power through staged ceremony and splendour. Reviving the mystical cachet of the king as a Christlike healer, for instance, he touched some 23,000 persons for scrofula, the skin disease thought susceptible to royal cure, in 1660–4. Over time, he would fashion a grandiose image of monarchy in his architectural projects, in the artistic decoration of Windsor Castle, and in his promotion of English theatre and music. Charles II was, in fact, every bit as capable of sustaining a majestic regal image as his father, whose court had been known for its aesthetic grandeur.

From the beginning of his reign, the king, his ministers, and his press guardians also worked tirelessly to disseminate a respectable public image of the court. According to them, a moderate, virtuous, and orderly royal government had replaced the ambitious, self-interested, and extremist republican clique of the 1650s. This message was tirelessly propagated in speech and print, in court-inspired drama and sermons, and in festive pageantry and poetry, including the heroic verse of John Dryden. Yet the reality of the cavalier court was quite different from the chaste imagery served up to the public. An assemblage of libertines, dandies, and intriguers without parallel in late seventeenth-century Europe, Charles's court was among the most wanton and wasteful of its age. His reputation as a "merry" monarch was not amusing to most contemporaries, who were shocked by stories about court shenanigans. Indeed, the integrative function of the court worked as much against Charles as for him: subjects of a variety of political and religious perspectives were united in their disgust at the behaviour of the king and his courtiers.[3]

Charles's own promiscuity set the standard for his courtiers, who trysted and turned from bed to bed. Marital fidelity was a rare commodity among Charles's friends and advisers. The Duke of York, whose sexual indiscretion had forced him into marriage to Anne Hyde, thereafter pursued one attractive court lady after another, indulged apparently by his wife. She compensated by ruling James 'in all things but his codpiece' and found other sexual partners for herself. The Duke of Buckingham, who had married the heiress of a puritan general when Charles's restoration seemed unlikely, shocked even Charles by installing the scandalous Countess of Shrewsbury in his London residence in 1668 and returning his wife of a decade to her father. (Of the countess, it was said that, 'although no man could boast of being alone in enjoying her favours, equally no one could complain of being refused them'.) The Duke of Lauderdale became intimate friends with Elizabeth Murray, Lady Dysart, while their spouses ailed. Elizabeth became the duke's mistress after her husband died, and she eventually replaced the declining wife with whom she competed.[4]

Such behaviour also caught hold among the lesser fry at court, who aped the mores of their superiors. Francis North, lord keeper of the great seal, was told that he must keep a mistress if he wanted to keep his career. Samuel Pepys, whose wife was ogled by York, was scandalized by the carryings-on of Lady Castlemaine, who was no more faithful to Charles than the king was to her, and of the Earl of Sandwich, his boss at the navy office. But Pepys himself went to the theatre as much to view the beauties as to view the plays; and he enjoyed his liaisons with the wives of some subordinates, who received his favour in exchange for the virtue of their spouses. 'We are fallen into a strange age', thought the Earl of Arlington, 'wherein even the appearance of good morality is become ridiculous'.[5]

Pleasure was the god of the courtiers and court ladies painted by Sir Peter Lely and other fashionable portraitists. From their pictures, they gaze upon us wrapped – or in the case of the mistresses, somewhat unwrapped – in lavish draperies, with elaborate coiffures, succulent fruits, and exotic pets. Charles and his ministers and friends were perfectly capable of hard work, as occasion demanded, of course; but they demanded few such occasions. The king sometimes played with his favourite spaniels at the Privy Council while ignoring his ministers, and the dogs whelped and suckled in his bedchamber. The court's passion for card games extended to the Sabbath; and everything was subject to wager, including the outcomes of military battles and ministerial intrigues. Even worship was converted into entertainment when Charles introduced a consort of 24 violins at the royal chapel, much to the disgust of John Evelyn, who thought they left the liturgy sounding more fit for a 'tavern or play-house than a church'. And lest any be unaware of their parts, courtiers and courtesans displayed themselves regularly upon the promenades of Hyde Park and in the formal dances at which Charles and Castlemaine delighted. Entertainments at palaces and townhouses were transferred to river barges when the heat and dust of summer made the Thames a more enjoyable venue than parks and drawing rooms.[6]

Charles II was not alone in demonstrating his power through consumption, display, and the visible enjoyment of wealth. Castlemaine's London entertainments rivalled those of her master; and despite the wealth Charles lavished upon her, her debts were said to have reached £30,000 by 1666. When Bristol sought to dislodge Clarendon in 1663, he entertained Charles at 'midnight revels', at which 'luxury and elegance reigned' and often led to 'other pleasures'. Arlington sunk his fortune into improving Goring House (now the site of Buckingham Palace) and Euston Hall in Suffolk. In 1671, he entertained much of the court at Euston Hall for two weeks, while Charles played the ponies at the nearby Newmarket races by day and 'toyed' with the newly acquired Louise de Kéroualle by night. Buckingham consumed a fortune of £26,000 p.a. on 'pleasure, frolic, and extravagant diversions'. His debts were thought to exceed £120,000 in 1671.[7]

Charles and his court were as addicted to witty repartee and discourse as they were to conspicuous sex and consumption. Buckingham, who had 'a peculiar faculty of turning anything into ridicule', preferred to dispatch his political opponents through satirical language and impersonations rather than through clever manoeuvres. Unfortunately, this practice generally left his opponents in power and him out of it: 'He laughed himself from court,' according to John Dryden. Charles also indulged the acerbic wit of John Wilmot, Earl of Rochester, another member of the 'merry gang' of stylish court rakes that included Buckingham. To Rochester in particular, Charles extended the customary licence afforded to court jesters, and he was well repaid. The earl once remarked to Charles that he 'never said a foolish thing, and never did a wise one', to which the king replied that he was only responsible for his words, for his ministers were responsible for his actions. Among the women at Charles's court, the lowborn Nell Gwyn rivalled Buckingham in her gift for mimicry and ridicule. She referred to the Duke of York, who suffered from a poor sense of humour, as 'Dismal Jimmy' and to Louise de Kéroualle, who suffered from poor eyesight, as 'Squintabella'. When Castlemaine was drawn to court in a new carriage pulled by eight horses, a number that would have been considered over the top, even for a king, Nell appeared in a cart drawn by eight oxen, shouting, 'Whores to market! Ho!'[8]

Such elaborate pranks and ruses were as plentiful as puns in the circles around Charles, although the stories have often gained somewhat in the telling. When Sir Charles Sedley and two other genteel blades dulled by drink mooned a crowd from a Covent Garden balcony in 1663 they provoked a riot. Whether this was because Sedley was also preaching an obscene sermon or because they had 'excrementized' the crowd below, or both, is unclear. When the Earl of Oxford became so obsessed with the actress Hester Davenport that 'he could neither gamble nor smoke', he overcame her reluctance about a relationship by taking vows of marriage to her before a minister and a witness. Only after sleeping with Oxford, did the happy 'bride' discover that the marriage had been a masquerade and the minister one of the earl's musicians playing a part.[9]

Matters were frequently carried too far at Charles's court, especially under the influence of drink, and often to the point of violence. Rochester, whose alcoholism shortened his life, was banished from court after assaulting another guest at a state banquet in the king's presence: departing for France, he was soon involved in an altercation at the Paris Opera. Sedley hired a thug to beat up an actor who had impersonated him on the stage. Buckingham punched another peer in a parliamentary committee meeting; and the scandal about his London installation of the Countess of Shrewsbury was aggravated by the convenient death of her husband, whom he had wounded in a duel. Challenges of honour were commonplace at the Restoration court, although Charles did his best to prevent duelling. His courtiers found a substitute for showcasing their honour, heroism, and manly dexterity in the orchestrated violence of the Anglo-Dutch naval conflict. Buckingham was mortified that York refused him command of a warship merely because he had no maritime experience. But he was more fortunate than Charles's favourite courtier, Sir Charles Berkeley, created Earl of Falmouth, whose blasted brains stained York's tunic at the battle of Lowestoft.[10]

The public language and gestures of Charles and his courtiers have a distinctly theatrical flavour, and that is not surprising. No English court has ever been so intimately associated with the theatre as that of the Restoration. The drollery, the elaborate ruses, the sexual escapades, and the violence of the Whitehall set often imitated the themes and episodes of the Restoration stage. The two theatres that reopened in 1660 did so at royal behest as the King's Company and the Duke's Company; and at Charles's warrant, women also appeared legally on the English stage for the first time. Playwrights, managers, actors, and actresses appeared regularly at court; and courtiers filled the seats of the two theatres by night. Buckingham wrote one of the best of all Restoration dramas; Rochester and Sedley, better known for their verse, also wrote plays. Nell Gwyn was not the only actress to play in Charles's privy chamber. In a society in which the roles of actress and prostitute were not yet fully differentiated, the theatre provided mistresses for other leading lights as well. Elizabeth Barry, the most accomplished actress of the age, became Rochester's mistress, for instance. Evelyn found this whole scene 'fowl and indecent' and complained about the wanton actresses who seduced men from the stage.[11]

The court was, however, an arena in which men generally preyed upon women, rather than vice versa. Still, the sexual obsessions of courtiers could provide women with opportunities to dominate, both through sensuality and through intelligence. Excluded from formal politics, some women at court were able to release themselves from the constraints of patriarchy and to enjoy a measure of power unheard of in the ordinary course of constitutional and family affairs. A shocked Gilbert Burnet wrote that not only did some of them 'have great power, but [Charles's] court is full of pimps and bawds, and all matters in which one desires to succeed must be put in their hands'. Barbara, Lady Castlemaine was among Clarendon's most dangerous enemies, for instance, because, although the chancellor could manoeuvre against his male opponents in public, she could work against him in the privacy of Charles's bedchamber. Bennet's appointment as secretary of state in 1662 was attributed to her, as was the rising influence of Sir Charles Berkeley, another of Clarendon's political foes. Barbara was adroit at employing both temper and tongue to move the king, though she eventually found a worthy rival in Nell Gwyn. 'Nellie' was equally gifted at manipulating Charles with colourful language and gestures, though she lacked Barbara's political finesse. Operating in a world that equated masculinity with rationality and femininity with feeling, Barbara and Nell mocked convention as they empowered themselves by exploiting Charles's passion. Indeed, Castlemaine and Frances Stuart, another royal paramour, each had herself painted as Minerva, perhaps thereby claiming both the assertiveness and the rationality of that Roman goddess in defiance of the patriarchal assignment of such attributes to men.[12]

Royal mistresses were not alone in the governing circles of Charles II in enjoying considerable freedom. Elizabeth Murray, Lady Dysart, turned her 'wonderful quickness of apprehension' to political ends after she became the Duchess of Lauderdale. Burnet loathed her as 'a profuse, imperious woman' who ruled the duke and dominated the northern kingdom, 'for all applications were made to her; she sold places and disposed of offices'. Burnet may have pushed the matter too far; but the duchess was Lauderdale's most trusted advisor, and others who sought to influence him and the making of Scottish policy often approached her first. Catherine Sedley, daughter of Sir Charles Sedley, had a portion of £6,000 and might have made an excellent match, despite her plain looks; but Catherine was what a later age would call a blue stocking. Commanding great wit and intelligence, she preferred independence to the constraints of marriage; and she retained it as mistress to the Duke of York, suffering 'no restraint in what she said of or to anybody'. The widowed Aphra Behn entered Charles's entourage after impressing Buckingham and York and exchanging espionage for drama. Among the most prolific playwrights of her age, she was the first English woman to earn a living through her writing; and she generally championed the right of women to make the same choices, sexual or otherwise, as men.[13]

Ironically, although some contemporaries and historians have accused Charles of advancing his prerogative over the liberties of his subjects, he afforded a liberty to some women at court that shocked the culture cops of his reign. Yet these women operated in a male-dominated hothouse atmosphere from which they were largely unable to separate themselves and their aspirations for autonomy and self-expression. Moreover, the culture of the Restoration court was definitely not the culture of any of Charles's kingdoms. His behaviour and that of his closest friends, confidants, and ministers were quickly exposed to the critical scrutiny of leading subjects whose personal values and expectations were quite different from those that prevailed at court. Charles confronted a rising tide of political disillusionment after the mid-1660s that was evident even among his most ardent supporters. Disillusionment was driven by disaster as well: The plague of 1665 and the great London Fire of 1666 bred public anger at an extravagant and frivolous court. Explanations of these massive misfortunes were as likely to focus on the sins of the great few, who lived in licence at court, as upon those of the great many who suffered obscure deaths or the loss of loved ones and possessions. Even Charles turned more sober by the late 1660s as the settlements of his kingdoms were challenged by disaster, disappointment, and dissent. Still, for much of the rest of his reign, his court was a political liability for him rather than the political asset that it might have been.

Disease and Disaster, 1665–7

Early modern British people were no strangers to terror. Villagers could be panicked into local witch scares by inexplicable misfortunes. Countless thousands died in fright and despair during the economic, social, and military disruptions of the civil wars. The plague was so frequent a visitor that children soothed their fears through nursery rhymes about a 'ring around a rosie' that could cause 'all [to] fall down'. Over 25,000 were killed by the plague in London in 1625, when one-fifth of the urban population died, of all causes, within a single year. Another 10,000 died in the next London plague outbreak a decade later. Despite their experience of mortality on a scale almost unimaginable to the post-modern mind, early modern people were no less traumatized by individual deaths. The grief of loss could easily disorder mind and heart, while fear of sudden death could disrupt entire communities. To Londoners who lived through 1665–7, the fears of all the years seemingly came together in a sequence of terrifying events. In addition to suffering through the third and last great plague pandemic in Western history, the survivors experienced the obliteration of their homes and businesses in an unprecedented urban firestorm, worried about foreign invasion, and were shocked by a Dutch assault on the English navy in their own backyard. Then as now, such calamities, both natural and man-made, produced political storms like the one that overtook the parliamentary session of 1666–7.

Plague claimed at least 70,000 victims in London's 1665 population of about 400,000. The heaviest losses were in the poorest and most densely populated wards that ringed the city's walls to the north and east. An exodus of those with the means to flee began in early summer, when weekly plague deaths were still numbered only in the hundreds. Eventually, perhaps 200,000 fled the city, thronging the roads out, compounding the fear and misery of those who remained behind (often because they had nowhere else to go), and producing alarm in the communities where they sought refuge. Charles and the court left in early July as the weekly plague toll spiked towards one thousand. Samuel Pepys remained until the end of August, by which time the weekly toll had reached its peak of 7000 deaths. By then, corpses were rushed to hasty night burials in mass pits on the outskirts of the city. Caregivers fled or died, and trade ceased. Many families suffered multiple deaths, as residents of infected houses were quarantined within them with their sick. Young adults and teenagers who had survived the perils of early modern childhood were struck down with the rest, dashing the hopes and spirits of friends and family. Pepys thought the few passers-by on the streets in August looked 'like people that had taken leave of the world'.

Some provincial towns had similar experiences when the pestilence reached them later in the year or in 1666. The richer sort abandoned Colchester, in Essex, which lost half its population of ten or twelve thousand. Yarmouth and Southampton were badly hit, and Cambridge colleges closed for six months. Villagers away from the main transportation routes were more fortunate but still edgy about outsiders and refugees, who they worried might bring contagion with them. 'How fearful people were, thirty or forty, if not an hundred Miles from London, ... of any person that came to their houses,' recorded Richard Baxter: 'every man was a terror to another!'[14]

Parliament met for a few weeks in October 1665, not at Westminster, because of the plague, but rather at Oxford, where some of the court and legal establishment had also taken up residence. Members focused on war finance primarily and paid little attention to the calamity that was spreading from London. Another £1.25 million in wartime supply was approved with directions that new tax proceeds should secure new loans for the war, rather than being used to retire old royal debts, and that new lenders would be repaid in the order of their loans. This proposal, which was copied from Dutch practice, came from Sir George Downing, onetime Cromwellian envoy to Holland. Shepherded through the Commons by the court's rising parliamentary manager, Sir William Coventry, the procedure was opposed by Clarendon, who feared it would damage the government's relationship with existing creditors, mostly urban goldsmith bankers. In the short-term, the measure ensured that money raised for the war went for the war; but in the long-term, the accumulation of old debts and new war expenses proved too much for the government's shaky finances. MPs also requested that those in charge of supplying the navy present their accounts in the next session, showing early signs of the suspiciousness about government corruption that would plague Charles for the rest of the Cavalier Parliament.

The other major legislative accomplishment of the session demonstrated that Anglican loyalists were so far unmoved by complaints about the vindictive spirit of the 1662 church settlement. The Five Mile Act required that expelled clergy either take an oath against armed resistance and against attempting 'any alteration of government either in church or state' or remove themselves, by at least five miles, from their former parishes or any incorporated town.[15] The act was a response to several developments since 1662. Many puritan clergy who had lost their livings three years earlier had remained in the communities they once served, much to the irritation of new incumbents seeking rapport with their parishioners. The plague damaged the reputations of the Anglican clergy in London, where they were perceived as having fled in large numbers, while the dissenting clergy were credited with remaining to minister to the dying and the bereaved. Furthermore, many Anglican gentry still suspected the expelled clergy of disloyalty in the wake of the Northern Plot and of another minor republican conspiracy. The act was promoted by the most intransigent Anglican loyalists in both houses rather than by the government or by the bishops. But an oath against efforts to change anything in either church or state was sweeping, to say the least. A move to extend it to all civil officers, including MPs, was defeated in the Commons; and the act narrowly passed in the Lords, where many peers preferred to accommodate Presbyterians rather than to persecute them.[16]

After returning to Westminster in early 1666, as the plague subsided, the government redirected its attention to a war that had widened considerably. The Dutch had been joined both by Denmark and by Louis XIV, who was concerned about the balance of power following the initial Dutch reverses. The royalist crusade to crush an isolated republic had ended in Charles's diplomatic isolation instead, and the English navy confronted a potential combination of the two most significant continental fleets. English merchants felt increasingly vulnerable to their competitors as war, privateers, and the plague damaged their trade. The navy was also short of manpower as the ranks of experienced seamen were thinned by battle, disease, and desertion: press-gangs searched far inland for replacements. To complicate matters further, proceeds from tax revenues increasingly fell behind the costs of maintaining the government and the fleet. The additional money approved at Oxford was only half of what was needed, but new loans did come in upon it. In the winter of 1665–6, those entrusted with supplying and equipping the fleet achieved a near miracle in readying English naval forces for the coming season.

The naval encounters of 1666 nevertheless proved far less glorious than the Lowestoft victory of the previous summer. York was removed from his commanding naval role prior to the season: as heir to the throne he could not be risked in battle again. The fleet was placed under the joint command of two civil war enemies: the Duke of Albermarle and Prince Rupert of the Rhine, a cousin of the royal brothers. In early June, Albermarle attacked a superior Dutch fleet without Rupert, who had sailed westwards, down the Channel, with a quarter of the navy to intercept a French squadron. The first reports of the ensuing Four Days' Fight (1–4 June) were hopeful. Yet, when all was accounted for, the Dutch sailed away with the loss of only five ships to the English ten, and with the loss of 3000 killed and disabled to the English 6000. Worse, the prospect of a union of the Dutch and French fleets appeared even more likely than before. Within a matter of weeks, however, the press-gangs restocked English decks, and the London bankers raised new money for the government. The county militias were called out against the possibility of invasion. New ships were found, and damaged vessels were refitted. 'The best fleet … that ever England did see' encountered the Dutch, again without French support, on 25 July and chased them back to the Netherlands with significant losses. Two weeks later, an English squadron destroyed or damaged 170 Dutch merchantmen, many of them fully laden, at anchor in the Vlie. But the renewed prospect of English victory finally brought out the French fleet; and the season ended in stalemate rather than success. Stalemate was better than defeat, but the debt-ridden government would now find it impossible to secure and organize the financial resources that success required.[17]

By the time parliament met again in late September 1666, London was also in ruins. It was destroyed not by any foreign enemy but rather by fire, the natural enemy of the timber and plaster in which the city was largely built. As Lord Macaulay suggested in his monumental Victorian history of the Restoration, nothing quite like the Fire of London had occurred in Europe since the conflagration that destroyed Rome in the reign of Nero.[18] The Fire erupted in the early morning of 2 September at the conclusion of an unusually hot and dry summer. Starting near London Bridge, in the oven of one of the king's bakers, it quickly overwhelmed initial containment efforts and consumed numerous adjacent precincts where combustible naval supplies like pitch, tar, resin, and hemp were stored. The near gale-force wind that blew the flames to the west was something of a mercy, however. Had they travelled eastwards, the magazines of the Tower and the warships in the Thames might have blown up, taking much of the city's dockyard area with them. That was little consolation to most of the population, however. As fire spread through the heart of the city, so did mayhem among a panicked citizenry, who rushed to hire every conceivable form of transport, by land or by water, to rescue themselves and their goods. And unlike the plague, the Fire threatened the rich more than the poor, for they had the most to lose.

Price gouging by porters and carters and the looting of deserted shops and premises threatened a descent into lawlessness and chaos. Charles called out the militia of adjacent counties, and the king and the Duke of York personally directed bucket brigades and water engines. Royal encouragement emboldened the fire fighters, but their efforts were largely in vain. In five days, fire consumed 85 per cent of the city within the walls and much of the incorporated area to the west, as far as the legal precincts at the Inns of Court. As many as 13,000 homes were destroyed, as were 87 parish churches, 52 guild buildings, the civic Guildhall, the Exchange, and the cathedral. Evelyn depicted the conflagration as a scene from hell: 'The noise and crackling and thunder of the impetuous flames, the shrieking of women and children, the hurry of people, the fall of towers, houses and churches was like a hideous storm, and the air all about so hot and inflamed that at the last one was not able to approach it'. Only a few people died in the flames; but Richard Baxter bemoaned the loss of books and libraries throughout the city, noting that the wind carried charred pages as far as Windsor. Hundreds of thousands of refugees of all social degrees camped, with whatever they had saved, in the woods and hills to the north as far as Islington and Highgate.

The Fire of 1666 had been preceded by decades of speculation that the year of the millennium and three sixes, which included the number of the Beast of Revelation, would produce some kind of apocalyptic event. But contemporaries also sought more tangible explanations. Charles had to send troops to protect Dutch and French denizens from mobs of enraged refugees who believed the

Fire was a deliberate wartime stratagem likely to be followed by a foreign invasion. Comparisons of London's fate to that of Sodom or to that of Troy suggested alternate explanations for the city's destruction. Evelyn and many others interpreted the Fire as a Sodom-like judgement against the ingratitude of Charles and his subjects after their providential rescue from civil war and anarchy and for the 'burning lusts' and 'abominable lives' that were epitomized by a 'dissolute court'. The Trojan analogy, with its suggestion of an attack from within by an external enemy, was, however, more politically acceptable to the governing elite. A parliamentary committee of investigation gathered and published evidence, most of it fanciful, suggesting that the Fire had originated in another Catholic conspiracy against the Protestant order. As the city was rebuilt over the next four years, therefore, so was the national hatred of popery. The Fire was incorporated into English historical mythology as a spectacular popish contrivance that, in its success, surpassed the Gunpowder Plot of 1605.[19]

The parliamentary session that began in September 1666 and that continued until early 1667 began well for Charles and his ministers. Recognizing the government's need for more money to carry on the war, the House of Commons quickly voted £1.8 million in additional taxes, despite issues with the government accounts that were delivered to it. This session would nevertheless prove quite different from any other since Charles's restoration. The government's need for money was more easily agreed upon than the means for finding it, and the extraordinary costs of the war pointed anew to the deficiencies in the king's ordinary revenues. The onset of an agricultural depression pinched the rents and incomes of gentry MPs, who were increasingly suspicious of the government's financial management; but they initially took out their frustrations on the Irish rather than upon the extravagant court. Charles tangled with the Commons over what he regarded as an important parliamentary encroachment upon his prerogative. The Duke of Buckingham became the central figure in a recognizable opposition, while tensions between Clarendon and ministerial rivals such as Clifford, Arlington, and Coventry left the government incapable of outmanoeuvring its parliamentary critics. Libertarian language that had recently been directed against the tyranny of the Rump and of the New Model Army was now redirected towards the government, as some MPs and country gentry began to fear that absolutist and intolerant politicians were a greater threat than the Dutch or the sects. Finally, a significant revolt of militant Presbyterians threatened the security of the Scottish Lowlands and of the northern kingdom's new Episcopalian order. Charles II was, in fact, about to confront his first serious crisis, one that accentuated both his fiscal and military weaknesses and one that also involved renewed attention to the religious divisions of all three kingdoms. The crisis would soon propel the king in new political, religious, and diplomatic directions.[20]

Like many wars, the Anglo-Dutch conflict exacerbated social and economic issues that might otherwise have been handled with greater facility. The MPs who gathered at Westminster in the autumn of 1666 remained committed to seeing the war through to a successful conclusion, but they were anxious about the strain of taking on the better-financed Dutch and the resource-rich king of France. Their tempers were also put on edge by the languishing of the agricultural economy upon which most of them depended for their incomes. English grain prices had begun to fall as agricultural improvements enhanced yields, while demand levelled off because of the population decline after the plague. Beef prices were also falling, as the importation of Irish cattle and sheep increased the supply of marketable meat. The country's overseas trade, which had only recently recovered from the ill effects of Cromwell's war against Spain, was severely disrupted again. The French drove English merchant vessels from the Mediterranean, while Danish entry into the war closed the Baltic; and Dutch privateers hovered about the English coasts. The plague also disrupted internal trade, and the fire consumed the largest tax base in the three kingdoms. By 1666, government revenues derived from all sources were in a freefall from their projected yields.[21] Moreover, London's goldsmith bankers and merchants were profiting from loans to a spendthrift court, and country gentry wondered why they should be taxed at levels that bore comparison to the hated imposts of the Interregnum.

The panacea for curing all these ills was a bill to prohibit the export of Irish cattle, sheep, and swine into England. The primary intent of the bill was to prop up the rents and property values of the gentry by relieving them of competition from Irish-bred animals, but its language also expressed the gentry's suspiciousness of favouritism and corruption at court. They condemned the importation of Irish beasts as 'a public and common nuisance'. This language was understood, constitutionally, to trump royal dispensations from the act for the benefit of courtiers and royal friends, such as Ormond, who was a major importer.[22] The bill was offensive to many Irish landowners and producers, for it hit at their principal overseas trade. It was equally offensive to Charles, who resented English parliamentary interference in his management of Ireland. Despite the efforts of ministerial spokesmen in the Commons, the bill was sent to the Lords with a sizable majority. Aroused by prints attacking court immorality, MPs then demanded that parliamentary commissioners begin an inspection of all government accounts since the commencement of the war. Charles believed this manoeuvre struck at his prerogative as significantly as the Irish cattle bill.

Buckingham, who had not hitherto cut much of a parliamentary figure, took the lead in orchestrating this 'Country' opposition. It included former Presbyterians such as Lord Ashley, Anglican royalist gentry such as Edward Seymour, and old enemies of Clarendon such as Bristol. Opportunistically attacking court corruption and immorality, of which he had more than a little firsthand knowledge, Buckingham hoped to turn his command of the opposition – and his long friendship with Charles – into ministerial office. Disappointed expectations about the war provided the duke and his allies with an excellent opportunity for criticizing both how the war was being conducted and who was conducting it. Moreover, the government's proposal of a general excise, to supply the £1.8 million the Commons had already approved, horrified MPs: many preferred even heavier taxes on their own properties to a tax that might enlarge the government's fiscal bureaucracy and its ability to intrude upon their localities. By the second half of November, the two houses of parliament had also come into dispute over the Irish cattle bill. The Lords adopted the bill without the 'nuisance' clause, while the Commons insisted upon it. As discussion about how to supply the king against his foreign enemies continued, the government was also briefly thrown into panic by a rising in the southwest of Scotland.

Too easily dismissed by English historians for its brief duration, its limited scale, and its crushing defeat, the Galloway or Pentland rising was nevertheless the first significant expression of resistance to the church settlement in Scotland. It was also a sign of much more to come. Archbishop James Sharp and his Episcopal brethren had moved after 1664, through a newly created church court, to enforce the settlement upon recalcitrant clergy and laity. Indifferent lords and gentry had distanced themselves from the bishops, however; and some Presbyterian spokesmen broke their silence with denunciations of both the church court and the settlement. Worse, the 'sullen and refractory' people of the western shires, who still felt bound to their covenants, also remained committed to their expelled clergy. Illegal conventicles of armed worshippers became more numerous and sizable in those areas, and new incumbents often faced declining attendance and revenues from their parishioners. The 'whigs', as the militant Covenanters became known, saw themselves as defenders of the true Reformed religion against Episcopalian declension. The Anglo-Dutch war was the final ingredient in turning their unrest into rebellion. Charles and Lauderdale had exploited all the crown's Scottish revenues for the benefit of the war, despite the wartime disruption of the Scottish economy; and, fearing the intervention of the Calvinist Dutch on behalf of the Presbyterians, the Scottish Privy Council decided in 1666 to act against religious dissent.[23]

The revolt broke out in November 1666 after soldiers had been sent to the western counties to fine dissenters under the Scottish Conventicle Act and to silence their preachers. Its rapid escalation and organization point to widespread discussions of resistance that had apparently extended to Scottish exiles in Holland and to Presbyterian militants in Ireland as well. A motley force of a thousand or so men with a few experienced officers, disaffected lairds, and preachers quickly occupied Dumfries and marched towards the Scottish capital. While professing loyalty to Charles, they demanded a renewal of the covenants, the restoration of their ministers, and the elimination of bishops. Resolute efforts by the Edinburgh government prevented the sympathetic rising within the city that the rebels had counted upon as they approached it. Taking a strategic Pentland hilltop position a few miles away, against a superior government force sent out against them, the rebels stood unsuccessfully for 'the God of Jacob' against those they believed had desecrated his church. The retribution that followed, with some 36 executions, failed to pacify the western countryside, failed to enhance the status of the Episcopal clergy,

and failed also to secure the Scottish settlement against the unrest
it had so far produced.[24]

In the meantime, the English parliamentary session continued at
Westminster. Wrangling between the Country opposition and the
court, as well as wrangling between the Lords and the Commons,
centred upon how to supply the crown and upon how the financial
accountability of the government could be achieved. Rumours
that Charles had initiated secret peace negotiations fed suspicions
among some MPs that the king was demanding supply not for the
war, but rather for a standing army or for some other injurious
purpose. In response, the Commons symbolically impeached the
governor of Windsor Castle, an old royal friend, for various cor-
ruptions. As deadlock ensued, one loyalist peer suggested, 'either
the kingdom will be reduced to a commonwealth' or the king must
'govern by some other medium' than parliament.[25] MPs seemed
as suspicious of the government's fiscal integrity and of its military
reliability as at any previous time under Stuart rule. Deadlock was
weakened when Charles offered his own accounts commission; and
it was broken when, over Clarendon's objections, the king accepted
the 'nuisance' clause of the Irish cattle bill. An assessment bill providing the crown with the funds already voted was finally adopted at
the end of January 1667, and parliament was finally prorogued.

The provocative Irish cattle bill made not a whit of difference to
the slumping English rural economy. It also damaged Ireland less
than might have been supposed, given that kingdom's economic
reliance upon its export trade to England. Over the long run, it
accelerated an ongoing diversification of Irish exports. Nevertheless the act foreshadowed subsequent efforts of English MPs to
subordinate the Irish economy to their own, and its passage was
accompanied by much anti-Catholic rhetoric. Historically, it is a
stark reminder of the insistence of the English landed elite upon
the dependent status of Ireland.[26]

The £1.8 million in additional financing that the crown had
secured also made not a whit of difference to the war's resolution, for, with Clarendon's encouragement, Charles had already
initiated private peace negotiations with Louis and would soon
enter into public discussions with the Dutch. Sick of parliamentary
whining, the king was as eager for an entente with France as he
once had been for war with Holland. Charles was also certain that
Louis would force favourable terms upon his Dutch allies. For his

part, Louis had now set his sights upon parts of the Spanish Netherlands, which he claimed by right of descent through his Spanish
queen. His new objective made the Dutch, who were hostile to
an expansion of France on their borders, an awkward ally; and it
made the English, who were equally concerned about the disposition of territories across the Channel, an awkward enemy. In light
of the prospect of peace, the Privy Council decided that the fleet
would not be equipped for another season: the great warships
were to be laid up in the Thames, while smaller vessels were only
to patrol the coasts. The decision proved catastrophic, however, for
the Dutch continued the war to tilt the negotiations, which opened
at Breda in May 1667, in their favour.[27]

In June, a fully outfitted Dutch fleet destroyed the English
defences at the opening of the Medway and proceeded up the
Thames to Chatham. There, the Dutch burnt three first-rate
warships, damaged others, sailed off with the flagship (the *Royal
Charles*), and set up a blockade of the most important English
commercial and military waterway. Unpaid for months, English
seamen deserted their places or surrendered. Nothing could have
been more humiliating for the government. It was the last straw
for London citizens who had survived plague, fire, and increased
taxation for the sake of the king and his immoral court. They now
again feared a foreign invasion. Crowds milled about Westminster,
demanding a parliament and destroying the windows and grounds
of Clarendon's new mansion in Piccadilly. Pepys reported that
many people thought it would 'cost blood to answer for these miscarriages' and were 'talking treason in the streets openly; as, that we
are bought and sold and governed by papists and ... are betrayed by
people about the king and shall be delivered up to the French'.[28]

Charles had little choice but to make peace on the best terms he
could manage and, in order to mollify public opinion, to summon
parliament before the October date to which it had been prorogued.
The recall of parliament was made over Clarendon's objections, a
strong sign that his influence continued to wane in comparison to
that of ministerial rivals such as Arlington and Coventry. Peace was
concluded at Breda, a few days before the new session began on
25 July, with better terms than might have been expected. The
Dutch ceded New Netherland to the English; and the English
relinquished Surinam in South America, which the Dutch had
recaptured in 1666. The Dutch improved their trading position in

the East Indies and West Africa at the expense of the English East India and African Companies. The French returned English St. Kitts in the West Indies as well as Montserrat and Antigua, all of which they had captured, in return for territorial concessions in North America. Far from crushing Dutch republicanism and enhancing the position of Charles's Orange relatives, the war also ended with a diplomatic recognition of the right of English and Scots republicans and dissenters to unmolested Dutch sanctuary.

The peace did at least permit Charles to send home, until October, the MPs who had assembled at Westminster. Some of them had arrived angry, suspecting that Charles intended to govern with a standing army funded by the new taxes they had approved. But they left angrier still, now worrying also that he intended, like his father, to rule without a parliament. The regime that Clarendon had established upon cooperation with parliament was in a shambles; and the increasingly unpopular chancellor, who had opposed the war at its inception, became the scapegoat for the series of disasters that had unhinged the government and the public since 1665. In August Charles dismissed him from office, hoping that, since Clarendon 'had drawn upon himself much envy and many enemies' over the long course of his service, he could thereby 'cover himself and the rest of the court'.[29] Charles also restored Buckingham, whose political antics had briefly earned him a room in the Tower, to the Privy Council, as he sought to mend his political fences before the next parliamentary session. In dumping Clarendon, Charles believed he had released himself from the past and all its troubles. He would, however, continue to be troubled by the consequences of his foreign policy, by the reputation of his court, and by doubts and fears about his political intentions. The disasters of 1665–7 had run their course; but they had also exposed all the weaknesses of the restored English state and some of the problems of governing multiple monarchies. The assertion of religious divisions would also now suggest the extent to which Episcopalian leaders had underestimated the difficulty of coercing dissenting Protestants into their churches.

The Culture and Politics of Dissent

Much has been written about the latter-day puritans or noncon-formists who, after 1660, preferred persecution outside the Church

of England to conformity to its strictures. The great British historian R. H. Tawney and the great German sociologist Max Weber
each pointed to the culture of dissent as providing the intellectual
environment in which the capitalist pursuit of wealth was transformed from a byway of moral temptation into a highway of Christian duty.[30] Despite much criticism of this argument, many scholars
have, since it was first offered in the early twentieth century, been
more interested in dissenting economic behaviour than in dissenting religious ideas. In American thought, writers from Nathaniel
Hawthorne to Arthur Miller have also developed a largely negative
cultural image of the nonconformists' New England cousins – and
especially of the puritan clergy – as guilt-ridden witch hunters and
killjoys. Such stereotypes routinely inform initial approaches to the
topic of Restoration dissent; and textbooks generally offer little
to offset them. Yet this same nonconformist culture provided, in
John Milton, one of the greatest of all English poets, and in John
Bunyan and Daniel Defoe, two of the finest English prose stylists.
Andrew Marvell, Richard Baxter, and William Penn – all writers of
no mean skill, whose work continues to be reprinted and studied –
were also among the principal spokesmen for Restoration dissent.
Moreover, far from centring upon arcane ceremonial disputes,
nonconformity was a principal issue of Restoration politics in all
three kingdoms. Indeed, more than any other shared problem, the
issue of dissent tied the politics of the three kingdoms together. In
England, Charles II and his ministers, followed by James II and his,
repeatedly stumbled as they navigated between the bishops and
their dissenting critics.

The modern denominational labels that historians have borrowed
to distinguish late seventeenth-century British Protestants of different persuasions from each other have only complicated approaches
to the culture of nonconformity. Such labels as Presbyterian,
Baptist, and Independent (or Congregationalist) artificially impose
tidy divisions upon believers with ambiguous and cross-grained
views and suggest that emerging religious structures could only
have developed in precisely the ways they did. In reality, the newly
re-established Episcopalian state churches and the nonconformist
communities were still at an early stage of defining themselves; and
even the dichotomy between conformists and nonconformists was
often not as clear-cut, especially in England, as the words suggest.
It bears repeating that between 1662 and 1688 the broad mass of

British Protestants of Reformed perspectives – that is, all those whose emphasis upon lay leadership, congregational discipline, and predestination were derived from Calvinist tradition – were divided between the established churches and nonconformity without losing old connections that crossed that divide. In England, dissenters who preferred the ministry of deprived or excluded clergy often followed them without separating from 'puritan' friends and kinsmen who continued to encourage preaching and godly behaviour, rather than ceremony, within their parish churches. Many who generally habituated either church or conventicle were more than occasionally found at the other. Presbyterian and Independent clergy who left their livings also still shared much with some Calvinist clergy within the church who had the same reservations about required ceremonies and Episcopal authority.

A tripartite division of British Protestants into Episcopalian or Anglican, Reformed or Calvinist, and sectarian is more helpful than the customary denominational nomenclature in understanding the culture of nonconformity. Most dissenters were Reformed Protestants, and many of them hoped to return to their parish churches at some point in the future after their reservations about the bishops and the liturgy had been resolved through church resettlement. Charles II encouraged them in these hopes, expressing both his preference for ecclesiastical healing and a calculation that stroking 'moderate' dissenters would deter them from more extreme courses. In England, Baxter and some other Presbyterian clergy regularly attended the parish churches they hoped to rejoin, thereby avoiding the appearance of schism and setting an example for their followers. Similarly, Denzil, Baron Holles, a leading nonconformist layman, maintained both Anglican and Presbyterian chaplains, while the Worcestershire Presbyterian Thomas Foley both patronized dissenting clergy and exercised his right of appointment to an Anglican pulpit.[31] Sectarian Protestants, on the other hand, saw their separation from the church as a necessary exercise of Christian liberty. The Quakers, most Baptists, and some Independents and Scottish Covenanters saw temporal direction of the church as an abomination incompatible with the Reformation. As separation continued, younger Presbyterian clergy, who had had little or no experience of the Cromwellian church, as well as many Independents, became more comfortable with dissent and less interested in comprehension in a reformed establishment.

Nonconformists faced opposite directions in the Restoration, then, as some looked back to the state churches from which they had withdrawn, while others looked forward to the separated churches they were creating. Yet many Reformed Protestants outside the church establishments continued to share more with fellow believers within the church than with sectarians. In England, the enormous grey area occupied by those who preferred their deprived former clergy, but who hesitated to separate completely from their parish churches, needs to be taken into account in considering nonconformist numbers. So does the behaviour of many who withdrew from dissenting meetings in times of strict enforcement of the ecclesiastical laws, only to return when times were better. In fact, at no time since the English Reformation had such a large proportion of the population sought and found Protestant ministry outside the state church. Speaking in 1662, Clarendon thought the English bishops had their work cut out for them in attracting 'the poor misled people' back to 'the bosom of their dear mother church'. The Presbyterian John Humfrey claimed in 1668, when many still feared to meet privately, that the English church settlement had 'so narrowed up' the church that 'the non-conformists ... outbalance[d] those that do conform.' In 1680, Algernon Sidney thought 'above a million of men [in England] ... go under the name of nonconformists.' A few years later, Andrew Marvell's nephew thought the 'collective body of the several dissenters is manifestly greater than the Church of England alone'; and William Penn complained, 'a national religion by law, where it is not so by number and inclination, is a national nuisance.' Each of these authors was arguing for the dissenting cause, of course; but even some Anglicans complained in 1680 that dissenting assemblies were 'more in number than the parish churches, by reason the penal laws are not put in execution against them'.[32]

Dissent was virtually absent from many English rural areas, especially in the North. In London, in regional centres such as Bristol and Yarmouth, and in market towns throughout the country, on the other hand, dissenters were numerous and involved in local government, notwithstanding their statutory proscription from office holding. English dissenters were in communication with dissenters from the established churches of Scotland and Ireland as well. Formal rejection of Episcopal establishments, or active dissatisfaction with them, was shared by much of the adjacent populations of Ulster and of the Scottish Southwest, where the disaffected certainly outnumbered the Episcopal interest. In Scotland, the 'general discontent' with the Scottish church settlement extended out of the Southwest into Edinburgh as well. Some new rectors were shunned in the Scottish kingdom's governmental centre; and bystanders there viewed an attempted assassination of Archbishop Sharp, in 1668, with indifference: 'It was but a bishop', they said. In Ulster, only a dozen conformists could be found in Antrim town in the 1660s, according to one report. Only one parish church in the entire diocese of Derry was suitable for worship, a condition that scarcely inclined the population to conformity. In Ireland as a whole, the dissenting groups, considered together, outnumbered Episcopalian Protestants and exceeded them in determination as well.[33]

Despite the continuing dissent of some great puritan aristocrats such as Lords Holles, Bedford, and Wharton and of country gentry such as Thomas Foley, dissenting leadership in England, as well as in Ireland, passed from land to trade after 1660. Some dissenters of most persuasions could be found in most social groups, but Presbyterians were especially numerous among overseas merchants and domestic traders, while Independents had strong support among the middling sort. One observer suggested in 1672 that 'Presbyterians have generally on their side the corporations [incorporated towns], and all formal men, which they are pleased to call the sober part of the nation,' while 'the Independents or fanatics consist only in artisans and the meanest of the land.' The Independents and the sects did, in fact, retain a significant following among ordinary people, like the members of John Bunyan's Bedford church, or the numerous conventicles of London's teeming outer wards. Yet the connection between trade and dissent was a fundamental assumption of many Restoration writers. Slingsby Bethel and other advocates of toleration insisted that nothing more discouraged the advancement of commerce than the church's persecution of dissent. Examination of the religious views of London's overseas traders confirms the connections that Tawney and Weber sought to establish between Calvinism and capitalism. Dissenters took the lead in the colonial trades, which is not surprising in light of their relationships and friendships with New Englanders. They were also heavily involved in the expansion and diversification of English trade to the Mediterranean, to the Levant, and to the Baltic that became noticeable during Charles's reign and that continued thereafter.[34]

Anglicans saw dissenters as a threat not only because of the role of puritan and sectarian religion in the recent civil wars but also because of the visibility of women within the dissenting milieu. Although the days of sectarian female preaching had passed even before the Restoration, the opportunities for women within the culture of nonconformity still surpassed those available within the Anglican fold. Some dissenting aristocratic ladies such as Elizabeth Cecil, the dowager Countess of Essex, for instance, were long-time patrons of leading nonconformist clergy. Similarly, the puritan gentlewoman Mary Speke presided at West Country conventicles, sponsored preachers, and bred a family of enemies to Anglicanism. Among dissenters of the middling sort were some women active in the publishing trades. When the Baptist Elizabeth Calvert's bookseller husband died in 1663, for instance, she continued without him as a principal publisher and distributor of unlicenced, 'seditious', and sectarian works. As the Quakers sought to order their ranks, and especially to subordinate women's meetings to male leadership, women nevertheless continued to act as organizers and missionaries. Margaret Fell's managerial skills surpassed those of her husband, George Fox, the nominal leader of the sect. The Quaker missionary Elizabeth Hooten lectured Charles II in St James's Park, preached in Boston, and died in Jamaica. Similarly, Joan Vokins defended women's meetings in Berkshire, toured New York, and ministered to slaves in Barbados. Overall, women outnumbered men at most dissenting meetings, perhaps by a factor of about three to two.[35]

Despite the many differences that separated Reformed nonconformists from sectarians, most British dissenters shared several religious perspectives that matured into a distinctive dissenting ethos in the late 1660s and early 1670s. Their rejection of the restored Episcopal structures of the Restoration as lacking in reformation was among these common denominators. One Presbyterian spokesman championed the English Reformation as 'the most perfect and complete' of its kind, for instance; but he saw the liturgical requirements of the 1662 prayer book as a 'retreat' from reformation. Dissenters objected to more than a perceived substitution of dull ceremony for lively preaching. They were especially critical of Episcopalian practices for insufficiently directing believers 'towards evangelical perfection and purity'. Richard Baxter and John Bunyan, one a Presbyterian and the other a sectarian, agreed that 'the soul of religion is the practick part', or the expression of individual faith in Christlike behaviour. They feared that the establishment's emphasis upon conformity merely produced outward Christian observance without changing the heart or transforming the believer. Presbyterians, Independents, and Baptists all sought to nurture personal faith and godliness through exhortatory preaching and extemporary prayer, through the application of scripture to individual experience, and through lay participation in church affairs. Similarly, the simple forms of Quaker worship enabled friends to share their experience of the divine presence and to encourage each other's pursuit of holiness.[36]

The greatest blemish of the Restoration church establishments, according to dissenters of all persuasions, was the persecution of individual conscience. Their definition of conscience and their defence of religious liberty (for Protestants, at least) became nonconformist contributions to modernity as important as their embrace of the sober, disciplined life that could advance trade and the accumulation of wealth. English dissenting spokesmen hammered out a definition of conscience as a faculty that requires each individual to come to a personal judgement about divine expectations for one's self. They argued that the expression of conscience is as essential to human nature as the use of reason, to which it is related. For them, obedience to conscience is obedience to God; and obedience to God takes precedence over the dictates of clerical and secular authorities. Indeed, the constraint of individual faith for the sake of conformity was, in the words of William Penn, 'a scandal to the Reformation'. According to the Quaker writer and to others, any coercion of belief challenges the sovereignty of God over conscience, violates reason, and reduces human beings to passive, uncritical 'bruits'.

The persecution of believers by a nominally Protestant state church was, moreover, a vestige of the spirit of 'popery'. If not checked, the persecution of Protestants would subvert the Reformation, threaten the state, and lead to Catholic recovery. Both Andrew Marvell and Richard Baxter argued that diocesan episcopacy, which had reached its apex in the Roman Catholic Church, had often produced an 'unchristian tyranny' over individual conscience. They believed also that lordly European prelates had frequently 'seduced' princes into 'ruling by constraint', thereby producing arbitrary government in church and state alike.

They blamed persecuting bishops for the divisions of British Protestantism that weakened it in its confrontation with the Catholic enemy. Dissenting anti-popery was more than a blind prejudice, however. It was a reading of contemporary and historical events that reflected a century of Protestant decline in the face of Catholic renewal and expansion, and it also expressed a commitment to limited monarchy in a century of mounting absolutism.[37]

Neither was dissenting anti-Catholicism an expression of insularity. Reformed believers outside the Episcopal establishments saw themselves as part of an international order of Reformed churches that extended from Geneva and the Rhineland through Holland and France to the British Isles and New England. This international outlook was reinforced among London dissenting merchants and clergy by ties of marriage, business, and friendship to the sizable Dutch and French Reformed immigrant communities in the city. Presbyterians and Independents were especially sensitive by the 1670s to the advances of Catholic France, for those advances often came at the expense of Reformed churches and Reformed traders abroad. Many sectarians were equally international in outlook. The self-educated John Bunyan was steeped in the treatises of Martin Luther, while Quaker missionary endeavours extended to the colonies of North America and the Caribbean as well as to the Islamic world of Egypt and Turkey. Dissenters viewed Charles II in this broad, international context as the most powerful European Protestant monarch and, therefore, as the natural protector of Protestantism against Catholic recovery. Despite their disappointments with him, they continued to hope that he might resettle the church in a more inclusive fashion, establish liberty of conscience for all Protestants, and claim his rightful role as the 'head of all the Protestant party in the world'.[38]

These elements of nonconformist culture were the perspectives of political and religious activists, not those of a defeated remnant. Characterizations of Restoration dissent as marked by quietism or a withdrawal from a corrupt world miss the mark, and they are too dependent upon a few brooding passages from Milton and Bunyan. In fact, Milton and Bunyan infused some of their principal literary characters with a combative spirit that is far more emblematic of nonconformist culture in all three kingdoms. Milton's Samson, for instance, smites the 'lords, ladies, captains, counsellors, [and] priests' of a decadent Philistine nation as a warning to Charles and his wanton set, while Bunyan's Faithful condemns the Prince of Vanity, 'with . . . his attendants' (including the Lord Carnal Delight, Lord Luxurious, Lord Lechery, and Sir Having Greedy), as fit 'for being in Hell'.

The rhetorical violence of such literature was matched by the forcible actions many dissenters took to protect their meetings and to promote reformation and godliness. In the London Easter riots of 1668, thousands of evangelical London apprentices, spiritually awakened by the kingdom's late disasters, attacked the bawdy houses, threatened to 'pull Whitehall down' (as the kingdom's chief brothel), and demanded liberty for conscience. Thousands of London dissenters again took to the streets in 1670 to defend their meetings against the efforts of London magistrates to enforce a new Conventicle Act. 'Heaven is inherited by the violent', argued one of their preachers, who turned the faithful into holy warriors against persecution, and who rejected 'moderation' as the counsel of the worldly. Dissenting perspectives might also reinforce surreptitious attachments to loosely republican principles, for the Reformed rejection of pomp and ceremony in the church could easily be translated into the commonwealth political language of hostility to waste, corruption, and the abuse of power. Most dissenters were not, in fact, republicans. Nevertheless, many of them admired the republican regime in the Netherlands and well remembered how the English republic and Protectorate had championed trade and godliness.[39]

The culture of nonconformity was, therefore, a breeding ground for convictions and actions detrimental to the forms of government in church and state in each of Charles's kingdoms. As the second Anglo-Dutch War concluded in a political train wreck in England, Charles and some politicians rightly worried that the continuing persecution of dissenters might destabilize the regime. Buckingham sought to take political advantage of the dissatisfactions of the nonconformists by presenting himself in 1666–7 as their public champion. When Charles took Buckingham into government at the war's end, many read this political rapprochement as a prelude to a more comprehensive resettlement of the church. Buckingham's associates were known to include other opponents of religious coercion such as Lord Ashley and Ashley's house intellectual, John Locke, who soon put his mind to arguments for toleration. Even Clarendon sought to separate himself from the punitive religious code that historians have unfairly named for him. Seeking to re-establish his position in the weeks before his dismissal, the chancellor opened conversations with leading Presbyterian and Independent clergy. As discussion of comprehension quickened, moderate and uncompromising bishops also began to divide over its prospects. All these developments pointed to the strength and spirit of dissent as well as to the unravelling of Charles's English government in the wake of military disappointment. For the remainder of his reign, Charles would engage in a complex *pas de deux* with his dissenting subjects in all three kingdoms, alternating between the near acceptance and the harsh rejection of their overtures. Now moving towards accommodation, he would prove unable to sustain one position or the other, leaving his realms exposed to unsettlement and confusion.[40]

Dealing with Dissent, 1667–72

The possibility of enlarging the Anglican church through the statutory comprehension of moderate dissenters was lost in the furious autumn 1667 parliamentary session that followed the Peace of Breda. Buckingham had been rehabilitated on the assumption that he and his political friends could secure an improved supply for a king who was now over two million pounds in debt. Unfortunately, the temper of the House of Commons had not improved during the summer prorogation. Re-assembling in October, the house quickly established a committee to investigate numerous examples of mismanagement and corruption during the war, while Charles's ministers nervously fingered each other as potential scapegoats. Although a bill to achieve a more comprehensive church settlement had been prepared in advance of the session and had attracted Charles's interest, it was never introduced. Instead, Buckingham attempted to redirect the Commons' fury against the fallen Clarendon, hoping thereby to get on the right side of the house's indignation and also to secure MPs' consent to financial expedients for the crown's benefit. A measure to impeach Clarendon for treason was held up in the Commons by reservations about the evidence. When it finally reached the House of Lords, the old chancellor's friends, including most of the bishops, opposed it. The earl soon fled abroad. Taking his flight as proof of guilt, parliament banished him for life. Charles then adjourned the session, already unhappy about Buckingham's inability to focus parliament's attention on his financial needs.

The government that eventually took shape in succession to Clarendon's ministry has generally been referred to as the Cabal. Current at the time, the label was based upon the initial letters of the surnames of five leading ministers and privy councillors: Sir Thomas **C**lifford, the Earl of **A**rlington (who served as principal secretary of state), the Duke of **B**uckingham, Lord **A**shley (Chancellor of the Exchequer), and the Duke of **L**auderdale (secretary for Scotland). The Cabal was not the tight-knit group the label suggests, however. It was more a style of government in which these and other politicians competed for power and influence, making short-term alliances to accomplish their goals and to reward their followers. Indeed, the years of the Cabal, from 1667 to 1672, were an era of political opportunism, intrigue, and deceit. Few practitioners of Cabal politics escaped with their reputations in tact. Marvell referred to Clifford as a 'tall louse', for instance, while Clarendon took revenge on his rival Arlington by recording that he 'knew no more of the constitution and laws of England than he did of China'. One recent authority has suggested that Arlington achieved pre-eminence in this government from the outset,[41] but Charles himself was the most successful politician of 1667–72, routinely manipulating his ministers and playing them off against each other. Governing by committee, Charles further diffused power by keeping some major offices (such as that of lord chancellor) vacant while assigning others (such as the Treasury) to commissions of multiple office holders. Buckingham was never trusted with an important administrative position, and he was kept on the Privy Council primarily to prevent him from becoming a political nuisance. Councillors who did become nuisances, such as Sir William Coventry, caricatured on the stage as 'Sir Cautious Trouble-all', soon found themselves without offices.

Diplomacy is generally given pride of place in accounts of the Cabal, but the domestic situations faced by Charles and his ministers in the three Stuart kingdoms are equally interesting. The Scottish rebellion of 1666, following other risings in England and Ireland, provoked a debate about whether coercive religious settlements could truly secure either church or state. Episcopalian hardliners believed the Pentland rising demonstrated the need for the complete suppression of non-parochial worship. Protestants of

Reformed perspectives within and without the established churches, on the other hand, believed the rebellion instead proved that coercion of Protestants would never secure domestic peace.

In England, the Cabal ministers largely subscribed to the latter view. Indeed, the need to moderate enforcement of the penal legislation against those outside the church establishments was virtually the only policy upon which they all agreed. None of them shared Clarendon's strong Anglicanism. Buckingham and Ashley had abandoned Presbyterianism without abandoning their Presbyterian connections. Ashley was drawn particularly close to London's dissenting traders though his involvement in colonial ventures in the West Indies and in the new Carolina plantation launched in the 1660s and 1670s. Lauderdale's past was Presbyterian as well, although he had more explicitly separated himself from it. Clifford was a secret Catholic; and Arlington, who had learned his style of diplomacy in Spain in the 1650s, was suspected of Catholicism long before his deathbed conversion. Clifford and Arlington hoped that a relaxation of the persecution of Protestant dissenters could be turned to the benefit of Catholics.

With Charles's encouragement, ministers responsible for affairs in the three kingdoms began to distinguish between moderate dissenters, who might be tolerated or accommodated, and extreme dissenters, whose defiance of political authority required a harsher response. Domestic policy in each kingdom exhibited a peculiar combination of moderation and repression as ministers focused upon both groups simultaneously. The details of this new approach to the religious issue varied from kingdom to kingdom, but by the early 1670s, Charles had adopted it as uniformly as he had accepted the Episcopalian policy of coercion in the early 1660s. For his own part, the king began the slow movement towards Rome that was completed only in his final hours, while his brother James explicitly abandoned Canterbury for the pope.

Both the proponents and the critics of coercion were ready for full debate of the matter when the English parliament resumed its work in February 1668. Buckingham had encouraged conversations among moderate Anglicans such as the former Cromwellian divine John Wilkins, leading Presbyterians such as Richard Baxter, and the Independent spokesman Dr John Owen. Charles personally assured the Presbyterians they would eventually be comprehended and encouraged them to practice greater discretion in their meetings.

One bill prepared prior to the session provided for comprehension of the Presbyterian clergy by relaxing liturgical requirements and by accepting their non-Episcopal ordination. Another draft bill provided an indulgence for sectarians who could not be comprehended. Pepys reported 'a great presumption that there will be a toleration', and Charles opened the session by requesting that a way be found better to enable his subjects of different persuasions to support the government.[42]

Unfortunately for Charles and his ministers, however, the parliament that met in 1668 remained the parliament chosen in the Anglican reaction of 1661. When he learned what was afoot, Archbishop Gilbert Sheldon organized the friends of episcopacy in the Commons in defence of the existing church settlement. MPs sympathetic to the dissenters, on the other hand, claimed they were 'a people in communion with us in doctrine' and argued that 'a more easy way' of church settlement needed to be tried because the 'strict government of the Church' had only increased nonconformist numbers. In the end, the house voted, with strong majorities, against any accommodation with dissenters and for a new bill against conventicles to replace the 1664 act, which would soon expire. Coercion was nevertheless weakened when the House of Lords failed to proceed with the new conventicle bill before the end of the session. Buckingham, Ashley, and other friends of the dissenters were largely responsible for this failure. They deliberately enflamed a minor jurisdictional dispute between the two houses, both to divert attention from the conventicle bill and to produce a hung parliament. They hoped thereby to persuade Charles of the need to dissolve the Cavalier Parliament, for they also believed a new election would produce a Commons more sympathetic to religious accommodation. Charles declined to dissolve parliament, but he also declined to enforce a new proclamation against conventicles that he issued to appease the churchmen.[43]

The advancement of religious accommodation in Scotland and Ireland proceeded without such parliamentary fireworks. Lauderdale resisted suggestions from some that the restlessness of the western shires required the continuing maintenance of regular troops in that area. Instead, the Scottish secretary worked with those privy councillors who thought the northern kingdom could be pacified by reclaiming 'peaceable dissenters' through leniency and through a more adequate provision of Episcopal clergy. But he also maintained punitive measures against the 'wilful opposers and condemners' of the church.[44]

In 1669, the Scottish government implemented a two-pronged policy of indulging moderate dissenters, while acting more forcefully against illegal conventicles. The scheme apparently originated with Lauderdale's youthful clerical protégé, the Episcopalian moderate and future historian Gilbert Burnet. Fines upon those who attended conventicles or who permitted illegal worship on their premises were increased. On the other hand, deprived ministers who applied to the Privy Council or to parish patrons were permitted to resume public ministry in vacant parishes under various terms, with those willing to accept Episcopal appointment given greater privileges. This indulgence was accompanied by the adoption of an Act of Supremacy by the Scottish estates that confirmed the king's ability, in terms abhorrent to some Presbyterians, to determine the church's form of government, and to superintend the clergy. Over the next year, some 40 of the deprived Scots clergy who were willing to acquiesce in these terms resumed full parish ministry, while dozens of others were also legally able to preach.

James Sharp, Archbishop of St. Andrews, and the bishops of the Church of Scotland accepted these measures only reluctantly, however; and they were rejected as well by faithful Covenanters, who persisted in worshipping outside the church. Deprived clergy continued to preach to large conventicles throughout the Lowlands; and 2000 worshippers, 'all armed', attended an enormous field conventicle in Fife in June 1670. Even some of the indulged clergy preached to conventicles outside the parishes to which they had been assigned, while many of them continued to reject Episcopalian forms of worship. The government responded by pushing the Clanking Act through parliament. It provided the death penalty for preachers at field conventicles, while fining attendees at house conventicles a quarter of their annual incomes.

Lauderdale also worked to comprehend moderate Presbyterian clergy within the church in order to split the religious opposition. Discussions between the leading indulged clergy and the Privy Council about such an accommodation began during the 1670 Scots parliament. When the discussions failed, Burnet, by then professor of divinity at the University of Glasgow, authored a proposal to indulge more of the deprived clergy and to fill vacant pulpits. Burnet's proposal became the basis of a second Scottish indulgence in 1672, a measure that permitted dissenting clergy to serve particular parishes in pairs. But it also restricted their preaching to those parishes; and like the indulgence of 1669, it was accompanied by measures to suppress the expression of nonconformity outside the church. Some 90 additional dissenting clergy were deemed eligible for service under this scheme, meaning that half the Scots clergy deprived in 1663 were now considered capable of returning to public ministry. A good number of these proved unwilling to accept the terms of their rehabilitation, but dissenting clergy soon served within 80 parishes of the Scottish church. Lauderdale thereby succeeded in splitting Presbyterianism through indulgence, and many lairds of Presbyterian sympathies were also reconciled through the government's moderation. What remained to be seen was whether most dissenting laity would follow the indulged pastors back into the church or whether many would reject all compromise with episcopacy in favour of the more intransigent dissenting clergy.[45]

The close cultural and religious ties between the Presbyterian populations of Ulster and Lowland Scots shires such as Dumfries ensured that conventicles were as large, belligerent, and frequent in Northern Ireland as they were in the Scottish Southwest. Three or four thousand dissenters attended an all-day field conventicle near Carrickfergus in 1670, for instance, listening to six sermons and receiving communion. Religious disaffection in Ulster was also fed by itinerant Scottish clerical refugees who bolstered Presbyterian commitments to the Solemn League and Covenant and to liberty for conscience. Dissenting gatherings in Dublin could be large as well: 3000 mourners, including the lord mayor and several aldermen, attended the funeral of a prominent Dublin Independent divine in 1666. In response, the lord lieutenant, Ormond, preferred mild enforcement of the Irish Uniformity Act to full-scale coercion, despite his own strong Episcopalian commitments, and despite the wishes of the Irish bishops. Ormond's replacement in 1669 had nothing to do with this leniency, but rather with his failure as a manager of the Irish revenue and with resentments about his ostentatious lifestyle and profiteering.

Three lord lieutenants followed Ormond, in short order, between 1669 and 1672, leaving the Irish government and Irish policy in some confusion, but also leaving Irish Protestant dissenters and Roman Catholics largely free to worship as they wished. Each of these viceroys was instructed by Charles to maintain the established Church of Ireland, but to do so in a moderating and reconciling spirit. Charles's desire for improved relations with Louis XIV of France also suggested a more benign approach to Ireland's Catholic majority, an approach from which Protestant dissenters also benefited.

The first of Ormond's successors, a onetime Presbyterian lord and long-time supporter of accommodation with the Presbyterian clergy, was so partial to dissent as to alienate the Irish Protestant bishops and their friends among the landed elite. The next viceroy, Baron Berkeley, a Roman sympathizer, provoked the common anti-popery of all Irish Protestants by implementing a more tolerant approach to Irish Catholics that really originated with the king. Catholic merchants expelled from Irish towns and cities by Oliver Cromwell were permitted to return and to resume trade. The Catholic clergy became more visible, and masses were publicly celebrated: Oliver Plunket, the Catholic Archbishop of Armagh travelled his diocese with impunity and even advised Berkeley on some matters. Catholic lawyers resumed practice; and some Catholics became JPs. At the request of leading Catholic landed men, including Richard Talbot, of whom much more would be heard later, Charles also appointed a commission to review the Irish land settlement.

The increasing Protestant unhappiness at these policies contributed to the demise of Berkeley, who was replaced in 1672 by Arthur Capel, Earl of Essex. Essex ignored the complaints of dispossessed Catholic landowners and quickly brokered an accommodation with moderates among the Ulster Presbyterian clergy. They agreed to restrain their language and to limit their meeting places; and in return, Charles agreed to the *regium donum*, an annual payment of £600 to them. This payment was made irregularly, and intransigent Presbyterian clergy refused to participate in the scheme. Nevertheless the Presbyterian interest in Ireland had been effectively divided and somewhat pacified, just as it had been in Scotland. Moreover, Presbyterians could often count upon the sympathy of local authorities, especially in Ulster: one Irish bishop complained in 1677 that the JPs were 'almost all Presbyterian'. Yet this de facto indulgence of moderate Irish dissenters did nothing for Quakers, Baptists, Independents, and uncooperative Presbyterians, who continued to worship in defiance of the Irish church establishment.[46]

Religious accommodation of a sort was also achieved in England by 1672, although it was not achieved easily. Anglican parliamentary efforts to replace the now lapsed Conventicle Act of 1664 were finally successful in 1670. Far more draconian than its predecessor, the new Conventicle Act permitted JPs, acting alone and without a public trial, to determine the guilt or innocence of those charged with attending illegal religious meetings. It also established fines for JPs who failed to take action against conventiclers. The dissenting poet MP Andrew Marvell thought the act represented 'the quintessence of arbitrary malice'. Already considering another English indulgence based on his prerogative, Charles reluctantly accepted the measure after getting a clause inserted that bolstered his ecclesiastical authority in a manner similar to the new Scottish Supremacy Act.

When the Conventicle Act came into effect in England in May 1670, it was met with rhetorical and physical opposition throughout the kingdom as dissenting meetings continued unabated. One pamphleteer suggested that when parliament adopted acts contrary to 'our English Rights' and Magna Charta, 'the People are obliged … to disobey' them in defence of 'our fundamental laws'. Recognizing that the act would be sustained or broken in London, old republican and sectarian leaders throughout the country flocked to the capital to join London dissenters of all persuasions in large conventicles. Hundreds were arrested in this 'battle of London', which coincided with the previously noted mammoth field conventicles in Scotland and Ireland. But little progress was made in dashing the spirits of thousands who defended their meetings against the city militia. William Penn, the young Quaker leader, was among those arrested. When he was tried for raising a tumult, he appealed to the nation in printed defences that claimed liberty of conscience was 'the undoubted birthright of every Englishman' and that the rights and privileges of all were put at risk by so reckless a law.[47] Sympathetic jurors insisted upon acquitting Penn, despite being imprisoned by the trial judge for giving a verdict contrary to his instructions. In doing so, they provided an important precedent against the judicial manipulation of juries.

Local efforts to enforce the act continued into 1671, but the dissenters broke it through their stout opposition; and Charles had never truly been behind it. As coercion weakened, the government sought to exploit the same division between cautious Presbyterians and other dissenters that had become central to Scottish and Irish religious policy. Moderate Presbyterians such as Baxter, who continued actively to hope for comprehension, were encouraged to abandon public meetings for private ones. But other Presbyterian clergy joined many Independents and sectarians in holding large public meetings in defiance of the law. The government sought to reach even to some of these more intransigent dissenters through the strangest of emissaries: Col Thomas Blood, the Irish Presbyterian leader involved in the 1663 Dublin Plot, was apprehended in May 1671 in the midst of attempting to steal the crown jewels in the Tower of London. For reasons not entirely clear, Charles pardoned Blood of his crimes, which also included various schemes against Ormond. The crown-stealer then turned informer, spying on some meetings and bringing several old republicans and New Model officers to terms with the government. But none of this eased government anxieties about the church. By November 1671, the under-secretary of state believed dissenting activity had more or less undermined the Anglican order: 'We are very loose and running into madness, if not brought to some [church] settlement', he thought.[48]

In early 1672, as Charles moved to seal a new alliance with Louis XIV through another Dutch war, he also therefore moved to appease the dissenting population, fearing its potential to unsettle English affairs even further. The instrument for accommodating nonconformists was the Declaration of Indulgence of 15 March 1672, which distinguished between peaceable dissent and seditious conventicles. Most penal laws formerly adopted by parliament against both Protestant dissenters and Roman Catholics were suspended, while the legal privileges of the Anglican establishment were affirmed. Dissenting clergy and spokesmen were permitted to register their congregations for public worship, while Roman Catholics were allowed to worship privately. The indulgence brought toleration rather than comprehension, which had proved impossible to achieve in England, as in Scotland; but it nevertheless represented a fulfilment of the efforts of Buckingham and Ashley to promote religious accommodation. Most dissenters accepted the indulgence, arguing that Charles's authority as supreme governor of the church permitted him to alter religious arrangements made by parliament, while noting that such authority did not extend to civil affairs. As many as 1600 dissenting congregations were licenced in England over the next year. But the declaration also indulged Catholics and suspended acts of parliament. Only time would tell whether either of those provisions would prove acceptable to Charles's Anglican-dominated parliament or to English public opinion.

Diplomacy and Deceit, 1668–72

The story of how Charles's kingdoms found themselves at war against the Dutch for the third time in 20 years has been told many times, but the story has lost none of its fascination in the retellings. Arlington's first great success as secretary of state was an alliance with the Dutch, agreed to in early 1668, and directed against Louis XIV's designs upon the Spanish Netherlands. When Sweden was brought into what then became the 'Triple Alliance', Charles appeared to be donning the leading European, anti-Catholic role for which English Protestant tradition had destined him. But Charles was neither following in the footsteps of the great Elizabeth nor addressing the political mistakes of his royal predecessors at the outset of the Thirty Years' War. In fact, he wanted an alliance with Louis. The Triple Alliance was, for him, a diplomatic feint intended to persuade the French king that he was a potential ally and continental player worth wooing. Charles not only admired his French cousin, but he also envied the ease with which the Sun King was able to subordinate estates, *parlements*, nobles, and bishops. Moreover, Charles's family history convinced him that monarchy and Protestantism could become uncomfortable bedfellows, and he was attracted to the divine right theories of leading French Catholic churchmen. The son of a French Catholic mother, the beneficiary of Catholic loyalty during his exile, and now husband to a Catholic wife, Charles II was soft on Catholicism, as was his brother. James secretly converted to Rome in 1669, attracted both by the orderliness of Catholic worship and by Catholic attention to authority in church and state. Previously notorious for its moral laxity, Charles's court was also slowly becoming associated with Catholicism.

Charles hoped to turn his new religious interests to diplomatic advantage as well. Having received little new money in the 1668 English parliamentary session in response to his Protestant alliance with the Dutch, Charles turned to Louis in 1669. He offered the French king a secret anti-Dutch alliance, which would not

require repudiation of the public Triple Alliance, and his conversion to Roman Catholicism. The price was a mere £200,000. Louis
was attracted by the offer and intrigued by Charles's duplicity.
The Sun King pursued negotiations with the English to draw
them into a war against the United Provinces and to secure the
Spanish Netherlands. As deceitful as Charles, however, Louis was
also simultaneously discussing a peaceful division of the same
provinces with the Dutch.

As Arlington focused on these external diplomatic dealings,
Lauderdale promoted conversations between the English and
Scottish parliaments intended to bring about a legislative union
that would simplify royal management of the multiple Stuart
domains. The potential wartime benefits of greater political
integration of the two kingdoms were obvious to the English. On
the Scottish side, a principal additional attraction was the prospect of the admission to England's colonial trade of the Scottish
merchants, who had been excluded under England's navigation
system. Some historians have also agreed with contemporaries
who thought the scheme was designed to strengthen Charles's
constitutional hand in a unified parliament. The 1669 proposals
provided for 30 Scottish MPs in a combined House of Commons
and left Charles free to determine the number and precedence
of Scottish peers in an enlarged House of Lords. Gilbert Burnet
thought Charles would have had a stronger hand in a combined
parliament, for Scottish members of both houses, less independ-
ent-minded than their English counterparts, could have been
counted upon to move legislative matters in directions Charles
favoured. The Scottish Militia Act of 1669, which authorized
the use of Scottish forces in Charles's other kingdoms, was also
regarded by some contemporaries as a sign of an authoritarian
design in Scotland that might be a blueprint for England. So
was the Scottish Supremacy Act, which better subordinated the
bishops of the northern kingdom to the crown. Indeed, after the
adoption of these acts, Lauderdale had actually informed Charles,
'never was [a] king so absolute as you are in poor old Scotland.'
Whatever the case, nothing came of the discussions about union
when commissioners for both parliaments met in 1670. Scottish
distaste for the recent Cromwellian union and English reluctance
to let the Scots into their parliament and trade proved insurmountable obstacles to union at this time.[49]

Charles had also lost interest in Scotland by 1670, for he had gained a far bigger prize in obtaining his alliance with Louis. He had received additional revenues from the English parliament by then, but Charles wanted and needed more than he got. In May 1670, he concluded his secret diplomacy with Louis under the guise of a family celebration of his birthday, at Dover, with his sister Henrietta (Louis's sister-in-law) as intermediary. Of Charles's cabal of ministers, only Arlington and Clifford, the two inclined towards Catholicism, accompanied Charles to Dover; and only they, as well as York, were aware of the details under discussion. Charles agreed to a joint attack upon the Dutch in which he would provide twice as many ships as the French king, while Louis's army attacked the Dutch on the ground. Charles's war expenses were largely to be reimbursed by Louis, to the amount of some £225,000 a year. England was also to receive three ports at the mouth of the Scheldt River, while acquiescing in Louis's annexation of most of the Spanish Netherlands. Finally, Charles agreed to a public conversion to Catholicism in return for an additional payment of £150,000 from Louis and for military assistance, should his subjects prove unhappy with his conversion. The agreement seemed to permit Charles to cut a continental figure with his expenses paid and without much of an army. Since the declaration of hostilities against the Dutch was made contingent upon Charles's prior religious announcement, Charles also thought he was in the driver's seat. By delaying his conversion, he could postpone the war, although he also lost his French windfall by doing so.

The conclusion of the secret Treaty of Dover was far from the end of the matter, however. Charles now pursued an elaborate diplomatic ruse designed to get the remainder of his ministers on board a French alliance without divulging to them his promise about converting to Catholicism. Because the recent alliance with the United Provinces had done nothing to end the commercial antagonisms between the Dutch and England, Charles expected that his ministers and many English merchants could be persuaded of the need for another war against the nation's principal trading rival. Given the role Louis had played in the last war, an alliance with France would obviously be perceived by many as beneficial. Flattering Buckingham, Charles manipulated him into proposing an alliance with Louis, as if it were his own initiative. Arlington and Clifford, who knew that Charles was already engaged to the Sun

King, endorsed Buckingham's proposal, and Lauderdale and Ashley also quickly fell in line. Buckingham, who had written for the stage, now unwittingly acted on one as Charles's emissary to Louis, who already knew his lines. The play ended with a second secret treaty between England and France for a joint attack upon the Dutch. This sham treaty made no mention of Charles's intended conversion to Rome; and the French payment for it was folded into his wartime subsidy. The Stuart king was now publicly tied to the Dutch in a defensive alliance against Louis and twice allied with Louis in secret offensive alliances against them.

Historians disagree about the extent to which Charles wanted another Dutch war in 1670 and about the sincerity of his conversion pledge to Louis. He was, nonetheless, in the happy position of playing his allies off against each other in order to extract as much as possible from each of them. From his French ally he demanded the reduction of new tariffs on English goods, while at the same time he pressed the Dutch for trading concessions for the benefit of the English East India Company.[50] Though he might congratulate himself for such cleverness, Charles was also taking enormous political risks. The secret conversion pledge had the potential, at any time it was leaked or discovered, to revive all the fears about popery that British Protestants had directed against the monarchy and their own bishops in the reign of Charles I. Moreover, although Charles II continued to act the Protestant, the heir to the throne – in the increasingly likely absence of any legitimate royal issue – was already a Catholic. Charles was playing with a religious fire that had the potential quickly to consume whatever advances he made in overcoming his fiscal and military weaknesses. And Louis had, in fact, secured power over Charles: the French king could at any moment undercut Charles at home by releasing the secret of Dover. Blinded by the lustre of the Sun King's court, Charles also failed to see that Louis was emerging as the greatest threat to the balance of power in Europe, and hence to his own kingdoms and their trade, as well.

Having deceived the Dutch, Charles now also proceeded to deceive the Cavalier Parliament. With his revenues still falling below his expenditures, and with his debt continuing to accumulate, Charles requested additional money from parliament in its 1670–1 session. He bolstered his argument by pointing to the probable cost of outfitting the fleet for possible employment *against* Louis XIV in keeping with the public Triple Alliance. This time, Clifford demonstrated his ability as a parliamentary manager in securing a subsidy for the navy, additional import duties on wine, an enlargement of the excise, and a tax on legal proceedings. But another bill that would have provided for at least £160,000 p.a. in increased duties on sugar and tobacco, the consumption of each of which was rapidly increasing, was lost in a dispute between the two houses of parliament.[51]

After Charles prorogued the session in April 1671, he also gave up on the possibility of securing additional funds from parliament before commencing the war he had promised Louis, and to which he now became increasingly committed. Once it began, Charles expected to profit from his French subsidies as well as from diverting Dutch commerce into English hands and towards his customs collectors. Yet he approached war without the means both to outfit the English fleet and fully to service his existing debts. The result was the January 1672 Stop of the Exchequer, which was both a sign of the crown's financial distress at the start of the war and a shoddy means of overcoming it. Clifford pushed the Stop against the opposition of Ashley, Chancellor of the Exchequer, who enjoyed good relations with London's bankers, and of other ministers.[52] It suspended payments on most of the debt for a year, with the promise of an interim payment of 6 per cent interest. It enabled the government to direct its resources to the war, when it came, a few months later; but it ruined a number of bankers and many depositors, for it left the former without the wherewithal to meet their obligations to the latter. Moreover, anyone who believed that Charles would, in the end, repay the debts he had rescheduled, was sadly deceived.

Charles had also exchanged his pro-Dutch ambassador to The Hague for the wily veteran diplomat, Sir George Downing. He instructed Downing to push all of England's commercial grievances against the Netherlands, knowing the Dutch government would not satisfy them. The English fleet was readied for war over the winter of 1671–2. In February 1672, a public Anglo-French treaty was signed that both covered the secret diplomacy of 1670 and signalled a joint attack on the Dutch. Having prepared for war themselves through a new alliance with Spain, the Dutch offered negotiations in March 1672. Charles would not compromise and instead declared war on 17 March. He happily took

Louis's subsidy for his public conversion to Catholicism; but both
monarchs recognized this was not the time to drop a religious
bombshell on Charles's subjects.[53]

Charles obscured his bankruptcy by going to war; and he
obscured his crypto-Catholicism through a Declaration of Indulgence that made a show of relief for Protestant dissenters while also
benefiting Catholics. But his success in all his deceits depended
upon achieving a better result in his new war than he had in the
last one. Influenced by traditions of Protestant anti-Catholicism,
public opinion was not really behind his alliance with the Sun
King, despite the commercial advantages to be expected from
beating up on the Dutch. 'Although the king may join France, his
subjects will not follow him', wrote one knowledgeable observer.[54]
Many merchants now also saw French tariffs as a greater threat
to their trade than Dutch competition. Finally, whether Charles's
cabal of ministers, who competed for power, and who were dangerously divided by diplomatic and religious secrets, could successfully prosecute the war also remained to be seen.

3 Church and Country, 1672–8

There has now for divers years, a design been carried on, to change the lawful government of England into an absolute tyranny, and to convert the established Protestant religion into downright popery: than both which, nothing can be more destructive or contrary to the interest and happiness … of the king and kingdom.

Andrew Marvell (1677)[1]

Introduction: Popery and Parliament

The seventeenth century was a Catholic century in Europe. Protestants found themselves continuously on the defensive. With its own reformation, Roman Catholicism had regained the initiative in the second half of the sixteenth century. Although the European centre of Catholic power gradually shifted from Spain to France thereafter, Catholicism did not again surrender the initiative to Protestantism. Only England, the Dutch Republic, and the Scandinavian kingdoms could have been counted as Protestant powers, even at the beginning of the seventeenth century. Thereafter the Thirty Years' War, which preserved Protestantism in some parts of Europe, nevertheless produced its collapse in areas like Bohemia and its constriction in many other German cities and territories, like the Palatinate. At the time of Luther's death in the mid-sixteenth century, half of all Europeans had become Protestant; but a century later, the proportion had probably fallen to about 20 per cent. Everywhere, the vigour of the Catholic Reformation, and especially of its clerical and monastic revivals, had swept back Lutheranism and Calvinism alike.

In the first half of the seventeenth century England had withstood the Catholic tide, but just barely so in the minds of puritans and many others. Calvinists had regarded the country's Protestant traditions as in crisis by the 1620s. James I's failure to aid the Reformed churches abroad at the outset of the Thirty Years' War had been followed by his son's preference for bishops whose ceremonialism and rejection of predestination was feared as a form of popery. In 1637–42, when rebellion broke out in Scotland and Ireland and civil war began in England, many British Protestants saw themselves as an embattled minority confronted by disloyal Catholic enemies at home, as well as by popish legions abroad. Only Oliver Cromwell's war against Spain had seemed finally to revive the Protestant advances of the great Elizabeth.

By the late 1660s, and especially by the 1670s, many British Protestants and their political spokesmen were persuaded that Protestantism was again in danger in their kingdoms. The Jesuits were as active in England as they had been before 1640, and the Fire of London was popularly blamed upon the Catholics, who were thought hostile to England's economic prospects. Ireland remained overwhelmingly Catholic, despite Cromwell's attempt to advance Protestantism there. The Scottish Highlands were an unreformed zone where the 'old religion' and folk superstition could blend together, and many Scottish Presbyterians regarded their bishops as popish accretions to a Reformed kirk. Abroad, both Louis XIV's curtailment of the liberties of French Protestants and his advancement of the Counter Reformation throughout Europe lent themselves to a religious reading of his motives. English Protestant patriots regarded Charles II as the natural head of an international Protestant interest opposed to these developments. Yet in 1672 Charles II led his kingdoms into war against the Netherlands, the one continental state best equipped to withstand Catholic France; and he did so in league with Louis XIV. In the meantime, the bishops in Charles's established churches seemed more determined to harass non-Episcopalian Protestants than to guard against popery. By the end of Charles's new war, many believed the threat from popery was as great as ever. If Charles was not prepared to take on this international Catholic threat, only one other British institution was capable of responding to it, and that was the English parliament.[2]

Reacting against the Whig interpretation of history, with its evolutionary narrative of the rise of parliament from the seventeenth century, some historians of Stuart England have lately been reluctant to place too much emphasis upon parliamentary opposition, electoral controversy, and clashes between the king and the

Commons. Consensus within the governing social elite and the integrating power of royalist and Anglican ideology have received much attention, both before 1640 and again after 1660. Such an approach is unhelpful, however, in looking at the politics of the 1670s. In that decade the conventional political idea, readopted in 1660, that government was by king-in-parliament, or by the king with the advice and legislative assistance of parliament, was subjected to much strain. After 1675, many MPs believed that the king's ministers and his bishops were involved in a conspiracy to undermine parliament and to subvert the Protestant civil and ecclesiastical order. They believed in an 'ancient constitution', traceable beyond Magna Charta to early medieval custom – a constitution in which the king respected the role of parliament, the common law, and the rights of subjects. These 'Country' MPs advocated vigorously for parliament's role in government and for the importance of popular liberties, both of which they believed were becoming as vulnerable as Protestantism. The parliamentary 'Country' saw parallels in the kingdom's political situation to that of the 1620s. The actions of the crown had then led to a similar expression of parliamentary concern and to the adoption of a Petition of Right in defence of the liberties of subjects. Some of the liberties advanced then, especially freedom from martial law and from the quartering of soldiers on civilians, now seemed in jeopardy again. Country MPs also looked with alarm on events in Ireland and Scotland. In Ireland, Charles's viceroys were lenient towards Catholics, and no parliament met after 1666. In Scotland, Lauderdale seemed to be advancing Charles's authority against the Scottish estates and his subjects. Finally, many Country MPs came to believe, by 1678, that the ruling family itself was at the centre of the threat to Protestantism and parliament.

War and Strife, 1672–4

Almost a year had passed since the last sitting of the English parliament when Charles II initiated his second war against the Dutch in March 1672. The king had temporarily solved his financial issues through the Stop of the Exchequer; and although war was expensive, Charles expected a magnificent victory against the republican enemy to guarantee parliamentary support and supply in a session planned for the autumn. A magnificent victory was obtained in

1672; but unfortunately for Charles, it was French rather than English. By the time parliament finally assembled, which was not until February 1673, popular anxiety about Charles's French ally was more pronounced than hostility towards the Dutch enemy.

The English navy was well prepared for the summer 1672 fighting season; and the Duke of York resumed his military career as lord high admiral. The major encounter came early, in May, off Sole Bay on the Suffolk coast, when the Dutch flung a 75-vessel fleet against a surprised and disorganized Anglo-French force of some 170 ships. In the ensuing confusion, the French failed to respond to James's signals, leaving the Dutch free to concentrate their attack upon the English. Both fleets were badly mauled; but the psychological victory went to the Dutch. The *Royal James*, the flagship of James's vice-admiral, was lost, together with its commander. More importantly, a planned English descent upon the Dutch coast was forestalled by the need to repair and resupply James's battered ships.

In the meantime, Louis XIV's massive army overran much of the Dutch Republic. The trading cities of the two major provinces of Holland and Zealand were preserved when their outlying lands were deliberately flooded. Although most of the urban population was thereby saved from French occupation, the Dutch government was overthrown: an internal revolution swept away the republican administration of the Grand Pensionary of Holland, who, with his brother, was murdered by an enraged mob at The Hague. Power passed to the young William, Prince of Orange, whose deceased mother was Charles's sister. William became *stadholder*, following in the footsteps of his Orange forebears who had, for almost a century, provided quasi-monarchical leadership to the country, despite its republican traditions. William had been the intended beneficiary of the anti-republican foreign policy of Charles and the English royalists; but, as he assumed command of the beleaguered Dutch forces, he adopted a patriotic stance against the invading French and their English allies.

The dramatic opening scenes of the war quickly gave way to a discussion of peace terms. William proved to be a stubborn Dutchman, however. He conceded little; and he cemented an alliance with the Holy Roman Emperor and the Great Elector of Brandenburg, both of whom were alarmed by Louis's disruption of the delicate balance of power. By early autumn, Charles and his ministers realized they would have neither a great victory nor a great peace with which to pry open the parliamentary tax coffers. Parliament was therefore prorogued until February 1673, and Charles sought to reinvigorate his ministry through a round of promotions. Ashley became lord chancellor and was advanced in the peerage as the Earl of Shaftesbury. Clifford became lord treasurer. Buckingham got a pension. Arlington, who had expected to become lord treasurer, got nothing, leaving him as suspicious of Clifford as he already was of Buckingham. Anglican anxieties about the Declaration of Indulgence were assuaged through other strategic appointments and favours. Ministers stroked MPs prior to the session and promoted the election of sympathetic men in numerous by-elections for vacant seats. The kingdom's military capabilities were broadened through the commissioning of new regiments and commanders for an invasion of Zealand.[3]

Charles opened the session in February with strong defences of the war and of the Declaration of Indulgence and with an appeal for money. The speech of the moment was that of the chancellor, however. Shaftesbury's denunciation of England's trading rival was long remembered for its employment of the slogan of the ancient Roman senator, Cato the Elder: *Delenda est Carthago*; 'Carthage must be destroyed.' Reciting a litany of stock arguments about Dutch economic competition, the earl suggested the Dutch were an 'eternal enemy, both by interest and inclination' and that the English must follow Roman example in securing themselves and their trade through the elimination of a dangerous rival. Shaftesbury's own involvement in England's developing colonial empire and his numerous ties to London's overseas traders made these sentiments a matter of personal conviction. Still, the House of Commons proved more immediately interested in the Declaration of Indulgence than in Dutch commercial competition; and, given the crown's financial issues, parliament had the leverage to manipulate the government rather than vice versa.

The Commons did decide quite early to advance new war taxes, but the house also resolved almost immediately, and by a margin of three to two, 'that penal statutes, in matters ecclesiastical, cannot be suspended but by act of parliament'. MPs' discussions also revealed a significant new interest in providing, through statute, the same 'ease for tender consciences' that the indulgence had provided through the prerogative, as well as in 'uniting Protestant subjects' to the church. In the meantime, Charles became convinced that a withdrawal of the indulgence was necessary to secure the supply the Commons had promised. Over the strong objections of some ministers, he cancelled his Declaration of Indulgence in early March 1673, ducking all the constitutional issues raised about his prerogative for the sake of money.[4] The debate about the declaration nevertheless revealed that an increasing number of moderate Anglican MPs had developed doubts about the coercion of nonconformists. Many of them were now willing to consider measures to comprehend moderate dissenters and/or to permit conventicles. Their determination to secure the church had not changed, but their consideration of the best means to do so had. Moreover, their anxiety about church security was now driven more by the favour the indulgence had extended to Roman Catholics than by its toleration of nonconformists.

Reacting to reports about Catholics at court and about Catholics holding commissions in Charles's military forces, the Commons addressed Charles against the 'growth of popery'. MPs also promoted a Test Act in defence of Protestantism, which was also quickly adopted by the Lords. The new act became the chief political guarantee of the Church of England's privileges for the next century and a half. It required that all civil and military office holders take the sacrament of communion, according to the Anglican rite, as a test or qualification for their positions. It further required that office holders renounce the Catholic understanding of communion as involving the transubstantiation of the bread and wine into the body and blood of Jesus. Charles swallowed this measure with some difficulty, but he was now accustomed to deceiving parliament and his ministers about his own religious preferences. Although the act was subsequently employed as much against Protestant nonconformists as against Catholics, dissenters accepted it at the time, both because measures to relieve them were still under consideration, and because many Presbyterians were also regular parish communicants.

In the end Charles got his money, an assessment expected to bring in about £1.25 million; but a bill to legalize dissenting worship had not been agreed upon when Charles adjourned the session, at the end of March, until autumn. The bill had become progressively less generous in response to concerns expressed by the more intransigent Anglicans, and it was drafted to benefit moderate dissenters only, to the exclusion of sectarians. The failure of the measure was a watershed for Anglicans and dissenters alike. One bishop expressed relief that the 'establishment of schism by a Law' had been avoided. Yet the Declaration of Indulgence had already accomplished the schism that ecclesiastical authorities feared. Since the preaching licences provided under the declaration were not withdrawn until 1675, JPs and magistrates throughout the country hesitated to interfere with nonconformist worship, and many dissenting congregations subsequently traced their beginnings to 1672. When parliament next seriously considered toleration and comprehension, in 1680–1, dissenting worship was far more institutionalized than it had been in 1672. The issuance and withdrawal of the declaration had hardened religious divisions rather than promoted Protestant dialogue. [5]

William of Orange had also opened a new front in the war, before the end of the session, through a propaganda campaign directed at English public opinion. The Dutch had discovered that the new coffeehouses springing up all over London, in response to the fashionable rage for caffeine, provided the perfect venue for turning public opinion against the government. Thousands of copies of *England's Appeal from the Private Cabal at Whitehall* were smuggled into the country, passed from hand to hand, and discussed over mocha and more. Writing in the guise of an English Protestant patriot, the anonymous author helped turn the English fear of universal monarchy against Catholic France. The *Appeal* pointed out that Louis's ambassadors at Catholic courts had depicted the current conflict as 'a war of religion … for the propagation of the Catholic faith' against 'heretics'. Moreover, according to the *Appeal*, Louis also sought to undermine the English parliament. The Cabal ministers were said to be on the French take, a charge that struck dangerously close to Charles himself. The ministers were also blamed for frequent prorogations that had saved the crown from bothersome 'parliamentary clamours'. Considering all the evidence, the author concluded that, despite the formal hostilities between the two Protestant states, 'it must be the chief interest of England to support the present government of Holland.'[6]

Such propaganda might not have taken hold had it not coincided with the pre-existent drift of English opinion or seemingly found immediate confirmation in English events. As office holders throughout the country rushed to qualify for their positions by taking the sacrament and declaration prescribed by the new Test

Act, all eyes turned to two at court who held off: Clifford and the king's brother. Rumours circulated that Clifford had been detected with a Roman priest in his carriage. In June 1673, he resigned as lord treasurer rather than qualify according to the test, retired to his country-house, and died a Catholic shortly thereafter. (Clifford's place was taken by a onetime protégé of Buckingham, Sir Thomas Osborne, who would soon emerge as Charles's principal minister.) The Duke of York's spectacular resignation as lord high admiral, which was anticipated after his Easter failure to take the Anglican sacrament, coincided with Clifford's departure. It served as public notice that the successor to the crown of the three Stuart kingdoms could not qualify for military office in England because of his Catholicism. James's religion would become a principal issue in British affairs for the next 15 years. Charles was also skating on thin ice: he was increasingly perceived as surrounded by Catholic relatives and mistresses while pursuing an anti-Protestant foreign policy.

The war got nowhere in the summer of 1673. New frustrations again suggested that the French were merely using the English for their own purposes. After York's resignation, the royal cousin Prince Rupert became overall commander of Charles's forces on land and sea. An army of some 10,000 assembled at Blackheath, near London, for an invasion of Holland, but some observers thought this force had been raised 'for another design', especially when one of Louis's generals replaced Buckingham as its leader. A successful invasion required Anglo-French control of the seas, but Charles's army languished on land after proceeding to Yarmouth. The major encounter of the season came in August, off the Dutch coast near Texel, when the combined Anglo-French fleet bore down upon their naval adversary. The battle ended in a draw, and Rupert blamed the disappointing result on the French admiral. The ensuing bickering could not obscure several unwelcome facts. The Dutch retained control of their coast. No invasion could be attempted in 1673, and Charles's case for more money in the autumn parliamentary session had also been ruined.[7]

A strong Francophobic and anti-Catholic reaction, embodied in 'a 1000 coffee-hous[e] reports and libels sans number', was in full swing by the time of the brief autumn 1673 parliamentary sessions. The worst fears of many merchants were realized when Louis declared war on Spain, which threatened to drag England into a broader conflict that could damage the expanding Anglo-Iberian trade. Abroad, William launched a successful counter-offensive against Louis's German princely allies, while the Dutch also recaptured New York from the English. Gilbert Burnet remembered the widespread complaint that 'we were engaged in a war by the French, that they might have the pleasure to see the Dutch and us destroy one another'. The government began to disintegrate as ministers turned against each other ahead of expected parliamentary recriminations, and as Charles and James turned against some of them. The simmering enmity between York and Shaftesbury, for instance, persuaded Charles that the earl was intriguing with the Dutch and working against the war. The furore was driven further by James's decision to take a second wife to replace the recently deceased Anne Hyde. His choice, Mary Beatrice, daughter of the Duchess of Modena was not only Catholic, but she was also the grand-niece of Cardinal Mazarin, who had governed France during the minority of Louis XIV.[8]

The adjourned parliament resumed its session on 20 October and immediately addressed Charles against the Modena marriage, demanding that York be married to no 'person but of the Protestant religion'. The address prompted a prorogation for a week. But the new session that then began proved no more satisfactory to the crown. Unimpressed by Charles's defence of his brother's marriage, the MPs again addressed against it, by a vote of two to one. They also considered a measure to make those who declined to take the test incapable of sitting in either house of parliament. They attacked Charles's wartime army as a threat to the nation's liberties, since it 'was not raised to maintain the war, but the war was made to have an occasion … to raise this army.' Some MPs complained against a 'betrayal' by 'evil counsellors' about the king, apparently intending to drive out ministers and to take their places themselves. Charles was offered money for the war; but it was approved with diplomatic strings attached that were intended to bring about peace instead. On 4 November, Charles again prorogued parliament, until January 1674, so 'that all good men might recollect themselves'. The short sitting was nonetheless momentous. The king's French alliance had raised suspicions about the royal family even among some of the most loyal MPs. On one occasion the Speaker of the House of Commons discovered a wooden shoe – a contemporary symbol of servitude – on his chair, with the arms of the English and French kings on opposite sides. Nothing could have more dramatically suggested the existence of a common Stuart and Bourbon design against European liberties. Charles took out his frustration on Shaftesbury, whom he removed from office. The earl had already begun his transformation from a principal minister to a principal contriver of opposition.[9]

Charles had disposed of his parliament for a while, but he hadn't disposed of his mounting troubles, which were also apparent in his other kingdoms. As was also the case for the previous Dutch war, the current conflict confounded the problems of managing multiple monarchies. Lauderdale, the Scottish secretary, was among the ministers most strongly disliked by the government's critics in the English parliament. When he presided over a session of the Scottish parliament, beginning in November, problems were apparent in that body as well. Lauderdale's increasingly autocratic tendencies, his venality, and his manipulative treatment of other nobles with political aspirations all contributed to the emergence of 'an organized parliamentary opposition'. So did 'industrious tamperings' from England, which Lauderdale blamed upon the Earl of Shaftesbury.

Led by William Douglas, Duke of Hamilton, the 1673 Scottish parliament declined consideration of Charles's request for money for the sake of the Dutch war before discussing the kingdom's grievances. Among these was the belief that the war 'was only for the benefit of England, for their trade and their plantations ... and that this kingdom could have no benefit whatever were the issue of it.' Monopolies granted to particular Scots grandees on the sale of salt, tobacco, and brandy – each exploited for personal financial gain – were equally unpopular. Lauderdale's opponents also challenged the domination of parliament by the lords of the articles. Wondering whether 'they were a free parliament or not', they sought to elevate a new grievance committee of their own. Regarding these tactics as similar to those that had driven the country into rebellion in the 1630s, Lauderdale outmanoeuvred the opposition through an adjournment and the cancellation of the offensive monopolies. When Hamilton and others subsequently travelled to Westminster to plead their case with Charles, he accused them of 'undermin[ing] the very foundation of his authority'. The Scottish parliament was eventually prorogued. Given the ruckus it had produced in 1673, it was not again summoned until 1681, which raised further anxieties about Charles's manner of government in England, as well as in Scotland.[10]

In Ireland, many of the Protestant elite continued to worry that their governors were too soft on Catholicism. As Irish viceroy, the Earl of Essex sought wartime rapprochement with Catholics as well as with Irish dissenters. Following his instructions from Charles, he prepared new guidelines for office holding in the Irish towns. These required magistrates to take the oaths of allegiance and supremacy, but they also permitted the lord lieutenant to provide dispensations from them, a proviso that Protestant leaders correctly surmised was intended to benefit Catholics. Essex also supported the other concessions that his predecessor, Berkeley, had extended to Catholic merchants, lawyers, and clergy. These steps merely intensified the anti-Catholic reaction among Irish Protestants that had begun under Berkeley, however; and they soon fed English anti-popery as well. Irish privy councillors and English MPs with Irish interests made Catholic activities in the western kingdom an issue in the Westminster parliament, which was already alarmed about Roman Catholicism. English MPs addressed the king in 1673 against any revision of the Irish land settlement. They requested the expulsion of Irish Catholic bishops and monastic heads, desired that Catholic officers in the Irish army and Catholic JPs be removed, and petitioned against the return of Catholic merchants and tradesmen to the towns. Charles strategically rescinded most concessions to Catholics; and the commission he had previously appointed to review the Irish land settlement for the benefit of Catholic families was terminated.[11]

Charles's decisions about Ireland failed to reassure either the Anglo-Irish Protestant elite or their friends in the English parliament, however. The 1674 English parliamentary session opened in early January with a heavy initial attendance of 400 MPs and with another political storm. Charles's second war ended the era of the Cabal just as surely as his first had destroyed Clarendon. Each of the three remaining Cabal ministers – Lauderdale, Buckingham, and Arlington – was savaged for complicity in 'a pernicious design to alter the government' by advancing the royal prerogative. An address to remove Lauderdale was carried after discussion of the allegedly 'arbitrary' purposes of the Scottish Militia and Supremacy Acts and of his preference for government through royal proclamation. The Commons similarly addressed Charles for the removal of Buckingham, and the Lords also condemned the duke for his adulterous relationship with the Countess of Shrewsbury. Charles was quite unwilling to part with his Scottish manager, but he took advantage of the address against Buckingham to dispense with an old friend who no longer served him well. Buckingham followed Shaftesbury into opposition.[12]

Charles also sought to regain the political initiative from the unruly Commons by personally appearing before the two houses, in late January, with new peace terms that he had received from the Dutch. When both houses signalled their acceptance of the Dutch terms, Charles rushed to peace, which was concluded in early February. The Dutch agreed again to the salute of English ships, to negotiations over trading disputes in Asia, to an indemnity, and to the return of New York. The peace was a far cry from what Charles had hoped for at the outset of hostilities; but the terms did at least suggest that he had withdrawn from the war, which Louis continued without him, with something to show for his efforts.

Those in parliament who had become suspicious of Charles, his ministers, and his army were not, however, quieted by the end of the detested alliance with France. Instead, both houses busied themselves with numerous measures that reflected the anti-Catholicism stimulated by the war and by York's conversion. Fearing a popish successor, the Commons were determined to strengthen the rights of subjects and to weaken the potential for arbitrary rule should James come to the throne. As one member argued, 'this is the time to take care against our coming under a bad prince' or against any repetition of the 'Marian days' of Catholic revival under Mary Tudor. In the Lords, some peers suggested that any member of the ruling family who married a Catholic without parliamentary permission be excluded from the throne. The proponents of divine right and hereditary rule shouted down this proposal, but the idea of excluding James from the succession had at least been aired.[13]

Charles's late-February 1674 prorogation of parliament until November prevented MPs and peers from proceeding with any of these measures, but it was also an admission by Charles that he lacked the ministerial talent and royal clout to manage the body. The fiction that he had been misled by malicious advisors did not at all conceal the rampant distrust of his brother. Suspicions that ministers in England, Scotland, and Ireland had aimed to promote popery or arbitrary government also reflected poorly upon the king himself. His government in disarray, Charles was in a real jam: the war had exposed all the weaknesses of his English regime, while contributing to Protestant anxiety in Ireland and to a parliamentary reaction in Scotland. Fortunately for Charles, he had also found a new fixer. Lord Treasurer Sir Thomas Osborne, created Viscount Latimer in 1673 and Earl of Danby in 1674, would soon re-establish the government on the firm foundation of the alliance between the crown and the established church that had been central to the politics of the early 1660s.

The Parliamentary Country

The English parliamentary opposition to Charles's wartime alliance with France in 1673–4 was better organized, more self-conscious, and more articulate than the outburst of opposition Charles had encountered in the sessions of 1666–7. The organization of the 'plain country men' of the 1670s, or the Country, as many historians have called them, was both more visible and more extensive. In the autumn 1673 parliamentary session, for instance, a 'great meeting' of opposition MPs agreed to stand by the objections they had already offered to York's remarriage to the Catholic Mary Beatrice of Modena. Opposition in the two houses of parliament was increasingly coordinated by January 1674, when Shaftesbury and other 'hotspurs' among the Lords worked in 'combination' with 'discontented and turbulent' Country members in the Commons. Votes against the ministry could attract as many as two-thirds of the members present in the House of Commons, while some 32 lay peers (out of about 150) formed a core Country group in the House of Lords. Such localities as London, Hampshire, Herefordshire, and Norfolk experienced political divisions parallel to those in parliament in 1673–5. Even in Scotland, the 'organized' opposition that Lauderdale encountered in 1673 was clearly connected to happenings in England. Although one recent authority has dismissed the Country as 'neither a party nor an opposition', but 'simply a tendency to raise awkward questions', other historians have debated the connections between the court and Country political followings of the 1670s and the Whig and Tory parties that wrangled in the 1680s.[14]

Defining and analysing the Country is nevertheless problematic, for politics in the 1670s, as always, turned on opportunities as well as on principles; and some politicians adopted new principles in the course of their careers. Moreover, some leaders of the Country, such as Shaftesbury and Sir William Coventry, had once been leading courtiers or office holders; and others would become such, with the passage of time. Not every MP who voted the Country position on some issues did so on all, and disagreements and rivalries could occur within the Country as well as between the opposition and the government.

Despite these qualifications, the political culture of the Country can by analysed by attention to three dominant characteristics, each of which reflected the increasing tensions and anxieties of Charles's reign. The Country was, in the first place, dedicated to the Protestant traditions of the English Reformation, including their expression by dissenters. The Country was prepared to defend those traditions against 'popery', broadly understood as the threat to Protestant religion from Roman Catholicism, from Catholic states, and from misguided leaders of the English church. Secondly, Country MPs were devoted to the liberties of parliament and to those of subjects in a 'mixed' or 'balanced' constitution, by which they meant a regime in which the crown legislated and taxed in association with the aristocracy and the parliamentary representatives of the people. Thirdly, the Country defended property by holding the government accountable to property owners and their MPs for the expenditure of taxes derived from them. Such taxes needed to be bearable, according to the Country perspective; and the state must also advance the interests of property owners by promoting domestic and foreign trade.

Of these three characteristics, historians have generally privileged the constitutional posture over the others; but as the foregoing political narrative of the Cabal era has indicated, religion was as important – perhaps even more important than the constitution – in the hardening of Country attitudes in parliament. The Duke of York's conversion and remarriage rekindled all the fears about Catholic recovery that had troubled the English Protestant elite since the 1620s when Charles I had married the Catholic mother of his sons. As Country MP Andrew Marvell suggested, 'such marriages have always increased popery, and encouraged priests and Jesuits to pervert his majesty's subjects.' Popish perversion extended, supposedly, to the advancement of arbitrary political principles antithetical to the government of king-and-parliament, to the elevation of clerical authority over secular powers, and to the discouragement of industriousness and enterprise.

When the House of Commons petitioned Charles against the growth of popery in March 1673, the petition was, therefore, a fundamental expression of concern about the well being of his three kingdoms. As one speaker argued, 'Popery spoils all.' The objection to the breaking of the Triple Alliance in favour of the league with France was, moreover, as much about Charles's desertion of two major Protestant states for an alliance with the chief Catholic king of Europe as it was about Louis XIV's threat to the balance of power. Country MPs had no objection to a war against another Protestant power, should that be necessary for the interest of Charles or his kingdoms. But MPs such as Sir William Coventry feared that the war of 1672–4 was actually a war 'against Protestantism' per se.[15]

If English Protestantism was threatened, according to Country argument, by Catholic intrigue at home and by Catholic advance abroad, it needed to be strengthened. The division between the established church and the dissenting persuasions needed to be healed, whether the healing took the form of comprehension for some, or only of a statutory ease for Protestants whose consciences required their dissent. In either case, the coercion of dissenters by the Protestant establishment must end so that bitterness and acrimony might give way to unity. By the mid-1670s, these arguments were advanced by a broad camp of MPs and peers within the Church of England, former Presbyterians like Shaftesbury and moderate Anglicans like Coventry and Edmund Waller among them. An eloquent spokesman for Protestant reconciliation, Waller hoped that Anglicans would not 'like the elder brother of the Ottoman family strangle all the younger brothers.' Coventry argued in 1673 for a parliamentary lifting of the impositions placed on nonconformists since the beginning of the Restoration. The Country divided over whether the king might employ his authority as supreme governor of the church to override parliamentary coercion of non-Anglicans; but Country MPs had, nevertheless, by 1673, abandoned the church's punitive safeguards against other Protestants. Episcopal leaders failed to make the same adjustment, and the Country would eventually come into collision with the bishops themselves.[16]

The Country was as devoted to parliament's role in the government of the nation as it was to the role of Protestantism in the national culture. Country MPs were suspicious of ministerial practices that weakened the independence of parliament in advising the king and supplying his financial needs or that eroded the representation of Charles's subjects in the making of laws. Many Country MPs had been ardent royalists in the 1650s, but they nevertheless understood that what they had restored in 1660 was a constitution in which the king made law and taxed with the full involvement of parliament, in contrast to the unrepresentative and authoritarian regimes of the Interregnum. They saw the English constitution as unique in this regard and as superior to continental systems in which ancient feudal practices had given way to 'arbitrary' monarchy, a form of government in which the will of the king often overrode the wishes of his people. In Country minds, Louis XIV was the prime exemplar of such objectionable rule. The French model of government was the antithesis of what the English had preserved in Magna Charta, the Petition of Right, and the Restoration settlement. In the words of Marvell, 'here the subjects retain their proportion in the legisla-ture; the very meanest commoner of England is represented in par-liament, and is a party to those laws by which the prince is sworn to govern himself and his people. ... His very prerogative is no more than what the law has determined.'[17]

By 1674, many Country MPs were worried, however, that some leading ministers sought to corrupt the government, to subordi-nate parliament, and to introduce French-style absolutism into the English constitution. Charles's Declaration of Indulgence was the initial source of much of the anxiety. What so frightened some MPs was Charles's determination to stick by an exercise of the prerogative that suspended over 40 statutes agreed to by previous monarchs and their parliaments. Willing to grant that the king might dispense with the application of single laws to individual persons, MPs read the dec-laration as an unprecedented royal abrogation or repeal of multiple laws. When Charles stood by the declaration after the Commons' initial address that penal statutes could not be suspended 'but by act of parliament', they informed him that the power he claimed was an innovation never exercised by any of his predecessors. Indeed, the suspending power that he claimed 'tend[ed] to the ... altering [of] the legislative power, which hath always been acknowledged to reside in your majesty, and *your two houses of parliament*'.[18]

Charles backed down, but the declaration had nevertheless so traumatized many MPs about the security of parliamentary government that they interpreted the upsets of 1673–4 and beyond in light of the fears it had aroused. They were deeply disturbed about the advice Charles had received regarding the declaration from his ministers. In fact, the more outspoken Country members came to the conclusion that the Cabal was engaged in a conspiracy to undermine the constitution. Upset that Shaftesbury had, as lord chancellor, issued numerous writs to fill up empty seats before the winter 1673 session – a responsibility usually exercised by the Speaker of the House of Commons – some MPs detected a ministerial design to protect the declaration by packing the Commons with court supporters. The Commons voted to void the chancellor's writs, fearing that if they stood, the house would lose its privilege of judging who was rightfully returned to parliament. In autumn 1673, some MPs revolted against the speaker himself, who was also a privy councillor and a naval treasurer, claiming he was a ministerial spy rather than a spokesman for the house. Disturbed that war against the Dutch had been timed for the long interval between the 1671 and 1673 sessions, some MPs also viewed the two prorogations of autumn 1673 as intended to release Charles 'from the advice of parliaments, which are now looked upon … as an encumbrance'.[19]

Above all else, it was the army Charles had raised to fight the Dutch that frightened Country MPs and persuaded them that their liberties and the independence of parliament were at risk. They were perfectly well prepared to countenance small standing forces to deal with troubles in Ireland and Scotland. But the sight of some 10,000 poorly disciplined troops assembling within proximity of London and Westminster was simply too reminiscent of the New Model Army for those who remembered the Commonwealth and Protectorate as thinly disguised military rule. They saw no reason for such forces, even in wartime, when the navy and the militia protected the country: 'Our security is the militia,' suggested one MP, which would 'defend us and never conquer us', because many of its officers were themselves Country MPs and their landed kinsmen. Yet Charles had not only raised an army but had also quartered troops on his subjects, the Petition of Right notwithstanding. He had, moreover, issued military directives for the governance and discipline of the soldiers, including courts martial and oaths of obedience. Some MPs feared these military practices would undermine customary legal processes, erode civil liberties, and breed soldiers indifferent to parliamentary government. 'Martial law has arbitrary principles and arbitrary power,' opined one parliamentary debater. When ministers were savaged in the Commons in February 1674, another MP asked 'who advised that the army should be appointed to draw up towards London, to awe this house, to make us vote what they please'.[20]

The Country also wanted the government held accountable for its expenditure of revenues derived from the taxation of Charles's subjects. MPs understood the liberty of being taxed by consent to involve a measure of parliamentary oversight over how tax proceeds were actually spent. As Country MPs turned against the war of 1672–4, against the French alliance, and against the English army, they also became wary of Charles's funding requests. Every parliamentary session of the war was marked by the holding up of votes for taxes, so that Country MPs might bargain for the redress of grievances, in both foreign and domestic policy, in return for more money. Wealthy landed MPs posed as 'poor country fellows' defending their counties and boroughs against the tendency of Charles's government to demand and to spend more money than it needed, both in war and in peace. The particular fiscal dynamic visible in these debates, which pitted the localities against the central government, was scarcely unique to Restoration England; but Charles's ostentatious lifestyle further damaged his efforts to raise money from frugal MPs. Many were also offended by the Stop of the Exchequer and wondered why anyone should lend to the king in the future. Some MPs were unwilling to supply Charles at all, fearing that the 'villainous counsellors' who had advised the war and demanded money, 'would have only a bank [of it], that they may carry on their design, and [then] use you no more'.[21]

Parliamentary reservations about governmental financial accountability and taxation were also driven by Country concerns over the state of the nation's trade. Many MPs found that the damages the war was inflicting upon foreign and domestic trade outweighed any supposed commercial advantages that might be wrested from the Dutch. Indeed, many in and out of parliament saw France, and not the Dutch, as the chief threat to the advancement of English trade. They were incensed by new French tariffs upon English goods. As one incredulous MP burst out: 'Fifty per cent [duty] upon our goods in France, and yet the war with Holland [is justified] upon account of Trade [!]' Just as the Country thought Louis XIV had dragged England into a war to facilitate his conquests on land, so many MPs believed he had pitted the English and Dutch against each other so that French merchants might encroach upon their trade. These anti-French commercial concerns were widespread among London's overseas merchants, especially its dissenting traders, who became a natural audience for Country ideas.[22]

The opposition that expressed these concerns in 1673–4 dominated the parliamentary sessions of those years. The Country fully exposed the military and fiscal weaknesses of the crown, while also drawing attention to the problem of Protestant disunity. Country ideas and perspectives would continue to flourish in British and Anglo-American politics for a century or more after the 1670s. Yet neither too much structure nor too much ideological coherence should be read into the emergence of the Country. Opposition did extend from the houses of parliament into the coffeehouses and the country houses; but parliamentary sessions were short, and political conversation in coffeehouses and country houses was not restricted to Country issues. The Country succeeded because it advanced popular, patriotic positions and sought to recall the nation to its first principles. Charles could also sell himself as the defender of patriotic principles, however; and his emerging political manager, the Earl of Danby, sought to reposition the monarchy, after 1674, on its initial popular foundations. But Danby and his Anglican following in parliament understood the kingdom's first principles in a somewhat different manner from the Country.

The Anglican Church

A variety of religious and political perspectives, including Country attitudes, flourished within Restoration Anglicanism, which was no more monochromatic in its complexion than Restoration dissent. The political posture of the restored church was nonetheless heavily defined by the suppression or persecution that the bishops, the Episcopal clergy, and their followers had experienced at the hands of puritans and republicans in the 1640s and 1650s. Indeed, a distinctive Anglican identity emerged during the Restoration as a response of the church's clerical and social leaders to that upheaval and to the fear that it might be repeated. The intransigence of Anglican gentry in the Cavalier Commons and in the counties had driven the intolerant religious settlement imposed on England in the 1660s. The triumphant adherents of Episcopal order in the localities and the clergy they supported had little time, however, to enjoy their political hegemony. It was seemingly threatened by rebellions and plots, as early as 1663, and by parliamentary and ministerial reconsiderations, beginning in 1668. As a result, the belligerent self-confidence of early Restoration Anglicanism gave way to a more anxious and defensive mood by the end of the decade. Frustration about the results of the church settlement motivated both those Anglicans who continued to call for the suppression of dissent as well as 'moderate' churchmen who called for accommodation, often on their own terms, with Protestants outside the church.[23]

More than the security of the church was thought at risk, however. Many Anglican writers and leaders also believed that the restored monarchy itself was increasingly endangered by the indulgence of dissent and by the revival of political ideas associated with Reformed Protestantism. For them, hereditary monarchy was the only form of government directly sanctioned by nature and by God, who 'did always govern His own people by monarchy only'. Charles II was God's vice-gerent, 'the father of the people', ruling the unsteady multitude in God's place and sacred in his 'person, crown, and dignity'. He was accountable to no power other than 'the supreme majesty of heaven'. Anglican writers followed Sir Robert Filmer, the pre-civil war advocate of monarchy and patriarchy, in perceiving the restored monarchy as the great antidote to the 'liberty without restraint' that the people naturally desired. Such 'lawless savage liberty' had cost Charles I his life, as the population was reminded in thousands of sermons delivered on the Restoration anniversaries of the royal martyr's execution. Moreover, as Anglican writers never tired of repeating, obedience to the king was required in all circumstances, for 'the bond of his subjects ... unto his sacred majesty is inviolable, and cannot be dissolved.' When kings err, their correction must be left to God; and if they become tyrants, the people should repent of those sins that may have disposed God to permit such misrule.[24]

Given their political convictions, most Anglican authorities became uncomfortable with the assertiveness of Country MPs, many of whom were actually committed both to the church establishment and to its enlargement. Church divines feared that Country behaviour in the Commons might reignite the quarrels of the 1640s. Behind such Country outbursts, they worried, lurked the ideas that parliament and the king were co-ordinate and co-equal constitutional partners and that the crown merely shared legislative power with the representatives of the people. In contrast to Country constructions about 'mixed' or 'balanced' monarchy, the Anglican clergy largely echoed Filmer in regarding the king as the sole 'foundation ... of all law', and entitled to 'the choice of those laws, by which he obliges himself to rule'. Parliament, on the other hand, was a historical contrivance of the monarchy, and 'all those liberties that are claimed in parliaments are the liberties of grace from the king.' The function of parliaments was to 'facilitate the government of the king' by giving 'consent and approbation' to 'laws which the king at their request, and by their advice ... ordain[s]' to the nation.[25]

The political thought of the dominant Episcopalian leadership in Scotland and Ireland was similarly outspoken in its exaltation of royal power. Episcopalian royalism in the other British kingdoms was directed both against the arguments for church autonomy of extreme Presbyterians and against the idea that the people should enjoy a role in their ruler's exercise of authority. Scottish royalist theory built upon the national myth that the Scots monarchy was the oldest in the world and could be traced back through two millennia. Indeed, it represented a nationalist reaction against the English republican intruders of the 1650s. The jurist Sir George Mackenzie of Rosehaugh, the most systematic Scots royalist theorist of the Restoration, grounded the hereditary succession of kings in natural law, dismissed any idea of popular acquiescence in royal authority, and insisted that Scottish kings were 'absolute monarchs, deriving their royal authority immediately from God almighty'. His royalist colleagues among the Scottish bishops echoed Mackenzie's arguments and those of their English counterparts against resistance. Kings, in their view, could be restrained only by God or by nature and certainly not by force.[26]

This exaltation of monarchy over parliaments and subjects was also part of a broader hierarchical understanding of the natural order of creation and of human society. In the Episcopalian political thought of the Restoration all men were understood as naturally ordered in graduated social ranks and degrees: kings and princes were on top, followed in descending order by the aristocracy, the gentry, the learned and commercial professions, the yeomanry, and mean artificers and rural labourers. Every man had a responsibility to respect those placed by God above him, just as he had a God-given responsibility to rule in his own household. Families were little monarchies in which 'every father govern[s] as a king', inculcating the natural principles of subordination and subjection to authority in his wife, children, and servants. Subjection was the cement of society, in the church's view, providing 'peace and immunity from sin', as all 'resigned' their 'will up to the command of others'. Indeed, only the practice of subjection permitted the establishment of law and government over the unbridled passions and self-interest that would otherwise prevent the achievement of community harmony and order.[27]

In England, such ideas were particularly appealing to the Anglican gentry and rural clergy who saw the Restoration as a recovery of order in parish affairs as well as in church and state. In their minds, Anglican squires had resumed their rule over local, organic communities in which the status and wealth of natural governors again assured deference from the lowly, while parsons led common prayers, reinforced order through their preaching, and were supported by the tithes and offerings of dutiful laymen. Moreover, just as gentry JPs brought the authority of the king into local affairs, so the Anglican clergy thought of themselves as operating locally under the apostolic authority that the bishops claimed. The maintenance of authority also required a well regulated press: the free flow of ideas in the 1640s and 1650s had contributed enormously, according to Anglicans, to the religious and political disorder of those days, as heretical works had circulated along side those that promoted revolution in the state. For much of the Restoration, the government's press licenser was the Anglican zealot Sir Roger L'Estrange, who pursued unlicenced books, their authors, and their printers as wanton incendiaries. Like his clerical friends, L'Estrange believed the press should only propagate ideas that reinforced subjection, subordination, and respect for tradition and hierarchy. Given these political and social assumptions, Anglican royalists were deeply shocked by the Cabal's reopening of the church settlement, by Charles's 1672 Declaration of Indulgence, and by the Country's clashes with the crown.

As had become increasingly apparent by 1667–72, the Anglican Church of the Restoration lacked the means to maintain the uniformity it desired. It relied upon the state to enforce acceptance of its doctrines and to prevent worship outside its precincts. Enforcement of parliamentary laws adopted in defence of the Episcopalian establishment at the local level was dependent, however, upon the willingness of local JPs and magistrates to harass and to persecute their dissenting or partially conforming neighbours. Coercion in the localities became increasingly uneven and half-hearted, even before Charles's indulgence, as dissent failed to fold under the weight of the punitive religious settlement. In numerous counties, only a few militant Anglican JPs carried on the struggle against dissent. Moreover, coercion was sometimes compromised by indifferent government agents, like the Lord Lieutenant of Hampshire, a client of the tolerationist Buckingham. After Charles's withdrawal of his indulgence, JPs in Surrey and elsewhere were unwilling to enforce the laws against conventicles without some explicit authorization from the crown to do so. In the towns, magistrates were often similarly hesitant to suppress dissenting conventicles or to act legally against those who attended them. Indeed, in many boroughs, the Corporation Act failed to eliminate nonconformists from government. The enforcement of conformity was rarely continuous in towns where occasional conformists or partial conformists held some magisterial offices.[28]

Neither, despite L'Estrange's best efforts, was the church able to monopolize the press. Parliamentary discussion of indulgence and comprehension was accompanied by discussion in the prints, as well, as dissenters launched a press campaign, beginning in 1667, against coercion and in favour of liberty for conscience. Challenging Anglican religious structures, dissenting authors encouraged open-ended enquiry into the claims of conscience in place of Anglican subjection to authority. Worse, from the churchmen's point of view, dissenting arguments circulated widely in the unrestrained discursive milieu of the coffeehouses, which were now spreading from London into provincial centres and spawning whole clubs of church critics. Few Anglican royalists had good words for the culture of the coffeehouses. Restoration loyalists perceived them as hothouses of disrespectful talk and agitation that turned 'every carman and porter' into a statesman, unlike the traditional alehouses, where good English beer produced a soporific acceptance of hierarchy and degree. Respect for clerical tradition and uniformity of thought were fractured as the press 'poison[ed] the clubs and coffeehouses with fanatic discourses, or even with atheism itself'.

But, like it or not, the church was confronted with the emergence of public opinion, informed by the press and inflamed by coffee, as a force it could not easily regulate.[29]

Churchmen took none of these challenges sitting down. The 1670s were as much characterized by a combative Anglican spirit as by dissenting resilience. Archbishop Sheldon's parliamentary efforts on behalf of the 1670 Conventicle Act were but the opening salvo in an aggressive Episcopalian re-launch, and dissenting arguments were answered point by point in the press and the pulpits. Samuel Parker, chaplain to the archbishop and a future bishop himself, ridiculed dissenting claims for conscience, suggesting that 'most men's ... consciences are weak, silly, and ignorant things ... imposed upon by their vices and passions.' L'Estrange joined Parker in backing the coercive religious laws of the state against dissenting claims for conscience. Penal laws were essential for the preservation of the 'prince's crown' and the order of society against rank individualists who would 'acknowledge no governor but themselves'. Should subjects prevail in dictating religious freedom to legitimate authority, 'the order of government [would] dissolve', as it had once before. Coercion, on the other hand, protected the state, protected orthodox Christianity, and protected believers from religious errors that imperilled their salvation.[30]

The crown's indulgence of both Roman Catholics and dissenters in 1672–3 reinforced another strain of Anglican apologetics; that is, the church's claim to represent the moderate Protestant middle against the opposite and extreme errors of popery and fanaticism. As one leading divine argued in 1673, the Church of England 'secure[d] men on the one hand, from the wild freaks of enthusiasm; and on the other, from the gross follies of superstition' propagated by Rome. Claiming the middle ground and painting all dissenters as extremists was a clever rhetorical strategy in the wake of Charles's declaration. It permitted the church to present itself within the Protestant rhetorical marketplace as the intended victim of an unholy league between the extremes. Indeed, not satisfied with fanning a revival of popular anti-popery in the wake of the Declaration of Indulgence, the church sought to rouse both anti-popery and anti-sectarianism in its defence. The papists were incapable of undermining the Protestant establishment on their own, according to Anglican argument; but they had come close to achieving their goal by using the obstreperous puritans of the 1640s as their unwitting accomplices in the murder of Charles I and the destruction of the church he headed: 'The Presbyterian was but the Jesuit's agent, and did that work for him, which he could not do for himself.' Although the church had recovered, the renewal of claims for Protestant conscience in the 1670s masked another Catholic attack upon the English establishment, according to Anglican royalist interpretation. The dissenters claimed to be as hostile to Catholicism as Anglicans, but why had they then so happily accepted religious liberty under an edict that provided it to Catholics as well? 'The Papists will accomplish the ruin of the church only through the activities of the dissenters, who are creating disorder and disturbance,' wrote Parker. Dissenters and their friends in the church were, in fact, merely the political dupes of Rome.[31]

For Anglicans such as Parker and L'Estrange, 'moderation' was a polemical stick with which to beat dissent. But another intellectual tendency within the church actually had a better claim to the practice of moderation. The 'latitude men' or 'latitudinarians' represented an alternate approach to the problem of religious diversity, an approach that was developing within the church by the 1670s but that would not fully mature until the 1690s. Although they neither constituted a theological school nor a movement, latitudinarian thinkers agreed upon the desirability of accommodation with their moderate counterparts among the dissenters, chiefly the Presbyterians. They also largely rejected the predestinarian teaching that had long informed Reformed Protestantism. Generally, they thought reason was critical in determining religious truth and that encouraging moral virtue was more important than requiring uniformity in religious doctrine or ceremony.

The principal latitudinarian spokesmen included John Wilkins, the natural philosopher married to Oliver Cromwell's sister, and Wilkins's younger associate, John Tillotson. Wilkins authored the proposal for comprehension promoted by Buckingham in 1668 and became a bishop; and Tillotson, eventually an archbishop, was involved with a similar proposal in 1674–5. Because both men came from moderate puritan backgrounds, they were able to retain friendships and intellectual dialogue with leading dissenting clergy. After the Restoration, Wilkins served as the vicar of St. Lawrence Jewry, the semi-official church of London's city government, where Tillotson supported him in his mid-weekly sermons. Their hearers included many former and continuing Presbyterians among city merchants, as well as John Locke, another advocate of religious accommodation. Wilkins and Tillotson were also in conversation with likeminded friends and associates at the universities, including the tolerant Cambridge Platonists. The latitudinarian spirit extended to the Royal Society of London, which had been chartered by Charles for the advancement of science, and where Wilkins was a guiding light. It seeped into English legal culture as well: both Wilkins and Tillotson held additional preaching appointments at the London Inns of Court, where most lawyers were trained, and where many young gentry picked up a smattering of the law. Finally, the latitudinarian outlook influenced some of the most reflective Anglican country circles, such as that presided over in Warwickshire by the philosophic Anne, Viscountess Conway. [32]

The latitudinarians did not, however, represent the public face of Anglicanism in the 1670s, which was instead marked by the harsh intolerance of the implacable foes of dissent. Moreover, even the latitudinarians were prepared to accept coercion to protect the establishment against unreasonable behaviour justified in the name of conscience. The belligerence of the Country in the 1674 parliamentary session had persuaded many observers that a new parliament – and a revision to the church settlement – could not be far off. These observers had not, however, considered the determination of militant Anglicans to preserve what they had restored. Churchmen, too, had caballed before and during the 1674 session; and as power passed to the Earl of Danby thereafter, he began to fashion a new church and court alliance from these gatherings. For Danby, the Restoration had become a shipwreck, and the wreck could be righted only upon its original bottom of uncompromising Anglican royalism. He determined, therefore, 'to keep up [the current] parliament, to raise the old cavaliers and the church party, and to sacrifice papists and Presbyterians'. The next session of parliament was put off until April 1675; and in the autumn and winter of 1674–5, Danby, the privy councillors, and the bishops met in closed sessions to devise an agenda that could reunite the country around the restored institutions in church and state.

Some of what Danby and the bishops agreed upon became apparent in the increasingly vigorous coercion of dissenters in some localities and in the encouragement of intransigent local governors. The preaching licences issued to dissenting clergy under the Declaration of Indulgence were finally cancelled. A few bishops were involved in comprehension discussions with some Presbyterians, but these discussions were primarily designed to weaken dissent by splitting off moderates like Richard Baxter. Many signs pointed to an enhanced role for churchmen and their views in English politics. One of the bishops joined the Privy Council. An ambitious scheme to expedite the rebuilding of St. Paul's Cathedral, still in ruins after the Fire, was announced. Plans were made to re-inter the body of Charles the Martyr in an impressive public mausoleum, where his cult might be advanced to greater effect. A statue of the late king was to be erected in Westminster, where resident aristocrats and Anglican gentry brought hierarchy into the urban environment. As the April 1675 meeting of parliament approached, Danby encouraged the attendance of Anglican royalist MPs, while Archbishop Sheldon sought to prep the bishops for their work in the Lords. Not since the days of Archbishop Laud, in the 1630s, had the church seemed so poised to exercise ascendancy in the conduct of government and public affairs.[33]

The Era of Danby: Court and Country, 1674–8

The Earl of Danby was a Yorkshire royalist tied to important northern lineages and a consummate politician. He rode Buckingham's political coattails into a lucrative place as a naval treasurer in 1668, but he broke with Buckingham thereafter, preferring religious coercion to Buckingham's toleration and also preferring friendship with the Dutch to the Cabal's league with France. John Evelyn, who knew him well, found 'nothing generous or grateful' in the new lord treasurer's 'haughty' character.[34]

As Charles's principal English minister after the collapse of the Cabal, Danby developed a parliamentary programme that included much more than the revival of Anglican influence. Recognizing that Charles's last war had destroyed his credit, revived fears of Roman Catholicism, and driven anti-French patriots into the arms of the opposition, Danby resolved to refashion the court's shattered image through fiscal probity and a Protestant foreign policy. Since becoming lord treasurer, he had retrenched government expenses and renegotiated contracts with the revenue farmers. He thereby answered Country concerns about property and taxation through government restraint, just as he sought to soothe Country anxieties about Catholicism through a revival of the Protestant establishment. But Danby's methods of promoting the crown's interest and of protecting the church gave the Country and nonconformists new causes for alarm. In attempting to exclude non-Anglicans from public life, the new lord treasurer sought also to create an Anglican confessional state. At the same time, his efforts to manage the Commons by reconstructing a loyalist following among MPs further provoked Country fears about arbitrary government.

Parliament met twice in 1675, for some two months in the spring and for another six weeks in the autumn. Despite his withdrawal from the Dutch war, and despite his reliance upon a new parliamentary manager, Charles might have been forgiven, however, for thinking that little had changed, politically. The sessions of 1675 brought new and sharper confrontations between the parliamentary Country and the court. Frequent 'hot discourses' in the Commons were, on one occasion, accompanied by spitting, shoving, and jostling for the speaker's mace, and by at least one half-drawn sword. Unusually, the Lords met long into many nights. Political rhetoric in parliament, in the press, and in public places suggested that the divisions the Restoration settlement had been intended to heal now instead threatened to unsettle both church and state. Charles and Danby placed much of the blame for this situation upon the Earl of Shaftesbury. The former minister not only rejected the lord treasurer's programme but also began to strengthen a loose opposition alliance of discontented lords, Country MPs, and dissenters.

When the first 1675 session opened in April, Country MPs largely ignored Charles's request for money for the fleet and instead returned to issues and projects similar to those they had advanced in 1673–4. They voted only narrowly to thank Charles for his opening speech, complaining, among other things, about the 'convention' of 'a few lords and bishops' that had pre-arranged the session. They again addressed Charles to discharge Lauderdale as a person whose 'pernicious principles' made him 'obnoxious and dangerous to the government'. They requested that Charles recall English subjects serving in the military of Louis XIV, so that France and its armies – still at war against the Dutch, the Spanish, and their German allies – might be less able 'to swallow up the world'. They considered additional measures for removing Roman Catholics from parliament, for preventing marriages between the royal family and Catholics, and for educating James's children as Protestants. They considered a bill to require MPs appointed to government places to quit the Commons so that new men might stand against them in by-elections. (This measure was prompted by a concern that, given the duration of the Cavalier Parliament, electors should be consulted again when men originally selected as MPs in 1661 chose now to accept government offices.) Finally, Lord William Russell and Sir Samuel Barnardiston, merchant MP of London, introduced articles of impeachment against the lord treasurer. They complained about his 'high and arbitrary manner', about his 'perverting' of Exchequer methods in ways that 'violated the rights and properties of the people', about his 'great gifts and grants from the crown', and about his high regard for royal proclamations.[35]

Despite much debate, the impeachment of Danby got nowhere. And despite the variety of issues pursued in the Commons, the real action of this session was in the Lords, where the lord treasurer introduced another test bill. Danby's test required all members of parliament and all office holders to make a declaration against participating in any form of armed resistance to the crown. It also required an oath against supporting any alterations to the form of government in either church or state. As its critics suggested, this was a sweeping measure that seemed to deprive parliament of any right to legislate adjustments to the country's basic institutions, which in the Country view, was among the most important functions of parliament. Indeed, Danby's opponents worried that the measure might drive some conformists, as well as most nonconformists, out of parliament and local offices. Danby's test made subscription to Anglican political principles a prerequisite for office holding; and it was the bishops' final answer to the Country's desire to fashion an accommodation between the church and its nonconformist critics. An oath against alterations to the church would forestall any modification of the establishment for the sake of comprehending dissenters.

Shaftesbury and his associates among the peers sought to talk the bill to death at every stage of its protracted 17-day consideration. They were, however, outvoted time and again – although by decreasing margins – by an alliance of Danby's supporters, Charles's friends, and the bishops. The king himself was frequently present to encourage his ministers in what became the 'longest debate in the House of Lords' that any observer could remember. In the end, though, the opposition lords gained a moral advantage through public attention to their entering of protests to the decisions of the majority in the Lords' journals. They claimed that Danby's bill would stifle freedom of debate in parliament, threaten the privileges of its members, and further weaken Protestantism by reinforcing the division between the church and dissent. Many of the protesting peers or their families had been supporters of parliament in the 1640s, a demonstration of how this quarrel was reviving the civil war divisions that churchmen so feared. Danby finally rid himself of his own measure, as well as of all the Commons' Country business, through a prorogation at the end of May.[36]

In the interval between the 1675 parliamentary sessions, Danby sought to secure the Commons through improved management; and Charles sought to secure himself against the Country through a new understanding with Louis XIV. The lord treasurer's preparations for the session included letters soliciting the attendance of over 100 MPs thought likely to favour the government's cause. He also provided pensions (under the anonymous cloak of secret service funds) to some 30 members with financial needs. Their votes were expected in return. Danby's unprecedented orchestration also involved efforts to secure the parliamentary attendance and support of his own numerous northern kinsmen, as well as of all MPs who held government offices.

For his part, Charles was so weary of MPs' indifference to his financial needs and of their attacks upon his French inclinations that he promised Louis to dissolve parliament if it failed to provide him with money. In that case, Louis promised Charles £100,000 each year until the next parliament. The French king's generosity was prompted by his fear that, as he continued the war he had begun in 1672, an anti-French English parliament might push Charles into an alliance with his enemies. At the same time, the French ambassador was passing out money to some opposition leaders, assuring them that France had no hostile intentions toward England and that Louis would use his influence with Charles to moderate Danby's domestic programme. Some Country spokesmen were, in fact, ready to offer Charles all the money he wanted if he would only agree to secure Protestantism through a statutory comprehension and toleration. Shaftesbury, on the other hand, was determined to paralyse parliament and to force a new election.

In the event, all political elements were to be disappointed when parliament met again in October and November. Danby's reinforcement of the 'moderate party' prompted a corresponding resolve on the part of the 'angry party'. Country MPs proceeded with their previous programme. Charles requested supply to pay off claims against his incoming revenue derived from his previous wartime expenses and to pay for new ships for the navy. The Commons rejected the first request. MPs agreed to fund new ships, but only half as many as Charles wanted. Moreover, they proposed that the expense be met, not from any new taxes, but rather from customs revenues that the government intended for other purposes. Danby's letters to secure a majority in the Commons were attacked, and some Country members proposed a test of their own, namely that MPs who took guineas from the government be ineligible to sit. In the end, Shaftesbury's strategy of provoking quarrels between the two houses addled the session, as he intended. Charles prorogued parliament for over a year, until February 1677. That left him without new taxes. It also left the Country without any of its bills, and it left Danby without much to show for two sessions.[37]

By the conclusion of the second 1675 session, the quarrel between court and Country had inflamed the press, the coffeehouses, and public discourse. The long interval before the next session in 1677 saw an intensifying debate in the prints about the future of the church and of parliament. Shaftesbury had initiated this appeal to the nation by publishing the *Letter from a Person of Quality* between the 1675 sessions. The argument of the piece was that the bishops had been engaged in a plot, ever since the days of Charles I and Archbishop Laud, to overturn the reformation of the church, the royal supremacy over it, and Magna Charta, by requiring that 'the government of the church' be 'sworn to as unalterable' in Episcopal hands. In return for support from the crown for their control of the religious establishment, the 'great churchmen' were prepared, according to Shaftesbury, to 'declare the government [of the state] absolute and arbitrary, and allow monarchy … to be *jure divino*, and not to be bounded by any human laws'. Danby's test was, according to this way of thinking, but the most recent initiative in an Episcopal conspiracy to wrest control of

the church from the monarchy and to safeguard it against any
parliamentary tampering as well. Furthermore, Anglican propagation of the doctrine of non-resistance, which would leave kings
unrestrained save for 'the fear of God', was part and parcel of a
design against the liberties of the people and of parliament. So
was Danby's filling of the Commons with 'courtiers, officers, [and]
pensioners' likely to fall in line with the plan for arbitrary rule.
Shaftesbury's arguments found further support in publications
from Andrew Marvell, Buckingham, and others. They argued that
a new election was required so that the people might be properly
represented, after 15 years of a 'standing parliament', and might
choose MPs devoted to Protestant liberties. The church could not
be safeguarded, moreover, without substituting accommodation
with dissent for the coercive policies of Anglicanism.

These Country propagandists redirected the popular fear of
plotting from sectarians to the very Episcopalian establishment
that stood behind the Restoration settlements in church and state.
They revived many of the quarrels of 1639–42 that had prompted
resistance to Charles I and his bishops. The impact of the Country's conspiracy theories was particularly notable in London, where
guildsmen, assembled in 1676 for city business, cheered a speech
demanding a new parliamentary election. Both Buckingham and
Shaftesbury had become active in the city by then. They recognized its potential, as in 1641–2, as an alternate or supplemental
political arena to parliament; and they cultivated connections to
the city's enormous and prosperous dissenting population.[38]

The government's initial response to the opposition's appeal to
public opinion was negative. Danby was concerned in particular
about the unbridled discourse that spewed out of the coffeehouses. The lord treasurer persuaded Charles to issue a proclamation in December 1675 that prohibited the retail sale of coffee
and such other stimulants as chocolate and tea. The coffeehouses
themselves were suppressed as places where 'false, malicious, and
scandalous reports' were 'devised' and disseminated, and where
tradesmen were tempted to neglect their work, to the detriment
of Anglican conceptions of order. This effort to stifle the country's
burgeoning public sphere was immediately critiqued in the streets
and in the shops, however, as a taking 'from the people the freedom of words'. Charles backtracked within a fortnight, replacing
his order for the suppression of the coffeehouses with one for

their regulation, in hopes that coffee, tea, and chocolate might yet prove 'liquors of peace'.

A more promising government response was to fight words with words. Over the course of 1676–7 the government matched Country publications with a propaganda effort of its own. Danby sponsored new Anglican treatises to reinforce the church's teachings about non-resistance, about the respect owed to princes and social superiors, and about the dangers from dissent. Royalist writers coloured the opposition to Danby's programme in the hues of 1640–1, reminding readers that the old enemies of monarchy had 'first found fault with the ... bishops' before 'overturning ... the throne itself'. Shaftesbury's record as a political survivor since the 1650s was turned against him: he was characterized as a slippery 'Dorsetshire eel' who could 'shift principles like shirts'. Lest it be accepted as a moderate, comprehensible form of dissent, Presbyterianism was also pilloried by Anglican writers as a menacing 'hydra' that had, in the past, spawned a 'many headed progeny [of] Anabaptists, Quakers, and Levellers'.[39]

The effectiveness of the government's propaganda – and especially of its suggestion that Country leaders were driving the country back to civil war – was apparent when parliament resumed its business in February 1677. After the king's predictable opening request for money, especially for the navy, Shaftesbury and Buckingham attacked the legitimacy of the parliament in the Lords. They claimed that the duration of the prorogation violated medieval statutes requiring annual sessions, and their associates in the Commons made the same arguments. The intention of these attacks was to force a new parliamentary election. Danby had shored up his support, however; and even many Country MPs were unprepared for so precipitous a course of action. Shaftesbury and Buckingham were sent to the Tower by the peers for contempt of the house. Both their fate and their absence curbed their more rambunctious followers thereafter. Charles got a quick Commons' vote of £600,000 for 30 new ships, to be paid for by a tax on land. This result was hastened by Louis's continuing successes on the continent and by a perception that he was increasingly likely to gain the Spanish Netherlands.

Danby's success proved short-lived, however. Distrust of Charles, of his international objectives, of his Catholic brother, and of the bishops quickly disrupted the session again. What Charles wanted was more money and the crown's traditional free hand in the conduct of foreign affairs. The Country was, in fact, prepared to provide more money. But Country MPs also wanted a war against France to prevent Louis XIV from overrunning the Low Countries and jeopardizing both English trade and English security. Indeed, they carried a motion to provide Charles with additional money only if he 'enter[ed] into a league, offensive and defensive, with the States General of the United Provinces [and their allies], against the growth and power of the French king, and for the preservation of the Spanish Netherlands'. Fear of France had driven the Cavalier Parliament from its earlier hostility to the Dutch into attempting to coerce Charles into a Dutch alliance. When Charles declined to have his sovereignty and his 'undoubted … prerogative of making peace and war' so 'invaded' by the Commons, another adjournment terminated all this Country trouble, including new measures adopted against Catholicism. Even the adjournment proved troublesome, however, when some MPs sought to seize the Commons' mace and to continue debate until the house had adjourned itself.[40]

As divided as they were over constitutional and religious issues, Danby and his Country critics agreed that the kingdom's future could only be secured in alliance with the Protestant Dutch against the Counter-Reformation French colossus. Such an alliance was also the key to Dutch security in the mind of William of Orange, who had so far been unable to check French military advances. With his leading critics still in the Tower after the parliamentary adjournment of May 1677, Danby maintained his credit with an increasingly Francophobic nation through public promotion of friendship with the Dutch and with William in particular. When Louis presented William with unreasonable terms for peace, Danby persuaded Charles to open diplomatic discussions with his nephew's government. Charles entertained William's personal envoy in the early summer, while plans proceeded for a state visit from the prince himself. By the time William arrived in October, his intentions included marriage to Mary, the elder daughter of the Duke of York, who, unlike her father, had remained steadfast to the Church of England. Charles agreed to the marriage, believing it would enable him to play the diplomatic role of arbiter of Europe; and James expected his new Protestant son-in-law to give him political cover for his Catholicism. Fifteen-year old Mary, on the other hand, wept for two days at her fate, for Dutch William had the mien of a warrior rather than the manners of a beau.

The contrasting 'great joy' of the 'whole nation' at this marriage nevertheless failed to give Danby any success in moderating Charles's obsessive desire for friendship with the Sun King. In fact, even as Charles entered the Franco-Dutch peace negotiations on William's behalf, Danby colluded in Charles's continuing pursuit of money from Louis, seeking to dash his master's hopes by demanding more money than he knew Louis would provide. Danby's duplicity proved unnecessary, however. The French king was so offended by the marriage of William and Mary that he cut off payments to Charles that he had already promised. For his part, Charles retaliated by entering into an offensive treaty with the Dutch that seemed to revive the objectives of the old Protestant Triple Alliance.[41]

When Charles met the Cavalier Parliament again in January 1678, the prospect had thus emerged that the king, his principal minister, both court-inclined and Country MPs, and the English public might finally converge in a great patriotic war against France. Instead, the parliamentary sessions of 1678 led the kingdom into a great Restoration Crisis that shook Charles's government to its foundations. Matters actually got off to a reasonably good start, as Charles informed parliament that his new arrangements with the Dutch satisfied their former demands for an anti-French alliance. He asked for a million pounds in new supply to ready 90 ships and 30,000 troops. For once, and despite attention to the usual Country concerns, the Commons agreed to the requested sum within a fortnight, though their formula for providing it eventually included a three-year ban on French imports that seriously cut customs duties. The potential for harmony was lessened soon thereafter, however, as Shaftesbury returned from the Tower to his place in the Lords, after making a strategic apology to the peers. As attacks upon Charles's ministers for their 'French counsels' began in the Commons, both houses also resolved in favour of a war with Louis. The lords were, at least, more respectful of Charles's prerogative in leaving the timing of a war declaration to him. Charles began to raise troops for a war, but some within and some without parliament now began to fear these troops were intended for use in England rather than on the continent.[42]

The Commons addressed the king in early May for the removal of ministers who had contradicted their previous advice, meaning especially Danby and Lauderdale. But Charles instead prorogued parliament for ten days and concluded another secret deal with Louis. In return for over half a million pounds, Charles agreed to disband his forces and to remain neutral, should the Dutch and their allies not accept Louis's peace terms. Danby remained involved in Charles's French bargaining through his instructions to Ralph Montagu, the English ambassador in Paris. The lord treasurer nevertheless stayed out of the final arrangements, other than to advise William of Orange to come to terms with the French as soon as possible. The Dutch prince did precisely that, agreeing first to a truce and, a few months later, to the Peace of Nijmegen.

When MPs returned to work in late May, Charles sought to keep up the forces he had raised as a safeguard to force Louis to peace. But the same MPs who had lately demanded war now demanded the disbandment of soldiers they feared 'may fight against Magna Charta'. They voted £200,000 to pay off the troops and to get rid of them. When Charles responded with a request for a significant enlargement in his ordinary revenue, Country MPs complained about ministerial mismanagement of existing revenues and expressed fears about a design to endow the crown so well that it would 'not need parliaments any more'. Charles got no additions to his ordinary income and lost his French subsidy as well when he stuck by William during the protracted peace negotiations.

MPs went home in July grumbling about the length of the session. They would have far more to grumble about by the time they returned in October 1678, however, for Charles used the funds they had voted to disband the army to retain some of it. The Country's fear of a standing army in England, which, like the New Model, might become an instrument of arbitrary government, seemed about to be realized. Moreover, despite extensive Commons' investigations into the danger from Roman Catholicism in England and Wales, parliament had accomplished little since 1673 to safeguard the country's Protestant traditions. The fear of popery would soon sweep all before it, engulfing Charles and James in a *grande peur* from which they would not easily be extricated.[43]

'Popery and Arbitrary Government': The Politics of Fear

Nothing in the history of seventeenth-century Britain is more off putting than the loathing of English, Scots, and Irish Protestants, of all persuasions, for their Roman Catholic fellow subjects. When the fear of Catholicism is placed in its Reformation context rather than judged by present-day aspirations for cultural tolerance, however, it can be seen as neither intrinsically irrational nor particularly bigoted. Like any popular fear, it was subject to manipulation and embellishment for political purposes, as was the case in 1678–81 and again in 1687–9. Yet British anti-popery itself was an understandable reflection of the vulnerability Protestants felt in a century of Counter-Reformation Catholic re-ascendancy on the continent. British Protestants saw their own possible fate in Louis XIV's promotion of Catholicism in the Low Countries and the Rhineland, in his exercise of an authority that seemed unrestrained by law or local liberties, and in his curtailment of the religious freedom of French Protestants. As one Country MP put it, 'our jealousies of popery, or an arbitrary government, are ... from the ill example we have from France.'[44]

The Catholic presence in the British kingdoms sustained anti-Catholicism as well. The best modern estimate of the number of committed Roman Catholic laity in England and Wales during the Restoration is about 60,000, or slightly more than 1 per cent of the total population of about 5.5 million. The Catholic population was unevenly distributed, however, both geographically and socially. In greater London, several thousand Catholics were sufficiently concentrated in Westminster and the western suburbs to give their faith an urban visibility that was alarming to Protestant neighbours. In four northern counties, including Lancashire, Catholics may have made up as much as 10 per cent of the population. Catholicism was also strong in some western and Welsh border counties, such as Herefordshire and Monmouthshire. In these peripheries, the survival of Catholicism in strength was partly an effect of the slowness of Protestantism to develop durable roots in overly large and poorly supplied parishes.

In many rural areas, Catholicism was also a 'household' religion maintained in the families of prominent Catholic nobles and gentry who could support priests, and who could also command the religious loyalties of servants, tenants, and villagers. In general, Catholicism had retained much more appeal for nobles and gentry – not all of them in remote counties – than for the population in general. Altogether, about 40 peers who sat in the House of Lords in Charles II's reign (15 per cent of the total) were definite or probable Catholics. Although few Catholics were chosen for the House of Commons, as much as 7 per cent of the English and Welsh gentry were Catholic. In Westminster and its environs, almost one-sixth of all Catholic recusants (those convicted of failure to attend their Protestant parish churches) were of gentle birth. The respectability of Westminster Catholicism was also enhanced by its residential concentration around the chapels of the French, Spanish, Portuguese, and Venetian ambassadors and those of Catholic members of the royal family, such as Charles's wife, Catherine of Braganza.[45]

But these numbers fail entirely to capture the cultural impact of Catholicism. English Protestants joined their Irish and Scots counterparts in facing a Catholic majority in rural Ireland and an unreformed population in parts of the Scottish Highlands, where many of that kingdom's remaining Catholics resided.[46] Moreover, Restoration Protestants believed that Catholic numbers in England were much higher than those given here and that Catholics were regaining lost ground. All British Protestants also shared a common historical memory in which Catholic monarchs and Catholic clergy were seen as enemies of the liberties of subjects and of parliaments. Mary Tudor *had*, in fact, burnt hundreds of English Protestants, and Mary Stuart *had* sought to undermine the Reformation in Scotland and England. English Catholics *had* plotted against the Protestant Elizabeth and had sought, in 1605, to blow up James I and the parliament at the opening of a session. Irish Catholics *had* killed Protestant settlers in 1641; and Jesuits and other Catholic priests had, contrary to law, maintained papal structures in Ireland and England. In the Restoration, as many as 650 Catholic clergy ministered in England: half of them were members of orders, and almost half of those were Jesuits.[47]

Furthermore, Catholics remained attached to their priests and to their religion despite a century of persecution under statutes intended to force their conversion. For Protestants who found parallels to the history of Christianity in the Hebrew Scriptures, Catholics were backsliders or apostates. They were also regarded as traitors to British national cultures that were Protestant by definition. In fact, however, most leading Catholics were loyal to the Stuart monarchy. Catholic gentry had defended Charles I during the civil wars and were often ardent royalists after the Restoration. But even minor office holding by Catholic gentry (in the militia or as JPs) was seen by Protestants as a first dangerous step in papal schemes to overturn the royal supremacy and the Reformation establishment in church and state. Those few English Catholics who had penetrated the highest counsels of government were also thought likely to promote authoritarian rule at the expense of parliament. This political reading of Catholicism contributed to the shock of spectacular conversions like those of Clifford and the Duke of York.

Country expressions of anti-Catholicism in the parliamentary sessions of 1673–4 were part of a broader anti-Catholic current that swept English opinion, especially in London, after Charles's 1672 indulgence of Catholics. The anniversary of the discovery of the Gunpowder Plot, for instance, was celebrated in London with a pope-burning procession on 5 November 1673, which marked the popular revival of that holiday. Another papal effigy was burnt in Southwark later in the month upon the arrival of Mary Beatrice of Modena, James's new Catholic bride. Convictions of Catholics for recusancy also increased notably in some parts of the country as local JPs took the initiative in enforcing the penal laws against them. Anglicans were initially as outspoken as dissenters in public expressions of anti-popery. After 1675, however, many Anglicans followed Danby in seeing dissent as the greater issue. Local adherents of Country principles, on the other hand, saw popery as the chief danger to the country. Anti-popery was a founding principle of the opposition Green Ribbon Club, for instance. It met, starting in 1674, in the West End of London and brought together parliamentary and civic critics of the government and of the bishops. Fear of Rome was evident at the 1676 London guild assembly, where speakers who followed the Country lead suggested that a Catholic succession would entail a loss of monastic property now in the hands of Protestant gentry and merchants. Urban pope burnings marked Queen Elizabeth's accession day (17 November) in 1676 and 1677, and the Gunpowder Plot was similarly commemorated in 1677 at the Fire Monument.[48]

By that time, fearing the 'popery' of their own bishops, Country MPs found dangers from Rome even in measures intended by Danby to safeguard the Anglican establishment in the event of James's succession.[49] Andrew Marvell's sensational *Account of the Growth of Popery and Arbitrary Government* (1677) brought all these fears to a head and further enflamed parliamentary tempers. Marvell suggested that

Danby, court MPs, and – reading between the lines – perhaps the king and his brother, were undermining church and state in order to bring in 'French slavery and ... Roman idolatry'. In 1678 Country MPs worried particularly about the number of commissioned officers in the newly raised forces who were said to be Irish Catholics or Highland Scots; and they demanded to 'be secured from those forces bringing in popery'. MPs learned from informants that mass had long been openly said in Monmouthshire, that Catholics were serving as JPs in some counties, and that statutes providing for the sequestration of the estates of Catholic recusants were instead being applied against Quakers. They pleaded with the Lords to adopt further measures to reduce the growth of popery. Finally, the Commons considered another test bill designed to prevent Catholics, including all peers, from sitting in either house of parliament.[50]

Events in Ireland had, in the past, reinforced the coupling in English Protestant minds of the dangers of 'popery and arbitrary government'. As English anti-popery mounted after 1675, Irish Episcopal churchmen became increasingly uncomfortable with the failure of the Earl of Essex, the lord lieutenant, to apply the full rigour of the laws against Roman Catholics and Protestant dissenters. Essex was replaced in 1677 by the Duke of Ormond, who returned to Ireland in alliance with Danby and the English bishops. Many expected him to pursue a policy of coercing those outside the established Church of Ireland more vigorously. Ormond failed to satisfy these Episcopalian expectations, however; and continuing Irish Protestant fears, especially about possible adjustments to the land settlement for the benefit of Catholics, made plans for a Dublin parliament imprudent as well.[51] As Ormond pursued the politics of moderation in Ireland, as he had before, Scotland instead became the focus of those in England who feared the spread of 'popery and arbitrary government' from Charles's other kingdoms.

The failure of Lauderdale's attempts to indulge middle-of-the-road Scottish Presbyterians and to separate them from their more intransigent brethren was clear by the mid-1670s. Conventicles continued in many parts of the kingdom, while some indulged Presbyterian clergy refused to take up ministry under Episcopal auspices. Armed confrontations between Covenanters, who sometimes possessed newly built meetinghouses, and troops sent to disperse them became frequent. At least two conferences of Presbyterian clergy were held to devise a common front between the indulged and the non-indulged. For their part, leading Episcopal clergy and the bishops divided between their own moderate and intransigent factions. The moderates included Gilbert Burnet and other advocates of accommodation with the Presbyterians. The intransigents included Archbishop James Sharp, who thought the Presbyterians would remain dissatisfied 'though the heads of all the bishops were given them in a charger'.

The Scottish church quarrel became interconnected with the political tensions of the northern kingdom as well. Lauderdale's principal antagonist, the Duke of Hamilton, was associated with the Episcopalian moderates, including Burnet, who had broken with the Scottish secretary. For his part, Lauderdale abandoned religious indulgence for repression. He was sure of Charles's support after the failure of his political adversaries in 1673–4, and he was soon in alliance with Danby and the English bishops. In 1674, the Scottish Privy Council authorized the use of both regular troops and militia to disperse illegal worship assemblies. Soldiers were quartered throughout those parts of the kingdom, especially the Southwest, where field conventicles had 'increased mightily' and often numbered thousands of people. Landlords were ordered to prevent their tenants from attending irregular worship. Urban magistrates were required to suppress conventicles in their burghs, and householders were made responsible for the religious behaviour of their servants. New appointments to Episcopal sees demonstrated the government's determined mood, while Archbishop Sharp cowed moderates within the church.

These measures failed, however, to reconcile equally determined Covenanters to the Scottish church. By 1677–8, Lauderdale embarked upon harsher measures yet that would eventually produce another rising and bring his own career to an end. The Scottish council authorized the taking of bonds from landlords in the southwest shires to ensure that neither they nor their households and tenants would attend conventicles or succour dissenting teachers. When many property owners declined to provide such security, their refusal was deemed treason. The area was declared to be in rebellion, and Lauderdale turned to the Highland clan chiefs to raise an emergency military force from their dependants. A 'Highland host' joined several Lowland militia units in an army of some 8000, who encamped 'at free quarter' in the affected shires for five weeks in January and February 1678. In effect, they requisitioned whatever they needed from the terrified population they policed. Lowland dissenters believed that their commitment to the gospel and to their preachers had unleashed upon them 'a host of savages ... more terrible than Turks or Tartars, men who feared not God ... [and] came ... to waste and destroy a plentiful country ... [and] make [it] as bare as their own'. Gentry and property owners known for their opposition to Lauderdale or for their Presbyterian sympathies were singled out for punitive confiscations of weapons and horses. Hamilton and several of his associates left for London, where they recounted tales of the wintertime pillage and spoliation of a rural population to leaders of the English parliamentary opposition. Although Charles authorized a convention of the Scottish estates to vote money for Lauderdale's military expedition, his confidence in Lauderdale's management had begun to erode.[52]

This Scottish confrontation did not, in fact, pit Catholics against Protestants, but it might just as well have. Many Lowland Presbyterians regarded Episcopalian services and tactics as a popery little different from that of Catholicism, and now they believed they had seen a demonstration of the prelates' malice that matched anything Rome had to offer. For many English MPs, the 'rapine and spoil' they saw in Protestant Scotland was no different from that inflicted on continental Protestant territories that fell to Louis's Catholic armies. The challenge to property rights by the Scottish Privy Council and the Highland clansmen, who were thought to have sacked the Lowlands like an occupying army, was exactly what Protestant tradition predicted from Catholics, should they ever regain power. Moreover, those forces were construed as the very standing army that the English Country so feared. 'In Scotland, if any man looks but discontented, then kill him, shoot him, eat him up,' thundered one outraged English MP.

Much of what was happening in the northern kingdom was also perceived at Westminster as a harbinger of what might be in store for England, should Lauderdale's understanding of law and government ever prevail there. Another Commons' address for Lauderdale's removal failed in May 1678 by a single vote. The victory was Pyrrhic for the government, however. Too many MPs had already come to the conclusion that ministerial manipulation of parliament and royal tolerance towards Catholicism threatened law, property, and the Protestant religion. 'Parliaments, and all laws, and government, and the Protestant religion … they are all one,' suggested one Country speaker, who thought if one fell, so would all the rest. No wonder MPs and the political public so easily credited a tale that began to circulate, in early autumn 1678, about a Jesuit conspiracy to assassinate Charles.[53]

The story itself originated with one Titus Oates, a young and emotionally troubled Anglican preacher and congenital liar who had feigned conversion to Roman Catholicism. He had been abroad for a year in 1677–8 at the English Jesuit colleges in Valladolid, Spain and St Omer in Artois, France. There he learned much about English Jesuit organization and personnel that he would employ to spectacular use. On his return to England, Oates teamed up with an obsessively anti-Catholic London rector, Dr Israel Tonge, and told him a complicated tale about being recruited to participate in a Jesuit plot to kill the king and the king's brother, who was to be spared only if he joined the scheme. According to Oates, details of the conspiracy had been agreed upon at a secret conclave of English Jesuits. Money had been provided by foreign Catholics, including one of Louis XIV's confessors; and failed attempts had already been made against the unsuspecting and largely unguarded monarch.

Tonge, who believed entirely in Oates's story, used court contacts to get it to the king shortly before Charles departed in August for Windsor, and then for Newmarket, to relax at the horse races. Charles initially proved relatively indifferent to the news: the king, Danby, and the Privy Council got around to interviewing Tonge and Oates only in late September. By that time, Oates had taken the precaution of swearing to the truth of his evidence before the respected Westminster JP, Sir Edmund Berry Godfrey. Godfrey, the brother of prominent London merchants, was connected to some of Danby's parliamentary opponents; but he also had Catholic acquaintances in high places. One of these was the convert Edward Coleman, formerly the Duke of York's secretary, and now secretary to James's duchess. Prior to facing the Privy Council, Oates had developed additional details, which he also swore before Godfrey. Among the names he now named was that of Coleman, who supposedly was involved in transmitting money from Louis XIV's confessor for the intended assassins.

Until this point, only Tonge was persuaded of the truth of the tale. But Oates, who had once been friendly with actors, gave a convincing performance before the council. He was able to draw upon his familiarity with the names of English Catholics in London and at court to enhance the plausibility of his fabrications. When Coleman's papers were seized upon Oates's evidence, they demonstrated that Coleman had indeed corresponded with Louis XIV's confessor, that he had received French money for distribution in England, and that he had made no secret of his hope that England might again become Catholic. Moreover, the disappearance of some of Coleman's correspondence suggested the possibility that more incriminating documents had been destroyed. Many of the London Catholic clergy named by Oates were rounded up, and the Privy Council began interviewing them to ascertain the truth of Oates's allegations. Coleman, who had probably been warned of the evidence against him by Godfrey, gave himself up, denying any involvement in such a plot but also acknowledging his correspondence with the French court.

What turned this affair into a cause célèbre, before the next parliamentary session began on 21 October, was the disappearance and death of Godfrey, just as public rumours about the Privy Council investigation began to spread. How Sir Edmund Berry Godfrey died is one of the greatest mysteries of British history. It remains unsolved despite the efforts of historians, popular writers, and even the philosopher, David Hume. The reclusive and unmarried Godfrey had a melancholy disposition, and he may have become frightened and depressed about the implications of his possible intervention on Coleman's behalf. Whatever the case, he was not seen after 12 October. His brothers and his friends soon claimed that he had been murdered by the Catholics to prevent the disclosure of further evidence about the plot. His body was found on the outskirts of London five days later, with a broken neck and with clear signs of strangulation, possibly by a rope or cord, but also with his own sword thrust through the torso. The jury at a coroner's inquest, influenced by Godfrey's family, found for murder, discounting evidence that instead suggested suicide and its disguise.

Only such a verdict would have been acceptable at the time. Godfrey and his brothers were well known; and the public had already concluded, 'in great spirit', that Godfrey had been murdered by the papists. His death was taken as verification of Oates's account of a vast, international Jesuit conspiracy to kill the king and to initiate Catholic risings in the British kingdoms. Indeed, Godfrey's murder was interpreted as the beginning of an intended 'horrid massacre and slaughter' of the inhabitants of the chief Protestant capital of Europe. Panic seized the London population, as it had during each of the disasters of 1665–7. The city militia was quickly put on guard, and neighbourhood watches patrolled the streets. Godfrey lay in state for a week before his funeral, which occurred a few days before the customary anti-Catholic solemnities of 5 November. A procession of 72 Protestant divines and a thousand mourners accompanied the corpse and were observed by a mass audience of aroused citizens. Godfrey's name quickly achieved iconic status and was added to the martyrology of the English Reformation.

Charles said little about the plot in his opening speech to parliament, but MPs could scarcely contain their own anti-Catholicism. Oates's story and Godfrey's death seemingly lent final credibility to the charges long made by Shaftesbury and Marvell about a conspiracy to impose popery and arbitrary government. A torrent of rumours, anti-Catholic publications, sermons, and public demonstrations kept London, Westminster, and the whole nation on edge as additional details of Catholic conspiracy spontaneously joined those offered by Oates. In some minds, James was transformed from a possible victim of the plot to a likely perpetrator, because Coleman – the chief suspect – had been in his retinue. According to one account the assassination had been intended to replace Charles with James, who would 'take the crown by gift from the pope'. Moreover, should 'any opposition ... be made the French were to be ready with an army and fleet', to invade the country, while 'the plunder of cities and towns' would be carried out by a 'rabble of Irish and French papists'. These stories prompted the disarming of Catholics throughout England and the imprisonment of five Catholic peers implicated by Oates.

Charges and counter-charges about the 'Popish Plot' would remain at the heart of the crisis that now overtook Charles's kingdoms for several years. In modern times, the plot has primarily been remembered as an unfortunate episode of religious and political hysteria. In that regard, it has remained part of the usable political past, even in the United States. In the early days of the Watergate investigation, for instance, the Nixon White House pointed to the

Popish Plot as an example of how false allegations could fuel a political witch-hunt. Similarly, in 2005, one notable blog defender of George W. Bush's embattled inner circle condemned an outspoken and influential public critic as 'our Titus Oates'. For its part, however, the English public of 1678–9 was fully persuaded that only parliamentary vigilance in unravelling a scheme to kill Charles II and to undo the Protestant Reformation would protect them from Catholicism.[54]

4   The Restoration Crisis, 1678–83

It was with exceeding great trouble that we were brought to the dissolving of the two last parliaments without more benefit to our people … We saw that no expedient would be entertained but that of a total exclusion, which we had so often declared … we could never consent to … We cannot, after the sad experience we have had of the late civil wars, that murdered our father of blessed memory and ruined the monarchy, consent to a law that shall establish another most unnatural war … And we have reason to believe … that if we could have been brought to give our consent to a bill of exclusion the intent was not to rest there but to pass further.

Charles II (April 1681)[1]

Introduction: The Crisis

An argument can be made that modern British politics began in the crisis of 1678–83. The initial issue was the future of monarchy. Many in the English parliament became persuaded that neither the monarchy nor Protestantism could survive the succession of a Catholic prince. Much of the English political public agreed, but others became persuaded instead that any alteration in the strict order of the hereditary succession would return the kingdom to the confusion of the civil war and Interregnum years. The realm became divided into hostile political parties that largely coincided with the religious division between committed Anglicans, on the one hand, and dissenters and their allies within the church, on the other. This political and religious division also dovetailed with a cultural division. The public sphere was invigorated by those who raised their voices on behalf of parliamentary and personal liberties as well as by those who really thought all subjects should instead defer to authority, order, and hierarchy.

The crisis extended to Ireland, and especially to Scotland, as well. Monarchy was just as much the issue in the northern kingdom, where the Duke of York was eventually sent by his brother to defang the English opposition by reducing the visibility of a Catholic successor. In Scotland, James worked with royalist nobles and lairds to re-secure Restoration institutions, both against Scots Presbyterians and against his English detractors.[2] In 1681, he obtained an uncompromising statement of loyalty to the monarchy and to the hereditary succession from the Scottish estates. Different from England in this emphatic parliamentary triumph of royalism, Scotland did mirror England in one other important respect: militant Scots dissenters were not reconciled to the Episcopal establishment, and their hostility to the bishops was even more intense than that of the English opposition. Indeed, unlike in England, where the Popish Plot was largely a fantasy, a real dissenting conspiracy in Scotland led to the assassination of the primate of St. Andrews. The murder of the archbishop was followed by a revolt of Covenanters in the Southwest. Although unsuccessful, this revolt was far more significant than the Galloway rising of 1666, and it challenged the king as well as the bishops. Ireland, on the other hand, was quieter, in part because its parliament had not met since 1666 and would not do so again until 1689. Nevertheless, Ireland was always in the background of the crisis. Fears about its Catholic majority fed opposition to the succession of a Catholic monarch in England, as did stories about the alleged participation of Irish Catholic leaders in the Popish Plot.

As is already apparent from this overview, the scope of the crisis that began in 1678–9 quickly expanded from the royal succession to the future of the religious establishments of England and Scotland and to other issues as well. Both kingdoms saw a collapse of the coercive religious order that had been put in place in the 1660s. Liberty of conscience prevailed, albeit briefly, in each kingdom; and in Ireland, Ormond's strategy of preventing disorder through the lenient treatment of dissent also provided a de facto toleration. The actions of the English House of Commons, which moved three times to eliminate James from the succession, frayed the governing connections between England and Scotland and threatened to put the two kingdoms on a collision course. The tensions inherent in the multiple Stuart monarchies could not have been more starkly revealed. Furthermore, in England, the royal dissolution of four parliaments, one after the other, in little more than two years, raised significant constitutional issues.

Some Commons' leaders feared that the place of parliament in the government was in danger.

Earlier histories of the crisis focused heavily on the English parliament and appropriately so. The eruptions of disorderly behaviour and angry words that had punctuated conversation between court and Country from the mid-1670s continued into the parliaments that sat between 1678 and 1681. Parliamentary politics also took on some of the trappings of more recent political ruckuses. Numerous committees in the Commons and Lords investigated the Popish Plot and allied concerns. Some MPs, such as Londoner Sir Thomas Player, sought to build public reputations by exploiting suspicions of a government cover-up about a frightful conspiracy. The king and loyal ministers, on the other hand, claimed that evidence about plotting had been exaggerated, fabricated, and distorted by the enemies of order and good government. Prominent figures like Danby were impeached. Several leading Catholics, including a few peers who were supposedly involved in the Plot, were subjected to public trials, and some were executed. Personal antagonisms between elite figures, like that between the king and Shaftesbury, further poisoned parliamentary proceedings.

Opposition leaders who sought to safeguard Protestantism fully developed parliament's potential as a public forum for national debate. Votes in both houses were closely calculated and much canvassing occurred about different measures. The 'people' – or at least those people who were electors – fully participated in the parliamentary dimension of the crisis. Three parliamentary elections in quick sequence gave electors opportunities to debate the issues and to express their views. Some parliamentary votes were printed for public information, and collections of proceedings and debates were printed after each parliamentary session. By 1681, some newly chosen MPs were also being handed lists of instructions from those who had elected them. Finally, by 1681, Charles sought to suggest that the danger to English traditions in church and state came not from the crown, as his opponents charged, but rather from parliamentarians. Like their forerunners of 1640–1, according to the king, they sought to expand their liberties at the expense of his prerogative.

More recent historical studies of the crisis have devoted as much attention to the English public sphere as to parliamentary politics. A variety of extraordinary political devices created a politics 'out of doors' that was as central to the crisis as politics within the doors of Whitehall and Westminster. Petitions, processions, electoral propaganda, and public feasts were among these devices. James's English detractors may have taken the lead in pioneering them; but the Anglican friends of hereditary succession quickly adopted them, and they were employed in Scotland and in Ireland as well. The politicization of the population extended well beyond the ranks of those who exercised the parliamentary franchise. In London, political crowds were swelled by the spontaneous participation of artisans, seamen, porters, and apprentices. Women as well as men were indicted for seditious speech.[3] These extraordinary political activities contributed to the emergence of extra-parliamentary parties in England. Opponents and supporters of the government had been referred to as parties even before the era of Danby. The Whig and Tory parties that emerged by 1680–1, however, had a better claim to that designation, in its modern, more organized sense, than the parliamentary cliques of the mid-1670s.

The debate and competition between these English parties was carried out as much within the public domain as within parliament. The press, coffeehouses and taverns, and pulpits and workplaces were all polarized by political dispute. Government efforts to limit and to regulate the press collapsed. Print output over the course of the crisis matched that of the 1640s. It included newspapers, periodicals, pamphlets, and political drawings that advocated about all the issues of the affair. The annual output of new English pamphlet titles rose from about 800 in 1677 to about 1800 in 1680, and many of them cost as little as a penny or two. The total number of copies of political pamphlets in circulation in England between 1678 and 1681 was somewhere between five and ten million. A significant portion of the population could access this material. Over 30 per cent of English men and over 20 per cent of English women were probably literate at the time. In London, 70–80 per cent of tradesmen and artisans could read, at least somewhat, as could 40–50 per cent of city women.[4]

The debate in the prints also drew forth the talents of the principal writers of the era. John Bunyan examined the probable consequences of a Catholic succession in *The Holy War* (1682), and Thomas Shadwell propagated the Whig view of the Popish Plot in *The Lancashire Witches* (1682). In the end, however, the Tories had the better of the literary contest. John Dryden savaged the

Whigs in *Absalom and Achitophel* (1681), which brilliantly reduced the issues of the crisis to caricatures of opposition personalities. Thomas Otway ridiculed Shaftesbury in *Venice Preserved* (1682). Aphra Behn attacked Whigs and dissenters in *The Roundheads or, the Good Old Cause* (1682) and *The City Heiress* (1682). John Crowne did the same in *City Politics* (1683).

The language of partisanship, which addressed critical constitutional and religious issues from opposite perspectives, made compromise almost impossible. Whigs thought Tories were dupes for popery and arbitrary government. Tories thought Whigs were agents of republicanism and fanaticism. Opponents in this crisis spoke different political languages, and they frequently spoke past one another. Anglican Tories held to their organic view of society: they regarded the king as a great father, as the source of law, and as a mystical embodiment of divine purpose. Instead, many Whigs saw monarchs as political contrivances: according to them, kings possessed powers negotiated over the centuries with a freeborn people and their representatives; and kings were bound to respect the liberties and properties of their subjects. One view was hierarchical; the other view was implicitly contractual. One view was consistent with an understanding of the church as the religious embodiment of a whole people. The other view understood religion instead as a sphere, somewhat distinct from the state, in which the claims of individual conscience took precedence over Protestant unity, which was otherwise desirable. One view looked backward to the Elizabethan worldview of the sixteenth century; the other looked forward to the 'liberal' Anglo-American worldview of the eighteenth century. The latter view found its most explicit expression in the work of the republican Algernon Sidney and of Shaftesbury's associate, John Locke. Sidney would lose his life for his unpublished *Discourses concerning Government* (which appeared only in 1698). Locke's manuscript defence of revolution, written to encourage crisis-weary Whigs, sent him into exile for fear of the same fate. His *Two Treatises of Government* (not published until 1690) would codify Whig language as a carrier of Restoration political experiences into the modern politics of Britain, Europe, and North America.

The political and religious institutions of the Restoration were, therefore, much in question in England in the crisis of 1678–83. They were also in question in Scotland and Ireland, given the political connections of the three kingdoms under one monarchy. The institutions of the Restoration had never fully settled any of Charles's kingdoms, but settlement unravelled in England after 1678; and it was challenged in Scotland as well. Historians have recently debated the most appropriate name for this crisis, which English historians have generally connected to the issue of exclusion. Given that exclusion was but one of several issues in England, and that exclusion gained much less traction in Scotland, 'Restoration Crisis' is arguably the most appropriate label for this multi-faceted British crisis. It is also the only label that captures the magnitude and the importance of these years for subsequent British and American politics.[5]

The Unsettlement of England, 1678–9

The eighteenth and final session of the Cavalier Parliament was shaped by the Popish Plot from beginning to end. Despite his managerial skills, Danby proved incapable of leapfrogging through the anti-Catholic parliamentary torrent. He had expended too much political capital, alienated too many MPs, and gotten on the wrong side of too many Country issues. He had also made too many enemies, even at court and in the government. The Plot revelations gave Country MPs all the incentive they needed to return to the anti-Catholic initiatives of previous sessions, especially one for imposing an anti-Catholic test on the members of both houses of parliament. When this second Test Act reached the Lords, the peers added an exception for the Duke of York, at his request. In the Commons, Danby promoted James's interest, despite his own suspicion of him, and maintained James's right to sit in the Lords by a scant two-vote margin. The debate nevertheless drew even more attention to the broader question of James's possible succession to the throne, despite his Catholicism.

Charles had ample reason to believe that a parliamentary assault upon James was in the offing, though nobody at first knew how far it might go. At Danby's prompting, Charles sought, in early November, to head off a confrontation over the succession by indicating his willingness to accept 'reasonable' bills for limitations upon a Catholic king's power. To the king's way of thinking, accepting such temporary limitations voluntarily was better than suffering any parliamentary interference with the prerogative or with the 'true line' of the crown's hereditary descent. Temporary limitations were an expression of royal grace, while parliamentary tampering with the succession assaulted Anglican royalist notions about kingship. But no Country consensus had yet developed about how best to proceed with the problem of a popish successor. MPs seemed reluctant, at first, to embrace the extreme solution of eliminating James as heir to the throne. Only gradually, through the course of events in 1678–9, did the exclusion of James emerge as the preferred opposition solution to the succession issue.[6]

Nothing was more damaging to James throughout this session than the preoccupations of parliament and of the public with investigation of the Popish Plot. Committees of both houses sat daily to gather evidence. To agitated parliamentary spokesmen, Oates had revealed a conspiracy that made the Gunpowder Plot of 1605 look amateurish by comparison. In their minds, the Plot was still ongoing, and it was directed as much at them as at Charles. Many members were persuaded that what they had learned so far was only the tip of an iceberg. Indeed, additional informants came forward in the next few months to expose for MPs what they suspected lay beneath the surface.

The most notorious of these new informants was William Bedloe, a onetime friend of Oates and a trickster with numerous Catholic contacts. Bedloe claimed he had seen Sir Edmund Berry Godfrey's body at the residence of Charles's queen, Catherine of Braganza. In fact, he claimed that Catherine's Jesuit priests and servants had murdered Godfrey. Not to be outdone, Oates suggested to the House of Commons that the queen herself had been party to the assassination scheme in order to revenge herself on a husband who had shared his bed with too many others. Bedloe then implied that James had known of Catherine's intensions. The examination, trial, and execution for treason of Edward Coleman, James's former secretary, provided further public plausibility for all these revelations. Some MPs muttered about impeaching the queen, and the Commons did address Charles to remove her from the court. Shaftesbury hoped the king would at least use the excuse of Catherine's alleged involvement in the Plot to divorce her, marry a Protestant, and produce a legitimate Protestant heir. Other MPs and privy councillors now followed Charles, however, in beginning to doubt the veracity of informers who, when pushed, seemed always to remember still more spectacular Plot details.[7]

By the end of 1678, Danby was in as much trouble as James and the queen, but he was undermined by a quite different set of revelations from those of Oates and Bedloe. He was targeted by a political alliance that brought together several notable Country MPs and Ralph Montagu, until recently Charles's ambassador to the court of Louis XIV. Montagu was in possession of important letters from Danby, with whom he had fallen out when the lord treasurer blocked his attempt to buy a secretaryship of state. Montagu was also in disgrace with Charles because he had abandoned his Paris post without Charles's permission after a disastrous affair with the Duchess of Cleveland, the king's former mistress. Montagu believed he could make a political comeback by ingratiating himself with the opposition by sharing his letters from Danby. These documents could be construed to suggest that the lord treasurer had been the instigator of Charles's requests for French cash.[8]

On 19 December, Montagu read to the Commons a letter of the previous March in which Danby, in pursuance of Charles's wishes, instructed the ambassador to offer Louis English assistance in his continuing war against the Dutch in exchange for a sizeable French grant. The letter was dated a few days after Charles had accepted supply from parliament, which had approved the money for the initiation of war *against* France in alliance with the Dutch. This startling revelation produced an immediate (and pre-concerted) move to impeach the lord treasurer for selling the nation and the Commons to Louis XIV. The arguments were obvious. 'Now we see who has played all this game ... and raised an army for no war,' pointed out one Country MP, who suspected the army was instead for domestic use. A second MP interpreted Montagu's evidence as yet another sign of 'the design on foot to destroy the government and our liberties', for it fit in with previous Country charges that a French supported conspiracy against Protestantism and parliamentary government had been afoot since 1675 or earlier.

The House of Commons rushed to approve articles against the lord treasurer. Even some government servants voted against him. But when the impeachment reached the House of Lords, the peers refused to authorize Danby's imprisonment. Fearing that an ugly deadlock between the houses might paralyse the government, Charles prorogued parliament for several weeks on 30 December. He probably worried that the attack on Danby might uncover his own duplicitous relations with Louis XIV. He may also have feared that additional allegations against James and the queen would emerge from the informers and witnesses parading before the parliamentary committees at the encouragement of Shaftesbury and Country MPs. Thinking first that only a cooling off period was needed, Charles eventually came to the conclusion that the situation required something more drastic. With Danby's agreement, Charles dissolved parliament on 24 January and called for a new one in March, finally providing the parliamentary election the Country had long demanded.[9]

The dissolution of parliament shocked the political public. In London, the prorogation had already persuaded many citizens that 'popery and arbitrary government is intended, [and] that a parliament is not to come again.' Danby's civic opponents had gathered 20,000 signatures on petitions calling for Charles to meet parliament again as soon as possible, with the intent of encouraging similar efforts elsewhere. Not since the early days of the Long Parliament had subjects petitioned on this scale. Coming in the wake of such petitioning, the dissolution of parliament 'terrified most people'. Some thought the popish conspirators were responsible for it, in order to prevent the disclosure of evidence and 'to gain time and to bring on the French assistance'. In London, many prepared to defend themselves. The streets were full of people, women as well as men, who had purchased newly manufactured daggers marked on one side with the Latin words 'for the Protestant religion', and on the other side, 'in memory of Godfrey, 12 October 78'. Numerous searches of Catholic premises by one JP produced popish propaganda, paraphernalia, and weapons assumed to have been put aside for use after the king's assassination. Mysterious fires in the legal quarters were blamed on the papists. Three of the Jesuits implicated by Oates were tried and executed, as were three Catholic tradesmen who were suspected of murdering Godfrey at the queen's residence. Shaftesbury wrote that most people 'hardly slept this winter, for fear of fire and massacring by the papists, whilst they suspect[ed] the government itself to be in the plot'.[10]

The election of MPs that occurred under these circumstances was a rout for Danby, the government, and the court. Seventeen counties and eighty-four boroughs had contested elections, twice as many as in 1661, and more than in either of the two subsequent elections of the crisis. Electors demonstrated hostility to the government in many places. Associates and relatives of Danby were hissed at the hustings. Charles remarked that 'the country would choose a dog if he stood against a courtier.' The bishops and the Anglican clergy were active in promoting loyalist candidates. The nephew of Gilbert Sheldon, the late Archbishop of Canterbury, was one of the unsuccessful London candidates, for instance. But nonconformists mounted a corresponding effort to block strong churchmen and to elect members committed to further reform of the church. The efforts made by candidates were often extensive, and the cost of these electoral efforts was often significant. Forty-five percent of the MPs chosen (235 of 522) were new to parliament. The number of government office holders in the House of Commons was cut in half. Opponents of the government outnumbered its supporters in the new house by a margin of at least three to two. The Duke of Ormond hoped that 'monarchy will not be struck at the root', in the new parliament, but he feared that 'it will be very close lopped.'[11]

Ormond was not the only political leader with political scenarios from the 1640s on his mind. The government was in disarray as a full parliament, with over 400 MPs in attendance, assembled in March. Before the opening, Charles supported an Anglican clerical effort to reconvert his brother to Protestantism. When that failed, he packed a reluctant James off to Brussels, both to defuse attacks upon him and to protect him from his enemies. But the king also met parliament with Danby still in office, a blunder of the first magnitude, given the animosity towards the treasurer that had been building throughout his tenure. After opening disputes, Charles retired Danby with a pardon, a large pension, and a promotion within the peerage; but he thereby merely added fuel to a revived move to impeach him. The earl went into hiding; but he resurfaced when the Commons moved to attaint him of treason in his absence, only to disappear again, this time into protective custody in the Tower. Charles put the Treasury in the hands of a committee, an acknowledgement in itself that no single individual in his government had the political skills necessary to contend with the mess that Danby left behind.[12]

With little government management of the Commons in evidence, Country MPs proceeded with the legislative programme that had emerged in the last years of the Cavalier Parliament. Measures were introduced to reduce corruption in the choice of

MPs, to replace MPs who accepted government offices, and to provide a biennial limit upon the length of any parliament. Another bill to strengthen the right of habeas corpus was introduced. MPs again provided Charles with money to disband the troops raised for the phantom war against France. William Penn and other dissenting writers took up their pens during the session to encourage a move towards toleration and Protestant accommodation. Both houses considered a measure to protect dissenters against prosecution under penal laws that had originally been adopted against Catholics. But this Country agenda also failed to gather momentum because of the continuing preoccupation of MPs and of the political public with the Popish Plot. Committees of both houses pursued their investigations, and the Lords published Oates's narrative. In April, a national fast day was held by order of parliament, and preachers throughout the country sought divine favour to 'defeat the wicked counsels and imaginations of our enemies'. When the five Catholic peers in the Tower were transported on the Thames to Westminster to plead to their indictments, anti-popish crowds 'flocked into boats' to harass them and threatened to get entirely out of hand.[13]

With his government adrift, with parliament obsessed with the Plot, and with a 'universal demand of reformation' and change threatening the foundations of the Restoration order, Charles finally acted decisively on 20 April. He reconstituted the Privy Council in order to regain the initiative for the government and to tame the opposition by naming several Country lords and MPs as councillors. Shaftesbury became lord president. The Earl of Essex, and several Commons leaders, including William, Lord Russell, also joined old courtiers on a council reduced to about 30 members. The prospects of Charles's political gambit largely depended upon how he and the council dealt with the succession.

A Commons debate about the succession began in earnest on a rare Sunday meeting a week later. Speaker after speaker suggested that York was at the root of the nation's ills, that his conversion had encouraged Catholic conspiracy, and that parliamentary government, liberty, and property were therefore imperilled. 'Most seemed to allow', according to one observer, 'that if a popish successor did enter there was an end of Protestant religion.' The Commons' secret committee for investigating the Plot was instructed to gather as much evidence as possible about James's suspected involvement. In response, Charles redoubled his efforts to retain the initiative, and he secured Privy Council endorsement for a more comprehensive scheme of limitations than that proposed in the previous session. Charles was willing to accept limitations upon a Catholic successor's right to make appointments of bishops, privy councillors, JPs, and military officers without parliamentary approval. He was also ready to agree that no popish successor should be permitted to begin his reign without the immediate assembling of parliament. In other words, in order to preserve the hereditary succession, Charles was prepared temporarily to accept parliamentary parity with a limited Catholic monarch.[14]

Only Shaftesbury, apparently, expressed strong reservations about these limitations in the council. The limitations scheme nevertheless foundered upon the depth of hostility to James and to Catholicism, both in the Commons and in the public, especially in London. When the limitations proposals were communicated to the Commons, one of Shaftesbury's associates immediately suggested that they 'will not do your work', for such measures could not guarantee that a Catholic successor, especially one with an army, would accept any abridgements of customary royal powers. The secret Commons committee of investigation, chaired by Sir George Treby, recorder (or chief legal officer) of the city of London, communicated the evidence about James they had so far collected. Other London MPs took the lead in directing the Commons towards more drastic remedies. One recommended that James be returned from Brussels so that he might be impeached for treason. Sir Thomas Player, the chamberlain or treasurer of the city government, moved a bill to exclude James 'and all papists whatsoever from the crown of England.' The house voted, late at night, and by a significant majority, to establish a committee to prepare such a bill. In Charles's mind, nothing could be more destructive to the future of monarchy than a parliamentary reassignment of the succession. All those imbued with the political philosophy of Anglicanism saw the situation the same way.

Shaftesbury has often been seen as the prime mover behind exclusion, whether from principle or from a desire to secure mastery of Charles's government. But exclusion could not have emerged without significant public and parliamentary support. Observing the political drama at Westminster, Londoners were particularly aroused and had been for some time. The loyalist lord mayor was worried about a revival of levelling political principles; and with good reason, for a popular movement to reduce the authority of the lord mayor and aldermen and to advance that of the electors and the annually elected common councilmen had emerged from the Country's London following. Player and the other London MPs spoke for this movement, which had dissenting roots, and which was also vehemently anti-Catholic. The urban Green Ribbon Club, which had been involved in the London pope burnings of recent years, was similarly supportive of exclusion and celebrated the Commons' move in that direction with bonfires. The Commons' consideration of exclusion also prompted another city petition that was clearly hostile to James.[15]

Many signs suggested, then, that London was reverting to the role it had played in encouraging and protecting the parliamentary opposition to Charles I in the early 1640s. When the Commons' exclusion bill was favoured by a vote of 207 to 128 at its second reading, some thought parliament was following in the footsteps of 1641–2 as well. MPs who sought to speak against exclusion were shouted down with cries of 'the bill, the bill!' Other matters had inflamed tempers by that time as well. The Commons had sent articles of impeachment against Danby to the Lords, who were also expected to try the five Catholic peers accused of complicity in the Plot. But the prospect of political trials in the Lords had raised another contentious issue, namely, the right of the bishops, who sat in the Lords as spiritual leaders, to vote in such critical temporal matters as political trials that carried the death penalty. The Lords narrowly rejected Shaftesbury's argument that the bishops should not sit for any of the proceedings against Danby, whom they were expected to favour, and instead maintained the right of the prelates to sit until such time as a capital judgement was to be rendered. This decision gave some Country MPs an opportunity to rehearse all their arguments against the bishops. Indeed, according to Gilbert Burnet, 'hot people began everywhere to censure them as a set of men who ... would expose the nation and the Protestant religion to ruin.'[16]

By 27 May Charles had had enough of the House of Commons, of the exclusion bill, and of the debate about the bishops. Expressing his disappointment in the session, he prorogued parliament until August, accepting the habeas corpus measure as virtually its only accomplishment. He had secured little money, and he had lost his principal minister. He had suffered the savaging of his brother in the Commons, and he had seen central assumptions of the Restoration order in church and state defied in parliament and in London. His whole system of government was unravelling at the centre. But his unexpected prorogation contributed yet one additional factor to the unsettlement of England. Parliament had not had time to consider renewing the 1662 act for the licensing of the press, which thereby lapsed with momentous consequences. The public sphere was soon saturated with sharp and divisive writing that assisted ordinary people in raising their voices about the numerous issues that confronted the kingdom. This liberty of the press eliminated yet one more prop of the cavalier order and yet one more safeguard of the Anglican ethos of deference and respect for authority. In London, the best-informed and most volatile locality in the kingdom, one loyalist observer worried that some 'would have risen' in reaction to the prorogation.[17] London remained quiet, however. Scotland, on the other hand, was in an uproar, while the Irish of all persuasions were forced to confront their religious divisions by events in both England and Scotland.

Settlement and Unsettlement in Ireland and Scotland, 1678–9

Given the fears of many Irish Protestants about any repetition of the Catholic violence they had experienced in 1641, they might have been expected to fall into a panic as great as that of the English over allegations about Catholic plotting. They were, after all, little more than a Protestant archipelago in a heavily Catholic sea; and the initial Plot rumours suggested that Irish Catholics would rebel in conjunction with their English counterparts. Not surprisingly, as rumours about Catholic plotting spread, Protestants in the counties of Cork and Kerry fled from the countryside into the security of the towns; and the people of Dublin were put as much on edge by stories about Catholic arms and conspiracies as Londoners. Ulster Protestants were alarmed by the continuing depredations upon their farms and villages by gangs of Gaelic bandits known as tories or raparees. As the Plot took hold of English politics, Ormond came under pressure from the Earl of Orrery and other Anglo-Irish Protestant grandees to launch a new assault upon Catholic landholding. At the very least, anxious Protestants wanted enforcement of the ban on Catholic residence in Irish towns. Had an Irish parliament been summoned at this time, Catholics might have suffered from additional measures directed against them. Ormond had, in fact, prepared the ground for a parliament after he returned to the lord lieutenancy in 1677. A parliament was made less necessary, however, by improvements in Charles's Irish revenues from duties on the kingdom's trade, which was expanding significantly.

Under the circumstances, Ormond's response to the Popish Plot was restrained and measured. He believed that Protestants held most of the cards in Ireland, despite their numerical minority. Many of the remaining Catholic landholders had bent over backwards to demonstrate their loyalty to the Restoration regime, and most of the Catholic peasantry were politically passive. Protestant towns were well garrisoned, and few Irish Catholics had military experience. Any threat to the Protestant establishment came primarily from the Catholic clergy, or so Omond thought. The lord lieutenant therefore directed his punitive measures largely against the Roman clergy. The Catholic hierarchy and all monastic clergy were formally expelled, and other Catholics were disarmed. The Irish army and militia were placed in readiness. Dublin and other towns were purged of Catholic residents without professional occupations. The Roman Catholic Archbishop of Dublin, who had been named as a conspirator in the original Plot revelations, was arrested and eventually died in prison. Oliver Plunket, the Catholic Archbishop of Armagh, was also apprehended and charged with attempting to raise 70,000 Catholics for a massacre of Ireland's Protestant inhabitants in conjunction with a French invasion.

Nevertheless, the anti-Catholic reaction in Ireland never really gathered momentum, despite the anxiety and increased suspiciousness of some Protestant leaders. The accusations against Plunket were so ill-grounded that even a packed Protestant jury found them incredible. Some county grand juries threw out charges that had been made against leading local Catholics. Ireland saw no executions of Catholics in the wake of the Plot, although Plunket was eventually shipped off to London, found guilty, and executed, despite Charles's sympathy for him. Orrery and other Irish Protestant leaders complained about Ormond's leniency to Shaftesbury and the English parliamentary opposition, but the lord lieutenant stood his ground against further reprisals directed towards the Catholic population.[18]

Matters in Scotland took a very different course in 1678–9. The issue that threw Scotland into crisis was not Catholicism but rather Protestant dissent. The withdrawal of the Highland host from the Scottish Southwest had ended none of the resentment among the population there or among Covenanters elsewhere in the kingdom. As Lauderdale felt his influence with Charles waning, he was driven further into the arms of the Scottish bishops. They insisted that coercion continue. Attendance at field conventicles was still a capital offence in Scotland, and the Scottish council also now sought to suppress house conventicles by transporting convicted conventiclers to the English colonies.

But neither these deterrents nor the bonds recently imposed on landowners and tenants against attending illegal worship weakened support for dissident clergy. Instead, the principal effect of continued repression was to intensify the militancy of those who saw the Covenants as binding and the bishops as apostates. Seven thousand were said to have gathered for a three-day field conventicle in Ayrshire in August 1678. As many as 14,000, guarded by armed gentry, were thought to have met near Dumfries in November. Small garrisons in strategic towns proved incapable of dealing with those travelling to or attending these enormous meetings; and when soldiers attempted to intervene, they were often repulsed. Troops who followed dissenters to a meeting in Lanarkshire in March 1679, for instance, were driven off by hundreds of armed conventiclers and horsemen. 'Farts in the king's teeth, and the council's', was reportedly their cry, 'for we appear here for the king of heaven.'

Disorder in the Lowlands was, in fact, becoming endemic by the spring of 1679. The lord mayor of Edinburgh was met with bullets and swords when he attempted to suppress meetings. Conformist clergy and sheriffs' officers were beaten and attacked in some shires. Pamphlets criticized Lauderdale and the bishops and called upon the godly to return to their allegiance to the Covenants. Militant nonconformist clergy stirred up the faithful wherever they went, often explicitly sanctioning resistance to authority for the sake of true worship. Dissidents were procuring weapons from the Netherlands and from London. Captured soldiers were sometimes dragged to sermons as punishment. Moreover, the disorder in Scotland threatened to spill out into Charles's other kingdoms. Ulster Presbyterians copied the worship practices of their Scottish brethren.

Large field conventicles across the North Channel, with thousands in attendance, disturbed the civil and ecclesiastical governors of Ireland. One Ulster parochial cleric reported that Presbyterians there expected 'a sudden demolishing of the present established church', and he feared that 'none of the established clergy shall be able to travel five miles … without peril to his life.' English authorities worried that dissenters in the northern counties would also be infected by the contagion of field conventicles.

Militants in Fife, north of Edinburgh, where troops had been especially active against conventiclers, were considering actions even more extreme. A group of several young men, two of them lairds, resolved to act in defence of their religion by ambushing the persecuting sheriff-depute (or deputy) of their shire. Missing their quarry on 3 May, when they had planned their attack, they discovered that James Sharp, Archbishop of St. Andrews, was travelling through the neighbourhood. Convinced 'that God now had delivered their greatest enemy into their hand', they gave chase. When their initial shots failed to kill the archbishop, Sharp's attackers dragged him from the coach and hacked him to death with their swords as 'an avowed opposer of the gospel and kingdom of Christ, and a murderer of his saints'. In England, a few days later, it was Lauderdale's turn to be savaged. The Commons again demanded his removal, attacking him as an abettor of arbitrary government who tolerated Catholics but threw 'whole armies' against Protestant dissenters.[19]

As the Scottish council issued a hue and cry after Sharp's murderers, they fled to the Southwest, where they consulted with Sir Robert Hamilton, a leading Covenanter, and with other disaffected lairds of Lanarkshire and Ayrshire. This group resolved to rise in defence of the Covenants and in opposition to the Episcopal usurpation over the church. They announced their intention with a proclamation on 29 May, Charles's birthday and the annual day for commemorating the Restoration. Describing themselves as 'faithful witnesses' to the 'interest of Christ', they demanded the repeal of all the laws adopted since 1660 that had produced a national apostasy from Reformed principles. In response, thousands of Covenanters assembled near Glasgow and sought unsuccessfully to take the city. When rebel numbers continued to grow, however, the Scottish council withdrew its forces, leaving the town to them.

The occupation of Glasgow pointed to the seriousness of the rebellion. Forty years earlier a Scottish rebellion had led to a political crisis in England. In 1679, the English parliament and Charles II were already in crisis. Fortunately for Charles, the Scottish nobles were overwhelmingly hostile to the Covenanters' cause; and the rebels lost the initiative when they split into contrary factions, compromising their ability to act together. Hamilton led a group of extremists who denounced those Presbyterian clergy who had returned to official ministry under the indulgences, and who also rejected Charles himself, as a turncoat to the Covenants. A larger group of moderates was more conciliatory towards the indulged clergy and the king. Their declaration of intent, published and posted in the towns, acknowledged reluctance to take actions 'which might import opposition to lawful authority'. They nevertheless cited the 'overturning ... of reformation' by the 'wit and malice of prelates' as a sufficient justification for 'this last [armed] remedy'. Fearing that inaction would leave the 'Protestant cause of Britain and Ireland' to decline further, they called upon Charles to summon 'a free and unlimited parliament, and ... a free general assembly' to restore 'the true Protestant religion, and Presbyterian government' of the Scottish church and the 'liberties of the kingdom'.

Only the approach of significant government forces prompted the more extreme rebels to fight together with the moderates. The Duke of Monmouth, Charles's illegitimate son, was the commander of these forces. Monmouth had become captain-general of the English army in 1678, and he had been sent north to deal with the Scottish rebellion. The Covenanters' quarrelling had given them little time to prepare for battle or to consider strategy. Their numbers were about 6000 and declining, as the bickering continued, while Monmouth had assembled an army of some 10,000. The rebels entertained hopes of the king's son, for he was thought to be sympathetic to the accommodation of dissent in England. As the two forces converged near the town of Hamilton, the rebels sought a conference to present their grievances. Monmouth demanded, however, that they first disarm as a sign of their goodwill, which the Covenanters refused to do. The two forces battled at Bothwell Bridge, over the River Clyde, on 22 June. Lacking discipline, artillery, and experienced commanders, the rebels were no match for Monmouth and his army. Several hundred were killed, over a thousand were captured, and the rest fled.[20]

Reprisals were limited, however. Monmouth promoted religious and political reconciliation in Scotland, returning to the policy that Lauderdale had rejected earlier in the decade, and one that many in England desired as well. For his part, Charles was happy to pursue a conciliatory course in Scotland. That suited his own instincts, as he had repeatedly demonstrated in each of his kingdoms. A general amnesty covered all but about 65 ringleaders of the rebellion. Most of those captured were released after taking out bonds for their good behaviour. A few hundred prisoners were to be transported to Barbados, as an example to the remainder; but they were largely lost at sea. Thirty-five rebel property owners were dispossessed. Only a handful of rebels, including two preachers, were actually executed in the wake of the rebellion.

Most importantly, another Scottish indulgence was issued within a week of Bothwell Bridge. Although field conventicles remained illegal, house conventicles were permitted throughout the Lowlands, except in and about Edinburgh, Glasgow, and a few other towns. Fines for ecclesiastical offences were generally remitted. Nonconformist clergy who offered security were allowed to preach; and several joined the ranks of the indulged, some of them taking up work in areas where few indulged clergy had previously served. All of this flew in the face of Lauderdale's recent actions and seemed to shift Scotland in the direction desired by the Duke of Hamilton and his associates. Yet Lauderdale retained his offices, at least for the time being. More ominously, Sharp's successor as archbishop was the chief advocate of coercion among the Scottish bishops.[21]

Whether Monmouth's reconciling policies would be given the time needed to pacify Scotland remained unclear, then. On the surface, Charles had seemingly rejected the intolerant and high-handed manner of government that had become characteristic of the Scottish Restoration. The northern kingdom was, in this way, experiencing an unsettlement of the accustomed order, even after the failure of the 1679 rebellion, as accommodation replaced coercion. Indeed, the Episcopalian policy of coercing dissenting Protestants seemed to be collapsing in all three kingdoms. Monmouth's new indulgence made legal in Scotland the de facto toleration that also now prevailed in England, where enforcement of the penal laws against dissenters had largely collapsed after the 1679 parliamentary election. In Ireland, Ormond hesitated further to strain relations among Protestants, in the midst of a crisis about Catholicism, by taking harsh measures against dissenters, despite the urgings of Episcopalians. As a preventative measure, he quartered most of the Irish army in Ulster at the time of the Scots rebellion. He nevertheless believed that toleration kept the peace, and Ulster Presbyterians largely rejected the rebellious example of the Scots Covenanters.[22] Episcopal authorities in all three kingdoms were upset about this suspension of state action on behalf of the established churches.

Monmouth's actions in Scotland also gave him a new role in the crisis in England. The bill to exclude James from the succession considered in the 1679 House of Commons had assumed that the crown would pass next to Mary, James's eldest daughter. But Monmouth, now 30 years old and the same age as Charles in 1660, had demonstrated both military and political ability in Scotland. A few years earlier he had been considered for the lord lieutenancy of Ireland, and he played a role in advising Charles's reconstruction of the English Privy Council. York viewed him as a threat and had become hostile to him. Hailed as a potential Protestant successor by London crowds in 1678, Monmouth was, on his return from Scotland, seen as such by some exclusionist leaders; and he was ready to take on the role. Moreover, Charles had not been without advice, over the years, to establish the legitimacy of a son he loved.[23] In 1679, such action would have further compounded his problems, however, providing a Protestant successor at the expense of scruples he shared with Anglicans about the hereditary succession. Monmouth's rising political star was, thus, another element in the unravelling of the Restoration order.

Confrontation in the Public Domain, 1679–80

Charles surprised the politicians and the public in early July 1679 by dissolving parliament, He called for a new one to meet in the autumn. After 18 years of the Cavalier Parliament, the kingdom had seen another parliament that lasted less then 18 weeks. For the second time in the same year, Charles tried to rid himself of the parliamentary opposition by ridding himself of a parliament; and electors were called upon to choose new MPs. The dissolution was a defeat for Shaftesbury, who had sought to impose exclusion upon Charles, and who was establishing connections to Monmouth as a potential successor. It signalled the Privy Council dominance of Essex and of two of Shaftesbury's nephews by marriage, George Savile, Earl of Halifax and Robert Spencer, Earl of Sunderland. All three had favoured limitations upon a Catholic successor rather than exclusion, and all three were developing ties to the Prince and Princess of Orange as the natural successors of James.

The dissolution was disturbing to many who construed it as yet another interruption in the parliamentary investigation of the Popish Plot. Those who thought Danby had sought to cover it up now had reason to believe that efforts to block the truth continued without him. The public executions of five Jesuits and other Catholics caught up in the Plot accusations served to stimulate the concern about popish conspiracy. Concern turned to panic in late August, when Charles suddenly fell gravely ill at Windsor; and the prospect of an imminent and disputed succession arose. As the legal heir, James rushed back to England from Brussels on the advice of Halifax, Sunderland, and Essex. For his part, Monmouth hovered about his father at Windsor and may have been in touch with city supporters engaged in secret meetings. Sunderland feared an exclusionist coup. When Charles recovered in early September, he sent the two rival successors out of the country again. James extracted a significant political price for his return to exile, however. At his insistence, Monmouth was stripped of all military offices in England and Scotland, before leaving for the Netherlands, as punishment for consorting with James's political enemies. James also returned to Brussels with a promise that he might soon exchange his Flemish exile for Scottish power. In October 1679, he moved to Edinburgh, taking Lauderdale's place as the king's principal representative in the northern kingdom and thereby also scotching the arguments of his English critics. When Shaftesbury orchestrated opposition on the council to James's political resuscitation, Charles dismissed him as lord president.[24]

Parliamentary elections occurred against the backdrop of these events. Electors did not know that the MPs they chose would not, in fact, sit for another year: Charles repeatedly put off the meeting of the new parliament, eventually until October 1680. The electoral results were discouraging to him and to his new ministerial advisors and dashed their hopes for a more moderate House of Commons. The king's decision to delay parliament merely intensified the crisis, however: many believed the postponement was another sign of a long-term conspiracy against Protestantism and parliamentary government. Indeed, the long interval between parliaments forced the nation's politics and the nation's politicians out of doors. The election that began in August 1679 provided the first in a variety of extra-parliamentary political venues in which subjects throughout the realm debated the issues before them and sought to act upon them. As the debates continued, and as all waited for a parliamentary resolution, the kingdom's politics became increasingly polarized. By the time parliament finally met, the building blocks of party politics had begun to come together.

Potential MPs and electors apparently returned to the hustings with relish after the 1679 parliament. The election featured 103 contested seats (in 16 counties and 61 boroughs), somewhat fewer than in the winter, but still more than in 1661 or in the next political crisis, that of 1688–9. Neither were all of these contests in the same constituencies as earlier in the year. Electors were in a determined mood in some places and unwilling to accept direction from their social superiors, as some landed candidates learned to their surprise. When two magnates, one a candidate, arrived in Coventry for that borough's election, for instance, the townspeople 'refused them entrance', fearing they had come to 'put some restraint upon their free choice'. In Essex, 8000 people, almost three times the number of eligible voters, showed up for a county election in which court and Country candidates arrived at the head of rival processions of supporters. The two hundred Anglican clergy in the loyalist procession provoked cries against 'Baal's priests, damned rogues, … [and] the black regiment of hell'. Voting went on for three days amidst the harvest, as freeholders entrusted their crops to providence rather than trust the outcome of the poll to anybody but themselves. Something extraordinary was clearly happening in Essex. In the end, the opposition candidates carried the election there. Overall, throughout the kingdom, three MPs hostile to James were chosen for every two loyalists. The evidence generally suggests that the opposition did better in the larger, less easily managed borough constituencies and in the counties, with the largest electorates of all, where court opponents took two-thirds of the seats.[25]

Although little is known about the extent of electoral participation across the kingdom, the experience of two parliamentary elections within six months could only have raised public expectations. So did the 'papers of all sorts' now flooding from the unrestrained

London presses and spreading from the streets and shops of the capital into those of the major provincial towns. Exclusion was not the dominant issue in the prints: it had not yet emerged, even in the minds of its supporters, as the sine qua non of the crisis. Instead, opposition publications focused on the broader issues that had provoked the Restoration Crisis in the first place, especially the fears of popery and arbitrary government. Opposition pamphlets – and electors who read them – railed against courtiers as the dupes of arbitrary rule, just as they had in the first 1679 election. Anti-Catholicism was pervasive; and the fear of the bishops, whose persecution of other Protestants was seen as a popish tactic, was particularly pronounced. The 'Episcopal party' was condemned in the most notable opposition pamphlet of 1679 as 'exclaim[ing] against our parliament's proceedings' and making 'even the very scriptures pimp for the court'. Only Protestant accommodation and liberty of conscience could preserve the nation from its enemies, according to opposition authors. Loyalist writers sought, in response, to discredit their opponents as advocates of the 'purest Reformed way' that had shipwrecked church and state once before. The contest was, in fact, largely between loyalist Anglicans, on the one side, and Protestants of Reformed background, some within and some without the church, on the other.[26]

Popular expectations aroused by the parliamentary election were dashed in October, however, when Charles issued the first of his prorogations and suggested that a session might begin only in late January 1680. The king largely followed his own counsel in making this decision, which cost him the ministerial services of Halifax and Essex. The first anniversary of the Popish Plot revelations passed, therefore, without any kind of parliamentary resolution. Aroused citizens in London nevertheless soon found a spectacular occasion upon which to vent their anti-Catholicism, affirm their support for a parliamentary sitting, and express their hostility to a Catholic successor. The massive London pope-burning procession of 17 November 1679 was an indication of how political gatherings and processions were starting to give ordinary people entrée into the troubled politics of the crisis.

Different reports suggest that between 100,000 and 200,000 people lined the streets and balconies of the London procession's route through major thoroughfares to the legal precincts beyond Temple Bar. Headed by images of Sir Edmund Berry Godfrey and a Catholic assassin, the parade included apprentices costumed as '6 Jesuits, 4 bishops, 4 archbishops, 2 patriarchs of Jerusalem and Constantinople, [and] several cardinals, besides Franciscans, [and] black and grey friars'. They were followed by an imposing representation of the pope, carried on his throne. Spectators shouted and sang anti-Catholic slogans and doggerel as the procession passed and climaxed in a great Protestant bonfire topped by the papal effigy. Charles himself sneaked into a goldsmith's shop to observe the show, and he could not have missed its political message. The affair enabled participants and spectators alike to act out the Protestant reading of the nation's history, and a statue of Elizabeth I, 'decked up with a Magna Charta', presided over the bonfire from above Temple Bar. The pope rather than James was the symbolic target, but the procession dramatized all that might be feared from a Catholic king. The considerable expense of the event was borne by the Green Ribbon Club, the membership of which was full of anti-Catholic supporters of exclusion. Although James's London enemies had contrived the pope burning, his critics could nevertheless point to it as a sign of popular hostility to his succession.[27]

Within a week of the London pope burning, Monmouth had returned to London without his father's permission. He was probably encouraged to return by Shaftesbury, who had been meeting with other peers to prepare for a session. News of his arrival was celebrated with spontaneous and unrestrained enthusiasm in London, where the church bells rang 'all the morning incessantly' and bonfires rivalled those set for Charles in 1660. Indeed, plebeian crowds forced people of quality out of their coaches to acclaim the Protestant duke. A furious king deprived Monmouth of most of his remaining offices and ordered him back into exile. But the son remained in town, defying his father as a visible Protestant successor, again with Shaftesbury's encouragement.

The continuing impact of the election, the manifest hostility of so many Londoners to James, and the return of Monmouth all persuaded Charles not to meet parliament under circumstances that could so obviously be exploited against his brother. He therefore put off the session again, this time announcing that a meeting would probably not occur until November 1680. He also kept his options open by moving towards that date through a series of short prorogations. In response, Shaftesbury abandoned all thought of returning to government and sought to force a parliamentary session on Charles by directing public opinion against the king's decision. Working with the leaders of the London dissenters and with civic activists like Sir Thomas Player, he launched petitions in the city for an immediate parliament, with the hopes that important constituencies throughout the country would follow suit. The petitions did not alter Charles's course, but they gave tens of thousands of people an additional opportunity to participate in the public sphere. The petitions also revealed that, despite their mutual fears of popery, Anglican loyalists and opposition adherents were not only divided about the succession but also becoming more entrenched in their division.

With some 16,000 signatures on its surviving rolls, the London petition, which was circulated in December 1679 and January 1680, was the largest and most provocative. The text did not mention exclusion because its authors hoped to attract signatures from all Protestant citizens, loyalists as well as government critics. It demanded that parliament sit on the late January date to which it had originally been prorogued in order to deal with the Plot, to secure Protestantism, and to attend to all the nation's grievances. This language did, under the circumstances, reflect popular fears about James and the succession. Tables were set up at the Royal Exchange for the gathering of signatures, and 'agitators' and 'choice party men' also hawked the petition throughout the neighbourhoods. They carried out their work despite a royal proclamation against tumultuous petitioning. The names on the petition rolls suggest that dissenters were eager to sign and that most Anglican conformists kept aloof from this effort to orchestrate public opinion against the king's express will. Less is known about the petitions from elsewhere in the country, but they did circulate in at least 17 counties and some boroughs. Those from Essex, Hertfordshire, and Wiltshire were reputed to have found eight, ten, and thirty thousand hands. Sometimes exclusionist leaders were involved in launching the petitions. Country MP Sir Samuel Barnardiston promoted the Suffolk petition, for instance; and a London committee may have coordinated efforts in different counties. Local initiative was equally important, however.

As in London, petitions in other localities enlarged the sphere of political activities and enabled many people beyond the parliamentary electorate to participate in the public discourse of the crisis. The country and borough petitions also proved as divisive as that of London. In fact, the petitions, which were reminiscent of similar mass subscriptions prior to the civil war, provoked the beginnings of a political backlash that would soon give Charles a party of loyal supporters in parliament and throughout the country. Some London petition rolls were seized and burned by loyalists, for instance. In Lancashire, most gentry balked at signing the county petition, despite its being presented to the county sessions by local notables. Such landed gentlemen preferred to see the nation's politics carried out within parliament rather than extended outside of parliament through popular petitioning. The puritan pedigrees of many families active in the petitioning aroused Anglican fears in some places. Gilbert Burnet believed that the petitioning 'alienated many sober and well-meaning men' who 'began to think' that advocacy of parliament and Protestantism in the public sphere was really 'under a pretence to alter the government, or to help the Duke of Monmouth into the throne'. Charles himself condemned the petitions as an attempt to 'animate people to mutiny and rebellion'. By the spring of 1680, courtiers and leading loyalists were cooperating in promoting local addresses to the crown that abhorred the winter's petitions as infringing upon the king's prerogative of summoning parliament when he thought best. The leading 'abhorrers' of petitioning generally preserved notions of hierarchy and degree by originating their addresses from official bodies like the county sessions or borough corporations. Indeed, for many loyalists, fears about a republican or sectarian revival were beginning to take the place of fears about popery.[28]

At the height of the petitioning campaign, several of the Country leaders on the reconstituted Privy Council of 1679 had resigned to express their unhappiness with Charles's unwillingness to meet parliament. This development further polarized the politics of the crisis. The government itself was now largely in the hands of a talented trio of younger political leaders: the ambitious Sunderland, the strongly Anglican Laurence Hyde (son of Clarendon and brother-in-law of York), and the capable Cornishman, Sidney Godolphin. Known as the 'Chits', because of their relative youth and inexperience, this ministerial triumvirate had revived the policies of Danby: hostility to France, friendship with William of Orange and the Dutch, and support for the Anglican establishment against nonconformity. With the assistance of this new ministerial team and their programme, which included a treaty with Spain for the defence of Flanders, Charles weathered the storm of petitions; and he was beginning to benefit from the arousal of loyalist concern.

The disappointing denouement for their petitioning effort left Shaftesbury and his associates searching for other means to maintain public support for a parliamentary sitting and for their strategy of exclusion. Just as fears of the Popish Plot appeared to be diminishing, Shaftesbury made a dramatic appearance before the Privy Council to reveal that new witnesses had come forward in Ireland who could demonstrate the existence of a separate plot in that kingdom. The French had supposedly pledged to assist a Catholic revolt there, to be accompanied by the burning of Dublin and a massacre of Protestants. Although most councillors thought the discovery of this new plot was simply too convenient, it quickly captured public attention, as Shaftesbury intended, and renewed public demands for government investigation of Catholic plotting.

Monmouth also remained much in the public eye as Shaftesbury and other opposition politicians stroked opinion in new ways, hoping to arouse the people through the sight of a Protestant successor. The employment of public feasts and processions for political purposes enlarged another continuing dimension of the crisis, as the opposition and the crown competed out of doors in promoting their rival kings-in-the-wings. When Monmouth visited Chichester in February 1680, for instance, he entered that cathedral town amidst a popular entourage of supporters. The bishop was unable to prevent his own staff from ringing the cathedral bells in honour of the 'Protestant duke'. The following month, Charles invited himself and James, who had returned from Scotland, to dinner with the Lord Mayor of London, hoping that a public viewing of the preferred successor would demonstrate that opinion had turned in James's favour. Bonfires and acclamations in the streets suggested that James had actually recovered much popular support. So did an attempt by loyalist Westminster apprentices to burn effigies of the Rump and of Cromwell in imitation of the November pope burning.[29]

Opinion about the succession had, in fact, become bitterly divided. New pamphlets promoting Monmouth's cause coincided with another royal illness in May. Hundreds of MPs then assembled for a previously announced prorogation, and some thought the opposition might initiate a session without royal approval. Sixty exclusionist MPs were on hand in London on 29 May 1680, the anniversary of the king's birth and succession, which they celebrated with a great dinner honouring Monmouth. In late June, scores of MPs were said to have processed, after Shaftesbury, into one of the central law courts, in support of an indictment of York as a common popish recusant. Many of these members were still around for another London fête of Monmouth that coincided with the next prorogation of parliament a few days later. In response, Charles and 'most of the court' dined in the city in July to emphasize the king's support for candidates loyal to James in London's choice of new sheriffs. Monmouth then took his show on the road, making an extensive progress through the West Country in July and August. Travelling through Wiltshire, Somerset, and Devon, he was treated by sympathetic gentlemen; and he even touched for the king's evil to demonstrate his royal authenticity. Thousands greeted him at Exeter. Loyalist writers thought he was shunned by many of the quality, but they had also missed the point. This showcasing was not for the benefit of the elite but rather for that of the people 'of all sorts, all sexes, all ages and degrees' that flocked to see him. In September, York returned to London for a feast of the loyalist-dominated artillery company, while Monmouth visited Oxford. There, the university officially ignored the king's son; but he was acclaimed by the bargemen with cries of 'No York, no Bishops, no University!'[30]

Even people who could not participate in or view such divisive political events could experience them vicariously through the flood of print that attended them. The summer parliamentary election of 1679 had seen the launching of two biweekly newspapers. The *Domestick Intelligence* was published by a Baptist printer with ties to John Bunyan and to Shaftesbury, and the publisher of the *True Domestick Intelligence* was both pro-court and a probable Catholic sympathizer. Many additional news ventures followed, despite government efforts in May 1680 to suppress them. As the initial rival newspaper titles suggest, the printing of political news during the Restoration Crisis was marked by competition among press entrepreneurs. They also deliberately sought to cater to the opinions of quite different audiences. As its satirical title suggests, for instance, *The Weekly Pacquet of Advice from Rome*, published by the dissenting publicist Henry Care, provided opposition readers with anti-Catholic fodder for five years, beginning in 1678. A variety of other genres of political writing and communication thrived during the crisis as well. Pamphlets and printed sermons were widely distributed through post or by private hands. Printed poems and ballads celebrated and condemned figures in both camps – Danby and Lauderdale, on one side, for instance, and Monmouth and Shaftesbury, on the other. Political poems, which could be purchased even by those of meagre means, personalized the issues and promoted divisive discourse in the taverns and coffeehouses. Among the most successful of the opposition poets was Stephen College, a carpenter who constructed effigies for pope burnings. Satirical cartoons and illustrated playing cards carried opposition and loyalist messages to different audiences as well. By October 1679, one observer suggested the press 'has already afforded such flames as if all the beacons of England were set on fire'. The impact of print extended beyond the ranks of readers, moreover, for those who could not read could talk with those who did.[31]

Loyalists were at first taken aback by the spread of sharp political discourse throughout all social ranks and throughout all parts of the kingdom. They accused the opposition of planting 'doubtful intelligence at each coffeehouse' in London; and they complained that cheap print had cheapened political talk as well. Access to the debates of their social superiors has 'of late made our citizens statesmen too', complained one defender of hierarchy in state and society, for 'every little ale-draper now can tell what the Privy Council intend to do a month hence.' When the dean of St. Paul's Cathedral printed a highly political sermon in May 1680, it was not only debated in print by leading dissenting clergy but also debated throughout the capital's clubs and dens of political talk. The dean complained that his words had become the 'sport and entertainment of the coffeehouses', as coteries of critics and loyalists parsed his meaning over their cups.

But loyalists also found strong voices in the prints as the petitioning campaign of winter 1679–80 peaked. Sir Roger L'Estrange, the press surveyor, no longer controlled the press under the terms of the 1662 Licensing Act; but he took the lead in crafting a campaign of printed words and images to match those of the opposition. As he was to say, ''Tis the press that has made them mad, and the press must set them right again … There is no way … but by printing, to convey the remedy to the disease.' The message conveyed by L'Estrange, John Dryden, and other loyalist authors built upon the whole body of Anglican writing since the Restoration and upon the propaganda that Danby had commissioned against the Country. The tenets of Anglican political philosophy – the sovereignty of the monarch, the king's exalted relationship to God, the subordination of parliament to the crown, the necessity of obedience to political and social superiors, the sinfulness of resistance to duly constituted authority – were each of them propagated anew. Not surprisingly, the crisis brought about the publication of Sir Robert Filmer's pivotal royalist text, *Patriarcha* (1680), which had circulated in manuscript for 50 years.[32]

This renewed loyalist emphasis upon political and social authority was not only a response to how strongly opposition writers had championed parliament. It was also a response to how deeply the people had again become involved in politics. Although Anglican writing was inherently hostile to the blurring of social distinctions in politics, L'Estrange, in particular, took the argument to the people themselves. His *Cit and Bumpkin* (1680), for instance, which condemned petitioning as an opposition plot to undermine established institutions, was written for a popular audience, in dialogue form and in colloquial language. L'Estrange was the most adept of several loyalist writers who suggested that the opposition of 1679–80, like the opposition of 1640, were the unwitting tools of the Jesuits and the pope in their attacks upon the established institutions of the Anglican church-state. He was the mind behind the satirical engraving, *The Committee; or, Popery in Masquerade* (1680), a six-penny sheet rich in historical iconography, that reflected the Country's conspiratorial projections back onto Shaftesbury and his followers. The print linked the language of Charles's critics in 1679–80 to the language of the crown's antagonists in the civil war, and it suggested the existence of a long-term dissenting conspiracy against church and state under the pretence of rooting out popery. The advocates of 'a thorough Reformation' had set 'the pulpits, and the presses ... ring[ing] of popery, grievances ... plots of all sorts, invasions, [and] massacres', but their real intention was 'to change the government' and the church. Moreover, Rome would derive the greatest benefit of all: the pope secretly drove the furore over the Popish Plot for Catholic advantage, hoping to reconvert the nation after weakening its Protestant institutions, as in the 1640s. The print successfully countered Shaftesbury's and

Marvell's charges about a long-term popish conspiracy driven by the bishops, and it utilized anti-Catholicism on behalf of loyalism. It marked a turning point in the literature of the crisis, as the loyalist message achieved a visual representation that was superior to anything so far devised by the opposition.[33]

By the summer of 1680 the political talk, print, and behaviour of the crisis had thoroughly aroused a greater proportion of the population than at any time since the civil war. As L'Estrange suggested at the time, 'the whole kingdom ... is again split into two parties; the one consisting of mutineers and schismatics, the other of loyal servants and subjects of the crown.' Adherents and detractors referred to opposition and loyalist followings with a variety of names. Gradually, however, during the parliamentary sessions of 1680–1 that followed, the names Whig and Tory established themselves over others. Each name was originally a term of abuse, and each was originally derived from the civil war experiences of one of Charles's other kingdoms. As Whigs, the English opposition acquired a name that originally referred to Presbyterian Covenanters in southwest Scotland. As Tories, English loyalists acquired a name that originally referred to the Irish Catholic rebels who terrorized Protestant settlers in the 1640s.

The establishment of these names was unplanned, just as the parties themselves owed as much to the uncoordinated expression of differences at every social level, throughout the realm, as to organization from the centre. Yet the connections between rival politicians at Westminster and London and rival partisans in the localities had firmed up considerably over 1679–80, during the long wait for a parliament. Moreover, some degree of organization had also been developed for the petitions, addresses, feasts, processions, and dissemination of political writings. To argue that the parties of the crisis had taken on the trappings of the mature British party organizations of the Victorian era would be absurd. On the other hand, some recent efforts to 'exclude' parties from analysis of the crisis fly in the face of too much evidence.[34] Moreover, unlike in the early 1640s, when Charles I had initially scrambled for active support against a broad parliamentary and puritan opposition, the Restoration Crisis featured two parties rather than one by 1680. Already highly visible in the public sphere, these two parties would now drive the crisis in parliament as well.

Confrontation in Parliament, 1680–1

Two parliaments met in England between October 1680 and March 1681, and both met under political circumstances that were radically different from those surrounding either of the parliaments of 1679. Many subjects were as aroused by the issues facing the politicians as the politicians themselves. As both Whig opposition leaders and Charles's ministers recognized, the press and public opinion had become independent factors in the crisis. Moreover, political happenings within parliament were far more transparent than had ever been the case before. Exclusion was the primary issue debated within and without parliament in 1680–1; but exclusion was part of a broader assortment of critical issues, and neither Shaftesbury nor Charles was entirely consistent about exclusion. Shaftesbury again pushed for a royal divorce and remarriage at one point, for instance, while Charles thought about abandoning York for Monmouth on more than one occasion. Over the two sessions, Shaftesbury and the Whigs would prevail within the House of Commons; but after March 1681, Charles and the Tories would prevail out of doors.

Despite the loyalist tide of 1680, Charles and his ministers knew, as they prepared for the autumn parliamentary session, that a majority of MPs were hostile to James. This realization, and the desire for a successful session, drove Sunderland into negotiations with Shaftesbury and Russell. The minister agreed to exclusion, and possibly to offices for the opposition leaders, in return for supply. Sunderland's shifting position split the Chits, for Godolphin followed Sunderland, while Hyde remained faithful to his brother-in-law, James. Charles's principal mistress, Louise de Kéroualle, Duchess of Portsmouth, sided with Sunderland in abandoning York, hoping thereby, as a French Catholic, to gain political protection. For his part, Charles drifted with events, agreeing to send James back to Edinburgh rather than face parliament with him, but otherwise keeping his own counsel. He opened the session on 21 October, recommending the Spanish alliance and requesting money, especially for the defence of Tangiers, the English outpost in North Africa. He indicated again his willingness to accept new measures to protect Protestantism that were consistent with 'preserving the succession of the crown in its due and legal course of descent'. The last proposal fell on deaf ears, as far as the opposition was concerned, since Charles offered no suggestions about the succession issue.[35]

Shaftesbury kept parliamentary attention focused on the English and Irish Plots in order to provide a rationale for the exclusion of James. The movement for exclusion in the House of Commons was not dependent upon Shaftesbury; however; and it was assisted by the frequent absences of scores of members who opposed it. Exclusion gained additional support from the Corporation of London, where civic Whigs had recently captured the mayoralty, the shrievalty, and the common council. Monmouth was treated again at the annual London lord mayor's feast at the end of October, a few days before Lord Russell re-ignited the exclusionist storm in the Commons. 'If the Catholics have such an influence upon the government under a Protestant prince, what will they have under a Popish?' inquired one of many MPs who moved a bill to exclude James. Its supporters made extensive references to the nation's historic struggle against Catholic foes and to the current menace from France. Some loyalists worried that an exclusion bill would merely lay the groundwork for civil war; but London MP Sir Thomas Player swept aside such objections: 'Let it be so, if there be no other way to prevent popery.'

When Charles sought to warn the Commons off their course, some speakers exploded about the prorogations that had impeded their work and the ministers who had advised them. As the third reading of the bill approached on 11 November, a mere nine days after its introduction, the city of London prepared to petition in support of it. When Tory speakers objected to the measure as 'reducing' the English crown into 'an elective monarchy', one outspoken MP suggested, 'if those things be true' that had prompted the bill, 'the duke has forfeited his life.' The Lords made short shrift of the Commons' bill when it was presented to them. With Charles in attendance, and with Halifax (who had resumed his ministerial role) taking the lead in condemning it, the bill was thrown out on 15 November by 63 votes to 30. All the bishops present voted against it. Undeterred, the opposition citizenry of London celebrated 17 November, Elizabeth's accession day, with another great pope burning. Sir Roger L'Estrange, depicted as fiddling amidst the Catholic firestorm, was one of those burnt in effigy.[36]

Exclusion was, however, but the most drastic solution to the problem of a Catholic succession; and the succession was only one of the issues before parliament. Parliamentary consideration of other issues and of other solutions to the succession – and even of exclusion in other guises – continued without interruption. Discussion of a legislative 'ease' for Protestant dissenters began in the House of Commons within a day of the decision to bring in the exclusion bill. In fact, parliament considered a variety of forms of relief for dissenters. Both houses adopted a bill to repeal an Elizabethan statute against sectarians that was notable for its draconian penalties. The Commons gave time and attention to measures to provide for the comprehension of moderate Protestant nonconformists and for toleration of those who preferred to remain outside the church. Although the details of each bill proved troublesome, one speaker suggested that 'there are not two in the house against' the idea of comprehension. Even some Anglican clerical leaders were persuaded that the time for comprehension had come. Other Whig-supported initiatives that drew on previous Country complaints included measures to ensure frequent parliaments, to secure judges against arbitrary dismissal by the crown, to prohibit 'standing forces', to repeal the Corporation Act, and to prevent the bribery of electors. The Commons also affirmed the right of subjects 'to petition the king for the calling and sitting of parliaments, and redressing of grievances'. Indeed, MPs censured officials, especially judges, who had sought to impede petitions, as thereby 'subverting the ancient legal constitution of this kingdom'.[37]

By the time the exclusion bill failed in the House of Lords, the court was in disarray. The Earl of Halifax had regained his leading voice in Charles's counsels without dislodging ministers of contrary views, including Sunderland, the secretary of state turned exclusionist. The defeat of their bill also left the opposition somewhat divided between moderates and hard-liners. Many of those who had voted for exclusion remained committed to it, although legally, exclusion could not be reintroduced in this parliament in the same form as in the defeated bill. Yet Charles could still be forced to accept something like it if he were deprived of any further supply, or so many hard-line Whig MPs believed. Convinced that the 'kingdom is sinking', they persuaded the house to address the crown to the effect that no supply would be provided until the kingdom had been secured against popery. In contrast, Halifax promoted limitations upon a popish successor in the House of Lords. The peers took the limitations proposal seriously. In fact, they eventually considered the most stringent restrictions yet proposed upon James's authority, should he become king. The Commons ignored this alternative, however, and retaliated against Halifax for his efforts against exclusion by addressing Charles for the earl's removal from office. Both houses also considered proposals to create national associations, modelled after the Elizabethan association of 1585, in which the political elite would swear to defend Protestantism and the king's person, by arms if necessary, against any who would seek to destroy them.

In early December, one of the five Catholic peers in the Tower, Lord Stafford, was tried before the House of Lords and sentenced to death for his alleged part in the Popish Plot. In its reaffirmation of the reality and continuing threat of the Plot, Stafford's trial both restored the initiative to the Whigs and renewed their unity. So Charles discovered when he appeared before both houses on 15 December, to reiterate his need for money and his willingness to consider reasonable measures to secure the kingdom other than exclusion. Monmouth's visibility as a Protestant successor had just been enhanced by another city treat, however; and in the House of Lords, Shaftesbury told Charles to his face that he could no longer be trusted. In the Commons, MPs voted for an association to preserve Protestantism and the king 'and for the preventing of any popish successor', especially the Duke of York. 'We can be never safe in our religion from a person that makes himself, by his religion, a public enemy to the nation,' suggested Lord Russell, in renewing the attack upon James.

On 10 January, Charles prorogued parliament; but learning what was afoot, exclusionist stalwarts in a thinly attended House of Commons adopted a series of truculent resolutions. They demanded that Monmouth be reinstated in all his offices. They condemned the prorogations of 1679–80. They declared the prosecution of Protestant dissenters on the penal statutes a grievance to the nation. They even considered defying the crown and continuing the session in the city of London, which they also thanked for its support. The session had failed to produce a single significant measure: Charles even undermined the repeal of the Elizabethan statute against sectaries, which had actually been adopted by both houses, by circumventing its presentation to him. Largely acting on his own instincts, Charles further dismayed exclusionists by dissolving parliament and by calling for another to sit – not at Westminster, but rather at Oxford, the civil war royalist capital – on 21 March 1681. Sunderland was dismissed from office as punishment for his support of exclusion. So was Essex, who had similarly backed exclusion and the association and opposed the dissolution.[38]

The parliamentary election that followed saw little change in the composition of the House of Commons. Noticeably fewer constituencies saw contests than in the elections of 1679. The opposition retained its majority in the Commons, with about 60 per cent of the seats, again doing best in the counties and in the larger, open boroughs. Yet some seats were vigorously contested, and both the press and electoral behaviour saw a hardening of the ideological divide between Whigs and Tories. No systematic orchestration of electoral efforts occurred on either side. Yet the Anglican clergy were noticeably active on behalf of Tory candidates, while some opposition grandees – including Shaftesbury, Monmouth, and Buckingham – promoted exclusionists in numerous places. Monmouth and Buckingham intervened in Southwark, the London urban borough on the Surrey side of the Thames, for instance. They sought unsuccessfully to secure the election of Slingsby Bethel, one of the London sheriffs and a dissenter with a republican past. As high steward of Oxford, Buckingham was similarly involved in that borough's election, where the sitting Whig MPs prevailed, as 'town' candidates, over Anglican Tories promoted by the university.

Mass assemblages and festive processions, like those that had occurred earlier in the crisis, were noticeable in some elections. Three thousand electors reportedly followed the Westminster Whig candidates to the poll at Westminster Hall, for instance. The Whigs claimed that 8000 disappointed electors stood in St. George's Fields, Southwark, on behalf of Sheriff Bethel, even though the total qualified electorate of the borough was less than half that number. The Oxford election featured a torchlight procession of the Whig MPs and popular chants of 'no universities, no scholars, no clergy, no bishops!' When one Bristol opposition MP returned for the election, 200 supporters rode out to meet him; but the arrival of a second opposition candidate provoked a Tory riot. In Chichester, 400 gentry were said to have greeted Monmouth in February 1681.

The hardening of opinion between the parliaments was noticeable in other guises as well, including the Whigs' promotion of 'instructions' to the newly elected members. The presentation of these written advices to MPs marked a new development in the relationship between electoral opinion and parliamentary behaviour. They implied a greater measure of accountability of MPs to those who chose them. Twenty-three constituencies, including London, Westminster, Chichester, and Essex instructed their representatives; and drafts were circulated elsewhere as well. Opposition instructions encouraged MPs to deal with the succession, with the Plot, and with the need for Protestant accommodation. Printed by the London newspapers, the instructions circulated far beyond the constituencies in which they were presented. They also prompted loyalist counter addresses in some localities that opposed any alterations to the church establishment.

As the time for the parliament approached, the politicians approached Oxford with considerable anxiety. Charles prepped the officers of his guard about how to respond to any disturbances in London during his absence. Fearing that Charles might militarize the crisis, the outspoken London Whig leader Sir Thomas Player attempted unsuccessfully to dislodge James as presiding officer of the city's artillery company. London's Whig MPs departed for Oxford in a grand procession: they were accompanied out of the city by scores of armed common councilmen and preceded by Shaftesbury, Monmouth, and other exclusionist leaders. Not to be outdone, Southwark Tories sent off their MPs to Oxford in similar fashion. Charles's arrival there was the occasion for the 'bonny youths' of the loyalist university to prove their mettle. Showered with hats and huzzas in the High Street, the king was greeted at Christ Church with an outpouring of bells and with evening bonfires, 'wherein were only wanting rumps and cropped ears to make the flame[s] burn merrily'.

Charles had intended, in moving parliament to Oxford, to separate MPs from the volatile public sphere of the capital, where members were so easily influenced by happenings out-of-doors. But Oxford proved as disorderly as London. Neither the town nor the colleges were capable of housing or handling the crush of servants, friends, relations, and hangers-on who accompanied members. Thousands milled about the streets and camped in the fields, where controversialists and booksellers hawked pamphlets, prints, and rumours about new Catholic threats. One of the entrepreneurs of this political street fair was the London carpenter and poet Stephen

College, who circulated satirical prints and ballads attacking both James and Charles, the latter for following the same courses against parliament as his father. In his opening speech, Charles complained that the previous parliament had sought to act contrary to law in promoting exclusion and indicated a willingness to consider a Protestant regency in the event of a Catholic succession. This suggestion, encouraged by Halifax, who thought the Prince and/ or Princess of Orange might rule for James, merely provoked the opposition, however. In the Lords, Shaftesbury argued that Charles should legitimize Monmouth and name him heir. In the Commons, Lord Russell and one of the London MPs took the lead in moving another exclusion bill.[39]

A week after parliament opened, as the Commons prepared to give a new exclusion bill its first reading, Charles shocked MPs and the Oxford throngs with a surprise dissolution. He was convinced that the intransigence of the Whigs had already demonstrated to the nation that parliament, and not the crown, was the principal threat to the Restoration order. Three times a new parliament had been elected to deal with the issues produced by the Popish Plot; and three times the Commons had run headlong towards a bill that implied a parliamentary right to alter the succession. Loyalist writers were already suggesting that the Oxford Parliament was not a free parliament at all. A political faction had hijacked the Commons, according to this argument; and instructed members were no longer independent agents. Charles quickly followed up on his dissolution with a *Declaration to all his loving Subjects* in which he presented himself as the victim of an opposition scheme to alter the established institutions of church and state. Donning the attractive Anglican garb of moderation, he reiterated his willingness to consider all necessary means to preserve the Protestant church and state against the immoderation of exclusion. Despite his disappointment in the last two parliaments, Charles also affirmed a commitment to 'frequent parliaments' as 'the only means to preserve the monarchy'. The *Declaration* easily achieved a national audience, for the Anglican clergy were required to read it from their pulpits.[40]

In fact, Charles had met the last parliament of his reign. He dissolved the Oxford Parliament without calling for another. The opposition had, from the beginning of the crisis, feared for the future of parliaments. Now Charles agreed, in his *Declaration*, that parliament was the issue. For Charles, however, parliament was the issue because the opposition had sought to employ it to attack the essential institutions of the Restoration. The response from Tories to this royal condemnation of parliamentary behaviour was enthusiastic. Loyalists believed that the Whigs and their dissenting allies had threatened hereditary monarchy and a church governed by bishops, the two cornerstones of the Anglican establishment. Whig critiques of Charles's behaviour at Oxford and of the *Declaration* merely fed the impulse of Tories to address the crown in support of its firm stand against an opposition rooted in the rebellion of the 1640s. Over the next six months, over 200 loyalist addresses poured into Westminster, some from boroughs and grand juries, others from apprentices and ordinary subjects throughout the kingdom. These English addresses were accompanied by some 40 from Ireland as well. Those who addressed proclaimed their respect for monarchy, for the hereditary succession, and for the established church as safeguards against Catholicism and 'arbitrary' parliamentary behaviour.[41] Tories would now prove as skilful as Whigs in smearing their political adversaries with the language of popery and arbitrary government. Ironically, the Whigs had actually insisted that all royal prerogatives be passed on to a Protestant successor, while Charles and some loyalists had been willing to compromise royal power in the hands of a Catholic prince. Such subtleties were lost, however, as the crown drove a reaction against the Whigs as rebels with a republican past.

Confrontations throughout the Kingdoms, 1680–3

Older accounts of the 'Exclusion Crisis' generally ended with the third and final failure of exclusion in the Oxford Parliament, but the Restoration Crisis was far from over. In Scotland, Charles and James would attempt to turn a meeting of the estates to royalist advantage, and the religious situation remained volatile. In England, Charles still confronted an opposition that was entrenched in London, in many other localities, and in the press and coffeehouses. The Whigs continued to demand another parliament to deal with the succession, to complete investigations of the Popish Plot, and to secure Protestantism through the accommodation of dissent. They fully expected that Charles's financial needs and Louis XIV's aggressive manoeuvres in Flanders would require another session.

The Whigs were mistaken in their expectations, however. Two developments had freed Charles from needing to face them in another parliament. The first of these was financial. Charles was able to maintain his government, despite his indebtedness, for the rest of his reign without needing additional parliamentary taxes. The Treasury commissioners who took over from Danby in 1679 had succeeded in drastically reducing the government's annual expenses. For once, Charles himself also accepted the need for economy. Furthermore, the crown's revenue from duties on commerce increased significantly, beginning in 1681, as the end of the 1678 parliamentary ban on trade with France contributed to a boom in England's overseas trade. Secondly, a few days before the Oxford Parliament, Charles made a new deal with Louis that seemed to make another parliament or another war much less likely. He promised Louis that he would neither aid Spain against France, despite his recent treaty with Spain, nor call a parliament to consider such aid. In return, Charles received almost £400,000 over the next three years, as well as the Sun King's assurance that France would not directly attack Spain in Flanders.[42]

Charles's growing financial security and his understanding with Louis gave him an independence from the English parliament that he had never enjoyed before. Indeed, his newfound financial stability was an important start in addressing the traditional handicaps of the Stuart state in England. Nevertheless, neither the king nor his loyalist ministers could feel secure as long as critics raged in the press and as long as the Whigs remained politically dominant in London and other localities. The crisis entered a new phase, therefore, as Charles and his ministers sought methodically to put down the opposition in church and state and to reimpose the Restoration civil and ecclesiastical order that had become unstuck. The 'Tory revenge' that followed was only partially successful, however, for it produced conformity only after many confrontations. Those who had hoped for a Protestant succession, for greater freedom for dissenters, or for further church reform struggled against measures intended to reduce them to compliance to the Restoration settlement. The compliance Charles finally secured from many of them was the acquiescence of the browbeaten rather than of the convinced. The Tory triumph crafted after 1681 was a somewhat hollow one, therefore, because far fewer of Charles's subjects were enthusiastic about him at the end of his reign than had been the case at the beginning.

The reimposition of Restoration norms began in Scotland, where Monmouth's indulgence of 1679 had temporarily stilled the troubled religious waters. In his first Edinburgh residence, in the winter of 1679–80, the Duke of York had accepted the indulgence, not because he liked dissenters, but rather because he thought it best not to provoke them while the kingdom was relatively peaceful. The Scottish government did not have to wait long, however, for further disturbances: they broke out almost immediately after James's return to England. The acceptance of the indulgence by most Presbyterians drove a minority of extremists into defiant actions that gave them far more attention than their numbers merited. These militant Covenanters converged, after Bothwell Bridge, around the clerical leadership of several outspoken preachers, including Richard Cameron, who lent his name to their movement. Acting on behalf of this faithful remnant, the Cameronian clergy began to issue *fatwa*-like religious edicts that acknowledged 'King Jesus' only and that declared war on Charles II as 'a tyrant and usurper'. Rejecting the succession of James, the Cameronians agitated for the reformation of the Scottish church and for a political regime without 'government by a single person'. The Cameronians' anti-royalism and their explicit endorsement of violence differentiated them from other Scottish dissenters. Cameron himself died during skirmishes between troops and armed bands of his followers in the summer of 1680. Several captured Cameronian leaders, including two women, were executed in the wake of the disturbances. Further efforts at suppression, however, succeeded only in providing extreme Presbyterians with new martyrs to emulate.[43]

In the meantime, the religious accommodation that Monmouth had brought to Scotland had been terminated through the influence of the Scottish and English bishops. They rejected the 1679 indulgence as an opening for schismatic ideas within the Church of Scotland and as the policy of a potential usurper to the thrones of both kingdoms. Back in England, James also threw his weight behind the move to reverse an indulgence that had enhanced the prestige of his rival. On the Scottish council, associates of the Duke of Hamilton, like William Douglas, Earl of Queensberry, sought to establish their respectability by distancing themselves from the cause of Scottish dissenters. In response to signals from all these quarters, Charles cancelled the most generous provisions of the indulgence in May 1680. The Scottish council adopted a tougher policy against conventicles, using the resistance of the Cameronians as a pretext. Scotland soon reverted to the disorder that had preceded the rebellion of 1679. Nonconformists in many counties defied the government in numerous field and house conventicles, some of them sponsored by landed families and women of quality. The conventiclers found encouragement in the attacks of the English opposition on 'popish' practices in the Church of England, and dissenters communicated and travelled across the border with relative ease.

Commissioned by his brother to resettle the northern kingdom, James returned to Scotland in October 1680 and remained for a year and a half. He not only pursued Lauderdale's hard-line policy of suppressing conventicles; but meeting with the Scottish parliament in August 1681, he also acted far more forcefully than his predecessor in re-imposing Restoration norms in church and state. As parliamentary high commissioner, James pushed through a Succession Act that, in contrast to English exclusion proposals, confirmed direct, hereditary succession to the Scottish throne as among the 'fundamental and unalterable laws' of the realm. Indeed, it condemned any attempts to alter the succession by written or spoken word as treasonous. James also promoted a Test Act that established everything for Scotland that Danby had sought for England with his test bill of 1675. Although James himself had been exempted from taking an anti-Catholic Scottish allegiance oath, the new Scottish test required all office holders, clergy, teachers, and soldiers to take an oath affirming the power of the king as 'supreme governor' in all matters 'ecclesiastical as [well as] civil'. The oath further required renunciation of all 'popish or fanatical' principles that limited royal authority, of any form of resistance, and of participation in any 'convenants ... or assemblies' dedicated to alterations of church and state. Finally, it required affirmation of the 1567 Scots confession of faith.[44]

Rushed through parliament despite debate and objections, the Succession and Test Acts were largely accepted by the great Scottish magnates who feared the Covenanters might otherwise take the kingdom back to civil war and attempt to re-establish clerical domination. The two acts were designed to re-establish uniformity of belief and to reinforce allegiance to the Restoration settlement in church in state. In fact, however, they had the opposite effect. The affirmation of the 1567 confession of faith was included in the

Test Act at the suggestion of the leading jurist Sir James Dalrymple of Stair, who may have designed its inclusion to wreck the bill. The 1567 confession was a classic creed of Reformed Protestantism, but it was one that 'none of the bishops' and 'scarce any one in the whole parliament had ever read'. It sanctioned the very resistance that office-holders were now required to forswear, and it implied limitations to the royal supremacy over the church that contradicted the Scottish Supremacy Act. Furthermore, in startling contrast to England, where limitations upon the authority of a Catholic prince over a Protestant church had acquired significant support, even among Anglican ministers of state, the Scottish parliament had entirely surrendered their Protestant church to a Catholic successor.

The Test Act, in particular, resulted in a legal and constitutional muddle that shook Scottish society from top to bottom. Many expected to take the oath had questions about its meaning. Most of the Episcopal clergy took the oath, but not without expressing reservations about 'obscure' expressions in the confession of faith. But at least 50 incumbent clergy, including the professor of divin-ity at the University of Edinburgh and many from the southwest shires, were deprived of their places for refusing the oath. Some of these clergy now joined the dissenters. The Test Act also pro-duced a few spectacular defections among the nobility. Archibald Campbell, Earl of Argyll, a leading privy councillor and the son of a Covenanting martyr of 1661, would take the oath only 'in so far as it was consistent with itself and the Protestant religion'. As clan leader of the Campbells, Argyll had both great power and much land in the Highlands. When James had him prosecuted for treason, English opinion was as shocked, as were the Scots: 'Many spoke of it, and of the duke that drove it on, with horror,' reported Gilbert Burnet. Halifax told Charles that the charges against Argyll would not hang a dog in England. Found guilty, Argyll escaped to London, where he consorted with Shaftesbury and the English opposition *incognito* in 1682, before joining other Scottish exiles, like Stair, who had also declined the oath, in the Netherlands. The Duke of Hamilton took the oath under pressure, but only to preserve his influence and his estates. In England, Charles pointed to the 1681 acts of the Scottish estates as an example of parlia-mentary support for monarchy; but the Whigs merely saw another example of arbitrary government at work.

When James returned to England in early 1682, power in Scotland passed to the imperious Queensberry, to the ambitious James Drummond, Earl of Perth, and to other royalist councillors determined to carry out the resettlement of Scotland on the basis of the new acts. Their persecution of Presbyterians surpassed anything attempted by Lauderdale. When some local magistrates declined either to take the Test Act oath or to act against conventicles, the council appointed extraordinary judicial commissioners to do their work. The militia was also purged. In Galloway, one of James's favourite Scots military officers, John Graham of Claverhouse, was commissioned to suppress dissent. That Claverhouse sought to do by vigorous means, including the quartering of troops, the fining of active dissenters, the imprisonment of the obstreperous, the taking of bonds, and an offer of amnesty to all who would return to church. Actions such as these filled parish services, even in the southwest. 'But it was more from the fear of the law than for the worship of God,' thought Burnet.

These strong-armed tactics also failed entirely to cow the Cameronians, who reorganized themselves as the United Societies of the true Scottish church. Claiming as many as 80 local groups, the Cameronians conducted guerrilla warfare against the armed posses the government sent out against them. Indeed, the societies sent delegates to regularly held assemblies that met in numerous places, including Edinburgh; and they took measures to provide for a succession of their own clergy by sending clerical students to the Netherlands for education. As repressive efforts continued in 1683, more retribution occurred than after Bothwell Bridge. The Scottish judges were sent out on circuits to enforce oath taking under the Test Act. Yet as deadlines for taking the test were imposed and extended, opposition continued, even from persons of high social standing; and conventicles persisted. Crowded prisons were emptied by transporting conventiclers to the colonies. Dissenters understandably believed the council's resort to unprecedented military and civil strategies already constituted the civil war the same authorities sought to avert.[45]

The Scottish acts of 1681 had clearly settled that kingdom far less successfully than the indulgence of 1679. Much of the population and most of the political elite eventually accepted the Test Act, but militants remained unreconciled. In Ireland, in contrast, Ormond maintained public order through de facto toleration as

Episcopalian fears about Catholics subsided before Episcopalian fears about dissenters. For once, Ireland was spared the religious and civil confrontations that were overtaking England and Scotland. The lord lieutenant remained anxious about contacts between the extreme Scots Covenanters and some Ulster dissenters, but he was reassured by protestations of loyalty from the leading Presbyterian clergy. Although the primate of the Church of Ireland continued to press for suppression of all Protestant conventicles under the Irish penal laws, Ormond doubted that statutes intended against Catholics could be applied to Protestants. He acted only against outspoken dissenting clergy suspected of advocating the Scots Covenants or of otherwise challenging civil authority.[46]

In England, Charles's Tory ministers and loyalist propagandists like L'Estrange worked together in 1681–2. Their goal was to turn opinion against the opposition by suggesting that the Whigs and dissenters had sought to destroy the Restoration church and state under cover of the Popish Plot. In April 1681 L'Estrange launched *The Observator*, a newssheet that hammered home loyalist themes three times a week for the next six years. Other Tory publicists quickly joined L'Estrange's campaign. For its part, the government arrested a number of London Whig activists in June 1681, hoping to gain maximum public benefit from charges that they had been engaged in treasonous activities. Among these was Stephen College, the carpenter and political poet. When the government's indictment against him was thrown out for lack of evidence, by a London grand jury empanelled by the city's Whig sheriffs, College was retried in Oxford, found guilty, and hanged. The last British poet executed for his poetry, he was also a symbol for Anglicans of how upstart plebeians had sought to turn the political and social order of the Restoration upside down.[47]

The College affair enabled the government to suggest that leading Whigs and dissenters, like the London sheriffs and their jurors, still hoped to damage the crown and the church through exclusion and toleration. The same charges were made against the Earl of Shaftesbury. Indeed, it was really Shaftesbury's head the government was after. The earl was arrested a few days after College and consigned to the Tower. The treason charges against him – which suggested that he had conspired to use force against Charles if necessary – did not reach a London grand jury until 24 November. Despite government efforts to orchestrate the result, the Whig sheriffs of London again selected a jury of leading dissenters and partisans who dismissed the charges. This result was greeted with pandemonium in the courtroom and with a night of bonfires, bells, toasts, and crowd celebrations throughout the city. Similar scenes occurred in some other localities as the news spread, but public opinion was also divided. Tory crowds had been active in the city on 5 and 17 November, for instance; and 'Jack Presbyter' had been burnt in Westminster.[48]

The government's difficulties in prosecuting College and Shaftesbury also pointed to how extensive an effort was needed to deprive Whigs and dissenters of their political clout and visibility in the press and in the localities. Whig and dissenting printers and authors had successfully employed the press to arouse public opinion about the succession and the church. Now the government acted to sanitize the public sphere by clamping down on opposition printers and authors. The government and loyalist politicians had used libel cases throughout the crisis to harass opposition publishers, but the legal intimidation of Whig printers intensified after the Oxford Parliament. The printer of the Whig *Protestant (Domestick) Intelligence,* for instance, was imprisoned for most of 1681 and 1682; and he was forced to give up publication. Henry Care and some other Whig publicists were more successful in publishing newssheets and pamphlets through 1681–2, despite increasing government prosecutions for seditious language. Still, Whig printers and writers were clearly on the defensive as loyalist authors argued freely and were able to fan popular fears of the sects to good advantage. The loyalist bonfires that greeted the Duke of York on his return from Scotland in 1682 were fuelled with copies of opposition papers. Norwich Tories celebrated Charles's birthday in May 1682 by burning Henry Care and other 'factious and seditious libellers' in effigy. As the public sphere began tilting rhetorically towards loyalism, Dryden published his anti-Whig masterpiece, *Absalom and Achitophel* (1681), released at the time of Shaftesbury's trial, while Aphra Behn contributed her *Roundheads* (1682).[49]

This cleansing of the public sphere of Whig print and talk was accompanied by stricter enforcement of statutes against dissenting worship. In London and some other boroughs, dissenters could count upon the active support of nonconformist and sympathetic magistrates. They were nonetheless subjected to an official campaign of harassment that began almost immediately after the Oxford Parliament. Initially, dissenting congregations often stood their ground, guarding their meetinghouses and protecting their preachers. Charles actually hesitated to employ the London militia against urban meetinghouses for fear of producing clashes in the streets. Even in London, however, many preachers were frightened by early 1682. Urban dissenting clergy, including the leading Independent John Owen and his Scots friend Robert Ferguson, accumulated some £10,000 in fines for illegal preaching in 1681–2. The ailing and aging Presbyterian leader Richard Baxter was eventually stripped of most of his goods, including his sickbed, for failure to pay the fines levied against him. Many clergy gave up preaching before the end of 1682, as gangs of semi-professional informers began harassing meetings and reporting (and often distorting) the words of sermons.

The campaign against dissenting clergy was reinforced by equally vigorous measures against the dissenting laity, who could suffer fines, the forfeiture of goods, and imprisonment for attending illegal worship. Alehouse keepers were threatened with the loss of their licences if caught at conventicles; and paupers were threatened with the loss of parish relief. Dissenters whose principles permitted them to attend church did so to avoid persecution, while Quaker leaders enjoined their followers to avoid coffeehouses and political talk. Still, some dissenters and their preachers remained obstinate. Four hundred London Quakers, probably only a fraction of those at meetings, were prosecuted as conventiclers in 1683; and several of John Bunyan's friends among the Independent and Baptist clergy continued to preach.[50]

The government's efforts to suppress dissent and criticism, to cripple the opposition, and to re-establish the authority of the Restoration church and state could not succeed as long as the Whigs controlled London. The site of most of the kingdom's print facilities and the centre of its coffeehouse culture, London was also home to over 100 dissenting clergy and a like number of meetings. For the government and for loyalist writers, the city was both the bulwark of exclusionist and tolerationist opinion and the chief example of how dissenters threatened to drive the kingdom back to the puritan excesses of 1640–60. Even before the Oxford Parliament, loyalist propagandists had succeeded in sparking an urban reaction against dissent that bred increasingly assertive Tory crowds. After the London grand jury's dismissal of the charges against Shaftesbury, the ministry initiated legal proceedings against the charter of the city of London. The government claimed the civic regime had trespassed upon royal prerogatives in its petitions for a parliament and had violated the terms upon which it held its extensive self-government. The charges were merely a pretext for the crown to reclaim management of the city in the interests of political and social order. Charles's intentions were to restrict the city's electoral processes, to reduce the size and influence of the urban electorate, and to enhance the ability of the government to intervene in civic elections and affairs. As the suit was prepared and brought before the central Court of King's Bench, the ministry also worked hand in glove with civic Tory leaders to recapture the city's political institutions from the Whigs.

The London and parliamentary Whigs and dissenters met the loyalist campaign against them head on. They relaunched their cause as well, in early 1682, with an urban campaign of neighbourhood fêtes and feasts involving Shaftesbury and Monmouth that was designed to keep up the pressure on Charles to summon another parliament. In June 1682, the government and the Whigs confronted each other in the city's election of sheriffs, which was contested by rival pairs of partisan candidates. The outcome was of critical importance, given the ability of the sheriffs to orchestrate the selection of jurors for politically charged trials and to facilitate or to disrupt the government's proceedings against dissenters and opposition printers. Ordinarily decided at a single meeting of the 8000 electors, this election required almost three months of crowded assemblies, polls, challenges of voter qualifications, and frequent confrontations between the ministry and urban Whig leaders. By September, the political focus of the entire kingdom was on the outcome of this one London election, which might make or break the crown's campaign against the opposition. Some Whig and dissenting electors and leaders came armed to Guildhall, on more than one occasion. The city's loyalist lord mayor employed regiments of the civic militia to police the election for the benefit of the Tory candidates. When the lord mayor finally determined the result in favour of the Tories, after manoeuvres of uncertain legality, the Whigs challenged the election in the courts. They also refused to recognize the authority of the new sheriffs or of a new Tory lord mayor.

Not until the winter of 1682–3 did urban and parliamentary Whig leaders accept that their cause was failing. The London elections of 1682 suggested that they could no longer arouse the commanding electoral support, even in London, that had provided them with clear Commons' majorities for exclusion and for Protestant accommodation. Assiduously propagated in the press, the Tory message was having an obvious impact on readers and electors throughout the kingdom. Shaftesbury fled the city and the country in November 1682, much 'broken [in] his understanding', according to Burnet. He died in the Netherlands a few months later. In the meantime, Whig efforts in the courts failed, as judges came under tighter crown supervision, and as the government launched new suits against Whig leaders. In June 1683, the King's Bench judges, their composition recently altered by the crown, found in favour of the government against the London charter. Charles then replaced several elected Whig aldermen with Tories, eliminated the city's elected common council, and deprived many London Whigs and dissenters of their electoral privileges. Some Tories who had proclaimed their party's 'moderation' worried the government had gone too far in London. Loyalist John Evelyn considered 'these violent transactions' highly imprudent.[51]

In the meantime, Charles sought to bring local institutions throughout England more effectively under royal control. He purged commissions of the peace and borough magistracies of all who were aligned with the opposition or were too sympathetic to dissent. The remodelling of the county commissions of peace had begun as early as 1680, as Charles reacted to the first exclusion vote and to the petitioning campaign of 1679–80. Altogether, about 50 MPs who had favoured exclusion and Country principles were removed from county commissions of the peace in this initial purge. The process was messy and imperfect, however; and additional alterations were required in some counties, as the crown slowly identified JPs of uncertain loyalty. Ministers were equally careful in appointing county sheriffs. As in London, the sheriffs in the counties played an important role in the selection of jurors. County lieutenancy commissions and militia leaderships were also regulated. By 1682–3, thanks in part to this significant intervention by the government, most counties were again securely in the hands of the Anglican loyalist gentry.

Stricter enforcement of the 1661 Corporation Act, originally intended to root nonconformists out of offices in the boroughs, had also begun in 1680. It was not entirely effective, however: younger office holders, who had never subscribed to the Solemn League and Covenant, had no difficulty in forswearing it, while many Presbyterians had no qualms about taking Anglican communion once a year to qualify for office. Neither could the Corporation Act intimidate Whig conformists; and opposition remained strong in some boroughs, like Yarmouth and Nottingham, through 1682–3. The complaints of local Tories seeking to overpower their Whig and dissenting rivals probably inspired the crown's most dramatic initiative in local government. Beginning in 1682–3, Charles began legal proceedings against the charters of boroughs and town corporations throughout the kingdom, with the intention of re-granting charters under terms that gave the crown greater control over local office holding. Although some towns were resistant, the example of London suggested that compliance was the better course. Some 134 towns, beginning with Worcester, Thetford, and Hereford were rechartered and remodelled over the next five years. They experienced a purge of office holders unparalleled in English history. Tories were soon as entrenched in the boroughs as in the counties, while Charles and his ministers exercised more influence over local government than any previous Stuart regime.[52]

As Charles and his government tightened their grasp upon local institutions and harassed Whigs and dissenters throughout the country, some Whig leaders and thinkers turned to the one course of action of which loyalists had always accused them. To their way of thinking, if parliamentary means to secure Protestantism in church and state had failed, perhaps only violent means could succeed. If the government was determined to destroy judicial independence and to abridge customary local liberties, perhaps resistance was in order. The Country had feared for the safety of parliament and Protestantism since the mid-1670s. Now Charles insisted upon a Catholic succession, prorogued and dissolved parliament repeatedly in order to frustrate the Commons' majority, and was employing the full extent of his prerogative to suppress all who disagreed with him or with his Anglican loyalist allies. Only an enlargement of his standing army seemed still necessary for the introduction of popery and arbitrary government.

When Whig leaders first began seriously to consider the option of armed resistance is not entirely clear; and neither is the extent of Whig conspiracy. Something may have been afoot when Monmouth travelled through the West of England in September 1682, drawing enthusiastic crowds wherever he went; and the Scots dissident, the Earl of Argyll, had secretive conversations with Shaftesbury about the same time. More likely, Shaftesbury, Russell, and the other parliamentary and London Whigs talked seriously about armed uprising only a few weeks later, in the wake of the disastrous loss of the London elections. By then they also understood that their hope for a parliamentary resolution of their disputes with Charles was unrealistic, since the king had no intention of summoning another parliament. Their assessment of the chances of success for an insurrection was not encouraging, however. Monmouth also had serious reservations about employing violent means against his father, while mutual distrust broke out between him and old republican hangers-on about Shaftesbury.[53]

Still, the talk of resistance was of great historical importance, for just as the politicians turned to it, so did their intellectual associates. John Locke, still a member of Shaftesbury's household, probably began the composition of his monumental *Second Treatise*, with its endorsement of resistance, at about this time. Algernon Sidney was connected both to some Whig activists in London and to urban republican remnants of old commonwealth-men and lawyers. He had probably begun drafting his *Discourses*, with their defence of resistance, in 1681; and he continued the work as the Tory revenge gathered strength in 1682. Neither were Locke and Sidney alone, among opposition thinkers, in turning in this direction. The influential London dissenting divines John Owen and Robert Ferguson also endorsed resistance in print in 1682–3; and the Scotsman George Buchanan's 1579 Latin defence of deposing a monarch, under some circumstances, was first published in English in 1680.

Both Locke and Sidney operated in intellectual frameworks much broader than the Restoration Crisis, and each sought to draw upon philosophical concepts to invest it with abiding significance. Yet their texts are littered with allusions and examples drawn from the events they had just witnessed. Both complained of how those defending their rights and liberties might easily be branded as political incendiaries, the very situation Whigs and dissenters had experienced from the government and its Tory propagandists. Both Locke and Sidney were appalled by what they regarded as the perversion of justice in the courts. Both saw the manipulation of legislative institutions by a ruler as a principal justification for resistance. Both wrote to encourage Whigs to consider resistance at the very time that many of them had given up hope for Protestant security and parliamentary government. In his chapter 'Of Tyranny', Locke suggested that the people now had the right to defend themselves against the 'several experiments made of arbitrary power' and against 'that religion underhand favoured' that 'is readiest to introduce it'. For his part, Sidney elevated parliaments, to which the people delegate their sovereignty, over kings. Indeed, he argued both that a parliament might now convene itself, on the basis of popular authority, and that the people and their parliament could justly 'change or take away kings'.[54]

These words of Locke and Sidney would bear much fruit; but they would bear little of it now. Charles had successfully outwitted his opponents and resolved the Restoration Crisis on his terms rather than theirs. In England, the monarchy and Anglican royalism had prevailed over their critics, and Charles had begun to address the traditional weaknesses of the Stuart state as well. In Scotland, the estates had affirmed the authority of the crown in the strongest language possible. The security of the monarchy and of the Episcopalian establishment had been enhanced in both kingdoms; but this enhancement was accomplished as much through confrontation as through parliamentary give and take, even in Scotland, where parliament had given the crown all it asked for. Reanchored upon their original cavalier and Episcopalian foundations, Charles's British regimes appeared firmly implanted, as the relatively peaceful state of Ireland also suggested. Yet the English and Scottish regimes were implanted upon the ruin of many who had once hoped to work with Charles to create quite different orders of government and whose acceptance of the current state of affairs was grudging at best.

5 Resettlement and Unsettlement, 1683–8

It ... hath of long time been our constant sense and opinion ... that conscience ought not to be constrained, nor people forced in matters of mere religion; it has ever been directly contrary ... to the interest of government, which it destroys by spoiling trade, depopulating countries and discouraging strangers; and finally, that it never obtained the end for which it was employed ... We have thought fit further to declare that we will maintain ... [our subjects] in all their properties and possessions, as well of church and abbey lands as in any other their lands and properties.

James II, 1687[1]

Introduction: Absolutism?

The seventeenth century was a century of absolutism. English Country and Whig politicians who looked to the continent in the 1670s and 1680s saw a Europe that was dominated by Louis XIV, and they also saw a Europe that was increasingly characterized by the style of government that Louis represented. Modern historians have stressed the continuing limitations upon the Sun King's authority, but they too have seen Louis as the central figure in a seventeenth-century decline of feudal and local institutions before the centralizing royalist state. With the aid of his administrative secretaries of state and his provincial *intendants*, the French king was increasingly effective in supervising regional diets, municipal governments, local law courts, and the nobility and clergy. At the centre, he held sway over the deferential *Parlement* of Paris, the kingdom's chief court of law. He never met the *Estates-General*, the French equivalent of the British parliaments, which was summoned by no French king between 1614 and 1789. Louis also used his extensive revenues to round out the state. He eventually maintained one of the largest European armies since the ancient Roman Empire. He gained increasing influence over the Catholic Church, and he sought to suppress Protestantism as an affront to his authority and an obstacle to the unity of his kingdom. Lastly, he directed the organizing power of the state towards the more effective development of the national economy.

Louis was not alone in representing the trend towards autocratic centralization in seventeenth-century Europe. Techniques similar to his had already been adopted in numerous German princely and ecclesiastical states and were progressively implemented by the electors of Brandenburg. Louis's mode of government was also observed and imitated by monarchs in Scandinavia and Russia. Throughout seventeenth-century Europe, medieval representative institutions generally experienced the same fate as the French *Estates-General*; and polities such as the Holy Roman Empire and Poland, in which local rights and privileges continued to dominate, declined and fragmented. Republican systems, in which power was diffused among noble or mercantile elites, also appeared to be a relic of the past. Venice had followed the other Italian Renaissance city-states into economic decline, and its political weaknesses were frequently the butt of royalist scorn in England. Only the example of the United Provinces suggested that republicanism might have a future. But even there, republicans had taken a back seat to the Prince of Orange since 1672, while Louis's animus against the Dutch state clouded its economic and political future.

In Britain, the Irish parliament had not met since 1666, and the Scottish parliament of 1681 had been more fearful about dissenting unrest than about the Duke of York's strong-armed legislative tactics. Neither of these institutions was as well established as the parliament of England, in which representatives of the localities retained an assertive role in central government, as the Restoration Crisis demonstrated. But in a broader European context, the English parliament was peculiar. Moreover, Charles II succeeded, after 1681, in defining the central issue of English politics as the obstreperousness of the House of Commons rather than the arbitrariness of the crown. Thereafter, his purging of local commissions of peace, his remodelling of the municipal boroughs, his alterations of the judiciary, and his avoidance of parliament could all be taken as evidence of a new style of government modelled after that of France. But did Charles II or James II, as the Duke of York became in 1685, consciously seek to undermine parliament and local liberties after the Restoration Crisis and to introduce French-style absolutism into their kingdoms?

The makers of the Revolution of 1688–9 had no doubt that such was the case. Many of them had feared popery and arbitrary government since the 1670s; and they eventually expelled the Catholic James for 'endeavour[ing] to subvert and extirpate the Protestant religion and the laws and liberties of this kingdom'. Whig historians from the contemporary Gilbert Burnet onward also had no doubt that the Revolution of 1688–9 preserved Britain from Stuart autocracy and permitted the evolution of parliamentary government and personal liberties in the eighteenth and nineteenth centuries. Carrying this tradition into mid-twentieth-century historiography, G. M. Trevelyan restated the old dichotomy between 'royal absolutism' and 'parliamentary government' and suggested that 'James II forced England to choose once for all between these two.'[2]

Some recent historians, on the other hand, have suggested that such a construction invests the decisions that Charles and James made in the 1680s with ideological motives foreign to their minds. To this way of thinking, Charles was reacting opportunistically after 1681, merely exploiting popular fears of civil war, which he in fact shared, to resecure his authority. Moreover, he and his Anglican allies conceived of their campaign against Whigs and dissenters not in terms of absolutism but rather in terms of law. They sought to protect established law against those who had jeopardized the constitution of king-in-parliament through their attacks upon hereditary succession, their setting of the Commons against the crown, and their flagrant disregard for the legal protections of the Church of England. Similarly, after 1685, James was concerned not with advancing royal prerogatives per se but rather with using those prerogatives, as necessary, to advance civil and religious rights for his fellow Catholics. His goal was toleration rather than 'arbitrary government'.[3]

Discussion of whether Charles or James sought to establish absolutism in England has generally paid little attention to evidence from Ireland or Scotland, which – at least in the case of James – does suggest an interest in keeping parliaments under royal check. But neither has the argument for Stuart absolutism taken much consideration of the inherent limitations of the British royal states, especially in comparison to Louis XIV's French regime. Even if Charles and James were influenced by French absolutism, and even if they desired to increase royal authority in their kingdoms, did they actually have the resources necessary to follow the example of Louis XIV? England must be central in any response to this question, for, in England, the state was far more developed than was the case in either Scotland or Ireland.

Some have suggested that, had James not offended the religious sensibilities of his Anglican subjects, he might well have succeeded in advancing the power of the English crown. Yet according to another line of reasoning, the seventeenth-century English royal regime was a somewhat fragile polity and prone to breakdown, as the events of the 1640s demonstrated.[4] Although the Stuart state had been put back together in the Restoration, it continued to suffer from the same structural weaknesses that had led to its collapse in the first place. Like their Stuart predecessors, for instance, Charles and James lacked the financial means to govern for lengthy periods without parliamentary assistance. True, Charles had overcome the financial difficulties of the early Restoration by the 1680s. But most royal income was authorized by parliament, and the crown's ordinary revenue was still insufficient to fund warfare on anything matching the scale that Louis had already attempted. The English precedents for the extraction of extraordinary revenues from subjects were also not very encouraging.

Furthermore, Charles and James were largely dependent upon unpaid local grandees for the administration of the counties; and the size of the central government, compared to that of France, remained small. The sense of political entitlement by the 'natural governors' of society had strengthened rather than weakened after the experiences of the civil war and Interregnum. The landed gentry and nobility who ruled the counties identified their influence with stability, tradition, and the proper ordering of the kingdom. Their resentment of the infringement upon local autonomy by the Cromwellian regime had contributed to the restoration of 1660 and suggested that too much central interference with county elites could prove hazardous to the state. The English understanding of lawmaking as a process that ordinarily involved representatives of the localities also established limitations on royal manipulation of parliament. Finally, the government's need to consider and to coordinate policy in three separate kingdoms, each with its own parliament, left the English state vulnerable to disorders originating in the other Stuart kingdoms, as the Country's appropriation of Scottish grievances in 1678 demonstrated.

The late Stuart monarchs were also limited by the thoughts and fears of their subjects, especially in England, where the constriction of the public sphere after 1681 did not soothe the minds of many subjects.[5] The extensive literacy of the English population and the continuing circulation of previously printed opposition and dissenting material counteracted the government's drive for uniformity and obedience. In all three kingdoms, widespread fears that parliaments and Protestant traditions were imperilled by events within Britain and throughout Europe were too old and too deep-seated to be eradicated. The actions of the crown after 1681 merely intensified those fears among some. The Episcopalian establishments upon which Charles leaned in the 1680s were better secured than in the 1660s, but the determination of nonconformists and sectarians to achieve comprehension and toleration had scarcely weakened. Persecution was a sign that Charles's regimes in England and Scotland had so far failed to command the beliefs of significant minorities. Coercion was a reflection of insecure establishments rather than of self-confident ones. And although James would far surpass Charles in the development of military resources, he did so only to revive the longstanding fears of local elites about forces under central direction rather than under their own control.

The narrative offered here will seek to explain why so many subjects in the Stuart kingdoms had come to fear, by 1687–8, that their king was attempting to impose 'popery and arbitrary government' upon them. The evidence frequently cited by contemporaries and by historians who have seen James's rule as a deliberate experiment in absolutism will be introduced. Whether that is the best construction for understanding James II will be left an open question, however. Evidence for an alternate hypothesis – that, in England, James stressed a somewhat fragile polity to the breaking point by ignoring the customary limitations of the royal state – will also be presented. In either case, what has already been said about fears of France that went back to the 1660s should be kept in mind, as should fears about arbitrary rule that went back to the 1670s, and ultimately to the 1630s. Ideas, fears, and perceptions were as important in returning the Stuart kingdoms to crisis by 1688 as the methods and motives of royal government.

Towards a Second Restoration, 1683–5[6]

The consideration of resistance by some Whig leaders and stalwarts did not end with Shaftesbury's departure for the Netherlands in November 1682. Indeed, in June 1683, as the ministry's campaign against dissent, the opposition, and the borough charters got into full swing, the government learned about a Whig conspiracy just as sensational as the Popish Plot. An informer revealed details of a scheme to assassinate Charles and James that had been hatched and abandoned a few months earlier. The assassination was to have occurred as the royal brothers, travelling from Newmarket to London, passed the Rye House at Hoddesdon, Hertfordshire. The government launched an immediate search for those believed to have been involved. Numerous London Whig activists were arrested, as were such parliamentary leaders as Lord Russell, the Earl of Essex, and Algernon Sidney. As the roundup continued, others wanted for questioning escaped to the Netherlands. Monmouth went into hiding, after being indicted for treason. He eventually joined the exiles in the Netherlands, after the failure of an attempt to reconcile with Charles. As the government acted, news of this 'horrid' conspiracy against the monarchy swept through the coffeehouses and the press, stunning many who had even favoured exclusion to preserve the Protestant church and state.

Loyalist propagandists such as L'Estrange had a field day with what became known as the Rye House Plot. They seemingly had all the evidence they needed to drive their opponents from the political field as a treasonous, regicidal remnant of the Cromwellian sects and commonwealth men. As interrogations and trials of accused conspirators followed in 1683–4, the press was flooded with transcripts of proceedings, confessions, and the last words of the condemned. The government proved as adept as the Whig opposition had ever been in swamping the public sphere with such publications. The established clergy read Charles's *Declaration* about the discovery of the plot from their pulpits. Sermons proclaimed that God had miraculously rescued Charles from the assassins in 1683, just as providence had miraculously restored him in 1660. A second divinely intended Restoration had thus begun; and the king was deluged with loyal addresses from the localities, as his hold on opinion strengthened.[7]

Charles's success in turning the Rye House Plot to his own advantage has been far more obvious than whatever plans actually lay behind the allegations of Whig plotting. Reacting to how the government deliberately massaged a series of 'show trials' for its own benefit, some historians have largely discounted the reality of opposition plotting. The executions of several government critics, including major parliamentary leaders, appear to be just too convenient. As many people eventually died for their alleged complicity in the Rye House Plot as were executed in the early 1660s for their part in the death of Charles I.

The first major figure to die was the Earl of Essex, the former lord lieutenant of Ireland and still a privy councillor. He was found dead in the Tower of London in July 1683, before any trial, with his throat gashed from ear to ear. The government claimed he died by his own hand; but the circumstances of Essex's death have proven almost as controversial as the death of Sir Edmund Berry Godfrey. John Locke and many contemporaries believed Essex was murdered, and so have some historians, arguing that the earl's broad, deep wound could not have been self-inflicted. 'An executioner could hardly have done more with an axe,' thought John Evelyn. One authority has even speculated that the power hungry Sunderland may have contrived the apparent suicide of Essex and sought to turn it to political advantage. Sunderland had made up with Charles, after voting for exclusion; and he had returned to office. But his standing with James, who was still smarting over exclusion, was shaky; and the death of Essex, whether arranged or not, conveniently eliminated two of James's adversaries with one stroke, the second being Lord Russell. The death of Essex occurred just as Russell's trial began; and prosecutors immediately took it as evidence that Essex had killed himself out of guilt for the treason of which both men stood charged.

Whatever the case about Essex, Russell – who had twice moved exclusion bills against James in the House of Commons – was found guilty within a few days and went to the block. Sidney's trial followed several months later, in November 1683. By that time the government should have found sufficient evidence of his alleged treason. Still lacking it, however, the prosecutors persuaded the jury that Sidney's unpublished writings, which called for resistance to a tyrant, substantiated his part in the proposed rebellion. In the meantime, the trials and executions of minor plotters, some of them with civil war pasts, kept the conspiracy constantly before the public eye.[8]

But had these figures – especially Essex, Russell, and Sidney – actually engaged in the treasons of which they were charged? The evidence does suggest the reality of a few loosely related conspiracies, involving different people and different plans, over the winter of 1682–3. Essex, Russell, and Sidney had been involved in secretive discussions with other Whig grandees. A separate group of London Whig activists and attorneys had met off and on for several months and had eventually brought numbers of sectarian tradesmen into their schemes. The Whig leaders were primarily interested in forcing a parliament on Charles. Assassination was more the game of the city group, who also planned a London insurrection. Sidney's presence brought republican ideas into the aristocratic conspiracy; and the London cabal also involved some committed republicans. But republicanism was not the principal engine of conspiracy in 1682–3, despite the attractiveness of plotting to old commonwealth men. Conspiracy was instead driven by disappointment about the failure of the Whig cause and by desperation among those, especially Londoners, who believed their rights and liberties were in danger.[9]

Unfortunately for the conspirators, their detection only fed the Tory reaction they had opposed, which became increasingly aggressive thereafter. On the very day of Russell's execution, for instance, the faculty convocation of the University of Oxford issued a decree condemning a variety of 'pernicious books' and 'damnable doctrines' deemed 'destructive to the sacred persons of princes, their state and government, and of all human society'. The government had little to do with this. The universities had been hotbeds of royalism since 1662, and the faculty were now determined to instruct and caution readers throughout the realm with an Anglican index of banned books. The Oxford decree condemned authors who proposed that government arises from consent, or that civil society rests upon contracts between rulers and the ruled, or that a tyrant might be lawfully resisted, or that parliament shared sovereignty with the king. These were all political ideas widely subscribed to by Whigs and dissenters. Oxford students and faculty were forbidden to read offending publications by

Richard Baxter, George Buchanan, Thomas Hobbes, John Milton, John Owen, and others. Banned books were removed from the Oxford libraries and publicly burnt in the Bodleian quad.

John Locke may have observed this last semi-official book burning in England, one directed against ideas that had influenced his own unpublished *Treatises of Government*. He quickly packed up his Oxford rooms and departed for the continent. Anglican loyalists, whose political ideas Locke so despised, on the other hand, came into their own in 1683–5. Robert Filmer's *Patriarcha* was printed again. John Dryden, the poet laureate, proclaimed Britain's recovery from its second flirtation with anti-monarchical principles in *Albion and Albanius* and other new works. William Sancroft, the strongly loyalist Archbishop of Canterbury, worked hand in glove with the king's Anglican ministers to promote like-minded men to vacant bishoprics and deaneries within the church. Thomas Sprat, whose earlier *History of the Royal Society* (1667) had celebrated Charles's patronage of science, authored an official history of the conspiracy and was rewarded with a bishopric. Latitudinarian clergy who had favoured comprehension of dissenters, on the other hand, were harried in the church courts and elsewhere.[10]

The Tory reaction that reanchored the monarchy was built not only upon the advancement of loyalist ideas in the public sphere but also upon the intimidation of all who thought differently. The executions of some Whig principals in the wake of the Rye House Plot were accompanied by other royal and ministerial reprisals. James had taken the lead, even before the detection of the conspiracy, when he sued a former Whig mayor of London for uttering libellous words against him and obtained a spectacular award of £100,000 in damages. In May 1683 several London Whig activists were fined for their part in the city's election of sheriffs in the previous year. Sir Thomas Player, who had spoken too frequently on behalf of exclusion in the Commons, was ejected from his office as the city of London's chief financial officer. Sir Samuel Barnardiston, the Country and Whig parliamentary leader, was tried and imprisoned in 1684 for expressing doubts about the government's evidence against some of the Rye House plotters. Titus Oates was arrested, fined, imprisoned, and eventually indicted for perjury.[11]

If this second restoration of royal authority rested upon a triumph of loyalist ideas, it also rested upon money, and especially upon the crown's expanding customs revenues. Indeed, it was partially, and ironically, built on the flourishing overseas commerce developed by Whig and dissenting merchants like the disgraced Barnardiston, a leading merchant in England's growing trade with Turkey. In no other period, probably, has the volume of English commerce ever mounted as quickly as in the era from the late 1660s through the 1680s. Merchants in all the kingdom's ports, but especially in London, responded vigorously to the increasing foreign demand for English cloth. They also catered to the mushrooming British and continental demand for the slave-produced sugar, coffee, and tobacco of the American colonies and for the fabrics of India. By the early 1680s, this expansion of the kingdom's trade positively assisted Charles in ruling without additional parliamentary taxes. Treasury Lord Laurence Hyde, now the Earl of Rochester, had enlarged customs revenues to tap on his behalf. Charles's overall income had previously lagged behind the £1.2 million p.a. the Convention Parliament had sought to provide in 1660. In the last four years of his reign, however, his ordinary revenue increased on an annual basis by over 25 per cent, from about £1.1 million to some £1.4 million, thanks in large part to taxes on trade.[12]

With his additional income Charles also embarked upon ambitious new building projects designed to provide striking embodiments of the royalist ideal of monarchy. Charles chose Winchester for the site of a new primary palace. The location was sufficiently distant from the troublesome citizens of London, and it was associated with Arthurian legend and mystique. The baroque structure that Sir Christopher Wren designed for the site imitated Louis XIV's palace at Versailles in providing an ordered environment in which Charles might limit access to his person and awe those who sought him out. Although work at Winchester ceased with Charles's death, Wren did complete another royal building project of the 1680s that presented a majestic royal image to those same troublesome Londoners. The royal hospital for aged and infirm soldiers at Chelsea was as much a political statement about baroque monarchy as the Invalides of Louis XIV. It was designed to showcase the compassion and largesse of a royal father for those who had served him well; and it was funded in part by the fines levied upon Whig plotters and politicians.[13]

Even as Anglican Tories celebrated the recovery of their monarch in this second restoration, their influence on Charles began to decline, however. The ministerial politics of Charles's last years are Byzantine in their complexity. Ministers jostled against each other, and Charles played all of them off against each other. The three leading ministers – Rochester, Halifax, and Sunderland – distrusted each other. A loyal son of the Anglican Church, Rochester was a better judge of money than he was of men. He and many other Anglican loyalists distrusted Halifax because Halifax had promoted limitations on a Catholic successor that contradicted their conception of monarchy; and he had sought also to establish an independent position above parties, as the kingdom's leading 'Trimmer'. Sunderland was the greatest political opportunist of the day. He had swung in the direction of exclusion when he thought it might prevail, but now he swung in the direction of an authoritarian crown. Of the three principal ministers, Sunderland was the most adroit politician but also the least committed to Anglican conceptions of law and constitutional propriety. York, Sunderland, and the Duchess of Portsmouth, the dominant mistress, came together as a working triumvirate. The team up was an odd one for James: his new political partner Sunderland had opposed his succession, while Sunderland's rivals, Rochester (James's brother-in-law through his first marriage) and Halifax, had worked to salvage it. But none of these three, or the three together, ever completely dominated the wily king.

In contrast to Rochester and Halifax, Sunderland also turned his back upon a Protestant foreign policy, thereby reinforcing Charles's own preferences. Already committed to Louis XIV through multiple secret arrangements, Charles now fell out with his nephew William of Orange, whom he blamed for sheltering growing communities of English and Scottish enemies of his regime. The Dutch were also at odds with the Danes. When France backed up the Danes, Charles – with Sunderland's assistance – showed his hand by accepting a proposal for the marriage of the Danish king's brother to the younger daughter of the Duke of York, the Princess Anne. Remaining indifferent to French pressure on the Spanish Netherlands, Charles kept to the sidelines when Spain (with Dutch support) declared a defensive war against France. Charles enjoyed his new solvency and was not about to risk it by getting involved either in a war or in the parliamentary session that war financing would entail. As Sunderland rose on Charles's French proclivities, Halifax – who was both pro-Dutch and a parliamentarian at heart – fell. When Halifax insisted in early 1684 that the Triennial Act would soon require a parliamentary session, whether Charles wanted one or not, he again put himself on the wrong side of the king's political agenda.

By then it was clear that York and Sunderland had achieved dominance. James resumed all the responsibilities of lord high admiral, the office from which he had resigned a decade earlier because of his failure to comply with the first Test Act. As James's star reascended, persecution of Catholics ceased, and some Popish Plot era prisoners were finally released. One sign of Sunderland's influence was the 1683 appointment of his protégé, Sir George Jeffreys, to the vacant place of chief justice of the Court of King's Bench. Jeffreys's opportunism, ruthlessness, and disregard for principle surpassed even that of his mentor. The following spring, Sunderland's associate Godolphin, another 'court artist', joined him as the other secretary of state. When Rochester's reputation was damaged by charges of impropriety in his revenue collection, Sunderland further advanced his position by getting Godolphin into the Treasury. Rochester remained at court as lord president of the Privy Council, and Halifax hung on thanks to Charles's pleasure in his wit. Still, Sunderland briefly enjoyed the kind of premiership in Charles's counsels formerly enjoyed only by Clarendon and Danby, the latter of whom was one of those released from the Tower in 1684.[14]

The authoritarian outlook of Sunderland had seemingly trumped the Anglicanism of Rochester and the constitutionalism of Halifax. We will never know how Charles's English regime might have functioned thereafter, however, for he died suddenly in February 1685, most likely of kidney disease. Most historians have argued that, by the time of his death, Charles had succeeded in resettling the kingdom on a more permanent and authoritarian foundation. The Whigs had collapsed politically after the failures of their parliamentary and extra-parliamentary programmes. JPs, magistrates, and militias kept dissenters on the run. The remodelling of borough charters was eradicating Whigs and nonconformists from local government. The ministry's reprisals for Whig plotting had 'crushed' what was left of the movement to reform the church and to advance 'parliamentary government'. Political institutions, both at the centre and in the localities, were as firmly in royalist hands as they had been in the early 1660s; and the crown had seemingly mastered public opinion. The royalist holidays of

30 January and 29 May were vigorously celebrated, while the Whig holidays of 5 and 17 November were discouraged.[15]

Yet against these signs of Charles's final success in England must be set others that suggest the issues of the Restoration Crisis continued to disturb the body politic, at least beneath the surface. Some dissenters persisted in illegal worship despite the harshest persecution of Protestants since the Reformation. Such coercion of dissent had been repeatedly attempted during Charles's reign; and coercion had not only repeatedly failed, but it had also regularly engendered protest and even resistance. Reformed and sectarian perspectives were as rooted in the experiences and language of the English Reformation as Anglican principles; and they could not easily be suppressed. Neither could the public sphere be cleansed of Whig ideas. Talk continued that the Rye House Plot was a government contrivance, for instance; and some Whig publications continued to attract attention. The surrender of charters throughout the country was proceeding despite much anxiety and some opposition. Yet every purge of the localities since the 1650s had miscarried; and many who had once been proscribed from participation or leadership had found ways to overcome such proscription. The rumours that continued to suggest that a parliament would be called also expressed a deep-seated Country hope that Charles would actually summon one. The Whigs had claimed to represent Country attitudes in their concern about the succession; but many Tories could also claim Country precedents for their attachment to law and constitutional order. The crown could, therefore, not easily ignore Country expectations about parliament and property.

Charles's resettlement of church and state also rested upon a loyalist reaction against the Whigs and their employment of parliament against the crown, but such reactions had limited staying power. The Cavalier reaction of 1660 and the anti-popish reaction of 1678–9 had been equally powerful, but each had eventually lost its momentum, as reactions tend to do. By 1684, the Tory reaction had been underway for a few years; and some evidence suggests that it was beginning to lose steam. Moreover, loyalism had largely flourished by energizing Anglican opinion rather than by converting Whigs.[16] Finally, Charles's reluctance to part completely either with Rochester and his Anglican legalism, or with Halifax and his balanced constitutionalism, in preference to Sunderland's 'continental ideal' of monarchy,[17] suggests that he too was still finding his way. Ever the pragmatist, Charles clearly desired settlement; and he had adopted some heavy-handed methods to achieve it. But his methods ran the risk of provoking a new reaction, just as had those of Danby and those of Shaftesbury. The potential for a lasting settlement was clearly present for Charles, as it always had been; but methods that could be construed as 'popery and arbitrary government' had so far demonstrated more potential to undermine settlement than to promote it.

James II and the Anglican Establishment, 1685–6

The succession to the throne of the Roman Catholic Duke of York had been the worst nightmare of the Whigs. But James II was not, in fact, the first Catholic on the Restoration British thrones, although few knew it at the time. As Charles II lay dying, he declined to receive communion publicly from his Protestant bishops. Instead, he received the last rites of the Roman church, in private, from a Catholic priest, finally making good on his long intended conversion.

Much has been made of the lack of any noticeable negative public reaction to James's accession. One loyalist courtier expressed astonishment, for instance, 'that so strong a party as had … appeared in parliament to exclude the Duke of York from the crown … should submit to his now coming to it with so great deference and submission.' Several circumstances contributed to the smooth transition between reigns, including Charles's removal of exclusionists from corporations and commissions of peace throughout England. Since the politicians and the populace were also taken by surprise by Charles's unexpected death, James was able to turn public shock and sympathy in his favour. To the element of surprise, as well as to the conventional respect for a new monarch, Whigs and dissenters added circumspection. Their painful experiences in 1683–5 hardly encouraged any expression of opposition. Moreover, they hoped that, given James's age of 51, he would rule only briefly before being succeeded by his Anglican daughter Mary, wife of William of Orange, now the nominal leader of Western European Protestantism. For his part, James was also a model of princely decorum. He immediately informed the Privy Council that he would 'defend and support' the established Protestant church and that he would uphold the 'laws of England'

and 'never invade any man's property'. To this he added that parliament would be summoned soon. Little wonder that loyalist magistrates and crowds acclaimed James's accession throughout his kingdoms.[18]

James's personality and outlook have been difficult to disentangle from the negative Whig judgements that have for so long been incorporated into historical writing. The new king could certainly act astutely, as his opening political moves suggest. Still, James was not as sharp mentally as his brother, and he lacked Charles's broad intellectual interests. Less willing to delegate and more determined to take the initiative in managing the government, he was more conscientious about the responsibilities of kingship. On the other hand, he was also less pragmatic and more stubborn in responding to developing situations. His conversion to Catholicism had intensified his piety. It also intensified his devotion to his Catholic wife, the same Mary Beatrice of Modena whose arrival had once outraged Country politicians, without diminishing his ardour for his Protestant mistress, Catherine Sedley. This personal tension contradicted James's bent towards tidiness, which also found expression in an aversion to his brother's extravagance and in his devotion to discipline and detail. After creating Sedley Countess of Dorchester in 1686, James packed her off to Ireland with a large pension, hoping thereby to simplify his life.

Above all, James was persuaded that he had come to the throne providentially: divine favour had overcome the obstacles his enemies had attempted to throw in his way. Persuaded that God was on his side, James acted boldly, and sometimes rashly, in ways that others could easily construe as inclining towards authoritarianism or 'arbitrary government'. He did have a high sense of his powers as monarch, and he expected his subjects to show the same respect for his authority as he showed for their rights and liberties. From the beginning of his reign, for instance, he collected the customs and excise duties that parliament had authorized for Charles, thereby deliberately asserting the primacy of his prerogative. Despite his assurances to Anglican leaders, moreover, he intended to release his fellow Roman Catholics from all civil disabilities and to encourage Catholicism as a visible faith that could compete with Anglicanism. Also expecting a brief reign, given his age, and expecting no further children from Mary Beatrice, James hoped to secure improvements in the status of Catholics that could not be reversed at the succession of the Protestant Mary. He had, therefore, become an advocate of liberty for conscience and an opponent of penal laws about religion. When he had acted to coerce religious minorities, as in Scotland, he was motivated primarily by his fear that dissenting defiance of law would lead to rebellion. His greatest shortcoming was an inability to understand that the attachment of many of his subjects to Protestantism expressed a religious devotion (rather than merely a political posture) as strong as his own. He always thought that, given a free choice and sufficient Catholic priests, his most dutiful subjects would follow him into the Roman fold.

James's succession also terminated the political alliance in which he had worked with Sunderland and Portsmouth. As the tripartite ministerial rivalry of Halifax, Rochester, and Sunderland re-emerged, James turned instinctively to his brother-in-law, who was as much the natural leader of Anglicanism at the beginning of James's reign as Clarendon had been at the beginning of Charles's reign. Rochester became lord high treasurer and the dominant figure in the government. Halifax hung on as leader of the Privy Council, acceptable not because of his onetime advocacy of limitations, but rather because his known devotion to parliamentary government gave the ministry a useful political complexion. James also appreciated Sunderland's political skills, but he had become somewhat distrustful of a minister who could so easily turn from exclusion to the prerogative. James kept him on as secretary of state, more or less on approval, while also placing him in charge of preparations for parliament. Disagreements among these ministers, with their quite different approaches to domestic issues, were inevitable. Moreover, unlike Sunderland, who admired Louis XIV, Rochester and Halifax preferred good relations with William of Orange and the Netherlands.[19]

The parliamentary election that occurred in March and April 1685 was an overwhelming Tory triumph. Only 57 Whigs were elected to a House of Commons of over 500 members, and few of the Whig MPs were dissenters. No seventeenth-century English government ever intervened so strongly or so successfully in a parliamentary election as that of James II in 1685. Sunderland wrote letter after letter to county gentry and borough magnates to encourage the choice of men well disposed to the government. Other courtiers sought to manage constituencies where they enjoyed influence. In the localities, Tory gentry and clergy acted to secure the election of those whose loyalty to hereditary succession and the church had been evident throughout the Restoration Crisis. In fact, the government of Charles II had been preparing for this election since 1682. The selection of MPs was strongly influenced by the installation of local Tory regimes in the remodelling of borough governments and by Charles's overhaul of county government. Local choices were similarly influenced by the government's long-term propaganda effort to paint Whigs and dissenters in the colours of civil war republicanism, a representation that gained greater credibility after the Rye House Plot. Indeed, electors responded in 1685 as strongly to this plot as they had to the Popish Plot in 1679. Outcomes were also influenced by the disinclination of some leading Whigs to stand for election, as well as by the disengagement of some Whig electors from a process with a foregone conclusion.

Nevertheless, signs of Whig life in the parliamentary election of 1685 ought not to be ignored. Contests took place for 100 seats, almost as many as in the second parliamentary election of 1679. Whig and dissenting energy was apparent in such towns as Bridgwater, Chichester, Huntington, and Taunton. Whig candidates in Cheshire were outpolled only through the manoeuvres of the loyalist sheriff and the presence of the militia: disappointed Whig electors retaliated by breaking Tory windows and shouting 'down with the clergy, down with the bishops.' In Bedfordshire, which had been represented in the parliaments of 1679–81 by the executed William, Lord Russell, Tories moved in procession to the election with decapitated cocks in disdain for Russell's brother Edward, who stood for his seat. After apparently prevailing in a show of hands, Edward Russell lost in a poll; but a moderate Whig nevertheless claimed one of the seats. Similarly, in Buckinghamshire, the Whigs secured one of the county seats, both of the Buckingham borough seats, and one of the Wendover seats. The last named was taken by Richard Hampden, an exclusionist whose son John Hampden was still imprisoned for his alleged part in the Rye House plotting.[20]

The contemporary Whig historian Gilbert Burnet ridiculed the members of the 1685 Commons as intemperate and obscure men who proved compliant to the court's every wish. Many of the members were new to parliament: over half had never sat before, and over half never would again. But Burnet's characterization of them is nevertheless inaccurate. The French ambassador was closer to the truth when he warned Louis XIV that the new MPs might 'easily become factious. They have an insurmountable hostility to the Catholic religion, and the greater part are hostile to France.' The House was as full of staunch Anglican gentry as the early sessions of the Cavalier Parliament. Whether their strong attachment to the Protestant establishment could be reconciled with their strong attachment to a monarch who happened to be Catholic remained uncertain. As county leaders, they preferred the customary autonomy of local governors to any centralized direction of local affairs. They preferred local militias to a standing army and prudent royal financial management to any additional taxation.

Tension between James and some Anglican leaders had already cropped up before parliament assembled on 19 May. Within a month of his accession, for instance, James was complaining to Archbishop Sancroft about the anti-Catholic preaching of some clergy. Halifax expressed legal concerns when James moved to stop prosecutions of Catholics under the penal laws and freed those imprisoned for violating them. Others were concerned about James's desire to repeal the Habeas Corpus Act of 1679. When James invited his ministers to accompany him to Easter mass, Rochester fled to his country home rather than compromise his Anglican religion. When James was crowned on 23 April, he omitted the Protestant communion, 'to the great sorrow of the people'; and the celebration of the coronation at Oxford was marred somewhat by a strongly anti-Catholic sermon at St. Mary's parish church.[21]

The first six-weeks' session of James's parliament was dominated by money and by rebellions. In his opening speech, James communicated the news that the Earl of Argyll had landed with a small force in the Western Islands of Scotland. Involved both in the Rye House plotting and in secretive discussions of English and Scottish exiles in the Netherlands, Argyll hoped his Campbell clansmen and the Lowland Presbyterians would flock to his standard. Instead, his rebellion and his life were both quickly over. Whether in response to this rebellion, or in response to James's warning against any effort to keep him on a short financial leash, parliament quickly approved James's collection of the same ordinary revenues enjoyed by Charles. But even as they moved to settle James's income, some MPs showed concern about the security of their church and of parliament. A grand committee of the Commons recommended an address to the crown to enforce the laws against Catholics and Protestant nonconformists. The king's angry response, however, turned the house towards a substitute motion to 'entirely rely' upon James's promise to support the established church. Still, Sir Edward Seymour, a former speaker of the Commons and a strong opponent of exclusion, declared in debate that parliamentary independence had been eroded by the rechartering of the boroughs and by the government's intervention in the selection of MPs.

James was nevertheless well on the way to securing additional revenues, to be raised from various impositions on trade, when news arrived of a far more serious rebellion. The Duke of Monmouth had sailed from the Netherlands and landed on 11 June at Lyme, in Dorset. He had planned a revolt in the West Country to coincide with Argyll's effort in Scotland. As Monmouth's rebellion developed, parliament continued to sit, attainting him for treason, and also voting James several hundred thousand pounds in additional short-term revenues. Before they were adjourned in early July, the MPs had nevertheless irritated James once more. A bill to broaden the definition of treason to include 'anything said to disparage the king's person or government' contained an exception for preaching against Catholicism. James preferred to adjourn parliament rather than to consider such a measure.[22]

Monmouth's rebellion ended with his crushing defeat at Sedgemoor, a few days after the parliamentary session ended, and with his execution in London on 15 July. But historians have generally been too quick to dismiss the rebellion as an ignominious failure. Charles's son was funded by some of the principal Whig exiles in the Netherlands, including wealthy London merchants; and veterans of the Rye House plotting accompanied him to Lyme. He chose to land in the West Country because of the support he had achieved there during the Restoration Crisis. His manifesto sounded all the right notes to arouse Whigs and dissenters throughout the country; and he had reason to expect sympathetic risings in the North and in London. Condemning the new borough charters, he called for a repeal of the Corporation Act, full civil and religious liberties for Protestant dissenters, the independence of the judiciary, annual parliaments, and a return of London's historic charter. Monmouth dismissed James as a tyrant who had burnt London, killed Sir Edmund Berry Godfrey, and probably poisoned Charles.

He initially left the future disposition of the crown to parliament, in deference to the republicans among his supporters; but he eventually claimed the throne.

The rebel duke quickly assembled a small force of some 3000, recruiting yeomen and young craftsmen from the towns of Dorset and Somerset, and putting to flight the local militias sent out against him. But the western Whig gentry, chastened by the events of 1681–5, remained aloof, leaving this the last 'popular rebellion' against the English crown. As James deployed royal troops, fears spread in London of a parallel rising 'of the factious party' there. Monmouth's expectations of local revolts elsewhere failed to materialize, however. Both he and his untrained troops were also discouraged by the news of Argyll's failure and by their own inability to take either Bristol or Bath. In one last effort to open the road to London, Monmouth staged a surprise night assault on the main body of royal troops at Sedgemoor. The royalist commander learnt of the attack just in time and was aided by a well-situated ditch that stopped the rebel advance. The attack failed, and the duke's forces retreated in disorder with great losses. Monmouth was eventually found hiding in the woods. He had, however, shown some of the same abilities as a commander that he had displayed in Scotland in 1679. James thought 'he had not made one false step'. The same courtier who had crowed about James's quiet succession thought that '*the disaffected were so numerous*', that, had Monmouth 'got the day ... they would have risen in other parts of England, to the very hazard of the crown.'[23]

Even in failure, Monmouth's rebellion had momentous consequences. The retribution exacted on his followers was severe. In September 1685, some 1300 of them were tried in the western counties. Baron Jeffreys, who had recently been elevated to the peerage and was shortly to become lord chancellor, presided over the 'bloody assizes', as they were dubbed in Whig polemic and history. The trials were hasty, and the results in little doubt, as Jeffreys exhibited his penchant for hectoring witnesses and juries. Many rebels pleaded guilty to the charges against them, hoping thereby to gain clemency. As many as 250 of them were nevertheless executed: James withheld pardons, regarding rebellion as the worst of sins against God and king. One of the first to die was the aged widow of a regicide who had given shelter to fleeing rebels. The public burning in London of Elizabeth Gaunt, a Baptist widow who had sheltered another rebel, ignited memories of the Protestant burnings of Mary I and was also the last such execution of a woman in English history. In order to deter future resistance, the quartered remains of the executed were dispersed throughout Dorset and Somerset for public display in the towns and villages from which they had come. Most of the remainder of those convicted were transported to the West Indies, some of them having been bought and sold like slaves prior to their departure.[24]

The treatment of Monmouth's followers was mostly in accordance with contemporary standards of justice and with the ordinary treatment of rebels. However, some contemporaries did not judge it by either of those measures. Just after the conclusion of the western assizes, English opinion was strongly impacted by the news of Louis XIV's revocation of the last shred of toleration for Protestants in France. Within months, England would provide refuge for thousands of Huguenots fleeing from state persecution. Although James sought to distance himself from Louis's actions, France nevertheless provided the context in which Protestant rebels could, in Whig and dissenting minds at least, be seen as victims of international Catholic cruelty. Moreover, many of James's leading Anglican Tory subjects were just as disturbed as Whigs and dissenters by another consequence of Monmouth's rebellion.

In light of the rebellion, James had begun an expansion of the English army. By the time parliament met again in November 1685, he had more than doubled it. By the end of the year, it numbered almost 20,000 men. In his opening speech to the houses, James pointed out the military lessons of the recent rebellions, stating that 'the militia … is not sufficient for such occasions; and … there is nothing but a good force of well-disciplined troops … that can defend us.' That message was hard for many to swallow, given widespread gentry hostility to a standing army. It was made even more difficult to accept because of James's employment of nearly a hundred Catholic officers to whom he provided dispensations from the 1673 Test Act. Moreover, when Halifax argued that retaining these officers violated the law, and refused also to support a repeal of the Test and Habeas Corpus Acts, James dismissed him. Suspecting that others might raise the same objections to Catholic officers whom he trusted, James told his parliament point blank that 'I will neither expose them to disgrace, nor myself to the want of them.' Indeed, he asked for an additional supply to maintain the enlarged army he had created.

James's actions and his words raised a storm of Country protests from Anglican MPs who wanted nothing more than to remain loyal to the monarchy. When the Commons turned to James's request for additional supply, the hall rang with speeches from 'country gentlemen' in defence of the county militias and in favour of a bill to improve their effectiveness. They were prepared to vote James additional revenue, but not for the sake of his army. The loyalist MP Sir Thomas Clarges, who was connected both to Halifax and to Rochester, and who had opposed exclusion, reminded the house that one of the strongest arguments of the exclusionists had been that a Catholic prince would create a Catholic army to intimidate his Protestant subjects. James's dispensations from the Test Act were a monumental 'breach of our liberties', according to him; and such dispensations might defeat the intention of the act by opening the power and influence of military and civil offices to the Catholic minority. Sir Edward Seymour agreed that if the dispensations for Catholic officers were accepted, 'it is dispensing with all the laws at once.' Over the objections of 'the court party', determined MPs moved quickly from denouncing a standing army to addressing James about the dispensations. They pointed out that Catholics could not 'by law' be employed in the army, and they argued that only an act of parliament could remove their ineligibility to serve. When the address was presented, James responded, 'with great warmth', that 'he did not expect' such behaviour from loyalist MPs. When his response was read in the Commons, it was followed by a 'profound silence', finally broken by one intemperate speaker, who barked that 'Englishmen ... are not ... frightened out of our duty by a few high words.' [25]

The breach that was opening between the king and Anglican opinion was as evident in the House of Lords. There, the king personally listened to denunciations of his dispensations from several peers and from Henry Compton, Bishop of London, whose speech prompted all the bishops present to rise in agreement. A mere two weeks after opening parliament, James prorogued it, forever as it proved; and he dismissed Compton from the Privy Council. He would probably have encountered Anglican objections even if he had only sought to move MPs in the direction of toleration for Catholics. His objective was not simply toleration, however, but rather the promotion of full civil rights for Catholics, as his dispensations for Catholic officers indicated. That was an objective contrary to a principal premise of the Restoration settlement, namely that a single Protestant faith should bind the officers of church and state together in a mutually supportive manner.

The collapse of the rapport between James and his Anglican parliament left Rochester exposed in his continuing struggle for ministerial dominance with Sunderland, who was more than willing to cooperate with the king's purposes. When James added the presidency of the Privy Council to Sunderland's offices in December 1685, he was clearly indicating a shift in Sunderland's direction. It took an entire year for Sunderland to regain the ascendancy he had enjoyed at Charles's death, however, and for the breach between James and the Anglicans to harden to the point where Rochester's service became untenable. In the meantime, the steady increase of James's ordinary revenues, especially those derived from trade, as well as the additional supply the 1685 parliament had provided, gave him an unheard of annual revenue of some £2 million.[26] With this financial freedom came considerable freedom of political action as well. James kept his options open by proroguing parliament repeatedly for short intervals, but he had no financial need for another session. With or without parliament, he was determined to proceed with his release of Roman Catholics from their civil disabilities.

In February 1686, after sounding out the 12 judges of the principal common law courts about the legality of his dispensations, James replaced two of the five judges who considered them illegal. Another four judges were replaced in April, just as the case of Godden *v.* Hales came before them. The government had designed the case as a trial of James's power to dispense from the 1673 Test Act. Sir Edward Hales had retained a military commission after converting to Roman Catholicism. He had also received one of James's dispensations, the legality of which was challenged, at the instigation of the government, by his coachman, Arthur Godden. In June, 11 of the 12 high court judges found for Hales and for the crown's dispensations. In July, James further set aside the Test Act by bringing four Roman Catholic peers onto the Privy Council. He thereby strengthened Sunderland's position against Rochester and also fulfilled the predictions of some MPs that his disregard for the Test Act would open civil offices to Catholic infiltration. By October 1686, a committee of the Privy Council was charged with a review of the commissions of peace throughout the kingdom, with the intent of eliminating Anglicans who would not agree to the king's understanding of his prerogative and to his religious agenda. Two hundred and fifty JPs were purged over the winter of 1686–7. The 500 new JPs added to the commissions included 300 Catholics. James also acted to encourage Catholic conversions among his courtiers and ministers.

Rochester was further weakened by the deterioration of détente with Holland, which he had promoted, and by tensions between James and the Anglican bishops. Relations between James and William of Orange had been strengthened, at the time of Monmouth's rebellion, when William temporarily returned the Anglo-Dutch brigade that had served in the Netherlands since the reign of Elizabeth.[27] All current accords between England and the Dutch Republic were publicly renewed in August 1685. Still, James was unwilling to employ his military resources in any serious effort to protect the Spanish Netherlands (and thereby the Dutch Republic) against Louis's continuing pressure. James's simultaneous expansion of both his army and his navy also eventually aroused William's suspicions. For his part, James was irritated by what he perceived as William's support for the growing body of English and Scottish opponents of his regime in the Netherlands.

Tensions between the king and the Anglican establishment came to a head in June 1686 when London Bishop Henry Compton declined to discipline a clergyman whose anti-Catholic preaching had offended the king. As supreme governor of the state church, James responded to this rebuff by creating a commission for ecclesiastical causes to exercise his disciplinary authority over the church, in place of the bishops. Rochester protested the creation of the commission. When he realized that James's mind was not to be altered, however, he accepted appointment as one of the commissioners in hopes of moderating the new body's actions. But among the commission's first decisions was a suspension of Henry Compton as bishop. The move was 'universally resented', according to Evelyn; and it raised the spectre of Archbishop Laud's pre-1640 Court of High Commission. Headed by Baron Jeffreys, the commission continued to restrain anti-Catholic preaching thereafter and to exercise a general supervisory power over the church.

In late 1686, James made clear to Rochester that only his conversion to Catholicism would preserve his place in the government. The earl was dismissed in January 1687 after declining to abandon

his faith. Sunderland had not yet publicly converted, but the secretary of state now commanded James's ministry and gave the king
numerous signs of his willingness to cooperate with the advancement of Roman Catholicism. The purging of staunch Anglicans
from local and central offices enabled Sunderland to promote
men whose loyalty he expected. James also hoped that the dismissal of Rochester and the purging of Anglican office holders
would provide sufficient warning of his resolve to move parliament
to repeal the Test Acts entirely. The king now turned even more
directly towards Anglican MPs and courtiers and began interviewing them, one by one, in hopes of gaining their agreement. These
'closetings' did not secure the compliance James desired, however,
while leading Anglicans were scarcely encouraged by the king's
strong-armed tactics.[28]

Ireland, Scotland, and the Colonies, 1683–7

James II was as determined to assert his authority in his other
kingdoms and dominions as he was in England. Ireland had been
relatively tranquil in the years of the Popish Plot and the Restoration Crisis, despite the grievances of its Catholic majority and the
fears of its Protestant minority. That would change dramatically
under James. He had no desire to alter the subordinate status of
his western kingdom, and he was as contemptuous of the Gaelic
Irish as most other Englishmen. Yet James had every intention of
rehabilitating the leading Old English Roman Catholic propertied
families, with land transfers if necessary, and of integrating Catholics into Irish civil and military life.

As James regained his political visibility in the last years of his
brother's reign, he allied with others who sought to terminate the
lord lieutenancy of the Duke of Ormond. Ironically, Ormond was
distrusted by the Episcopalian interest in Ireland for his leniency
towards Protestant dissenters, while James perceived him as too
strongly aligned with that same interest to be helpful in the relief
of Catholics. James was confirmed in this view by his old Irish Catholic friend Richard Talbot, brother to the late Catholic Archbishop
of Dublin, who had died in Ormond's custody. An intemperate
and ambitious man, Talbot had been instrumental in securing revisions to the Irish land settlement in favour of Catholics in the early
1660s; and he had aroused Irish Protestant and English Country

fears when he pressed for further adjustments in landholding in the early 1670s. As a survivor of Cromwell's massacre at Drogheda, he burnt with a passion to right the wrongs inflicted upon Catholic Ireland since 1641. He even dreamt of reachieving Irish independence, fearing that James's reign would prove but a brief interlude in a succession of Protestant monarchs hostile to Irish Catholics.

Before his death, Charles announced his intention to remove Ormond as lord lieutenant and to replace him with Rochester, whom Sunderland was trying to get out of the way at Westminster. Charles's death left Rochester in England, however, where James wanted him at the Treasury; and it left Ireland without a viceroy, since Ormond's commission expired with the king's demise. As two Irish lord justices assumed temporary administration of the kingdom, Talbot arrived as a regimental commander in the Irish army with one of the first military commissions given by James. Preoccupied with parliaments and with rebellions in his other kingdoms, James did not appoint a new lord lieutenant until September 1685, turning then to Henry Hyde, the second Earl of Clarendon and the elder brother of Rochester. By the time Clarendon arrived in Dublin in early 1686, Talbot, who had by then been created Earl of Tyrconnell, had wrested control of the Irish army away from the lord justices. Exploiting anxiety about the 1685 rebellions as well as James's distrust of militias and of the Ulster Presbyterians, Tyrconnell also persuaded the king that arms were too widely dispersed among Irish Protestants. The Protestant-dominated local militias were therefore disarmed as a precautionary measure, as were numerous Protestant landowners. Some Protestant soldiers were purged from the army. Eight hundred Roman Catholics were recruited to take their places, making the army about 10 per cent Catholic by the end of the year.

Clarendon was as staunch a defender of the Episcopalian interest in Ireland as his brother was in England. He was immediately at odds with Tyrconnell, who coveted the Irish viceroyalty for himself. Clarendon fought a rearguard action, however., His only real accomplishment was that of maintaining James's Irish revenues. His influence with the king declined with that of Rochester, while his rival took advantage of James's natural sympathy for Irish Catholics. Making Tyrconnell lieutenant general of the army, James stripped Clarendon early on of the military responsibilities usually associated with the lord lieutenancy. Tyrconnell also persuaded the king to appoint one Catholic judge to each of the three central Irish law courts. He further secured James's agreement to a relaxation of all restraints upon Catholic office holding, a decision followed by the appointment of 11 Catholics to the Irish Privy Council.

The following year, Tyrconnell continued his purge of Protestants from the Irish army, dismissing entire companies of officers and soldiers to make way for Catholics. By the end of 1686, two-thirds of the soldiery were Catholic, many of them Gaelic. So were two-fifths of the commissioned officers, some of them not only from old landed Catholic families but also French-trained and French-inclined. Dismissed Protestant troops rioted in Dublin to no avail. The military balance between Protestants and Catholics that Ormond found so reassuring during the Popish Plot had proven fragile indeed. 'I believe it was never yet known, that the sword and the administration of justice were put into the hands of a conquered people,' complained the English Clarendon. Although James probably did not originally intend to use this Catholic army outside Ireland, Gilbert Burnet and other contemporaries believed it was designed to assist him in England, should he need it.[29]

More than the military balance was at stake in Ireland, however. The Irish Catholic hierarchy and clergy quickly became as visible and as 'established' as they had been since the Reformation, and the weaknesses of the Protestant Church of Ireland became more apparent than ever. Mass was publicly celebrated in Dublin for the first time in 40 years. James kept vacancies in the Protestant episcopate empty in order to divert church revenues towards salaries for the Catholic bishops. The king himself assumed the right of appointing to vacancies in the Catholic hierarchy, and the pope quietly obliged him. Dominicans, Franciscans, and Jesuits opened new schools for the Catholic youth; and a Benedictine convent was established in Dublin. Catholic crowds extinguished Protestant bonfires in the Irish capital on holidays such as 5 November. The Catholic clergy hoped that lands and buildings that had been at the centre of Protestant ministry for 150 years would soon be in their hands.

Given Ireland's violent history, fears spread among Protestants that their properties and lands were no longer secure, while a rash of robberies and assaults suggested a return to the conditions of 1641. Tensions between Catholic soldiers and Protestant inhabitants were evident in many localities. The Protestant response was nevertheless largely passive. The Episcopal establishment was as committed to the hereditary succession and to non-resistance as the Church of England. Flight was a more common remedy than opposition for merchants and landowners who worried about their goods and lands, and who began drawing in their wealth. Some departed for England, and Clarendon's secretary reported that 'those who can fly out of the country, either to Pennsylvania [just established], Virginia, or other places'. As the kingdom's formerly flourishing trade plummeted, rumours spread that Tyrconnell would act to prevent more Protestants from fleeing, with or without their assets, as Louis XIV had done in France.[30]

Clarendon sought to reassure Protestant landowners by persuading James to confirm current titles upon the payment of fees into a fund to relieve former Catholic owners. This scheme got nowhere, however., Dispossessed Old English Catholics wanted their lands, not Protestant money; and Tyrconnell was pledged to their cause. In England, Sunderland and James's Catholic peers and advisers feared Tyrconnell was pushing Irish matters too fast and sought to restrain him. Yet James dismissed Clarendon in November 1686 and replaced him with Tyrconnell, 'to the astonishment of all sober men, and to the evident ruin of the Protestants in that kingdom', thought Evelyn.[31] The first Roman Catholic governor of Ireland since the Reformation, Tyrconnell was given the lesser title of lord deputy. James declined to offer Protestants a reassuring proclamation about the Irish land settlement to accompany the appointment. While he thereby kept his options open, he further alarmed landowners in Ireland, and in England as well. Some Catholic tenants discontinued paying rents to their Protestant landlords and tithes to the established Protestant clergy.

The new lord deputy quickly carried out a systematic transfer of power to Ireland's Catholics under the auspices of an Irish indulgence for their benefit that was also extended to Protestant dissenters. The recreation of the army as a Catholic force was completed, and it was expanded to a total of 10,000 men. Major administrative positions like the offices of lord chancellor and attorney general were given to Catholics. Catholics gained a majority of places on the Irish Privy Council and in the judiciary. With only one exception, the county sheriffs were replaced with Catholics, and Catholics took over the county commissions of peace. The charters of major Irish parliamentary boroughs, starting with

Dublin, were challenged in the courts. The process of remodelling the boroughs, which had previously been accomplished in England for the benefit of Anglicans, was now implemented in Ireland for the benefit of Catholics. They took about two-thirds of the offices in most towns. Places as magistrates and burgesses were also opened to Protestant dissenters, including Quakers, in the hope of gaining their cooperation against the Episcopalian interest. Politically ousted Protestant gentry and merchants also believed that a social revolution was in process, pointing to the lesser status and wealth of those who replaced them. Catholic office holders were, however, more often merchants, lawyers, and substantial tradesmen than former employees and servants of the Protestant elite.

Old English Catholic families in Ireland were euphoric about these changes in their fortunes: they 'talk of nothing now but … bringing the English [Protestants] under their subjection' recorded one observer. The Gaelic Irish dreamt of expelling the English entirely. 'Behold … the Gael in arms every one of them, they have powder and guns, hold the castles and fortresses; the Presbyterians, lo, have been overthrown,' or so boasted one Catholic poet. But struck with 'anxiety and terror', many Protestants thought they had succumbed to the regime of 'Turk-conel'.[32]

Tyrconnell's long-term hope was that an Irish parliament elected by Catholic-dominated localities would initiate a wholescale revision of the 1662 Act of Settlement, the basis of the Protestant landed ascendancy. As his Catholic attorney general advised him, nothing could more support the Roman faith in Ireland, 'but to make Catholics there considerable in their fortunes, as they are considerable in their number'. Although the king himself became uneasy about his Irish deputy's agenda, fearing that it might produce disorder, he agreed in principle to a modification of the land settlement and to a meeting of the Irish parliament to consider one. Tyrconnell was, in reality, more the master of Ireland than the king was; but James saw only that, in at least one of his kingdoms, his co-religionists had regained much of what they had lost since the Reformation. Indeed, by 1687, Protestant England faced a renascent Catholic kingdom in the west; and the foundations of Irish Restoration society, government, and religion had been overturned. The rapidly growing city of Dublin, with some 60,000 inhabitants, and now the second largest city in the British Isles, appeared to be emerging as a new Catholic capital in a European

Protestant fringe already diminished by Louis XIV's suppression of the Reformed churches of France.[33]

In Scotland, where James ruled as James VII, he assumed authority over a kingdom in which Protestants remained divided against each other, and he sought to turn this situation to the advantage of Catholics. James's initial goal was to reduce the disorder and violence he blamed upon militant Presbyterians. That disorder had continued in the final year of Charles's reign, as the government imposed the new Test Act oath on the recalcitrant, and as the Cameronians or United Societies issued a new *Apologetical Declaration* in justification of their resistance. The Scottish council responded by ordering the immediate execution of any who declined to repudiate the *Declaration*, by removing some indulged Presbyterian clergy from their pulpits, and by redoubling its efforts to impose the oath. In what became known in Presbyterian martyrology as the 'killing time', thousands were fined, imprisoned, and transported for their refusal to take an oath that, in their minds, enslaved the church to the state and undermined the Reformation. The Southwest was placed under martial law again, and privy councillors acted there as judges in extraordinary tribunals. The government's procedures severely strained Scottish law. Some who refused to renounce the *Declaration* were summarily executed, but dissenters who had maintained their distance from the Cameronians were actually the chief victims. Many deaths were popularly attributed to the rough methods of James's friend, John Graham of Claverhouse. Among the hundred or so executions were those of the 'Wigtown martyrs', two women – one a teenager – who were tied to stakes in Wigtown Bay and left to drown in the rising tide.[34]

James had three objectives in his first Scottish parliament, which met in April 1685. He wanted to secure a reassertion of the 1681 legislative declarations about royal authority, to settle his Scottish revenue, and to criminalize further any religious behaviour that defied the state. Members were seemingly happy to respond to the lead of James's parliamentary commissioner, the Duke of Queensberry; and they quickly assigned excise duties to the crown in perpetuity. They readily acknowledged the 'sacred, supreme, and absolute power' of James as the last in an 'uninterrupted line of one hundred and eleven kings' provided to the Scots by God. They also adopted a new act imposing the death penalty for attendance at field conventicles. Another act provided the same penalty for witnesses who declined to testify against suspected field conventiclers, and a third act extended the obligation to take the Test Act oath to additional elements of the population. Allegiance to the historic Covenants was declared treasonous. Still, neither the condemnation of 'all preceding rebellions' nor James's placing of the militia in readiness deterred Argyll from attempting to mount a national rebellion. That unhappy lord departed the Netherlands, shortly after the session began, with three ships and 300 men.

On the face of it, Argyll's rebellion should have caused James more trouble than it did. Both Argyll's name and his message could have aroused Scotland's Covenanters for a great crusade on behalf of reformation. But Argyll, who had little actual military experience, frittered away his chances. He landed first in the Orkneys before establishing a base in Argyllshire, giving the government plenty of time to dispatch troops against him. His windy, wordy declaration was a catalogue of the misdeeds of Charles II that had spoilt the Scottish church and state. It only slowly got around to the problems at hand, namely, the succession of a Catholic king and the coercion of Protestant dissenters. Even the call for a rising against James to restore 'the true, reformed protestant religion' and to restore 'all men to their just rights and liberties' was long on rhetoric and short on detail. It failed entirely to mention the Covenants. The Cameronians condemned Argyll's declaration; and most Presbyterians held back, many feeling they had already suffered enough. Only language that could have reunited the fragmented Presbyterian factions might have turned the trick. Argyll was able to recruit far fewer men than had fought at Bothwell Bridge. When he advanced from Argyllshire, his forces disintegrated in their first encounter with royal troops. The harsh treatment of those who followed Argyll, like those who followed Monmouth, was further proof of James's loathing for any who defied the law. Yet like his brother, James had no political quarrel with nonconformists whose dissent did not extend to active defiance of authority in church and state.[35]

Buoyed both by the loyalist spirit of the Scots parliament and by Argyll's abysmal failure, James proceeded to initiate the same programme of Catholic rehabilitation that he was launching in Ireland and would soon accelerate in England. He was assisted in Scotland by his lord chancellor, James Drummond, Earl of Perth and in England, by Perth's brother John, soon made Earl of Melfort, the Scottish secretary of state. Their embrace of Roman Catholicism initiated a small wave of elite conversions, which staunch Protestants regarded as opportunistic. The Drummonds supported James's religious agenda against the Protestant Queensberry, who was allied to Rochester and Clarendon, his English relatives by marriage. As in Ireland, James also placed control of the Scottish army in the hands of Romanists: one Catholic earl became commander in chief; and the Catholic Duke of Gordon was placed in charge of James's forces in the Highlands. Dispensations from the Scottish test were granted to Gordon and to other Catholics to serve as commissioners for the collection of taxes in their shires. The government employed James's ecclesiastical powers under the 1669 Supremacy Act to justify all such departures from the church settlement. As in England, the council also placed pressure upon the Protestant bishops to restrain the anti-Catholic preaching of their clergy, and it disrupted the distribution of anti-Catholic printed literature.

James's programme of advancing Catholicism was handicapped by the relative paucity of Scottish Catholics – only a few thousand in the Lowlands and probably not much more than 2 per cent of the population overall. It was also stymied by the prevalence of anti-Catholicism among Protestants of all stripes. Perth's establishment of a Catholic chapel at Holyrood Palace, the principal royal residence in Edinburgh, provoked a week of rioting early in 1686, just as Laud's 'popish' innovations had prompted rioting in 1637. Students, apprentices, tradesmen, and women interrupted the celebration of mass at Holyrood, destroyed the furnishings of the chapel, attacked Catholic worshippers as 'papist dogs', and broke windows in the homes of Catholic nobles. Some soldiers sent to quell the initial disturbances joined the rioters in subsequent episodes. James took out his frustration upon the Protestant Queensberry, permitting the Catholic Perth and Melfort to gain dominance in the Scottish government. Queensberry was deprived of his positions as parliamentary commissioner, treasurer, and governor of Edinburgh Castle, although he remained on a Treasury commission headed by Perth. The Catholic Gordon was placed in charge of military forces in Edinburgh, and another Catholic convert met James's Scottish parliament again, in April 1686, as high commissioner.[36]

James's second parliamentary session in Scotland was no more successful than his second parliamentary session in England. Just as the regime's harsh measures against Presbyterian dissenters seemed finally to have coerced most Covenanters into submission, James opened a new breach in his northern kingdom. He instructed the lords of the articles to secure the removal of all anti-Catholic penal legislation, thereby placing Catholics on the same civil footing as other subjects. As an inducement to cooperation, James offered free trade between England and Scotland, which he optimistically promised could be achieved 'in a short time'. But many of the usually compliant lords of the articles baulked. Some of them even had trouble with the idea that Catholics, given their allegiance to the Roman pope, could be considered 'subjects'. The bishop of Edinburgh provided a sermon for the opening of the session in which he urged compliance with the king's wishes, in keeping with the doctrine of non-resistance. Most of the rest of the Scottish bishops were unpersuaded, however, as were many other shire and burgh commissioners. They could easily construe what James wanted of them as a demand that they forswear themselves, because they had already taken the oath required since 1681 against 'popish or fanatical' principles. Most members were reluctant to oblige the Catholic king with what they regarded as a weakening of the Protestant state church, believing, as one of them subsequently recollected, that 'the finger of God' directed their opposition. The most that James could get was liberty of conscience for Catholics, with no right of worship outside private homes. Because that was not good enough for him, he first adjourned and then prorogued parliament. He also began dismissing Protestant office holders who had opposed his wishes.

But James had altered the terms of political debate in Scotland, and he had managed to turn his cooperative Scottish parliament into a confrontational one. As he replaced some privy councillors with Catholics, other office holders demonstrated their loyalty to the Church of Scotland by voluntarily relinquishing their positions. They regarded resignation as the only way to avoid direct opposition to a monarch who demanded compliance with measures their consciences condemned. James's efforts to prevent anti-Catholic preaching by the Episcopal clergy were also defied by preachers, and even by bishops. One intrepid divine reportedly preached that he would as soon 'believe the moon to be made of green cheese ... as believe [in] transubstantiation.' In the summer of 1686, a bishop who had spoken against removal of the laws against Catholicism was suspended by Perth, in a move similar to that of the English ecclesiastical commission against the Bishop of London. Another bishop was threatened with suspension, and a third was forbidden to preach. The Archbishop of Glasgow was deprived of his see in January 1687 after apparently arranging the publication of an anti-Catholic sermon by a preacher he had actually been ordered to discipline. Such opposition from men of a loyalist bent convinced James that he could not secure the toleration of his co-religionists without breaking the political and religious establishment.

In September 1686 James employed a Privy Council order to permit Catholics private worship in their homes. He also forbade royal burghs from proceeding with municipal elections so that he could replace numerous local office holders with Catholics and even with a few Presbyterians. He dissolved parliament in October 1686, hoping that new elections from politically altered burghs would produce a more compliant body. Finally, in February 1687, he employed his prerogative to provide, through a Declaration of Indulgence, the toleration that parliament had declined to legislate. In addition to the religious and civil relief it provided for Catholics, the declaration permitted private worship for 'moderate' Presbyterians and public worship for Quakers. Presbyterians who sought to take advantage of this indulgence were required to take a new oath against resistance and to acknowledge James's 'absolute' authority, but few of them were prepared to accept toleration on such terms.

The royal prerogative had not been much of an issue in Scotland since 1681. But James's indulgence made the prerogative an issue by employing it in a way that seemed not only to challenge the Protestant establishment in parliament but also to undermine the Scottish Reformation. Some privy councillors, including the Duke of Hamilton, refused to have anything to do with James's declaration. One Covenanter preacher, safely in Dutch exile thundered that James's manner of rule surpassed 'all the lust, impudence, and insolence of the Roman, Sicilian, [and] Turkish ... tyrants'.[37] A recent historian of James's reign in Scotland agrees that he was trying to turn his absolute authority in theory into an absolute authority in fact. Whether James had successfully resettled the turbulent northern kingdom as his brother's representative in 1680–1 is debatable, but that James as king had now fully unsettled Scotland is beyond dispute. His policies had provoked the hostility of the very Episcopalian elite upon whom the Scottish restoration in church and state was anchored.

James's prerogative also became a general issue for English colonists in North America. They experienced little of his promotion of Catholicism, but many of them became suspicious of his manner of government and downright hostile to his principal administrators. James well understood the importance of the Southern and Caribbean colonies, especially of Virginia and Barbados, in the expanding English trade in sugar, tobacco, and other tropical crops. As governor and a major investor in the Royal African Company, from its founding in 1672, he was also personally involved in the slave trade upon which the prosperity of these colonies rested. As king, however, James focused primarily upon New York, of which he had been proprietor for 20 years, and upon New England. His involvement in the Restoration Hudson's Bay Company, founded to open the Northern fur trade to England, had sharpened his awareness of the danger to English North America from France. James was much better informed about the colonies than his brother, but his perspectives about colonial government nevertheless proved far from reassuring to the 125,000 settlers who resided in the Middle and Northern colonies.

With a population of about 70,000 by the reign of James II, the New England colonies were the most heavily settled of these. Massachusetts dominated the region, which also included Plymouth (the original 'Pilgrim' plantation), Connecticut, New Hampshire, and Rhode Island. These were the most commercially advanced and diverse of all English colonies. The merchants and merchant marines of Boston and nearby towns were already heavily involved in transporting regional agricultural and fishing surpluses to the West Indies in return for sugar, rum, and molasses. The New England merchants traded these commodities in other colonies and in Europe as well, often in violation of the Navigation Acts. All the New England colonies except New Hampshire were largely self-governing under charters granted by the crown. Property ownership and participation in elections for colonial assemblies were widely distributed. Most men participated in the affairs of their towns and villages as well, which also contributed to an egalitarian and individualistic ethos that James and English officials strongly disliked. John Evelyn, who had once served on a government council for the plantations, thought the New Englanders 'were a people almost upon the very brink of renouncing any dependence of the crown'. James's suspiciousness of the New Englanders was further fanned by the religious connections between the region's Congregationalists and dissenters in the British kingdoms.

The Middle colonies were dominated by two proprietorships, New York and Pennsylvania. New York had been captured (twice) from the Dutch and assigned to James, as Duke of York, for its administration. With a heterogeneous population of 15,000 or more Dutch, English, and French settlers, the colony already had a troubled history. Tensions between the Dutch and the English were compounded by unhappiness about the framework of government James had instituted. Concentrating power in the hands of a governor appointed by him and of a council appointed by the governor, the 'duke's laws' provided for no representative assembly and for no town meetings. James's governor between 1674 and 1680 was Sir Edmund Andros, a military officer with an authoritarian manner. Andros became embroiled in disputes with merchants seeking to expand the colony's trade. He also imposed taxes on the colony's towns; and on James's orders, he rejected requests for a colonial assembly. Andros was eventually recalled because of complaints about these matters. James replaced him with an Irish Catholic brother-in-law of Tyrconnell, who was finally authorized to permit elections to a colonial assembly. In 1683, the New York assembly drafted a charter of liberties and privileges that claimed all the rights of Englishmen and assigned supreme legislative power to the settler's own representatives. This new framework of government arrived in London in the midst of the attack upon borough charters, however; and James never implemented it.

In New York, James permitted religious freedom to all Christian persuasions. The heavy Dutch Reformed presence required such a broad approach, but it also reflected James's developing attachment to liberty for conscience in purely religious matters. Liberty for conscience was also a founding principle of William Penn's Quaker colony, which was launched in 1681 and attracted some 10,000 immigrants in its first decade. The odd friendship that developed in the 1680s between Penn, an outspoken advocate for the civil and religious rights of English dissenters, and James, so often interpreted as inclined to absolutism, is further evidence of James's genuine endorsement of religious toleration, even when few Catholics were on hand to benefit. A de facto toleration also prevailed in the Chesapeake colony of Maryland, the northern-most of the Southern colonies. That colony's politics and assembly were nevertheless troubled by tensions between its predominantly Protestant inhabitants and its English Catholic proprietors, the Calvert Barons of Baltimore.[38]

The French threat to English North America became more obvious, in the first years of James's reign, when French traders and the Quebec governor sought to drive the English out of Hudson's Bay and attacked New York's Iroquois allies. Even before the danger from France increased, however, the fragmented character of England's North American domains struck the tidy, bureaucratic James as no way to run an empire. He was involved in efforts, starting in the last years of his brother's reign, to provide a more coherent and effective style of colonial administration. At the behest of James and others, the charter of Massachusetts was attacked in the English courts in 1684 and suffered the same fate as the charter of London: it was revoked, and the elected government of the colony was eliminated. The colonies of Massachusetts, New Hampshire, and Plymouth were combined in 1685 under a single royal governor and an appointed council, without a representative assembly. The charters of Rhode Island and Connecticut soon suffered the same fate as that of Massachusetts. Those colonies, too, were incorporated with the others into a single Dominion of New England under the governorship of the same Sir Edmund Andros who had already administered New York. By 1688, the Dominion was extended to include New York and East and West Jersey as well. Andros headed an administrative structure that included a subordinate government in New York, crown revenue collectors, and a 'standing army' of a few score regular soldiers. Indeed, Andros presided over a vice-regal form of government little different from that employed by the French and Spanish in their New World empires.

James's Dominion of New England as effectively terminated the political autonomy of the North American puritans as Tyrconnell's Irish regime eliminated the ascendancy of that kingdom's Protestant minority. As he had done in New York, Andros levied taxes without any local approval, and he prosecuted opponents who claimed his levies violated Magna Charta and the laws of the land. He frightened landowners by questioning the legality of their purchases and grants from Native Americans, and he offered confirmation of titles only upon payment of feudal quitrents. He restricted town meetings to the annual election of local office holders. He censored the press. He enforced the Navigation Acts, and he required all commerce to be conducted through a limited number of ports for the easier collection of customs duties. An admiralty court was introduced for the prosecution of merchants who violated the maritime codes; and it could operate without a jury. In other cases, juries empanelled by local sheriffs replaced juries chosen by townsmen. New Englanders believed they had taken their English rights and liberties with them to the New World. James and Andros, on the other hand, saw the New Englanders as having separated themselves from the English realm and therefore as being subordinate to royal administration.

Finally, Andros established the same liberty for conscience that James was promoting in his British kingdoms, and he thereby challenged the Congregational church establishment in Massachusetts and Connecticut. Ironically, toleration in the puritan colonies worked primarily for the benefit of the few Anglicans, for there were virtually no Catholics to tolerate. The use of town rates for the support of the Congregational clergy was eliminated. An Anglican rector arrived to minister to a Boston following dominated by Andros and other appointees to Dominion offices. Boston's South Church was required to share its building with these representatives of the very Anglican order puritans 'came over to avoid'. The Anglican holy day of Charles the Martyr was observed in Boston; and a maypole was set up, torn down, and set up again in Charlestown in 1687. At the governor's insistence, the Anglican rector occupied the pulpit during the 1687 commencement of Harvard College, the nursery of the puritan ministerium. The New England Congregationalists felt as threatened by Andros's promotion of Anglicanism, as many English, Irish, and Scots Protestants felt threatened by James's promotion of Catholicism. One puritan cleric believed that 'the foundation of all our good things', or of everything the colonists had laboured to produce, 'was destroyed' through the 'exercise of an arbitrary government'. Nothing in over two generations of colonial experience had so obviously unsettled New England's inhabitants as James's political and religious policies.[39]

The Politics of Indulgence, 1687–8

In April 1687, James II confronted the Protestant establishment in England even more directly. Having already issued a Declaration of Indulgence for Scotland, and having instructed his governor in New England to implement a liberty for conscience there, James proclaimed toleration in England as well. His English Declaration of Indulgence benefited Roman Catholics and Protestants dissenters alike. The penal laws were lifted, and pardons were offered to all individuals under prosecution for having violated them. Oaths and tests for office holding were generally suspended. All persuasions were permitted to worship in public places, provided that no preaching 'alienated' hearers from their obedience to the government. James assured the Church of England that he would preserve its establishment and protect its lands and properties. But he blamed the disorders of the four last reigns, stretching back to Elizabeth, upon misguided efforts to impose 'an exact uniformity in religion', perfectly pinpointing how religious divisions had for long disturbed the English state and kingdom. Toleration, James hoped, would better promote peace and trade.

Although James had always distrusted leading dissenters as crypto-republicans, he had also come to accept the need to tolerate religious dissent per se, as opposed to the disloyal political expression of dissent. The declaration was, therefore, a logical outcome of his beliefs. It also owed much to Sunderland, who encouraged its extension from Catholics to dissenters, and to the Quaker William Penn, who was involved in drafting it. Its proclamation reflected James's growing conviction that his heavily Anglican parliament would never agree to repeal the Test Acts unless Tory politicians were forced to compete politically with Protestant nonconformists and Roman Catholics for his favour. Although his toleration rested upon the prerogative, he nevertheless hoped for the 'concurrence' of parliament. But he prorogued parliament again, this time until November, in order to continue pressuring Anglicans, at every level of government, to accede to his religious programme. Neither could he disguise the fact that his new polity of toleration represented a new 'foundation' of government. He had abandoned an essential assumption of the Restoration, namely, the idea that the state needed to coerce on behalf of religious uniformity for its own security. His toleration edict also contrasts remarkably with Louis XIV's 1685 edict suppressing the historic liberties of the French Reformed churches.

But was James's toleration really a commendable effort to establish religious freedom? Or was it instead a trick intended to 'ruin' the Church of England, which its leaders regarded as the only safeguard for English Protestantism? 'The design was well understood,' claimed one of James's erstwhile Anglican friends: 'to divide the Protestant churches, that the popish might find less opposition.' This question troubled the politics of the kingdom for the next 15 months, especially since, in issuing the declaration, James let slip the impolitic wish that 'all the people of our dominions were members of the Catholic Church.' He genuinely believed that many of his subjects conformed to the Protestant establishment for political reasons only. Toleration, he expected, would remove the obstacles to massive defections to Rome. Many ordinary people, he hoped, would follow the lead of those English and Scots courtiers who had already converted.[40]

In fact, however, James's closeting of Anglican courtiers and parliamentarians continued to prove disappointing. Not even Sunderland was yet prepared to own Catholicism publicly, and additional Anglican notables were dismissed from office for point-blank refusals to change their religion. For their part, court Catholics were divided into rival factions. The Catholic peers were mostly cautious moderates, but ambitious zealots like the Scots Earl of Melfort and the Jesuit Sir Edward Petre threw caution to the wind in encouraging James to drive on with the re-establishment of visible Catholic church life. The king himself remained confident that he would eventually secure a compliant parliament. The continuing Anglican rebuffs merely persuaded him to dissolve the existing body in July 1687 to permit a parliamentary election under the new circumstances of toleration. Yet his hopes for Catholicism had ironically come to rest upon the cooperation of his old Whig and dissenting antagonists.[41] To what extent, therefore, were they actually prepared to work with the popish successor they had once loathed?

Within several months of the 1687 declaration, many dissenters would seek to distance themselves from James's toleration. Taking their cue from later dissenting apologists, historians have generally suggested that the dissenting response was lukewarm, with only sectarians truly embracing indulgence. Such an approach conflates the attitudes of the Restoration Crisis with the circumstances of 1687, however. Dissenters had experienced nothing but coercion and retribution since the Oxford Parliament. Beginning with the Rye House trials and continuing through the aftermath of Monmouth's rebellion, hundreds of English dissenters had been executed for treason. Thousands had been prosecuted, fined, and imprisoned under various penal statutes. This persecution was carried out by the state, but dissenters blamed it not on the state itself but rather upon the Anglican principles from which the king had now firmly separated himself. James provided relief in 1687; and most dissenters were happy to take it, even if they were astonished to take it from a king they had never wanted. Like John Bunyan, many dissenters believed that the same deity who had benefited the ancient Hebrews through pagan rulers such as Cyrus and Darius might relieve them through the popish James. Despite their hostility to 'arbitrary government', dissenting political writers had also generally distinguished between the civil prerogative and the authority English monarchs enjoyed as supreme governors of the church. They believed the declaration could be justified according to the latter. Finally, James had endorsed liberty of conscience on many of the same grounds that dissenting authors had laid out, and he had expressed a desire that his indulgence be grounded in an act of parliament.

The initial dissenting response was, therefore, one of qualified enthusiasm, but enthusiasm all the same. Many dissenters expressed gratitude to James. At the same time they assured themselves and Anglicans that liberty for conscience could be employed to promote Protestantism rather than to destroy it. In the next six months, James received dozens of addresses thanking him for the declaration from dissenting groups of all persuasions. These dissenting addresses frequently repeated the king's own suggestion that the indulgence be confirmed by statute, but they made no reference to James's desire to remove the tests for office holding. Neither was such enthusiasm restricted to England. To the north, Presbyterians had not benefited to the same extent as Catholics and Quakers from James's initial Scottish Declaration of Indulgence. But a second Scottish declaration of June 1687 placed Presbyterians on the same footing as other dissenters. Assembling in Edinburgh, Scots Presbyterian clergy not only addressed James in thanks but also proceeded openly to organize a revived national

Presbyterian church outside the state establishment. Only the extreme Cameronians or United Societies held aloof. Similarly, the Massachusetts and Plymouth puritans thanked James for his English declaration, perceiving in it a check to Anglican intrusions on their churches. When Tyrconnell issued the English declaration in Ireland, Quakers and Congregationalists joined the Presbyterians of Ulster and Dublin in thanking James for it. In each of James's dominions, dissenting enthusiasm was, however, neither for the king himself nor for the relief of Catholics. Dissenters were instead simply enthusiastic about the permission they had to worship freely.[42]

The Anglican response to the Declaration of Indulgence was rather circumspect, considering that James had overturned much of what Anglicans had worked for since the beginning of the Restoration. They were, nevertheless, mostly horrified. When James pressed the English bishops to support the declaration, only four of them could be found to thank him publicly. The parish clergy and the Anglican laity were largely unsympathetic as well. The Scottish indulgence provoked a corresponding hostility from most of the bishops and parish clergy of that kingdom. Church writers might have been expected to excoriate dissenters who thanked James for an indulgence that also benefited Catholics, and some of them did so. Dissenters who had thanked the crown had, after all, opened themselves to the old Tory canard that, given half a chance, they would cooperate with Catholics to destroy the Protestant establishment. Other Anglican writers reached out to the dissenters, however, hoping to detach nonconformists from what churchmen feared was a popish ruse. James's former minister, Halifax, was the most notable of these. His anonymous *Letter to a Dissenter* appeared in the summer of 1687. He suggested that nonconformists were 'hugged now' by friendly Catholics only that they 'may be the better squeezed at another time', when Rome had secured the upper hand and could again persecute. Appealing to dissenting regard for 'the public safety', Halifax encouraged nonconformists to stick fast to their 'old friend Magna Charta' against James's employment of the prerogative. He assured them, moreover, that the Church of England had turned from 'the spirit of persecution' towards 'a spirit of peace, charity, and condescension'.[43]

James further alienated Anglican opinion by promoting Catholicism at the universities, the intellectual redoubts of the Protestant establishment. Catholicism had gained a foothold at Oxford, early in James's reign, when the master and three fellows of University College defected from the Church of England to Rome and opened a Catholic chapel. They retained their positions with dispensations from James. He also supported their efforts to set up a Catholic printing house, to secure academic appointments for other Romanists, and to recruit Catholic students. Undeterred by the negative Anglican reaction to these developments, James appointed a Catholic as dean of Christ Church (an Anglican cathedral as well as a college), and he filled the vacant bishopric of Oxford with the sycophantic Samuel Parker. By 1687, a few fellows at four other Oxford colleges had also converted. At Cambridge, James imposed a Catholic master on the fellows of Sidney Sussex and demanded that the university grant the MA to a Benedictine monk. When the university rejected this demand as likely to open degrees generally to non-Anglicans, the ecclesiastical commission suspended the university vice-chancellor.

The case of Magdalen College, Oxford, provided the most spectacular confrontation between James and Anglican academics. The king required the fellows to elect as their president a suspected Catholic with marginal credentials and a reputation for debauchery. The fellows claimed that James's man was not eligible according to college statutes, and they elected an anti-Catholic Anglican instead. When the ecclesiastical commission voided their election and required them to elect Oxford bishop Samuel Parker, they refused. James confronted the recalcitrant dons in person at Oxford in September 1687. Their continuing defiance provoked him to fury: 'Is this your Church of England loyalty?' he thundered, before threatening them with 'the weight of their sovereign's displeasure'. The Magdalen fellows stood their ground, however; and the ecclesiastical commission eventually deprived the ringleaders of their fellowships, which were reassigned to Catholics. By then, James's desire to promote Catholicism at Oxford and Cambridge was producing the impression that Anglican ministry, provided primarily by college graduates, was imperilled by popish infiltration of the universities. Furthermore, academic defenders of Anglican statutory privileges were behaving in ways that strained the church's teachings about passive obedience and non-resistance. These university episodes also permitted staunch Anglicans to present themselves as public defenders of Protestantism against the Catholic threat, while dissenters could be criticized as taking advantage of Catholic largesse at the expense of their Protestant brethren.[44]

Doubts about James's intensions were also shared in the Netherlands by William of Orange and his wife, Mary, James's daughter and successor. They had so far proven deaf to James's request that they support a repeal of the 1673 Test Act. As disturbing rumours about James's purposes continued to reach The Hague, William sent a personal envoy to England, early in 1687, with instructions both to mend fences with James and to encourage politicians who opposed James's promotion of Catholicism. Such meddling further poisoned the prince's relations with his father-in-law. William was willing to endorse a statutory toleration and a repeal of the penal laws, but neither he nor his devoutly Anglican wife were prepared to abandon the sacramental test that preserved the Protestant establishment's political position. Already friendly with such expatriates as Gilbert Burnet, the renegade Scots divine and future Whig historian, William and Mary also hosted several disaffected English dignitaries and nobles in 1687–8. Moreover, such leading Anglican politicians as Danby and Daniel Finch, Earl of Nottingham initiated regular political communication with the prince, hoping that he might serve as a restraining influence on James. For his part, William sought to protect his wife's inheritance. He also feared that James might provoke an internal rebellion that would eliminate England as a European player and potential ally against France.[45]

Neither William nor Anglican opinion was much reassured by James's dissolution of the English parliament in the summer of 1687. The dissolution was the opening move in a systematic royal campaign to manipulate local institutions to produce a parliamentary majority on behalf of toleration. Viewed ever since as an effort to 'pack' parliament, James's efforts were even more systematic and coordinated than his brother's overhaul of the localities in 1682–5. Indeed, his regulation of the boroughs represented the most heavy-handed intrusion of the central government on the parliamentary constituencies since the Reformation. Starting with London, Anglicans and Tories who had been placed or retained in corporation offices in Charles's remodelling of the boroughs were subjected to a new loyalty test: Would they support the Declaration of Indulgence, repeal of the sacramental test and penal laws, and cooperative parliamentary candidates? These so-called three questions were at the centre of English politics for the next year, and they were asked of appointees and office holders throughout the realm. The questions were administered by local agents of a Privy Council committee dominated by Catholics and headed by Sunderland, who now completed his conversion to Rome.

The results of this second royal regulation of the boroughs were staggering, both in their magnitude and in their implications. Throughout the kingdom, the many Anglicans who gave the wrong answers to James's questions were purged from the governing boards and magistracies of corporations. In London, a few Catholics were added to the city's governing body of aldermen, but two-thirds of the new aldermen were dissenters once involved in efforts to prevent James's succession. London's electorate was also remodelled again: many Whig and dissenting electors purged under Charles now resumed their rights at the expense of Anglican Tories. In Exeter and Oxford, some of John Locke's Presbyterian friends and relations assumed or returned to borough offices. Throughout the kingdom, 2200 corporation members in over 100 towns were cashiered. Seventy-six per cent of the local governors of those communities were replaced. In borough after borough, the victims of Charles's earlier purges now ousted the very Anglican loyalists who had triumphed after 1681.

A parallel overhaul of the county commissions of peace yielded similar results. By the time the issuance of revised commissions concluded, in the summer of 1688, a quarter of the JPs and deputy lieutenants of the county militias were Roman Catholics, as were a significant proportion of the county sheriffs. Almost every Catholic landowner in the kingdom had assumed some responsibility. Even more remarkable were the replacements of Anglican loyalist JPs by old exclusionists, dissenters, and even a few of Monmouth's recent followers. The Bishop of Norwich complained that 'all the most considerable gentry in the county' were purged from the Norfolk commission of peace. James had, in fact, removed the 'natural governors' of society from their places, dismissing the Anglican squirearchy whose political triumph of 1660–2 had shaped the politics of the entire Restoration. In county and borough alike those who had argued for liberty of conscience and for a more comprehensive Protestant church were instead placed in power, together with Catholics. Finally, the rehabilitation of Whigs and dissenters was extended to the press and to the public sphere. James employed some dissenting writers such as Henry Care to massage opinion with tracts on behalf of toleration. Other dissenters independently took up their pens on behalf of parliamentary confirmation of James's liberty for conscience.[46]

The assignment of local power to those who would support toleration was accompanied by a redoubling of Catholic efforts in each of James's kingdoms. Catholic ministry became more open in England than at any time since the reign of Mary Tudor, as James sought to make good on his wish that more of his subjects return to Rome. Local Catholic families followed the royal lead in financially supporting Catholic ministry, especially in the towns. By 1688, Catholic secular priests, as well as Jesuits, Benedictines, and Franciscans, were providing mass in almost every county town of any significance. York had eight Catholic chapels; London had 18. The Roman vicar apostolic was said to have confirmed 20,000 converts in 1687 in the North and in the Midlands, a figure that probably better measures Protestant fears than Catholic success. Crowd hostility to Catholic clergy and worshippers was another index of Protestant fear, but no deterrent to the increasing visibility of the king's religion. In the same year, a papal nuncio took up residence in London; and in 1688 the Catholic hierarchy was re-established through the division of the kingdom into four regions, each under its own vicar apostolic. When Oxford bishop Samuel Parker died, Magdalen College finally got its Catholic president, who began transforming it into a Roman seminary.

In Scotland, James began the conversion of the abbey church at Holyrood into a Roman chapel. It was especially to be used by the revived order of the Knights of the Thistle (or of St. Andrew), which was made up of the same Catholic nobles who now dominated the kingdom's government. Mass was sung there for the Feast of the Conception in December 1687 with the assistance of female vocalists imported from France. Jesuits and Benedictines arrived and feuded with other priests for leadership of the Catholic community. The Jesuits opened a school in Edinburgh, as they had in London; and a Catholic printing house operated at Holyrood. In Ireland, Tyrconnell's Catholic revival was now directed against Protestant property. As the deputy lieutenant continued preparations for a Catholic-dominated parliament, he secured James's approval to draft a proposal for the redistribution of land. The proposal that eventually emerged was that Protestants granted land since the Cromwellian era should return half of it to the Catholics from whom it had been taken in the first place.[47]

In England, Whigs and dissenters who accepted toleration and offices from James did so to check Anglican-inspired persecution rather than because of any comfort they had with Catholicism. As frightened as Anglicans by the increasing Roman presence, they also found security for Protestantism in the prospect of the succession, in the not too distant future, of the very Protestant Mary. If only the Anglican leaders could be persuaded to abandon persecution, all would be well. Such sanguine hopes were blasted in the winter of 1687–8, however, as dissenters and Anglicans alike came to terms with the possibility that Mary might not succeed James after all.

Queen Mary Beatrice had survived ten pregnancies in the first decade of her marriage to James: six had ended in miscarriages, and of her four live births, only one child had lived as long as five years.[48] In November 1687, the crown confirmed rumours that she was again pregnant. James prayed for a son. His assumption that his subjects would be thankful for the birth of a new male heir, one who would be brought up as a Catholic, and who would take precedence in the succession over his Protestant daughters, was optimistic, to say the least. As the pregnancy continued through to the birth of James Francis Edward, on 10 June, the calculus of politics altered dramatically. By then, the fear of a popish succession was again as much the driving force of British politics as it had been in 1679–80. The birth of James's son threatened to consign the three Stuart kingdoms to rule by a continuing Catholic royal line. At the same time, James's efforts to eliminate all who opposed his religious programme from parliaments and from local government had also confirmed long-standing fears about an arbitrary government.

James at Bay, 1688

Most historians believe James's new polity of toleration had little chance of success in England. How could a regime that rested on the social and political extremes of dissent and Catholicism, neither of which was well represented within the country's governing elite, prevail against the Anglican majority, and especially against the Anglican aristocracy and gentry? Moreover, the refusal of most Anglicans to support toleration left James attempting to manufacture a House of Commons in which the few who had generally been excluded from parliament took the places of the many who had generally filled it. James's regime was, therefore, a house built on sand. It could not have withstood the anti-Catholic and anti-sectarian phobias of most of the English population and its leaders.

Such arguments are often too boldly stated, however. For one thing, they unduly minimize the proportion of the population drawn to dissent prior to the Anglican reaction of the 1680s; and they maximize the Anglican commitments of ordinary people. Furthermore, the likelihood of James's success in securing toleration also changed, always for the worse, as his methods became more heavy-handed. What if James had settled for toleration of dissenting and Catholic religious worship, without removal of the 1673 Test Act, which provided political protection for the Protestant establishment? He might thereby have retained the initial enthusiasm of nonconformists and also have attracted support from moderate Anglicans who had reservations about coercive methods to achieve uniformity. He could still have used his dispensing power, generally acknowledged as legal, to except Catholics whose services he desired from the test. From the Netherlands, William and Mary were prepared to support such a compromise, which would have decriminalized worship outside the Anglican Church. This formula would also appear to have been acceptable to leading dissenters: several new Presbyterian and Independent aldermen of London, for instance, actually insisted upon taking the sacramental test, prior to accepting office, as a way of demonstrating their commitment to Protestant unity.[49] Moreover, indulgence with the test was also close to what was actually implemented in England after 1689. Many in the kingdom were clearly ready for a religious settlement along these lines.

Or what if James had been less intrusive in his preparations for parliament? What if he had left the election open, merely encouraging Whigs and dissenters to compete with Anglican Tories for seats on their old programme of liberty for conscience and a comprehensive reform of the Protestant establishment? Much of the increasing opposition to James's agenda is more attributable to his invasion of the localities, to his displacement of local elites, and to his attempt to pack parliament than to his hopes to establish

religious toleration. Or what if James had offered alternative protections for the Church of England? William Penn, Henry Care,
and other dissenting advocates of James's indulgence promoted
'expedients' or alternatives to the sacramental test to reassure
frightened Anglicans that their church would be safeguarded.
Care supported a parliamentary confirmation of all the Church of
England's privileges other than those that rested upon coercion.
Care, Penn, and other sectarian authors also called for parliamentary adoption of a 'great charter for liberty for conscience'.
What they had in mind was a bill that would establish liberty of
conscience as 'part of the constitution of this kingdom' without
dislodging the Church of England. It would, they thought, protect
the religious rights and properties of all and function like Magna
Charta or a bill of rights. James did occasionally use such language
himself in 1687. As opposition to his declaration intensified, however, he abandoned libertarian rhetoric that might have countered
the developing assumption that he intended to establish 'popery
and arbitrary government'.[50]

Such hypothetical considerations are not beside the point: they
suggest that James may have been undone in England more by his
means than by his ends. Moreover, his means alienated not only
uncooperative Anglicans but also many of those whose cooperation
he counted upon after the 1687 declaration. Leading Presbyterians
and Independents drew back from active cooperation with James in
early 1688, both because of doubts about his intentions and because
of his reliance upon sectarians in his regulation of the boroughs
and in his propaganda. Presbyterians, in particular, had long sought
to act with like-minded kindred in the Church of England in order
to broaden the establishment to include themselves. Given James's
failure to provide substantive guarantees for Anglicanism, they began
to wonder, however, whether any Protestant establishment would
be left for them to join. They also distrusted 'old cankered sturdy
sectaries' who had no interest in comprehension. As distrust of James
mounted, a number of overtures towards finding common ground
were initiated by Presbyterian and Episcopalian clergy in the winter
of 1687–8. One Presbyterian diarist hoped that 'sober churchmen'
might 'coalesce with the sober dissenters'. Some nonconformists
placed in local offices also declined to act in them, fearing that James
sought to engineer a Catholic triumph through Protestant division.
From the Netherlands, William sponsored English propaganda that

sought to maintain Protestant unity through the advocacy of toleration without repeal of the Test Act.[51]

Reacting to these new signs of opposition, James reissued his
Declaration of Indulgence in April 1688. He sought to reclaim
dissenting support, to redivide Anglicans and moderate dissenters,
and to recover the initiative for his campaign to secure parliamentary repeal of the Test Act. The new declaration announced
his intention to meet parliament in November in order to enact
the indulgence as a statute. Both in order to advertise his intentions and to defuse Anglican opposition, James also required the
established clergy to read the declaration from their pulpits on
appointed Sundays in May and June. Ironically, in imposing this
unwelcome task upon the clergy, James facilitated the convergence
of Anglicans and moderate dissenters against him. Archbishop
Sancroft led six other bishops in personally presenting a petition
to James, which suggested that the reading of the declaration
would require the church to break the law. The bishops pointed
out that the suspending power upon which James had offered
his indulgence had twice been declared contrary to law in the
House of Commons. They could not in good conscience read it,
they claimed, without appearing to condone an illegal action; and
neither could their clergy. The petition was offered after consulta-
tion with leading London dissenting divines, to whom the bishops
made reassurances about comprehension.

When the prelates sprang their petition upon an unsuspecting
James, the king recoiled in anger at what he perceived as an affront
to his prerogative: 'This is a standard of rebellion,' he shouted at
them; and he was right. The bishops had endorsed the view that
the prerogative upon which the king's declaration and his entire
new polity of toleration rested had been employed illegally. With
relatively few exceptions, the Anglican clergy followed the seven
bishops in refusing to read the declaration from their pulpits.
James retaliated by charging the bishops with seditious libel and
clapping them in the Tower of London to await trial before the
Court of King's Bench.

The Restoration church and the Restoration state were now at
war in the courts. The Restoration settlement of the realm was
coming unstuck, and James was also losing control of opinion.
The seat of rebellion in 1641–2, and the heart of opposition in
1679–81, London rallied to the bishops in 1688. So did the nation,

as Protestants of many persuasions took alarm about the recent birth of James's son. Awaiting trial, the bishops were visited by a sympathetic delegation of dissenting clergy. Released on bail, they were mobbed by supporters seeking their blessing. The Reformation paradigm of Mary Tudor's reign had been re-established as bishops took the lead in Protestant opposition to the dictates of a Catholic monarch. The trial of the bishops at Westminster Hall on 29–30 June was a government fiasco. Nobles and gentry who might have sat in parliament sat instead in support of the prelates. Thousands again filled the streets and hissed the arriving Sunderland. The judges could not agree on whether the bishops' petition constituted a libel and threw the matter to the jury, which was entirely Anglican after a few dissenters picked for it declined to serve in favour of their conforming brethren. The jury's acquittal of the bishops touched off scenes that 'looked like a little rebellion in noise'. The shouting carried all the way to Hounslow Heath, where James's encamped army (still largely Protestant, despite some indulged Catholic officers) joined in the celebrations.

Bonfires celebrating this Protestant triumph were lit throughout the kingdom. The fires in the streets also stoked smouldering resentments about the birth of James's son. Many wondered whether Mary Beatrice's pregnancy had really been a sham intended to foist an impostor on the nation as a Catholic successor. Most importantly, the bishops had regained their stature. A few years earlier, opposition politicians and pamphleteers had treated them as symbols of 'popish' persecution; now they were Protestant heroes. One Presbyterian worried that the prelates had 'got such an universal interest in the nation as they never had nor were likely [otherwise] to have recovered'. Most Presbyterians and Independents, concerned about the appearance of their initial enthusiasm for James's toleration, fell in line behind the Anglican opposition to James's employment of his prerogative. The Anglican church was riding as high as in the early 1660s.[52]

The prosecution of the bishops also coincided with the climax of a conspiracy against James. Seven Anglican leaders invited William of Orange to intervene in England in defence of the kingdom's constitution. William had not been short of advice to do exactly that from some of the hundreds of prominent English and Scottish exiles in the Netherlands. Indeed, he was himself encouraging conspiracy through Henry Sidney, brother of the executed Algernon Sidney, whom he knew well as Charles II's onetime envoy to his government. Henry Sidney was critical in the new conspiracy: he secured the signatures on a letter to William of six other notables. These included the Earl of Danby (as strongly committed to the Anglican church now as in the 1670s), suspended London Bishop Henry Compton, and a cousin of the executed Lord Russell. They requested that William intervene with arms, noting both that the 'religion, liberties and properties' of Protestant subjects had 'been greatly invaded' and that 'a packed parliament' would lead to even 'worse' results. They appealed to William's desire to protect his wife's interest in the succession by suggesting that James and Mary Beatrice had concocted an elaborate ruse to produce a spurious Catholic heir. 'Not one in a thousand believes [the baby] to be the queen's,' they assured him. Finally, they echoed their exclusionist predecessors in fearing for the future of 'parliamentary government'.

The conspiracy was, thus, a reaction both against James's parliamentary methods and against a Catholic succession. The birth of James's son was seen as just another Jesuit trick to undo the Protestant establishments of his kingdoms. The letter to William was sent on the very day of the acquittal of the seven Anglican bishops. It reflected a growing alarm about James's intentions that had spread even among officers of the army and the navy such as Baron John Churchill, once James's comrade in arms. Other Anglican leaders like the Earl of Nottingham knew of the conspiracy but could not sign the letter, finding solicitation of an armed intervention incompatible with their principles of passive obedience and non-resistance. No dissenter was invited to sign it. Yet some dissenters, including John Hampden, who had narrowly escaped execution for his part in the Rye House conspiracy, were working independently to encourage William's intervention in Britain.[53]

Unaware of the conspiracy, James was determined to press ahead with his plans for a parliament to confirm his declaration. He rejected Sunderland's suggestion that he settle for religious liberty with retention of the Test Act of 1673. He had for some time considered creating a majority in the House of Lords in favour of toleration by creating new peers pledged to his indulgence. As for the House of Commons, his election agents continued their efforts to secure candidates committed to the repeal of the sacramental test. Their optimistic reports about the prospects of sympathetic candidates for many borough and county seats were, however, wide of the mark. They failed to take into account the movement of public opinion against the court, and they largely overlooked the increasing caution of Whigs and dissenters whose cooperation had been assumed. Indeed, a growing number of Whigs and dissenters were sidelining themselves from politics and from the government's hunt for prospective parliamentary supporters. Some prospective MPs eventually found by the court, or believed by the court, to oppose the Test Acts were without the social standing of their predecessors. Others were actually Anglican loyalists who had given disingenuous answers to the three questions. Still others were sectarian dissenters whose indifference to comprehension raised suspicions among Presbyterians. The influence of these candidates in the localities they were intended to serve was also often unclear. Furthermore, in many boroughs, as well as in London, the management of local affairs was collapsing, as dissenters failed to act in offices that had been assigned to them. The electoral machinery the government had set up through regulating the boroughs and purging the commissions of peace was grinding to a halt. James's English regime was already beginning to implode.[54]

Moreover, the visibility of sectarians among James's continuing supporters, as well as the convergence of moderate dissenters and Episcopalians against him, recreated the political and religious dynamics of 1659. Once again, a strong internal reaction in favour of a 'free parliament' and of settlement was emerging against a central authority with a standing army that had unsettled the kingdom. Fear of the sects and fear of the Catholics were again arousing those dedicated to the historic association of a Protestant church establishment with a Protestant state. This time the reaction was reinforced by obvious naval and military preparations in the Netherlands. James at first refused to believe these preparations could be directed against him, despite numerous warnings from Louis XIV. Instead, he initially thought Louis was attempting to poison relations between him and his son-in-law in order to drag him into another French war against the Netherlands. By late summer, however, his concern about William's military build-up grew. He then decided to proceed with the parliament he had planned as the best means of retaining his subjects' support in the event of a crisis with the Dutch. He issued writs for a parliamentary election in mid-September.

Within a few days of authorizing elections, James was persuaded that William was indeed preparing an invasion. He responded first by announcing that the parliamentary election would be free, and then by cancelling it altogether. He reopened dialogue with the Anglican bishops and politicians whose support he now thought necessary again. The bishops drove a hard bargain. James had to agree to abolish the ecclesiastical commission, to reinstate the Bishop of London, and to restore the fellows of Magdalen College. He returned the charter of London, re-establishing the city's self-government; and he began replacing the new borough charters with those that had been surrendered a few years earlier. New commissions of the peace were issued for some counties, restoring the Anglican landed elite; and Catholics were removed as deputy lieutenants of the county militias. Still, major Anglican figures such as Rochester, Halifax, and Nottingham remained aloof. Even the bishops refused to sign a document abhorring an invasion. James had reversed course too late.

As James's polity of toleration was uprooted, his government split apart. A panicking Sunderland distanced himself from the Catholic zealots. Father Petre was dismissed from the Privy Council; but so was Sunderland, at the end of October, when James learned that William's invasion fleet had been driven back by winds. William was not to be deterred, however; and he landed at Torbay, in the Southwest, on the Devon coast, on 5 November, the most auspicious day of the English Protestant calendar. His invasion manifestos – one for England and one for Scotland – catalogued a variety of evidence to suggest that both kingdoms had fallen 'under arbitrary government and slavery'. They called for the election of a 'free and lawful parliament' in England, under the 'ancient' charters and traditional franchises, and for a parliamentary settlement in Scotland as well. Suggesting the need for a 'good agreement between the Church of England and all Protestant dissenters', the prince recommended an end to the religious persecution of any, including Catholics; and he encouraged an investigation into the birth of 'the pretended Prince of Wales'.[55]

6   The Glorious Revolution and Its Aftermath

Whosoever uses force without right, as every one does in society who does it without law, puts himself into a state of war with those against whom he so uses it; and in that state all former ties are cancelled, all other rights cease, and every one has a right to defend himself and to resist the aggressor.... Whereby it is evident, ... that ... all resisting of princes is not rebellion.

John Locke (1689)[1]

Introduction: Invasion

William of Orange's intervention in the domestic affairs of James II was the last successful invasion of the British Isles. It quickly led to the establishment of revolutionary regimes in England and Scotland. It soon led as well to the reimposition of the Protestant ascendancy in Ireland and to the creation of new regimes in some major North American colonies. Contemporaries understood these events to be of critical importance. Yet the Revolution of 1688–9 has never acquired much stature in the historiography of revolution, where it has been largely overshadowed by the modern revolution-ary upheavals in France, Russia, and China. This neglect may be partially attributed to the invasion with which it began; but the event's supposed lack of bloodshed and its preservation of many traditional institutions have also struck some historical observers as distinctly unrevolutionary. Even in modern British historiography, the era of civil war in the 1640s and the ensuing Interregnum have drawn far more attention as a time of revolution than the episodes of 1688–9.

Such relative neglect would have astonished many eighteenth-century European intellectuals and public figures, and especially those of their trans-Atlantic counterparts who created the American republic. For them, the events of 1688–9 and the institutions that emerged from those events were models of how a prosperous and free people might preserve political liberty and the autonomy of private property owners against tyrannical rule. Eighteenth- and nineteenth-century Whig interpreters on both sides of the Atlantic may have exaggerated the libertarian intentions of those who made the Revolution. They were not incorrect, however, in believing that it provided both ideas and precedents that might be used and reused in the political debates of their own day. Misconstrued or not, the Revolution of 1688–9 does retain an important place in English, Scottish, Irish, and early American history. That place will be outlined here by examining the Revolution itself and by selectively analysing the history of the next quarter century in light of both the Restoration and the Revolution. Discussion of the Revolution and its aftermath helps to explain the triumph, in subsequent British and American history, of such ideals as liberty for conscience, accountable government, the political restraint of military establishments, individual rights, and the encouragement of economic enterprise. It also assists in understanding how parliament secured its place in the British constitution, how England and Scotland were soon merged into a single polity, and how a new British state overcame some of the weaknesses of the old Stuart regimes.

The Revolution began with an act of war against James II; but the success of William's military intervention in England was no sure thing. The last attempted invasion, made a hundred years earlier by Philip II of Spain, did not suggest encouraging odds. What inclined William to embark upon so hazardous an undertaking was probably not the attachment to free parliaments that he proclaimed in his manifestos but rather his concern about the European balance of power. William had counted on keeping a Protestant England on the Dutch side in the event of a general war. His wife's place in the succession had seemed to support such expectations until Mary Beatrice's pregnancy. Although James had actually maintained his distance from Louis XIV, William nevertheless read the Catholic advances in James's kingdoms as an indication that James might well ally with France, when the next conflict came, just as Charles had in 1672. Should James's differences with his subjects instead prompt civil war, which also seemed a strong possibility to William, the effect on the Netherlands would be the same: the loss of an English alliance in the event of a war with France. William intervened in England, then, not so much to save the English from 'popery and arbitrary government' as to save England for the Dutch cause. Neither did he contemplate, at least initially, the overthrow of James or his own ascension to James's thrones. His invasion was intended to back the English parliament in negotiating domestic issues with James and to bring England into the European balance against Louis.[2]

Resolving on an invasion by May 1688, William had put together a force of 14,000–15,000 men by September. Some 3000 of the infantry, as well as many officers, were actually James's own subjects, members of the Anglo-Dutch brigade that had historically served in the army of the United Provinces. They were accompanied by numerous English and Scots exiles; and the fleet that ferried them to Britain was commanded by a popular English admiral whom James had cashiered for opposing repeal of the sacramental test. William's force was also quite cosmopolitan in complexion. It included many Huguenot troops and officers and even 200 Africans from the English and Dutch colonies. William could, then, claim that he was leading a liberating force of British and Protestant soldiers rather than a Dutch invasion. His path to England was cleared in September when Louis decided that no seaborne invasion could be launched so late in the season and mounted a strategic advance of his own in the Rhineland. No longer having to worry about French interference, William committed his armada of 50 warships and 200 transports to the winds. They treated him roughly on his first departure. Turning from west to east, however, they sped him from the Netherlands to Devon in early November, while keeping the English fleet bottled up behind the sandbars of the Thames estuary.

Within days of landing, William had taken Exeter, to the jubilation of the area's Whig and dissenting inhabitants, who began flocking in to take up the arms the prince brought with him for additional regiments. As William prepared for an advance on London, James completed the defensive preparations he had already set in motion. James's resources were far superior to those of the invader. He had begun an enlargement of his standing army of 21,000 in September to create a sizable field force without having to abandon local garrisons. The small Scottish army was drawn down to England, and regiments of the Irish army began entering the country through Chester and Liverpool in early October. As soon as the western location of William's disembarkation was determined, James began assembling his forces on Salisbury Plain to protect London and the Southeast and to meet William head-on. By mid-November, when James arrived at Salisbury to command this force, it numbered 29,000–30,000 men, including 3000-strong contingents from Scotland and Ireland. James, therefore, had an army twice the size of William's. As experienced a commander as his son-in-law, James also had the advantage of fighting on his home ground. William, on the other hand, was cut off from further Dutch reinforcements and supplies, as well as from flight, by the English fleet, now nicely positioned between the West Country and the Netherlands.[3]

The pitched battle that both camps were preparing for never occurred, however. James's military and political position disintegrated, even before his arrival at Salisbury, as major political figures and officers began defecting to William's cause. These defections had been pre-arranged by the prince and by those who had conspired against James in order to damage James's morale and that of his army. The most spectacular of the early desertions were those of James's nephew, Edward Hyde, Viscount Cornbury, who was commander of the royal dragoons, and of the West Country Tory MP Sir Edward Seymour, whom William immediately appointed governor of Exeter. Cornbury and Seymour were pillars of Anglican propriety, and their example encouraged other Tories to rethink their attachment to absolute non-resistance. Only one of the officers who deserted James's army managed to take his regiment with him, but both James and his officer corps were nonetheless unnerved by such treachery. The camp at Salisbury was soon in turmoil as officers who were supposed to fight alongside one another began instead to wonder who would desert next.

Elsewhere in England a series of local revolts and risings broke out, some of them again pre-arranged. The Earl of Danby, one of the conspirators against James, had expected the prince to arrive in the North, where he had prepared his friends among the Yorkshire gentry to receive him. Still hoping to resuscitate his political fortunes by aiding William, Danby led those same gentry in seizing York for a 'free parliament and the protestant religion'.[4] Plymouth was secured for William by the very magnate James sent to hold the town. Derby and Nottingham saw local gentry rebellions inspired by the desire for a free parliament; and Chester was raised by a Whig peer, the son of the leader of the county's 1659 rebellion against the Rump. Indeed, the parallels to 1659 were many. James was as stymied by the desertion of local elites demanding a free parliament as the republican regime had once been; and like the Rump, his government faced a wily general who played his cards close while encouraging the localities against the central government. In some areas, the revolts represented a recovery of leadership by the natural governors of society who had earlier been pushed out of their places by James for their opposition to repealing the test. For them, rebellion was a means to reordering and resettling communities that had been thrown into confusion by James's promotion of Catholicism and dissent.

Arriving at his camp on 19 November, James was plagued by nosebleeds that were symptomatic both of his anxiety and of his disintegrating position. At a council of war a few days later, he accepted advice from his principal general to order a retreat from Salisbury towards London. The decision was a concession that he could no longer defeat William by force of arms. As James returned to London, he suffered further staggering losses of personnel and allegiance. Lord John Churchill, once his friend but now a conspirator, as well as two other peers who were regimental commanders, went over to William's side. So did James Butler, the second Duke of Ormond and grandson of Charles II's Irish viceroy. Most shattering to James's confidence were the desertions of his younger daughter, Anne, and of her husband, Prince George of Denmark: the royal patriarch of Britain was now at war with both his daughters and both his sons-in-law. In the meantime, emboldened by these fresh examples of royalty in revolt, additional towns and assemblies of county gentry defied James by declaring their support for William's goal of a free parliament. With his government collapsing, James issued a proclamation on 30 November calling for a parliament to meet in January 1689; and he offered a general pardon to all who had defied him. He also opened negotiations with William.[5]

William and James's negotiators agreed to a meeting of parliament as summoned by James, to the positioning of both armies outside the capital (to ensure parliament's freedom), and to the removal of Catholics from all offices. This deal, in which William negotiated with James as a monarch in full possession of his kingdoms, had already been overtaken by events, however. Occasional anti-Catholic rioting had begun in both England and Scotland in late September and October, well before William's arrival. These popular disturbances were directed neither against James nor against his government, but rather against Catholic properties and personnel. In London, crowd attacks on Catholic chapels had broken out during the first week of the invasion. In Scotland, a few weeks later, University of Glasgow students celebrated 30 November (St. Andrew's Day) with a pope burning that rather ominously included effigies of the Protestant archbishops of St. Andrews and Glasgow. Students at the University of Edinburgh followed suit within a few days.

These episodes were but the beginning of an explosion of the phobic anti-Catholicism that so many English and Scottish Protestants had suppressed for the previous three years. The transit of Irish Catholic troops through England further stimulated Protestant fears. So did a spurious declaration put out in William's name that suggested Catholics were again conspiring to burn London. The result was a 'great fear' or alarm that produced waves of anti-Catholic violence in both kingdoms. In London, on 11–12 December, crowds reportedly numbering 20,000 assaulted most of the Catholic chapels; and several of them were completely destroyed. The Spanish ambassador's residence was sacked, as were the facilities of the king's Catholic printer. Further popular anti-Catholic violence had broken out in Edinburgh a few days earlier, again on rumours that the city was in danger of being burned. Three nights of street battles broke out between apprentices and royal guards, producing several casualties. When all was over, the royal Catholic chapel at Holyrood was destroyed. The city's Jesuit residence and the homes of prominent Catholics (including that of Lord Chancellor Perth, who fled) were ransacked, and many Catholic worship accoutrements were ritually burnt in the streets.[6]

The actions of country nobles and gentry on behalf of a free parliament had so far been orderly local coups without much crowd action. These street episodes suggest, however, that a new popular dimension to the crisis was developing. Although crowd disturbances were so far directed against Catholics, they might easily turn against authority associated with Catholicism, as the Chancellor of Scotland had already learnt. James feared for his own safety and for that of his family. He well remembered how a hostile army, a hostile city, and a hostile parliament had disposed of his father. He managed to get Mary Beatrice and the infant Prince of Wales out of the country and off to France. He followed himself on 11 December, but not before contributing further to the disorders that climaxed that day. He ordered the disbanding of the army, thereby sending masses of demoralized troops out among already frightened local populations. He recalled his writs for a parliamentary election in England and destroyed those that had not been delivered. He tossed the Great Seal of England into the Thames, as he departed, to prevent its use in authorizing parliamentary writs thereafter. His motive in all these actions was to make government in his absence impossible and thereby to insure that he would be recalled on his own terms.

Nevertheless both kingdoms were now effectively without a king. In England, authority was assumed by a body of peers, largely Tory, who had begun to meet with James as the crisis developed, and who established themselves at the London Guildhall. The London common council, which had been elected in November, after the return of the city's charter, also became more active, as crowds threatened to get out of hand. The city government surpassed the peers in enthusiasm for William and his purposes, and it requested that the prince proceed to London as soon as possible. William recognized that he could no longer negotiate the kingdom's future with a king prepared to abandon it, and he was worried also about the country's descent into disorder. His way forward was clouded, however, by James's return to London, under the protection of the loyalist Guildhall peers, after he was recognized and detained on the Kentish coast. James's resumption of authority nevertheless proved brief, for he was determined not to function as a captive king. Neither was William prepared to continue dealing with him. James soon fled the country a second time, and this time he made it to the court of Louis XIV.

England and Scotland confronted their second effective interregnum in 40 years. After much debate, the Guildhall lords, functioning as a provisional English government, requested William to assume the administration of the kingdom and to summon a parliamentary convention to resolve the national crisis. But William, who had now decided to seek the throne for himself and his wife, and who distrusted some of the loyalist peers, strategically sought approval for the summoning of a convention from a broader representation of the political nation. On 26 December, he convened an assembly of some 300 MPs from the 1679–81 parliaments who had come up to London since the invasion, and who sat with the lord mayor, aldermen, and 50 common councilmen. At the request of this body, William summoned a convention for 22 January with a House of Commons elected at his behest, rather than on James's writs. A few days later, William met with over 100 Scottish peers and lairds who had also come to London. They requested that he assume administration of the northern kingdom and summon a convention of the Scottish estates to meet in March.

William was clearly acting as a de facto king of both kingdoms. He had also just as clearly slighted James's Tory-dominated English parliament of 1685, the MPs of which were not invited to the 26 December meeting. The 'popery and arbitrary government' from which England and Scotland were being rescued was, therefore, in William's mind and in the minds of many Whigs, not merely James's programme of 1687–8. It was rather the entire sequence of royal decisions that had followed the English and Scottish parliaments of 1681. Tory and Whig leaders in England had so far acted together to restrain James, but whether these old antagonists could now cooperate in reconstructing a government – either under James or under William – remained to be seen.[7]

The Revolution in England

The English Convention met less than a month after William called for the election of MPs. It was the free parliament that William had demanded in his manifesto and that James had promised. The lack of intervention by any strongly established central regime left electors as free of outside interference in their choices as had been the case for any election since 1660. The issues before the electors were of the greatest concern to the future of the realm. Whig electoral propaganda that encouraged the choice of MPs sympathetic to William's purposes was answered in print and sermon by Church-Tory arguments against precipitous changes. Archbishop William Sancroft and leading Anglican politicians such as the earls of Nottingham and Rochester expressed deep concerns that any move to depose James in favour of William would compromise the legitimacy of the restored monarchy and of the church associated with it. Thanks in part to James's attack upon them, the archbishop and his Episcopal colleagues had gained much greater popular influence than they had enjoyed in the parliamentary elections of the Restoration Crisis. Moreover, not all English people were enthusiastic about Dutch William's invasion or about accepting a second 'William the conqueror' as king. Few had imagined such an outcome, even after the invasion began.

Despite the gravity of the issues, the parliamentary election of 1689 was marked by fewer contests than had generally been the case since 1679. This was in part because of the haste in which it occurred and also in part because of confusion in the constituencies after James's reversal of his remodellings and purges. Some 70 seats were contested in 50 constituencies, but these contests were often more about local rivalries than about the issues that divided Whigs and Tories. The results nevertheless reflected the bitter divisions of the recent past: 174 MPs chosen in 1689 were experienced Whig parliamentarians; 156 were old Tories. 183 new members were chosen in 1689; and although many of them had Whig or Tory inclinations, the new members also included men whose minds would either be made up or changed by the events that followed. MPs who were now or who had once been associated with nonconformity of one kind or another made up almost one fifth of the membership of the Commons. The house noisily rejected the Tory Sir Edward Seymour for Speaker. Its choice instead of an experienced Country leader of the 1670s, one who had also been a moderate Whig, was a good indication of its political complexion. Still, the division of the house was narrow, and the large number of new MPs left the Whigs' majority rather fragile.[8]

The Whigs did not, however, have a majority in the House of Lords, which had rejected exclusion in 1680. In the first ten days of the Convention, the Commons and the Lords seemed again to be proceeding in different directions. On 28 January, when the Commons debated the state of the nation, members focused upon James's behaviour as king and upon the implications of his flight for his kingship. Whigs and Tories could agree that James had threatened the kingdom's constitution and the Protestant establishment. Whigs and Tories could also agree that they now found the throne empty. But was the throne empty as a result of James's behaviour as king, or was it merely empty because James had fled the country and its government? Many Whigs argued that

James's wrongful behaviour as king – his violation of the laws of the kingdom – had irreversibly deprived him of his kingship. As the argument was put most strongly, a king can 'forfeit' his kingship 'if he break that pact and covenant with his people', upon which government rests, thereby abdicating his rule, which then 'is devolved into the people'. According to this argument, James had dissolved his government through his actions and had forever forfeited his kingship. The meeting of the Convention therefore represented a radical break with the past and an opportunity to create a new regime.

Leading Tories strongly disagreed with this reasoning, fearful that it would damage both the principle of hereditary succession and the legitimacy of Restoration institutions. They argued that James's flight was the equivalent in law of the 'demise' of the crown through the death of the monarch. James's departure had produced an 'interruption … in the administration' of government only, which needed to be remedied. James had not been deposed, and the government had not been dissolved. For parliament to act as if James had been deposed would suggest that the monarchy was elective. For parliament to accept that the Restoration government had been dissolved left the way open for the establishment of another republic or commonwealth. The Tory position, on the other hand, would enable parliament to establish a regency for Mary on behalf of her withdrawn father. Alternately, parliament might accept the succession of Mary as the legitimate monarch, in hereditary succession to her departed predecessor, on the convenient assumption that the infant son of Mary Beatrice was not James's natural offspring.

The resolution that the Commons eventually sent to the Lords about the state of the realm pointed to the Whigs' success in that house. It employed contractual language that had been explicitly condemned by the Oxford dons in 1683. It also went beyond the comfort level of many Tories by turning James's flight into an abdication: 'King James the Second, having endeavoured to subvert the constitution of the kingdom, by breaking the original contract between king and people, and … having violated the fundamental laws, and having withdrawn himself out of this kingdom, has abdicated the government, and … the throne is thereby become vacant.' Tory peers could not accept the resolution in this form and soon rejected the ideas that the throne was 'vacant' and that James had 'abdicated'. Indeed, the day after the Commons' debate about the state of the kingdom, a loyalist proposal for a regency was lost in the Lords by a scant three votes, 51 to 48. Those who supported the regency were a roll call of the Church-Tory elite, including Rochester, Clarendon, Nottingham, Godolphin, and most of the bishops. On the other hand, Danby now favoured the succession of Mary outright.[9]

As discussions continued in each house and between the houses, the Whigs staked out an innovative rationale for the radical changes they were proposing. Their arguments about a forfeiture of authority, about contractual relationships between governors and the governed, and about the dissolution and recreation of governments were not new. These ideas were, however, being drawn together in a coherent justification for revolution, as they would be again and again by subsequent revolutionaries. The Tories just as clearly had the stronger argument in describing the actual circumstances of the kingdom. James had not, in fact, abdicated. He was across the channel in France, still claiming to be the legitimate monarch of the three Stuart kingdoms. If James had not abdicated, neither could the throne really be considered 'vacant'.

This debate might have gone on interminably had not the London citizenry begun to show renewed signs of restlessness and, more importantly, had not William intervened again. The prince informed the politicians that he would withdraw with his army unless the crown was offered to him. He was not prepared to accept the sole rule of Mary, whose claim to the throne he had until recently defended without reference to his own. Now he would neither be his wife's 'gentleman usher' nor 'reign by her courtesy'. He agreed with those of his supporters who believed that 'the husband ought rather to rule the wife, than the wife the husband' and that the reversal of those roles 'is not possible, nor ought to be in nature'. With their strongly patriarchal political orientation, most Tories could scarcely disagree with these sentiments. When Mary, on her way from the Netherlands to Westminster, conveyed her refusal to rule without her husband, the matter was largely settled. Moreover, Tories in both houses had already joined with Whigs in agreeing 'that it hath been found, by experience, to be inconsistent with the safety and welfare of this Protestant kingdom, to be governed by a popish prince'. That position further assisted many Tories in distancing themselves from James and from the claims of his 'pretended brat beyond the sea'.

A sufficient number of Tory peers were thus able to bend their principles for the Lords to drop their objections to the idea that the throne was 'vacant' through James's 'abdication'. Tories assuaged their Anglican consciences with the thought that the 'absolute necessity of having a government' required them to make the best of a bad situation. They were further accommodated when new loyalty oaths were prepared that merely required them to acknowledge that William and Mary were monarchs in fact rather than in right. Yet most Tories were uneasily aware that they had agreed to accept in 1689 what they had refused to accept in 1679–81, namely, the alteration of the hereditary succession by parliament.[10]

One other critical matter accompanied parliament's movement towards the acceptance of William and Mary as joint monarchs. Early in the session, Whig and Tory speakers in the Commons had suggested the need for a statement about what powers the crown actually possessed. A committee chaired by the London Whig lawyer Sir George Treby was appointed to prepare such a document. The draft 'Heads of Grievances' that were quickly returned to the house were a catalogue of the practices of James – and of Charles as well – to which objections had been made ever since the parliamentary clashes of the 1670s. Indeed, the Heads were the ultimate expression of the Country legislative programme that had emerged before the Restoration Crisis, now enlarged in response to the events of the 1680s. The document denied that the crown's prerogative included any right to dispense with or to suspend parliamentary legislation or to maintain a standing army without parliamentary authorization. It declared James's commission for ecclesiastical causes illegal. It affirmed the rights of subjects to petition and of Protestant subjects to hold arms. It called for frequent parliaments and for the free election of MPs. All of these pronouncements were thought by most MPs of both parties merely to restate the legal boundaries for the exercise of the prerogative. They were mostly wrong about that, however. The legality of the dispensing power had been upheld in King's Bench, for instance, albeit by judges chosen for their partiality to the crown. Moreover, although the House of Commons had, in the 1670s, condemned both the suspension of statutes by the crown and the keeping of a standing army, Commons' resolutions did not have the force of law.

If the draft Heads of Grievances proposed new law in these respects, they clearly did so in others as well, as Tories noted at the time. The obvious innovations included condemnations of the crown's attacks on borough charters and of its use of prorogations to prolong a parliament or to abbreviate a session. The Heads also included an extensive assortment of grievances arising from the crown's political employment of the courts in the 1680s: the removal of judges without sufficient cause, exorbitant fines and bail, and the manipulation of juror selection. Taking Tory reservations about too expansive a statement into consideration, the Commons chose to emphasize, for the time being, only those limitations on the crown thought already to have the force of law. The result was a new document entitled the Declaration of Rights that also incorporated the language about James's 'abdication' and the 'vacancy' of the throne that had been agreed to by both houses.

The Declaration of Rights was presented to William and Mary on 13 February 1689 at the time of their proclamation as monarchs in the Banqueting Hall of Whitehall Palace, near the site of the execution of Charles I in 1649. Some Whigs thought that William and Mary should affirm the declaration prior to their receipt of the crowns, but this idea was rejected, both by William and by the Tories. The contractual implications of such an arrangement were too obvious for William, who had no desire to weaken the crown he was accepting. Any suggestion that the new monarchs were replacing their predecessor because of James's violation of a contract with his subjects was also removed from the declaration.

Some Whigs at the time and some historians since then have nevertheless interpreted the Banqueting Hall ceremony along contractual lines. Yet no such interpretation is necessary to advance the revolutionary character of the succession of William III and Mary II and of their acceptance of the declaration. Parliament (as the Convention soon declared itself to be) had, in fact, deposed a monarch. It had also arranged a succession not in accordance with strict hereditary principles, even without considering James's son, for William was assigned the 'sole and full exercise of the regal power'. He was to continue as monarch, should Mary predecease him, regardless of her sister Anne's superior hereditary claim to the throne. Mary's untimely death from smallpox in 1694 actually brought that scenario to pass sooner rather than later. By then, the Protestant hero of 1688–9 had been revealed to be a dour and uncommunicative European, every bit as stubborn as James, and as capable of duplicity as Charles. Still, William's rule was secure, even if secured by rules he had not made.

In fact, despite MPs' insistence that they were merely resettling the government 'as near to the ancient constitution as can be', the Declaration of Rights enhanced the rights of parliament and of subjects; and it did so in language that would have been unacceptable to all previous English monarchs. These innovations were confirmed when the declaration was enacted as the Bill of Rights in the second session of the Convention Parliament, later in 1689. In limiting the crown in new ways, the declaration represented a sharp break with the Restoration settlement. It deprived the crown of powers that both Charles and James had utilized to manage parliament and to outmanoeuvre their critics. Indeed, the declaration was intended to prevent the crown from ever again manipulating parliament and the law in ways that both Whigs and Tories found incompatible with 'parliamentary government'. The crown was certainly left in 1689 with many remaining powers, including the rights of summoning parliaments, of appointing the chief civil and military officers of the realm, and of formally making war and peace. The Declaration of Rights nevertheless initiated a series of diminishments to the crown's freedom of action that would be made over the course of William's reign. Finally, the events of 1688–9 saddled the Tories with the internal contradiction of continuing to profess allegiance to hereditary principles they had actually violated. That contradiction would contribute to the Tories' eventual weakening as a party and to the emergence of a quite different political paradigm in the Whig ascendancy of the mid-eighteenth century.[11]

The Glorious Revolution in England might have been revolutionary in one other respect as well. The Heads of Grievances called both for the toleration of sectarian dissenters and for the comprehension of those nonconformists who might be included within the 'public worship'. The Toleration Act subsequently adopted by the Convention Parliament, in May 1689, has often been depicted as both a reward to dissenters for supporting the church against James and a leap forward into the Enlightenment toleration of religious minorities. In fact, it was neither. The act provided moderate dissenters with far less than what they had expected after the Anglican overtures of 1688, and it perpetuated the religious division that many in the Convention sought to heal.

William was partially responsible for this result. The Anglican Earl of Nottingham had taken the initiative in the Lords, as he had in 1680, in promoting measures to provide both toleration and comprehension, while retaining the sacramental test or some equivalent for office holding. William, who had defended the test against James in 1687–88, indicated in March 1689, however, that he preferred its elimination in order to enjoy the services of all his Protestant subjects. Such a proposal was simply too much for many churchmen, who had already swallowed their hereditary principles, and who distrusted William's Reformed religious background as closer to that of the Presbyterians. They feared that, without the sacramental test for MPs and other office holders, the Anglican Church would be as vulnerable to political alteration under a Calvinist prince as it already had been under a Catholic one. The Anglican response to William's initiative was, therefore, largely negative. One aroused MP hoped measures for comprehension would 'lie on the table until Doomsday'. Scores of Whig MPs joined with their Tory counterparts in defending the test as necessary for the preservation of a Protestant establishment. The Toleration Act, which had been designed for sectarians only, was adopted and applied to all Protestant dissenters, who could now worship openly. They were still legally ineligible for office, however, since neither the Corporation Act nor the 1673 Test Act were repealed, despite the efforts of some parliamentary Whigs to do just that. Comprehension was assigned for further discussion to the clerical Convocation of the Church of England, which, meeting later in 1689, quickly consigned the idea to oblivion.

The parliamentary toleration of 1689 was, thus, less generous than the indulgence with full civil rights that James had offered, through the prerogative, in 1687–8. The coercion of Protestants was gone, to be sure; and over 1200 dissenting places of worship were licenced soon after the adoption of the act. Yet the sacramental test continued as a pillar of the state, and as an enduring legacy of the Restoration, into the nineteenth century. Protestant dissenters nevertheless found various means for getting around the test; and their success in doing so would contribute significantly to the party tensions of the next quarter century. Moreover, in accepting toleration, the Anglican establishment had finally, if painfully, relinquished its Restoration goal of being the church of all Protestant subjects.[12]

The Revolution was, then, a compromise between the parties: the Tories salvaged their church, while abandoning their king; and the Whigs deposed a king they had never wanted, while accepting critical elements of a national church they disliked. Because the achievement of this compromise was hard fought, the settlement left party politicians as distrustful of each other as they had been in the early 1680s. Indeed, by perfectly satisfying nobody, the Revolution's 'settlement' of the issues of church and state ensured that party conflict would continue through the 1690s and for years to come. The rhetoric of each party quickly suggested that the kingdom's future could not safely be entrusted to the other. Even before the end of the Convention Parliament, for instance, the Whigs unsuccessfully attempted to proscribe from further political service all Tories who had cooperated in Charles's remodellings of the boroughs. The parliamentary election of 1690 was also accompanied by the circulation of rival blacklists of candidates whose commitments to monarchy or to the Revolution were questioned by the other party.

That election was the first in almost a dozen, over the course of the next quarter century, in which the parties contested with a fury that troubled both the public sphere and numerous localities. Lacking some of the organizational features of modern parties, the Whigs and Tories of the late Stuart era were nevertheless recognizably different from each other; and as parties, they were taken as seriously by contemporaries as their modern counterparts have been. The Tories remained the party of staunch Anglicanism; the Whigs remained the party of dissent and of English puritan tradition. The Tories remained the party of the old cavalier squirearchy; the Whigs remained the party of trade, business, and finance. William sought to trim between the parties; but his efforts to keep a mixed ministry of Whig and Tory leaders were regularly adjusted to the changing balance between the parties in his parliaments.[13]

If the Revolution was a turning point in the establishment of parliamentary government, it did not, therefore, represent a complete break between the political world of the 1680s and that of the ensuing decades. Many of the issues and the party structures of politics remained the same. The relationship between the parties and some issues did nevertheless change, primarily because of the quarter century of warfare that began in May 1689. William then took his new kingdoms into a general war against France in alliance with

the Netherlands and a collection of anti-French states and principalities. This War of the League of Augsburg continued until 1697.
It required parliamentary taxation on a scale undreamt of during
the Restoration, and it reignited the tensions that had erupted in
the era of Danby's ministry between the government and MPs with
Country perspectives. Those tensions continued into the reign of
Queen Anne (1702–14) as well. The international contest then
re-erupted in the War of the Spanish Succession (1702–13), in which
Louis sought to draw Spain and its colonies into the French sphere,
through the succession of his Bourbon grandson to the Spanish
throne. The Country ideas that had developed in the 1670s were, by
that time, flourishing anew as a legacy of both the Restoration and
the Revolution. Country ideas endured, despite the achievement
of parliamentary government, because the wars that followed the
Revolution also established the sizable military and civil administration the Country had always feared.

The Whigs saw vigorous prosecution of the wars as necessary
for defence of the Revolution they had just made. This was because
one of Louis XIV's objectives was the re-establishment of James II
(d. 1701), and then of his son, James Francis Edward, on their Stuart
thrones. The Tories, on the other hand, resented England's entan-
glement in the long-term defences of the Netherlands and of an
international balance they thought primarily benefited continental
interests. To win the wars, the Whigs were prepared to maintain the
largest land army England had ever seen and to take the lead in
offensive operations in Europe. The Tories, who believed that the
country's allies needed to assume the principal costs of the wars,
instead preferred a limited English commitment based upon the
contributions of the navy. Many Tory gentry also came to believe
that the incessant fiscal demands of a growing state and military
establishment threatened the autonomy of the localities, the independence of parliament, and the wealth and social hegemony of the
landed elite. Whig commitment to the wars and Tory reservations
about them combined to produce an odd ideological and polemical
reversal of the roles the parties had taken in the Restoration Crisis.
The Whigs gradually embraced the needs of central government,
and they became less likely than the Tories to employ the Country
language they had once espoused. The parties' departures from
their Restoration roles were already becoming apparent by the end
of William's reign.

By then parliament had met every year since the Revolution, a pattern of annual sessions that has continued until the present. The Bill of Rights encouraged frequent parliaments, but only warfare on the unprecedented scale that began in 1689 required annual sessions for discussion of the ways and means to fund it. Having experienced a financially independent crown under James, parliament sought initially to keep William on a short financial leash. But by 1690, when his civil revenues were settled and his invasion expenses were funded, William already required another £1.8 million for the fleet; and he needed £2.3 million to raise an army to assist in the continental containment of France. Those expenses were only the beginning. Year by year, throughout the war, MPs met to consider the government's financial needs and to devise the taxes necessary to support them.

James's government had cost the country some £2 million a year; but William spent almost £50 million between 1689 and 1697, three-quarters of it for the war. After 1693, the mainstay of revenue collection was the land tax, a levy on land and real estate that became as unavoidable as a modern income tax and that produced a similar measure of happiness on the part of those (chiefly the landed gentry) who paid it. The land tax was accompanied by a host of taxes on trade; and the government's financial needs were also supplied by public loans, especially those generated by the new Bank of England authorized by parliament in 1694. The implications of this 'Financial Revolution' will be considered below. The point to make here is that war required the annual meeting of parliament to approve expenditures, taxes, and loans. Parliamentary government was ensured as much by the financial realities of warfare as by the high-minded Bill of Rights.[14]

The growth of the kingdom's military, however, touched raw nerves for many MPs schooled in Restoration debates about standing armies. So did the growth of central revenue departments charged with the raising of funds. The combined average annual strength of the army and navy during William's war was almost 120,000 men. Between 1690 and 1708, the number of employees in the revenue collecting departments of the government also almost doubled, from about 2500 to about 4800. Few who had supported William's invasion had imagined at the time that it would lead to an army that dwarfed James's, to taxes greater than Cromwell's, or to the most fiscally intrusive government in English experience. Indeed, the Revolution and the ensuing warfare solidified the state far more effectively than any of Charles's or James's divisive efforts to strengthen the Stuart regime through the prerogative. The Revolution and its wars thus corrected some of the military, administrative, and fiscal weaknesses of the once fragile English state. England (as well as Ireland and Scotland) would remain lightly governed in the eighteenth century, at least by some continental standards; but a more cohesive and effective 'fiscal-military' state was nevertheless emerging.

As the English wartime state achieved this durability, many Country-minded MPs worried that the size of the military and civil establishments controlled by ministers might threaten the parliamentary independence they had worked to secure. As had been the case in 1675, they especially worried that scores of placemen in the Commons might enable ministers to influence parliamentary outcomes. As early as 1692–3 the Commons included some 130 MPs whose retention of civil or military offices depended upon ministerial favour. Whigs took the lead in the early 1690s in promoting legislation to reduce or to eliminate the danger to the independence of the legislature from these placemen. Their attachment to old Country phobias about placemen waned thereafter, however, as the collective Whig ministry known as the Junto, which governed from 1694 to 1699, wedded itself to the growing military and civil bureaucracy. Hostility to placemen would now become a Tory attribute.

Similarly, frequent parliaments had been an old Whig and Country shibboleth. However, the successful endeavour of 1693–4 to turn the call for regular parliaments in the Bill of Rights into a new Triennial Act produced mixed feelings among some Whigs. They worried about the danger to wartime government initiatives from insular MPs and reactive electors. Thereafter, as the Whig Junto 'became preoccupied with the processes rather than the principles of government', Whig interest in guarantees of parliamentary independence or in parliamentary oversight of state resources weakened. That was not the case for many Tories, however. In the peacetime interval of 1697–1701, Tories, rather than Whigs, took the parliamentary lead in attacking the size of William's army as a threat to the national interest. Tories impeached Whig ministers for complicity in a Williamite foreign policy they disliked. Tories, rather than Whigs, attacked the prerogatives of the crown in the Act of Settlement (1701), which assigned the throne to the Protestant electoral family of Hanover, should the direct Stuart line die out with Anne, as it did.

Some Tory adoption of Country ideas was a matter of short-term political tactics, and some Whigs could still wrap their 'revolution principles' in Country rhetoric. Yet Tory employment of Country language was often a genuine expression of local hostility to the leviathan the Whigs had created at the centre, whereas the same Country language often stuck in the throats of Whigs dedicated to the transformation of the state and of its military services. Many Tories saw the growth of the state as a threat to the domination of the kingdom by its natural governors, the Anglican gentry, who they believed should rule at Westminster, just as they did in the localities. One-time supporters of the Stuart prerogative, Tories became critics of the executive departments that increasingly surrounded and sometimes overshadowed the crown.[15]

This transformation of the parties carried critical ideas of the Restoration forward into the eighteenth century; but such a transformation could not have been predicted in 1688-9. It was, nevertheless, an import part of the transition to the rather different political paradigm that emerged after 1720. What did not change during this transformation of the parties was the centrality of parliament to the nation's politics. That was an accomplishment that could be traced back to the Country ideas of the 1670s, back to the Whigs' efforts to alter the succession in parliament in 1679–81, and back to the Tories' defence of the integrity of parliament against James II. Moreover, Country MPs and county gentry who worried about the potential manipulation of parliament by the crown and its ministers after 1689 were expressing the same commitment to free parliaments that had led to the restoration of Charles II in 1660 and to support for William's invasion in 1688. Yet, although parliamentary government would look different in the hands of the Whig oligarchs of the 1720s than it did in the minds of Whig exclusionists in the 1680s, it was still a far different polity from the 'popery and arbitrary government' the Country feared in the 1670s.

The Revolution in Ireland

The Glorious Revolution was just as important a turning point in Ireland and Scotland as it was in England; but the revolution in England did not determine the course of events in the other Stuart kingdoms. Under its new Catholic regime, Ireland rejected the Protestant revolution in England, while Scotland experienced its own Presbyterian revolution against the political and religious structures of the Restoration. The resettlement of the Stuart kingdoms in the wake of the English deposition of James II required the reconquest of Ireland through warfare that scarcely supports the usual depiction of the Glorious Revolution as bloodless. In the end, Williamite success in Ireland involved the re-establishment of Protestant ascendancy, the political suppression of the Catholic majority, and a reaffirmation of Ireland's dependent status.

That Irish affairs would turn in these directions was scarcely apparent in 1688. Tyrconnell's Catholic government held firm as James's English and Scottish regimes disintegrated. In some areas, remaining Protestants established defensive military associations for their self-protection. Protestant flight from the countryside to the towns and cities or for England also continued, however, especially as rumours of impending Catholic massacres spread. A writer in County Kerry could scarcely find 20 English residents in April 1689, and none of them 'had the value of sixpence left'. Neither were all Protestant Irish cheered over the winter of 1688–9 by the news from England: Irish Episcopalians were as caught as their Anglican counterparts between loyalty to James as king and disgust with his policies. For his part, Tyrconnell was determined to maintain the Catholic state he had created. His banner over Dublin Castle read 'Now or Never, Now and Forever'.

James II arrived in Ireland in March, his nerves and his determination restored in France. After subduing any opposition in Ireland, he intended to use his western kingdom as a springboard for attacking William and recovering both England and Scotland. In the end, however, the 'war of the two kings' that James unleashed was largely an Irish civil war, and Irish Catholics would join their Catholic king as its chief victims. The details of the war have not been forgotten in Ireland, either in the Republic or in the North. These events confirmed animosities between the Protestant and Catholic populations of the island that have never been healed.

The Jacobite menace from Ireland was real; and the outcome of the war was far from certain. Tyrconnell quickly built up the Irish army to some 40,000 men, although this force was more impressive for its size than for its discipline or experience. Protestants in Dublin were disarmed; and the Protestant military associations were either subdued or defeated. Only the Ulster towns of Enniskillen and Londonderry, where over 30,000 refugees were soon under siege, held out against the Jacobite army. The English navy proved incapable of disrupting French convoys that supplied James with a military arsenal, with French advisers and troops, and with Catholic officers of Irish, Scots, and English extraction. After arriving, James summoned an Irish parliament, the first to sit since 1666; and he met it in May. Never before had an English monarch actually convened his Irish parliament in person, an occurrence that would be repeated only once, in the equally delicate year of 1921.

By meeting a parliament and by proclaiming his attachment to liberty for conscience, James sought to give the lie to Williamite claims that he was an arbitrary king. Yet, this was a parliament packed with Old English Catholics returned under Tyrconnell's new borough charters. Ulster was scarcely represented. A few Protestant peers and bishops took up their places in the House of Lords, and another handful of Protestants appeared in the Commons, among some 230 MPs. The 'patriot' parliament, as some sympathetic writers have called it, quickly repealed the 1662 land settlement. Rejecting Tyrconnell's previous plan for an equal division of disputed lands between old and new proprietors, parliament instead restored to Old English Catholics everything they had lost since 1641. Additionally, the properties of over 2000 'rebels' and departed Protestants were declared forfeit. Still attached to the property rights of all his English subjects in Ireland, James reluctantly agreed to these measures in return for the taxes he needed to support his army. He also agreed to a measure that liberated the Irish parliament from English parliamentary and legal jurisdiction. He baulked, however, at an attempted repeal of Poynings's Law, which maintained the general superiority of the English government over Ireland. He also broke with the Catholic hierarchy by promoting an act for toleration and by refusing to overthrow the Protestant Irish establishment for the sake of the Roman Church. James feared that any such disestablishment would further alienate his Episcopalian subjects in England, whose allegiance he still hoped to recover.[16]

Even before the conclusion of parliament, however, Jacobite momentum was slowing; and the parliamentary session had diverted James's attention from carrying on the war. In July 1689, the siege of Londonderry was broken by an English relief expedition, just as the last rations were distributed; and the Protestant townsmen of Enniskillen mauled a Jacobite force sent against them. In August, English troops began disembarking near Belfast. They were officered by Irish Protestants who had been cashiered by Tyrconnell, and they were commanded by a Huguenot general who had defected from Louis XIV to William. English penetration beyond Ulster was initially stalled by disease and by James's advance with the bulk of his Catholic army. The climactic battle of the war did not occur until July 1690. By then the new English king had himself arrived in Ireland with sufficient reinforcements to bring his Irish army up to 37,000.

The two armies encountered one another on opposite sides of the River Boyne, a few miles upstream from the symbolically significant town of Drogheda. William narrowly escaped death on the eve of the battle when a stray Jacobite cannon shot grazed his shoulder as he surveyed the area. The ensuing Battle of the Boyne was both the largest military confrontation ever to occur in Ireland and a genuine battle of the nations. In addition to Irish, English, and Scots troops, the two armies included French (both Catholic and Huguenot), Dutch, Germans, Danes, and Walloons. The encounter was one of European significance as well. Louis's hope of tying William down in the bogs of Ireland depended on the battle's outcome, as did William's hope of mopping up in Ireland in order to block Louis on the continent. James, Tyrconnell, and William each commanded critical regiments. The result turned on James's misreading of a Williamite feint, which drew too many of his troops away from the main English attack.

A major defeat for James, the Battle of the Boyne has been celebrated by Northern Irish Protestants ever since. Yet the Boyne was not a devastating defeat for Catholic Ireland. James fled back to France, and William liberated eastern Ireland and Dublin, to the relief of its Protestant inhabitants. But the Jacobite army regrouped in the west, at Limerick, and most of Munster and Connacht remained in Catholic hands. William lost much more of his army in an unsuccessful siege of Limerick than he did at the Boyne. He returned to England in September 1690 without the complete subjugation of Ireland he had sought. Irish Protestants were nevertheless cheered again, in the autumn, by the fall of Cork and Kinsale to another English force commanded by John Churchill, now Earl of Marlborough. These victories deprived the Jacobite army of the ports that had served as conduits for French supplies. In the meantime, William's Irish government began to operate in Dublin. Numerous Catholic leaders were indicted in the courts and suffered a legal forfeiture of their properties. The west of the country filled with impoverished Catholic refugees. Catholic irregulars or rapparees nevertheless remained a threat to Protestant lives and properties in many areas nominally under control of the Williamite government.

The war ended the following year. Athlone fell to a Williamite siege at the end of June 1691, and a Jacobite force of some 20,000 was broken on the point of victory at Aughrim when its commander was killed. A third of the Jacobite force died in the ensuing panic and rout. The final western towns in Jacobite hands surrendered – Galway almost immediately, and Limerick after another siege, protracted negotiations, and the death (from natural causes) of Tyrconnell. The Treaty of Limerick brought resistance to William's regime to an end throughout the kingdom. It permitted 12,000 Irish Catholic troops to depart with honour to France, where they continued to serve under James II in the army of Louis XIV. Catholic property-owners in areas still under Jacobite control were required to take an oath of allegiance to William and Mary to retain or to be restored to their lands. Catholics were also assured of such religious liberties as were not prohibited by law under Charles II, and William's emissaries at Limerick promised to secure agreement to these terms from an Irish parliament. Twenty-five thousand had died in the fighting. More had probably died of disease and malnourishment in the midst of sieges, plundering, and the disruption of agricultural life by troops and rapparees. The Irish rural economy, which had flourished through much of the two previous decades, was devastated. The Catholic revival was over, and the work of the Jacobite parliament negated. Irish Protestants were about to establish an ascendancy that would not be challenged again for a century, until the era of the French Revolution.[17]

William III hoped that the conciliatory provisions of the Treaty of Limerick might be incorporated into the resettlement of Ireland. His generosity towards defeated Catholics was a reflection of his own commitment to liberty for conscience. He pardoned numerous Jacobite landowners who had been attainted before the Irish courts. The leaders of Protestant Ireland, who had experienced their old nightmare of a return to the 1640s, were in no mood for

William's reconciliation, however. They were determined never again to permit a Catholic political recovery. An initial effort at Irish resettlement in the parliament of 1692, assembled by Henry Sidney, William's first lord lieutenant, was a fiasco. The crown's conciliatory agenda collided with that of Protestant gentry and townsmen who had returned to their estates and to their local hegemony. An exclusively Protestant body, as dictated by an English law of 1691, the Irish parliament declined to endorse William's toleration. Moreover, in asserting its sole right to initiate financial legislation for Ireland, the Commons proved as bent upon overcoming the legislative shackles of Poynings's Law as its Jacobite predecessor. This was a parliament of landed men influenced by English Country ideology, and they were determined to ensure that Ireland would never again be ruled without an Irish parliament. They were prorogued within a month, leaving the Irish government without an income and Sidney without William's confidence.

The settlement of Ireland did not take legislative form until 1695. A new viceroy with impeccable Protestant credentials, Lord Henry Capel (brother of Essex, the Whig martyr and former lord lieutenant) then exercised more political adroitness in dealing with a newly elected parliament. By taking the leading intransigents of the 1692 Commons into office, Capel succeeded in funding the government and in saving Poynings's Law. He did so at the cost of William's hope of conciliating the Catholic majority, however. Capel accepted acts that prohibited Catholics from possessing arms or even owning horses worth over £5. Catholics were forbidden to send their children abroad for education. An act to ban members of Catholic orders from Ireland was rejected by the English Privy Council, but it was accepted when readopted and enlarged in 1697 to include the Catholic bishops. Moreover, when the Treaty of Limerick was finally accepted by the Irish parliament in that year, the clause promising Catholics the same measure of toleration they had enjoyed under Charles II was omitted.

The discriminatory legislation against Catholics was steadily enlarged by successive Irish parliaments through the early eighteenth century. In 1698, for instance, Catholics were prohibited from practicing law. A 1703 measure was designed to destroy concentrations of wealth in Catholic landed families by requiring partible inheritance, while also preventing Catholics from purchasing Protestant land or even leasing it on long terms. New Catholic clergy were banned from entering the kingdom after 1704, while priests already in the kingdom were obliged to register. And finally, in 1728, the Dublin parliament completed its anti-Catholic penal code with a measure restricting the right to vote in parliamentary elections to Protestants. The harshness of these measures was legitimized, in part, by the failure of most Catholic clergy to abjure the legitimacy of James III, as James Francis Edward became, in Jacobite minds, upon the death of his father. A principal result of the Glorious Revolution in Ireland, then, was the political proscription and social ostracism of Catholics; and the Irish Catholic Church remained a distinctly Jacobite organization.[18]

The Anglo-Irish gentry who dominated Irish affairs after the Glorious Revolution were little more favourably disposed to the kingdom's Protestant dissenters. Their hostility was especially directed towards the Ulster Presbyterians, the largest and most assertive of the Irish dissenting communities. The bishops of the Church of Ireland, who had come to see the Presbyterian clergy as dangerous competitors, were equally hostile. Presbyterian enthusiasm for William had exposed the mixed feelings of staunch Episcopalians, and William had responded by reviving and increasing the royal payment to the Presbyterian clergy that Charles II had introduced in the 1670s. The Presbyterians of Ulster were, moreover, largely of Scots extraction; and the fate of the Scottish bishops at Presbyterian hands in 1689 (still to be examined) left the Irish bishops apprehensive about the future of their church. When the Ulster Presbyterians organized their presbyteries into a general synod in 1691, they appeared to be setting themselves up as a rival establishment. Indeed, with clerical stipends from the crown, the Presbyterians had achieved quasi-establishment in the north of the kingdom.

The Revolution's legacy for Irish Protestants was, therefore, a hardening of divisions rather than the Protestant unity and accommodation that William preferred. Ulster Presbyterians dug in at the local level, and their numbers increased dramatically in the 1690s. Thousands of Scots Presbyterians then relocated to Ulster's greener pastures as a significant dearth afflicted the Scottish Lowlands. At the opening of the eighteenth century, Presbyterians made up a majority of Ulster's population, and they outnumbered the conformist population almost everywhere in the northern counties. They were actively involved in the civic governments of Londonderry, Belfast, and other Ulster towns. With dissenters from other persuasions, Presbyterians were heavily involved in trade throughout Ireland; and they dominated the expanding linen industry in the north. They generally worshipped freely and openly, in violation of the Irish uniformity act.

Irish nonconformists were unable to secure even the modest legal toleration enjoyed by English dissenters, however, and nothing like the freedom of worship they had been granted by James II. Toleration bills supported by the crown failed regularly in the Irish parliaments of the 1690s. The Episcopalian interest insisted that an Irish test act, restricting office holding to those willing to take the sacrament in the established church, be adopted first. In 1704, such a test was finally adopted, but without any measure of toleration, leaving dissenters technically disqualified from local office. Not until 1719 did the Irish parliament legally countenance the de facto toleration of Protestant dissenters that actually prevailed. By then the religious division between Protestants had become a factor in the rivalry between the Irish Whig and Tory parties, just as it had been in England since the 1680s. The Church of Ireland remained the respectable church of Ireland, but it also remained a weaker and less effective church body than Protestant accommodation might have produced.[19]

Irish Catholics were far more aggrieved than Irish dissenters, however. The Glorious Revolution returned them to a state little better than what they had experienced under Cromwell. When the Dublin parliament accepted the landed provisions of the Treaty of Limerick, it restricted the broad protections the treaty had originally offered Jacobite property owners. Although adjudication of land disputes in the next few years was fair to Catholics, Catholic landownership was still drastically reduced as a result of wartime forfeitures. Catholic ownership fell from 22 per cent of all Irish land to a mere 14 per cent. In only five of Ireland's counties – two of them in the west – did it still exceed a quarter. Thereafter, the discriminatory legislation against Catholics took a further toll, as many landowners converted to Protestantism for the sake of political and social acceptability. By the end of the eighteenth century, only 5 per cent of Irish land remained in Catholic hands.

The Protestant squires of Ireland had, then, largely succeeded in emasculating their Catholic counterparts and in securing the ascendancy they sought to establish in the Restoration. In the European eighteenth century – a 'century of aristocracy' in which political structures were generally dominated by landed elites – Ireland was singular as a Catholic country with a Protestant aristocracy. The Irish Catholic hierarchy was similarly attenuated. Hundreds of Catholic clergy and several of the bishops departed in the 1690s, as the first of the new penal laws took effect, leaving about 1000 clergy behind to minister, most without much supervision by their superiors. No effort was made by the Protestant state to prohibit Catholic worship, but with limited clergy and with few resources, Catholicism was often reduced, outside the towns, to the status of folk religion. Catholic merchants and traders fared better, but they operated on the political and social fringes. Although some old English Catholics struggled to retain their social visibility, the Gaelic Irish were the largest submerged culture in Britain. Indeed, the Catholic Irish were among the most significant marginalized peoples in Enlightenment Europe.[20]

Ascendant over Catholics, the Protestant elite of Ireland nevertheless dominated a dependent kingdom; and Ireland's subordinate status within the broader British polity was strongly confirmed over the course of William's reign. William and Mary had become monarchs of Ireland not by any proclamation of the Irish parliament, but rather because rule over Ireland was bestowed upon them at Westminster, in 1689, by an exclusively English parliament. In English thinking, Ireland's status was not much above that of the colonies. English writers saw the Irish parliament as inferior to their own and as akin to the colonial assemblies of North America. The constitutional inferiority of Ireland was brought home in 1699 when the Westminster parliament prohibited the foreign export of Irish woollens in order to protect West Country woollen interests. In this instance, the subordination of Ireland to English economic priorities was as clear as it had been in the 1667 adoption of the Irish cattle act. Some Dublin politicians and writers responded that Ireland was a sovereign kingdom and that it could not be obliged by the acts of an English parliament in which it was not represented. Their claims for parliamentary autonomy were almost as strong as anything Tyrconnell had contemplated for his Catholic state, and they were equally unacceptable to English politicians. The Westminster parliament condemned all such Irish assertions with a ringing confirmation of its authority 'to bind the kingdom and people of Ireland'.

So strong were Irish resentments about English treatment of Ireland as a mere dependency that many Irish landowners came to feel a constitutional union, in which both kingdoms were represented in the same parliament, as in Cromwell's day, would better advance Ireland's interests. English disdain for Ireland and for the Irish (Anglo or otherwise) made that solution to the tensions between the two kingdoms impossible for another century. Despite its subservient status, Protestant Ireland therefore developed its own vigorous parliamentary culture and its own party system in the early eighteenth century. Both were fruits of the Glorious Revolution and of the ensuing wars, which required heavy and regular taxation in Ireland as much as in England. The regularity of Ireland's parliamentary sessions after 1692 also contrasts sharply with the vice-regal pattern of governance that Charles II and James II adopted for their western kingdom. Only after the Hanoverian succession in 1714 did party competition give way to an effective system of Whig parliamentary management.[21]

The Revolution in Scotland

If Ireland gained a parliament through the Glorious Revolution, Scotland eventually lost one. The Revolution led, by 1707, to the parliamentary union of Scotland and England in a new Kingdom of Great Britain. In this creation, the Scots exchanged sovereignty for representation in the Westminster parliament and entrée into the English trading empire. The union both simplified and strengthened British government; and it facilitated economic growth and the expansion of trade as well. Such a result was as unexpected as many other consequences of the Glorious Revolution.

From its beginning, the Scottish revolution proved more drastic in its outcomes than events to the south. It produced more vigorous assertions of parliamentary independence than anything seen since 1640–1. The formerly dominant Episcopalian elite in church and state was dislodged by Presbyterians who showed as little tolerance after 1689 for churchmen as churchmen had once shown for them. The Episcopalian establishment was destroyed, and new political leaders emerged who were relatively free from the taint of association with it. These grandees were, however, often as interested in advancing their own interests as in serving the state. The aggressive spirit of the Scottish revolution eventually carried into the adoption of a royal succession that was at variance with that of England. By 1706–7, the danger of an entirely independent

Scotland that might even revert to its medieval French alignment stampeded English politicians into embracing the unpredictable risks of union for the sake of their own kingdom's security.

The anti-Catholic activities that broke out in Scotland in the autumn of 1688 eventually took an anti-Episcopal direction. James's indulgence of Presbyterians had seriously weakened the Episcopal establishment in the Lowlands and had revitalized Presbyterian worship and local organization. Neither had the Scottish bishops and churchmen benefited from an upsurge in popularity like that experienced in 1688 by the persecuted English bishops. Instead, as crowds in the Scottish cities attacked the signs and symbols of Catholicism, parishioners throughout the Lowlands also drove Episcopal clergy from their churches and manses. These popular 'rabblings' took the form of ritual cleansings of the church: vestments and prayer books were ceremonially burnt as popish trappings, and Episcopal ministers were publicly shamed as apostates from Scottish Reformed tradition. Surviving Presbyterian clergy who had been excluded a generation earlier, or who had secured various forms of indulgence over the years, were returned to their former places by popular acclaim. Some 200–300 Restoration clerical incumbents were evicted by the summer of 1689, as Presbyterianism apparently experienced the same kind of popular revival in Lowland Scotland that Anglicanism had experienced in many parts of England in 1660. Presbyterian clergy assembled in Edinburgh in January 1689 to address William as the 'Lord's chosen ... servant' for their 'deliverance' from the 'yoke of prelacy' and for 'the restoration of the Presbyterian church government'.[22]

When the Scottish estates met in Convention in Edinburgh in March 1689, they met, therefore, in a rhetorical environment in which many anti-Catholic Scots were celebrating a recovery of the Reformation from prelacy and popery alike. The Convention did include Episcopalians who wanted to abandon James's promotion of Catholicism without abandoning James himself; and Edinburgh Castle remained in the hands of James's commander, the Catholic Duke of Gordon. However, numerous Presbyterian burgh commissioners, chosen with the 1681 Test Act in abeyance, wanted no more truck with the Catholic king who had indulged them or with the 'popish' bishops who had persecuted them.

English events had probably already cost James his Scottish throne; but the Scottish politicians were relatively free to work out their own future. An absent William was unable to influence the course of events in Edinburgh as significantly as he had at Westminster. He sent the Duke of Hamilton to the Convention as his commissioner. Hamilton's victory over an Episcopalian lord for the presidency of the body was the first sign that James was about to lose the original Stuart kingdom. An intemperate letter James sent to the Convention further damaged his cause. Within days, the leading Jacobite present, John Graham of Claverhouse, now Viscount Dundee, withdrew from the Convention to organize resistance on behalf of his king. As other Jacobites followed Dundee's lead in walking out, and as Presbyterian influence increased, the Convention overturned the foundations of Restoration government in church and state.

In April 1689 the estates agreed, with few dissenting voices, upon a Claim of Right that surpassed the English Declaration of Rights in employing language that sharply broke from the past. The rule of James VII was invalidated, regardless of his behaviour, on the grounds 'that by the law of this kingdom, no papist can be king or queen,' a statement that seemingly overturned James's right to the throne under the 1681 Succession Act. Without any of the ambiguities or compromises of the English Declaration, the Scottish document boldly declared that James had also 'invaded the fundamental constitution of the kingdom, and altered it from a legal limited monarchy to an arbitrary despotic power'. This characterization of the Stuart monarchy as 'limited' would have surprised many Scottish Restoration politicians and Episcopal apologists. Nevertheless the Convention concluded that, 'the throne is become vacant,' since James had, through his arbitrary rule, also 'forfaulted the right to the crown'.

The Claim of Right also condemned many governing practices of Charles and James, including both the severe methods employed against Presbyterians in 1683–5 and James's claim of a prerogative authority to 'annul and disable laws'. It further declared an end to the Episcopal settlement of the church: 'Prelacy', it argued, is 'a great and insupportable grievance and trouble to this nation, and contrary to the inclinations ... of the people, ever since the Reformation ... and therefore ought to be abolished.' An accompanying set of Articles of Grievance attacked the 1669 Supremacy Act that had confirmed Charles's and James's oversight of the national church. Citing a right to frequent parliaments and a right to freedom of debate within them, the Articles of Grievance also called for an abolition of the lords of the articles, which had managed the Scots estates on behalf of the crown throughout the Restoration. On the whole, the Convention was moved by a vision of government in church and state drawn from the Covenanting movement of 1638–43 and from parliament's reduction of the prerogative in 1640–1. Having redefined the monarchy and called for a new church, parliament offered the 'regal power' to William, and a throne to Mary, in the 'entire confidence' that these monarchs would 'preserve' the 'rights which they have here asserted'.[23]

When William and Mary accepted the crowns of Scotland in May 1689, many makers of the Scottish revolution understood that they had entered into a contract with their new governors. They had asserted that the Scottish monarchy was a limited one, and they believed that William had agreed, in taking the crown, to the adoption of legislation to implement the Claim of Right and the accompanying Grievances. William did not understand the revolution in contractual terms, however; and he also sought to maintain the prerogatives of the Scottish crown he now held. The revolution was not settled without a parliamentary struggle, in 1689–90, between the new king and the Scots revolutionaries. William managed to salvage his authority as monarch, but only by conceding most of the other institutional changes the revolutionaries wanted. This parliamentary struggle coincided with two additional confrontations that continued into the early 1690s. First, a military contest pitted William and the revolutionaries against those who continued to regard James VII as their king. Second, the now dominant Presbyterians worked, often against William's conciliatory instincts, to rid the church of all remnants of the fallen Episcopal establishment.

The parliamentary sessions of 1689–90 well illustrate the political obstreperousness that would plague the monarchy and the monarchy's Scottish ministers until the 1707 union. Scotland was settled politically by 1690, but just barely. A 'Club' of militant Presbyterians – many of them drawn from the Covenanting heartland in the southwest – dominated these sessions. They promoted measures to abolish episcopacy, to eliminate the royal supremacy over the church, and to free parliament from supervision by the lords of the articles. The Club also wanted to incapacitate politicians who held offices under James and who, not incidentally, now held offices under William that Club spokesmen coveted for themselves. The Club was as well organized as Shaftesbury's opposition bloc in the English parliaments of 1679–81, and Club leaders such as Archibald Campbell, the tenth Earl of Argyll, were determined to elevate the Scottish parliament over the prerogatives of the crown. William accepted the abolition of episcopacy. He actually preferred Protestant accommodation in Scotland, just as he did in England; but the failure of all the bishops and many Episcopal clergy to acknowledge him as monarch left him with little choice. He baulked, however, at being deprived of his power in the church, as its supreme governor, or of his ability to manage parliament, through the lords of the articles. The session ended in August, in a frustrating abortion, as the government sacrificed any hope of supply for the sake of maintaining royal prerogatives.

By the next session, in 1690, William had replaced Hamilton as his commissioner to parliament with the moderate Presbyterian, George, Earl of Melville, who was also Secretary of State for Scotland. William and Melville undermined the Club by offering places and responsibilities to some of its leaders while ostracizing others. The revolutionaries of 1689 were accommodated by the king's agreement to abolition of the lords of the articles and to the repeal of the royal supremacy. In return, the king got the wartime taxation he needed and retained some authority in the church. William thus lost most of the parliamentary battles of 1689–90. Melville was nevertheless beginning to lay the foundation for more effective administration by playing the factious and ambitious Scottish grandees off against each other and by drawing some of them into government. Melville's style of parliamentary management would also be employed by his successors, over the years, with varying degrees of success.[24]

Scottish politics would, in fact, prove a kaleidoscopic nightmare for William and for the Scottish and English ministers of 1690–1706. The political energies and leadership of the great Scottish magnates, with their anarchic and feudal rivalries and their surviving clientage systems, were not easily harnessed to the needs of a wartime state. No matter who was brought into government, some rival with the potential of causing trouble was always left out; and if too many grandees were brought into office, they paralysed government with their quarrels. The crown's management practices were also quite capable of igniting defences of parliamentary independence in language and behaviour similar to that of the 1689–90 parliamentary Club or to the Restoration English Country opposition. William actually proposed a union of the two kingdoms as early as the Scottish Convention to alleviate the ministerial stress of managing multiple parliamentary systems. The eventual union of 1707 was, in part, a sneaky English way to eliminate a Scottish parliament that took too much time and art to manage. Preoccupied with war and with European affairs, William contributed to the problems of Scotland by his own relative disinterest. Being king of Scotland was the least of his worries, and he readily consigned the affairs of his northern kingdom to whichever Scottish politicians seemed most capable of managing them.[25]

The parliamentary struggle of 1689–90 took place against the backdrop of a Jacobite rebellion. James retained a reservoir of support among the Highland clans, some of them still notable for significant Catholic attachments. Jacobitism would prove a far more threatening political issue in Scotland over the next half century than in Ireland; but the Jacobite threat was initially more easily contained in the northern kingdom. Hastily assembling a few thousand clansmen and their chiefs, Dundee overwhelmed a larger Williamite force sent out against him at the Pass of Killiekrankie in July 1689, only to lose his life in the battle. A few weeks later, the Cameronians played a key role in the defeat of Dundee's leaderless Jacobite army. In 1690, the government successfully carried its military campaign against Jacobitism into the Highlands, where James's supporters missed the supplies and troops he kept in Ireland for his climactic encounter with William.

James's return to France after the Battle of the Boyne took the wind out of active Jacobite resistance in Scotland. Their path sweetened by money, the clan chiefs accepted William's authority, for the most part, despite government missteps such as the 1692 Glencoe massacre of 40 of the MacDonald clan. Jacobitism nevertheless retained a powerful, nostalgic following north of the Tay. It was fed by history, by Catholic and Episcopalian resistance to the revolutionary order, and by the kingdom's absorption into Great Britain. In 1715, major Scottish clans would rise again for another Stuart claimant to the throne, James Francis Edward, the 'Old' Pretender, and against all that had followed in the wake of the Glorious Revolution.[26]

The religious settlement of Scotland further complicated relations between William's principal kingdoms by giving them quite different state churches, each hostile to the other. The re-establishment of Scottish Presbyterianism on an exclusive basis was fuelled by the understandable anger of many about the persecution they had experienced under Charles II. But the new Scottish church settlement also fanned the fears of Anglicans to the south that the destruction of episcopacy would follow any reduction in the political safeguards for their church. An act of the Scottish parliament in 1690 legally returned all Presbyterian clerical survivors of the Episcopal purge of 1662 to their parishes. The general assembly was re-established as the church's governing body; and in its first meeting, only the clerical survivors of the pre-1662 kirk and their junior associates joined lay presbyters in it. The Scottish national church had, in fact, been handed over to a committed religious minority, just as it had been a generation earlier. The presentation rights of lay patrons within the church were also abolished (with compensation); and the future selection of the clergy was largely placed in the hands of elders and property owners in each parish. The Reformed confession of faith agreed to by the English and Scottish churches in 1646 was readopted. The Covenants were not revived, much to the dissatisfaction of the Cameronians, who continued as a sectarian splinter outside the national church. Needless to say, the Catholic following that James had worked to revive was broken up. Roman clergy were imprisoned or banished, some following James's Catholic ministers to France.

The real problem the new Church of Scotland faced, however, was neither the few Cameronians nor the even fewer dispirited Catholics. It was rather the many Episcopal incumbents. Their scruples about resistance and their oaths to James discouraged bona fide allegiance to William and Mary, just as their attachment to Episcopal orders and worship prevented acceptance of the new church. In contrast to England, no toleration was adopted by the Scottish parliament for the sake of those Protestants who could not accept the terms of the new religious settlement. Indeed, the church's general assembly overrode William's express desire for restraint by removing additional scores of Lowland Episcopal clergy who refused to conform. Within a few years of the revolution, over half the Scottish church's clergy were expelled, and the universities were purged as well. Many Episcopalians did hang on north of the Tay, where they were protected by local lairds and ministered in their parishes without acknowledging the new kirk.

Tensions between William and the Presbyterian assembly about the treatment of the Episcopalian remnant were resolved only in 1695 when a new act permitted an indulgence to Episcopalian parish clergy who swore allegiance to William and Mary as de facto monarchs. Over 100 of them then secured their positions by accepting the revolutionary state, without being required fully to accept the new religious order. Still others retained their places without accepting either. The adherence to Episcopal worship practices by these clergy was complemented by a strong Episcopalian streak among some landed families who, by Queen Anne's reign, formed a distinct 'Cavalier' parliamentary faction with Jacobite proclivities.[27]

William's problems with the new Presbyterian church were nothing, however, compared to the problems produced by the greatest Scottish trading endeavour of his reign. The Company of Scotland Trading to Africa and the Indies was established by parliament in 1695. Its creation represented a reaction by Scottish merchants and landed men alike to a perception that the trade of their kingdom had suffered immeasurably during the Restoration, while that of England had gone from strength to strength. Without colonies of its own, and legally excluded from direct trade to the English colonial sphere by the Navigation Acts, Scotland was, in fact, in economic decline. At the same time, the kingdom was fighting an expensive war against France that was believed to be more beneficial to English trade than to the Scots. The 1690s were also a decade of poor harvests and rural dearth in Scotland, with portions of the population experiencing malnourishment and a major demographic crisis. The Company of Scotland became the panacea for all these ills. The brainchild of William Paterson, the Scots financial wizard whose ideas had already spawned the Bank of England, the company chose the isthmus of Darien, in Panama, as the site of its initial colonial venture. A successful colony there was thought likely to permit the Scots to straddle the New World, to tap both the Pacific and the Atlantic trades, and to compete successfully with all rivals, especially the English and the Dutch. Loaded with privileges by the Scottish parliament, including an exemption from customs duties for 21 years, the new joint stock initially seemed as likely to attract English capital as Scots money.

Unfortunately, the 'Darien scheme', as it was known, became just another Scottish disaster rather than the great national enterprise its backers had projected. Potential English investors withdrew when the English East India Company and the Westminster parliament condemned its customs exemption as likely to divert trade from English ports. William, moreover, could scarcely afford the embarrassment of Scots squatters in the Spanish New World domain. He was involved in delicate diplomacy over the future of a Spanish Empire thrown open by the impending death of the last heirless Habsburg king. He had agreed to the act that created the company without paying much attention to it, but he soon directed his European ambassadors to discourage continental subscription to the company's stock. He also ordered English colonial officials to give no assistance to the expeditions sent out to Panama from Scotland in 1698–9.

The failure of the Darien colony, through inadequate planning and a Spanish attack, was blamed in Scotland squarely on William and on the machinations of English politicians and merchants. The Scottish reaction was furious. All the accumulated envy of the weaker kingdom, joined for so long to a domineering southern neighbour through the union of crowns, was expressed in popular rioting and in parliamentary uproar. The parliamentary management of James Douglas, the second Duke of Queensberry, and his ministerial associates was competent; but the increasingly Anglophobic and nationalistic Scottish Country was further outraged in 1701. The Westminster parliament then assigned the succession to the English throne to Anne's Hanoverian relatives, in the failure of her own issue, without so much as bothering to inform the Scottish estates, who were simply expected to follow suit.[28]

Scottish antagonism was contained for a time by Queensberry's management and by William's revival of the idea of a parliamentary union; but after William's death, Country and Cavalier members of Anne's new Scots parliament did the unthinkable. In 1703–4 they adopted an Act of Security that threatened to terminate the union of crowns that bound the two kingdoms together. The act stated that the next Scottish monarch, after Anne, would be a Protestant member of the Stuart dynasty, but not necessarily the Hanoverian successor chosen in England. *Only if* the English ended the exclusion of the Scots from their trading empire, and *only if* the freedom of the Scottish estates from ministerial manipulation was conceded, and *only if* Scottish religious and political traditions were protected against English interference, would Scotland accept the Hanoverian line. Even then, the next Scottish monarch would need to reacknowledge the Claim of Right and to surrender to the estates the right to determine war and peace. The Act of Security and accompanying legislation took Scotland back to the political circumstances of 1688–9. Indeed, the aggressive Country opposition demanded even more concessions from the crown than the revolutionaries of 1689 had imposed upon William, including a triennial act and additional limitations upon the prerogative. The prospect of a dynastic rupture finally concentrated English parliamentary minds on the constitutional union of the two kingdoms, an idea that had gained little political traction since Lauderdale's 1669 scheme.

Explaining this sudden English about-face on the subject of union with Scotland is not difficult: the Scottish Act of Security threatened to undermine much of what England was fighting for in the War of the Spanish Succession. Even most English Tories eventually came round to the union, although they fretted about their church and were more sceptical than Whigs about its benefits. How the Scots could so quickly change course is more difficult to explain. The Treaty of Union, which was negotiated by commissioners from both kingdoms, was generous to the Scots and went far to address their grievances. It provided them with 45 seats in the united House of Commons and 16 places in the united House of Lords, the places in the upper house being elected by the Scottish peerage. It also provided Scottish merchants with free trading access to England and within the English colonies, now a common British colonial empire. The Scots were, moreover, given concessions about taxation, compensation for the bankruptcy of their trading company, and money for the promotion of domestic industry and manufacturing. The Scottish kirk was guaranteed its privileged position in the north, as well as freedom from any Episcopal interference from the south; and the separate Scottish legal system was also maintained. These inducements split the Country and Cavalier (Jacobite) followings within the Scottish estates. The court also employed the customary inducements of offices, honours, and money to draw enough of the opposition towards the treaty to secure its adoption by a comfortable parliamentary margin.[29]

Tensions between the Scots and the English did not disappear in the new kingdom of Great Britain. Elements of Scottish opinion remained strongly hostile to union, and a new toleration act adopted by the Westminster parliament in 1712 for the benefit of northern Episcopalians troubled Scottish Presbyterians greatly. Still, the anxieties of the Scots about their economic future were eased by their entrée into what was now the largest free trading area within Europe. Similarly, English worries about the Hanoverian succession, which was incorporated into the Treaty of Union, were resolved. The new union lacked many features of modern state centralization, but it nevertheless brought greater order and coherence to British government. It survived an early challenge in the Jacobite invasion of 1715 and the strains of many subsequent wars against France. The common experiences of Scottish and English people who had opposed 'popery and arbitrary government' in the Restoration also fed the shared British attachment to Protestantism and parliamentary government that tied together the eighteenth-century British Atlantic world.

The Revolutions in Empire, Trade, Finance, and Foreign Policy

If a revolution can be considered an 'imperial' event, the Glorious Revolution certainly qualifies as one. It was a turning point in the history of the first British Empire, the collection of colonies and trading institutions that expanded in the Restoration and that soon became central to British political identity and economic development. The Glorious Revolution was also a turning point in the contest for empire among the principal early modern European states. The wars that it spawned weakened the French and Spanish Empires and enabled the British to surpass their Dutch allies in the colonial sphere. By 1713 Britain had emerged as the leading imperial and commercial power of Europe with far-flung colonial possessions scattered about the globe. In the North American colonies, now home to a quarter of a million people, political institutions came to reflect the parliamentary legacy of the Glorious Revolution; and the trading classes there interacted extensively with their metropolitan counterparts. Indeed, American farmers and craftsmen, as well as colonial planters and merchants, saw themselves as denizens of the same political and economic world as other British subjects. Their attachments to their own trade and assemblies would become a principal cause of the next British revolution, the war between the North American colonies and the Westminster government that began in 1776 and that drew heavily upon the language and experiences of 1688–9.

The protection of Protestantism and the rejection of 'arbitrary rule' were as much a part of the Glorious Revolution in the colonies as in England, Ireland, and Scotland. In Massachusetts, Governor Andros was deposed in April 1689 after the circulation of William's English invasion manifesto and the spread of rumours about the English revolution. When many Boston inhabitants began to mutter about defending their 'liberties against the arbitrary rulers that were fleecing them', a body of the leading 'sensible gentlemen' organized a rebellion themselves, lest things otherwise get out of control. They found evidence of an 'absolute and arbitrary' regime in Andros's taxes and fees, in his treatment of land titles, and in his manipulation of justice in the courts. They acted to reclaim their cancelled charter and to recover 'the privileges of Englishmen' under Magna Charta; and they defended the 'pure exercise of the Protestant religion' against a perceived Catholic conspiracy. The Dominion of New England was dissolved by local action. The government of Massachusetts passed first to a council of safety, and then to the old colonial assembly.

In New York, Andros's deputy was overthrown in May 1689 by the civic militia acting under Capt. Jacob Leisler, who headed a provisional government for the next two years. Revolutionary consensus against the 'tyranny, popery and slavery' of an 'arbitrary' regime quickly gave way in New York, however, to the expression of cultural tensions within the colony. Old Dutch and Reformed inhabitants, reacting to the Anglicization of the colony, looked to Leisler for leadership; but more recent English settlers came to see Leisler's governing clique as a new despotic regime. The Maryland revolution, on the other hand, was a much cleaner affair. As news of the revolution in England and of the revolts to the north spread, an overwhelmingly Protestant population had little difficulty uniting in July 1689 against their absent Catholic proprietor, Charles Calvert, Lord Baltimore, and his officials. The colonial government's failure to proclaim William and Mary fed speculation about a Catholic conspiracy to betray the colony to the French and the Indians. The rebels' condemnation of the proprietorship as characterized by 'injustice and tyranny' expressed long simmering tensions between the Calvert family and the colonial assembly.

Somewhat suspicious of irregular colonial governments that claimed his own actions as their inspiration, William moved quickly to normalize his colonial administration. Although he and his advisers might have preferred tighter control of the colonies, they settled issues throughout the American colonies in ways that balanced royal authority with the sensitivities of local assemblies. They also acted quickly, given the need to draw colonists into their own defence against France. Massachusetts received a new royal governor and a new royal charter rather than its old one, but it retained its elected assembly and absorbed the Plymouth colony. Connecticut and Rhode Island, on the other hand, returned to their former autonomy under their original charters. New York received a new royal governor, who promptly executed Jacob Leisler; but neither he nor his successors were able to resolve the ethnocultural tensions that afflicted that colony's politics and its assembly. In Maryland, the crown assumed the right of appointing the colonial governor; but in Pennsylvania, Penn's proprietorship continued, despite the increasing assertiveness of the colony's assembly. This emerging pattern of government by locally elected assemblies and royal governors also characterized Virginia, where Sir Edmund Andros reappeared as William's governor, and the West Indies plantations. It also often produced the same court and Country political dynamics that were characteristic of other British parliamentary systems, as governors and crown appointees wrestled with independent minded assemblymen. [30]

The colonists did assist in their own defence, both in the war of William's reign and in that of Anne's. Although invasions of Quebec and of Spanish Florida, mostly organized by the colonists themselves, failed to achieve their objectives, 25 years of European warfare ended in 1713 with a significant consolidation of British power and trading advantages in the New World. Contrary to the hopes of Louis XIV, the French and Spanish crowns were kept separate, in different branches of the Bourbon family, as were the colonial possessions of the two kingdoms. Moreover, France surrendered Newfoundland, maritime Acadia, and its claims in the Hudson's Bay to Britain, which thereby gained greater control of North American fishing, naval stores, and fur. In the West Indies, which fed the vital sugar trade, the French portion of St. Kitts passed to British control. From Spain, Britain obtained the *asiento*, the right to import African slaves into the Spanish colonies, a concession, formerly possessed by the Dutch, that British merchants would flagrantly abuse to overcome Spain's restrictions on other trade with its colonies.

Despite major losses of ships and cargoes to French privateers, Britain emerged in 1713 with most of its trade in tact and with less damage to its merchant marine than either France or the Dutch. The largest and most professional navy in the world also protected the country's expanding trade. Overall, the volume of English trade grew from less than £8 million p.a. in the 1660s to £14.5 million p.a. after the War of the Spanish Succession, an increase of over 75 per cent. That trade had also diversified significantly. A wartime alliance with Portugal, for instance, gave British cloth exporters important trading opportunities within the Portuguese Empire. Similarly, Britain's acquisition of Gibraltar and Minorca from Spain facilitated consolidation of older Mediterranean markets. In India, the Dutch East India Company overextended itself against the French, and its trade began to decline; but the English had, in the meantime, secured their trade within the Mogul Empire. The progressive enlargement in the share capital of major English joint stock companies during the wars was yet another sign that English merchants, especially those of London, were poised for even further commercial advances. After the union of 1707, Scottish merchants also became increasingly (and legally) involved in British overseas commerce, especially in sugar and tobacco. Glasgow emerged as an entrepôt in the finishing of colonial goods. Scottish soldiers and colonial administrators followed a rush of Scottish immigrants to the American shores over the next 75 years.[31]

The 'Commercial Revolution' that began in the expansion of trade under Charles II, and that filled both his customs coffers and those of James, continued, then, into the eighteenth century. In fact, by the War of the Spanish Succession, taxes on trade – both customs and the excise – provided the state with over 60 per cent of its revenue. The wealth that London merchants were accumulating by the time of the Glorious Revolution also contributed to the emergence of an English wartime state that was far stronger financially than its Restoration predecessor. Investments in the state by London merchants were critical to the military defeat of Louis XIV, and they established a new relationship between city money and the government. The creation of the Bank of England in 1694 became the centrepiece in a Financial Revolution that enabled the state to turn the wealth of rising merchant families into a critical military resource. The original £1.2 million share capital of the Bank, purchased by individual investors on a joint-stock subscription basis, was lent to the government for a period of 12 years at a fixed rate of interest. The most prominent Bank subscribers and directors were drawn heavily from the ranks of London Whig and dissenting merchants. Many of them, like the Bank's first governor, a nephew of the 'murdered' Sir Edmund Berry Godfrey, had close family ties with the exclusion movement of the early 1680s.

The Bank loan dwarfed previous loans the crown had raised piecemeal from city merchants. As the government commenced repayment with interest, its need for additional wartime loans found an enthusiastic response from confident investors. A variety of wartime lending schemes followed. Additional money was raised from the Bank, from the sale of annuities and lotteries, and from new joint stock companies, including both a new East India Company (which eventually merged with the old company), and the ill-fated South Sea Company. Almost one third of the cost of all government expenditures in the two wars of 1689–1713 – some £46 million of £143 million spent – was raised through public borrowing, always on clear terms, and generally to the profit of lenders. Public creditors (those who lent to the government) numbered 10,000 by 1710 and 30,000 by 1720. These developments in public credit were so phenomenal, and they contrast so remarkably with the jiggery-pokery of Charles II's wartime financing, that the label of Financial Revolution is no exaggeration. The financial embarrassment from which the Stuart regimes had regularly suffered had finally been addressed in an innovative manner that was advantageous to the state and to investors alike. The British government continued to borrow on a significant scale throughout the eighteenth century. Indeed, the willingness of creditors to lend again and again became a principal asset in war after war against the cash-strapped French state.[32]

Old Tories and Country politicians who feared the social consequences of this Financial Revolution in England were right to do so. It provided many commercial Whig families with opportunities for greater influence, both in parliament and in a central administration focused on the raising of money. The Commercial and Financial Revolutions together challenged the national ascendancy of the landed leaders of local society who had dominated

Restoration politics and who saw parliament as their preserve. After 1689, old cavalier values were confronted by the commercial values of rising mercantile elites in London and regional centres such as Bristol and Glasgow. Moreover, the tensions between land and this new 'moneyed interest' fed the party rivalries that continued into the early eighteenth century. The percentage of MPs who were drawn from overseas trade doubled from the Restoration parliaments to the parliaments of William and Anne. When all MPs drawn from mercantile, banking, and manufacturing pursuits are considered, the business element in parliament approached one fifth of the Commons membership after 1690.

Country MPs had always worried about the influence of money on government. They were especially sensitive after 1689 to the political influence of commercial *arrivistes* who had prospered on government loans, while the rural gentry struggled with a land tax that hovered around 20 per cent for almost two decades. These tensions between land and money erupted as early as 1701, when ten investors and directors of the new East India Company were expelled from the Commons for bribing electors. Tory MPs also reacted against the Whiggish politics of the overseas trading community from which so many mercantile MPs and politically influential stock company directors were drawn. Too many of these 'moneyed men' came from dissenting families or from the naturalized families of Dutch and French Reformed immigrants. These Tory concerns fed bills to strengthen the sacramental test by eliminating the occasional conformity of dissenters for the sake of office holding, and they also drove an effort to require that MPs qualify for office by owning land.

Such measures proved abortive in the end, and they also proved unnecessary. Parliament remained a body overwhelmingly made up of local landed men. Wartime taxation did drive many declining 'mere gentry' from the land; but substantial landowners more often than not bought up their properties. The eighteenth century would prove the most aristocratic of all British centuries. An increasing proportion of land was concentrated in the hands of the greatest county families, and their wealth was exhibited in the new houses they put up all over the countryside. These great magnates maintained the stable social hierarchy once presided over by the old cavaliers, while often absorbing the enterprising values promoted by the Financial and Commercial Revolutions.

The 'big bourgeoisie' as yet offered no real challenge to the dominance of this landed aristocracy. Through the War of the Spanish Succession, moneyed men kept their wealth in the stocks and public loans. Thereafter, many followed the long established social pattern of raising their families into the ranks of landed society through intermarriage and the purchase of country property.[33]

The chief political victim of the Commercial and Financial Revolutions would not be the 'natural governors' of society, then. It would instead be the crown, which gradually lost control of the determination of Britain's external relations. The prosperity of the post-1689 commercial empire and the security of a state in which so many had invested were simply too important for parliament to leave the making of foreign policy to the monarchy. Like some other effects of the Glorious Revolution, this development was not apparent at first. Indeed, the European-minded William III had to force many of his more insular subjects to confront the problems of the continent. Both Louis XIV's continuing support for James II and his recognition, in 1701, of James Francis Edward as James III assisted William in drawing his kingdoms into European affairs. People of all social ranks came to believe that defence of the Revolution required tackling the French military colossus. After the long war of 1689–97, some would have preferred a long peace. Yet fears about French commercial aggrandizement within the Spanish Empire, as well as fears about French threats to the European balance of power moved the British kingdoms inexorably towards a second war.

By 1713, the extraordinary cost of warfare, the magnitude of what could be gained or lost abroad, and the wartime requirement of annual parliamentary sessions made the secretive royal diplomatic style of Charles II almost impossible. So William discovered in 1698–9, when he sought to avoid another war by negotiating treaties with Louis to partition the Spanish Empire – treaties that he did not share with the English parliament. After the ensuing parliamentary ruckus, the making of foreign policy required much greater transparency. Indeed, after William's death, ministers more often guided monarchs in the making of war and peace than vice versa. The secretaries of state, who took the lead in foreign policy, sought to maintain parliamentary support for their objectives and to keep public opinion in mind in making both war and peace. Their diplomatic objectives were understood as being in the interest of the British kingdoms, their people, and their trade rather than in the dynastic interest that Charles II and James II had followed. [34] As striking was the new role of Britain in Europe. England had played no part in the last major European settlement, that of 1648. Britain's premier place in the diplomacy that ended the war of 1701–13, on the other hand, prefigured the role it would play in every major European diplomatic settlement through the Napoleonic era and again in 1919.

The Revolution in Discourse, Opinion, Religion, and Ideas

The Glorious Revolution was also a watershed in the history of ideas in Britain. The events of 1688–9 occurred in the midst of a transition from a mental world dominated by the unresolved issues of the Reformation to the mental world of the Enlightenment. The Restoration debate between the advocates of toleration and the proponents of religious coercion was one sign this transition was already occurring. Writers on behalf of conscience announced some of the themes of an emerging intellectual paradigm in which religious argument would sometimes draw as much upon reason as upon dogma and history. Furthermore, the adoption of the Toleration Act of 1689, no matter how grudging and limited, marked an official abandonment in England of the idea that force rather than reasoned persuasion should direct minds and hearts away from error and towards truth. Indeed, the Toleration Act represented an acceptance by the state of an intellectual and religious diversity, within a Protestant discursive framework, that Restoration Anglican thinkers had generally thought undesirable. Restoration governments in church and state had instead regulated intellectual life and the press in order to prevent the spread of ideas that challenged established institutions. They were, moreover, suspicious of the undisciplined talk percolated in the clubs and coffeehouses of London and some provincial centres.

The Glorious Revolution, however, was a particularly wordy event that shattered these efforts to control political and religious discourse. It provoked numerous pamphlets and treatises on a variety of issues that had to be settled in each kingdom. Although Anglican Tories sought to minimize the political disjuncture that had taken place in England, the ouster of James II and the accompanying efforts at military and commercial defence were experienced by most, despite the language of 'settlement', as one of the most unsettling events since the Reformation. Political discussion once again, therefore, spilled over into the world of print and public debate in all the heady ways that Restoration authorities had sought to prevent. The annual output of the English press, which had reached some 1800 titles by the time of the Restoration Crisis, dipped only slightly during the 1680s before continuing to increase after 1689 towards an annual total of over 2400 titles by 1710. In 1695, after much consideration, parliament permitted the Restoration Licensing Act of 1662 to lapse. The resulting freedom of the press was a triumph for the purveyors of printed ideas over those who sought instead to mould minds in support of approved conventions. The press contributed to the enlargement of a public sphere of discourse and debate in Britain that had few continental analogues, except in the Netherlands. After 1689, print helped make politics out of doors as ordinary in Britain as politics within the doors of parliamentary chambers, country houses, and borough corporations.[35]

The print culture that shaped the public sphere after 1689 developed firmly on its Restoration foundations. The style of professional journalism exemplified by Henry Care, Sir Roger L'Estrange, and other partisan writers and printers of the Restoration Crisis matured in the era of party conflict and warfare that followed. As in 1679–82, the newspaper was central to the media revolution of 1689–1714. By 1710, 18 different newspapers were being published in London alone, one of them on a daily basis; and 13 additional papers were published in nine different English provincial towns. Some of these papers had considerable circulations. The London *Post Boy*, which averaged 3000–4000 copies per issue in Anne's reign, probably passed from hand-to-hand or through reading out loud to some 50,000 people. The total number of copies of all periodical publications in print in England reached an annual total of over two million in the earliest years of the eighteenth century. These newspapers and their printers were often even more obvious in their partisanship than the prints of the Restoration Crisis. Their news columns provided selective and coloured accounts of politicians, electoral contests, and political decision-making. Newspapers were, however, merely the core medium of a political press that also provided partisan pamphlets, poems, broadsides, petitions, and addresses and that attracted some of the era's best writers, like the Tory Jonathan Swift and the

Whig Daniel Defoe. Much of this political output was cheap and affordable even to those of mediocre means.

The cumulative effect of all this political writing, reading, and listening was to produce the best-informed (or at least the most frequently informed) public in Europe. The audience for print was drawn into politics in various ways, and the partisan attitudes that originated in the issues of the Restoration intensified. Coffeehouses and public houses, and the clubs that met at them, as well as homes and workshops became political venues, as men and women alike debated the issues, with varying degrees of civility and understanding. Politicians on the hustings appealed to the public with handbills and manifestos, and politicians in parliament learned not to act beyond the boundaries suggested by public opinion. The rowdiness of some parliamentary contests of 1679–81 was almost institutionalized after 1689, as a quarter-million electors, seeped in print and partisanship, turned out for general elections held more frequently than has ever again been the case in Britain. Rhetorical abuse and misrepresentation became as central to electoral debate as it has been in more modern times. After 1695, this 'license of the press' released all the political antagonisms that had come to the surface in 1679–81 and that had been only temporarily driven beneath the surface thereafter by ministerial efforts at control. No wonder some Tory MPs and Anglican clergy who had never truly accepted an unregulated press wished, by the end of Anne's reign, to see press licensing re-established, in the interests of order and deference.[36]

Tory MPs and Anglican clergy still devoted to Restoration ideals had much else to worry about by then as well. The Revolution permanently fragmented English Protestantism and crippled efforts against non-Protestants, both Catholics and the heterodox. The failure of comprehension in England in 1689 marked the collapse of the last serious effort at an accommodation between Anglicans and Protestant nonconformists. Although the established church continued to include Protestants of Reformed heritage who had never dissented from it, the bulk of the old puritan following was now left permanently outside it. Elderly dissenters who had once identified with the Cromwellian state church, and who hoped that the Anglican Church might yet be reformed for their benefit, were rapidly dying off. The younger dissenting generation who took their places were accustomed to the idea of separated congregations. The dissenting clergy were also largely trained for separate denominational ministry after 1689, at nonconformist academies or at foreign universities.

Although the Toleration Act protected dissent, many Anglican clergy never fully accepted the idea of other Protestant churches functioning alongside their own. Church leaders were taken aback by the number of dissenting congregations, especially in urban areas, and by the size and opulence of some of these. They were stunned by the effrontery of dissenters who qualified for office by taking the Anglican sacrament only as often as was necessary. One dissenting London lord mayor, who had so qualified, even processed to a conventicle in 1697 in full official regalia. The self-confidence of such assertions of dissenting political identity incensed high-flying Anglican clergy like the Oxford don, Henry Sacheverell. He called upon churchmen to 'hang out the bloody flag' in defence of the sacramental test against 'a party which is an open and avowed enemy to our communion'.

Dissent did not really grow after 1689, however. After the Revolution, many fewer Protestants stood in the ambiguous middle ground between the national church, on the one hand, and separated clergy who had once been a part of the national church, on the other. The dissenters' own numbering of themselves in the early eighteenth century suggests that they represented 10 per cent of the population, at most, a figure considerably less than what appears to have been the case through the early 1680s. Moreover, as dissenters organized themselves in separate denominations, they also separated from each other. Efforts to maintain a common dissenting identity floundered. The organization of a common national political committee by Presbyterians, Independents, and Baptists in 1702 was really an effort to overcome divisions that had been less apparent in the Restoration Crisis.

Ironically, toleration tamed English dissent far more effectively than the coercive strategies of the Restoration. The end of persecution moderated dissenting enthusiasm and energy. It deprived nonconformist communities of hallowed victims, of the need for vigilance, and of the righteous spirit of defending threatened traditions and preachers. The fiery, spirited dissent of the early 1680s was gradually transformed by toleration into the more complaisant dissent of the wealthy and respectable meetings that emerged by 1714 in London, Bristol, Exeter, and other towns. The material success of so many dissenting merchants, investors, and traders after

1689 also gave them a strong stake in the settled order – so strong a stake, in fact, that many of them abandoned dissent for the greater respectability of conformity. The same pattern is observable among those landed families still connected to dissent at the time of the Glorious Revolution. The number of definite or probable dissenting MPs in the Commons of 1690–1715 never approached the proportion of between a fifth and a quarter that had been the case in the parliaments of 1679–81 and in the Convention. Indeed, dissenting numbers in the Commons eventually fell to a handful, leaving the Whig leadership much less strongly connected to the dissenting cause than before. Whig commitment to repealing the Test and Corporation Acts in the early eighteenth century was correspondingly half-hearted. Finally, the new dissenting denominations were all weakened by internal theological conflicts. The Presbyterians and the General Baptists, in particular, were divided by the spread of anti-Trinitarian ideas that left many of their clergy distancing themselves from previous tradition and practice.[37]

If the splits among Protestant persuasions produced separate denominations after 1689, the Church of England was itself damaged by internal division. Perhaps most crippling to the church was the loss of Archbishop William Sancroft, several other bishops, and 400 parish clergy. They had sworn oaths of allegiance to James II, and they had fully subscribed to the tenets of non-resistance and passive obedience. Like many of their Scots counterparts, but unlike most of their English and Irish colleagues, these clergy would not take the new loyalty oaths to William and Mary, even as de facto rather than as *de jure* monarchs. As nonjuring clergy who would not accept the Revolution in the state, they could not serve in a church governed by monarchs whose legitimacy they declined to acknowledge. Their failure to take the new oaths was followed by voluntary resignation or deprivation from their places. In number, the nonjurors were less than four per cent of the Episcopalian clergy, but they included some of the most respected figures of the Restoration church. Five of the seven bishops tried by James II in 1688 became nonjurors, for instance; and the nonjurors were supported by some of the most stalwart Anglican laity, including the Earl of Clarendon. As far as the nonjuring clergy were concerned, the establishment was in schism from Anglican principles; and they provided for their own succession in a 'true' Episcopalian church.

The nonjurors had many clerical admirers within the church as well. Indeed, the established church was shaken to its core as many clergy took the new oaths with mental reservations or with persistent doubts about the legitimacy of the new regime. Open to charges of hypocrisy, some assuaged their guilty consciences by venerating the nonjuring bishops whose examples they had failed to follow. Others were unsettled by the selection of new Episcopal leaders. Two-thirds of the dioceses of England lost their bishops in the first two years after the Revolution through death, resignation, or deprivation. William and Mary filled the vacancies with moderate men, like the historian Gilbert Burnet, who would have preferred accommodation with dissent rather than a mere toleration. John Tillotson accepted appointment as Archbishop of Canterbury. He had been a puritan before 1660 and still enjoyed connections to Presbyterians. Tillotson had also long been a bright light in latitudinarian circles, and he was a close friend of John Locke.

Many Anglican clergy responded to this reorientation of the Episcopal leadership with a false perception of their own bishops as lukewarm timeservers. From their doubts sprang the church's principal internal tensions of the next generation. The 'low church' clergy favoured the new latitudinarian and tolerationist approach, while 'high church' divines instead reacted strongly against dissent and subscribed still to the Restoration ideal of the crown and mitre as coupled symbols of authority. Filled with distrust and recrimination, the Church of England was a church divided in the decades after the Glorious Revolution. Dyspeptic high churchmen defended the authority of the clergy, of the church courts, and of their Convocation in particular; and they backed Tory politicians as strongly as ever. Low churchmen, on the other hand, followed the lead of William and his bishops, preferred moderation to polemic, and developed ties with the Whigs. High churchmen believed in divine right and hierarchy; low churchmen subscribed instead to 'revolution principles' in church and state. High churchmen believed the church was 'in danger' as a result of the Revolution; low churchmen thought it was instead secured.[38]

As English Protestants divided into camps and again turned their hostility against each other, Roman Catholics largely escaped further harassment. Not beneficiaries of the 1689 toleration per se, they were nevertheless spared serious persecution thereafter.

As the fear of popery eased, high churchmen were, however, seized by a new fear of anti-clerical and anti-Trinitarian ideas. Indeed, high churchmen believed the religious establishment was imperilled by a rising tide of blasphemy, heresy, and 'atheism', on the one hand, and by dissent, on the other. Anti-clericalism had been an element of opposition thought in the 1670s, even before the emergence of the Whig movement in the Restoration Crisis. After 1689, the expression of anti-clericalism was released by the Toleration Act and by the lapsing of the Licensing Act; but now it also took the form of attacking seminal Christian doctrines that were upheld by the clergy. Although the Revolution had occurred in defence of Protestantism, the Revolution also ironically opened Protestantism to attack by intellectuals who had defected from orthodox Christianity entirely. Yet another division opened in the fragmented religious world of post-1689 Britain.

Within a year of the establishment of freedom of the press, for instance, the freethinking John Toland, born an Irish Roman Catholic, produced his *Christianity not Mysterious* (1696). Toland denied the truth of any tenet of Christianity that contradicted reason. While John Locke had sought in his *Reasonableness of Christianity* (1695) to suggest that most of the faith could be reduced to principles capable of rational demonstration, Locke had preserved the status of revealed truth. Toland was less circumspect: the so-called mysteries of the faith were nothing but fables invented by priests to manipulate the laity. Toland had, in fact, become a deist, a non-Christian believer in a unitary God. In his rejection of the Trinity, he was part of an intellectual tendency towards deism and Unitarianism that had proponents both within the Church of England and in the dissenting persuasions. Outspoken deists like Toland savaged orthodox Christianity as a perversion of a more simple ancient religion corrupted by the clergy, Catholic and Protestant alike. Reacting against 'priestcraft', they were fascinated with Islam as a modern expression of the ancient monotheism founded by Moses, reformed by Jesus, and recovered by Muhammad.

The ranks of deists and freethinkers converged with those who championed republican principles as well. If reason could be employed against the pretensions of the clergy, it could also be used to cut through the pretences of royal courts and ministries that dominated the people and corrupted civil society. The posthumous publication of Sidney's republican *Discourses concerning*

Government in 1698 was part of this broader intellectual challenge to those Restoration foundations that still undergirded the established church and state. Some coffeehouses and clubs became centres of anti-clerical and 'commonwealth' talk, and both the Blasphemy Act of 1697 and the high-church move to reimpose press controls were directed against all those who defied political and religious conventions. But heterodoxy and free thought had entered the public sphere to stay.[39]

The effect of the Revolution upon religion in England, then, was to harden the old Protestant divisions, to create new ones, and to weaken the stature and political influence of the clergy. Moreover, these religious divisions became less hazardous to the state as they multiplied. This picture of religious fragmentation needs to be qualified, however, with an emphasis upon the continuing centrality to British politics and culture of a shared Protestantism. Deism had few adherents, after all; and after 1689, most people identified as strongly with Protestant tradition as during the Restoration. The propaganda of the Williamite state in England also dwelt upon the Revolution as a providential intervention in almost the same terms in which loyalists had once depicted the restoration of Charles II. William and his new bishops saw the Revolution as an opportunity to perfect the Reformation in Britain. They portrayed the events of 1688–9 as a 'godly revolution'. A righteous William and a pious Mary had, according to this construction, reversed the advance of Catholic falsehood; and they would lead a virtuous people in recovering their government, reviving their Protestant culture, and reforming their society.

Such celebrations of a renewed Protestant agenda drew a ready response. Many committed Anglicans were prepared to work with committed dissenters, across their divisions, to reform the public sphere in the new societies for the reformation of manners that sprang up in the 1690s. These groups of high-minded clergy and laity in London and elsewhere were as dedicated as the puritans of old to cleansing public and private life of foul language and indecent behaviour. Furthermore, after William's death, high-flying divines found in Queen Anne a Protestant monarch suited to their tastes. Respect for the Anglican Anne enabled many high churchmen to overcome their scruples about the revolutionary state. Finally, although some deists pointed to British empirical science in defending their abandonment of revealed truth, most naturalists and theological writers continued to find nothing incompatible between Protestant Christianity and the developing new science. If anything, Sir Isaac Newton's explanation of a complex universe according to a few simple natural laws seemed to confirm the reality of a pre-existent divine intelligence behind it all.[40]

The discourse of politics had nevertheless changed. Divine right and strict hereditary principles hung on among high churchmen and Tories, their persistence reinforced by the hierarchical ethos of British society. Still, the acceptable language of political discussion had been extended by a revolution in which a monarch had been successfully deposed, however that deposition was defined, and in which new limitations had been placed on his successors. Before 1689, the language of resistance and contractual government had been officially proscribed. Algernon Sidney had died for writing in such a language, and John Locke had fled after writing in the same manner. After 1689, however, the language of resistance and contractual monarchy competed successfully in a broader field of political discourse. It was spoken within an intellectual milieu that also still included the Country language of parliamentary government, a commonwealth and republican outlook influenced by Sidney, and high-church conceptions of monarchy indebted to old royalist ideals.[41]

The practice of politics had changed as well. Although historians have lately stressed how much authority post-1689 monarchs retained, none of them ever governed in the manner that Charles II and James II had adopted in the 1680s. Even William, who fought a rear-guard defence of his prerogatives, and who frequently ran afoul of partisan parliamentary blocs, largely recognized that the revolution had altered the balance of king-in-parliament in parliament's favour. In fact, the political assumptions about parliament, Protestantism, and the crown that Charles sought to suppress after the Oxford Parliament become the operating assumptions of the state, after the Glorious Revolution, despite Tory reservations about them. Jacobitism preserved royalist Stuart assumptions through the early eighteenth century, but Jacobitism proved a waning creed as revolution principles gradually triumphed in Britain, Ireland, and the colonial dependencies. Indeed, after the Hanoverian Succession, veneration of the Revolution often eclipsed veneration of the monarchy, as the Glorious appellation suggests. That, perhaps, was the greatest long-term achievement of the Restoration advocates of parliamentary government.

Abbreviations

AHR	*American Historical Review*
BIHR	*Bulletin of the Institute of Historical Research*
Bodl.	Bodleian Library, Oxford University
CJ	*Journals of the House of Commons*
Clarendon MS	Clarendon Papers, Bodleian Library
CSPD	*Calendar of State Papers, Domestic*
CSPVen	*Calendar of State Papers, Venetian*
EcHR	*Economic History Review*
EHD	*English Historical Documents*, D. C. Douglas, gen. ed., 12 vols (New York, 1955–77).
EHR	*English Historical Review*
HJ	*Historical Journal*
HMC	Historical Manuscripts Commission
IHS	*Irish Historical Studies*
JEcH	*Journal of Ecclesiastical History*
JMH	*Journal of Modern History*
LC	Library of Congress
Newdigate	Newdigate Newsletters, Folger Shakespeare Library
ODNB	*Oxford Dictionary of National Biography*, H. C. G. Matthew and B. H. Harrison, eds, 60 vols (Oxford, 2004).
POAS	*Poems on Affairs of State; Augustan Satirical Verse, 1660–1714*, G. deF. Lord [*et al.*], eds, 7 vols (New Haven, CT, 1963–75).
SHR	*Scottish Historical Review*
TAPS	Transactions of the American Philosophical Society
TRHS	*Transactions of the Royal Historical Society*

Notes

1 Revolution and Restoration, 1658–65

1. Bishop Gilbert Burnet, *History of His Own Time*, abr. Thomas Stackhouse, Everyman Classics (1979), pp. 32–3.
2. C. Russell, *The Causes of the English Civil War* (Oxford, 1990).
3. After 1660, some adherents of the Anglican Episcopal order also claimed the Reformed label, but their claims were less convincing to continental Reformed Protestants.
4. For elaboration of these perspectives, see: L. Stone, *The Causes of the English Revolution 1529–1642* (New York, 1972) and J. Scott, *England's Troubles: Seventeenth-Century English Political Instability in European Context* (Cambridge, 2000), pp. 43–88.
5. D. Underdown, 'Settlement in the Counties, 1653–1658', in G. E. Aylmer, ed., *The Interregnum: the Quest for Settlement, 1646–1660* (1972), pp. 165–82; G. E. Aylmer, *The State's Servants* (1973), p. 305; D. L. Smith, 'The Struggle for New Constitutional and Institutional Forms', in J. Morrill, ed., *Revolution and Restoration: England in the 1650s* (1992), pp. 15–34; R. Hutton, *The Restoration: A Political and Religious History of England and Wales, 1658–1667* (Oxford, 1985), pp. 3–6.
6. A. Hughes, 'The Frustrations of the Godly', in Morrill, ed., *Revolution and Restoration*, pp. 70–90; Hutton, *Restoration*, pp. 6–11; D. Underdown, *Revel, Riot, and Rebellion: Popular Politics and Culture in England, 1603–60* (Oxford, 1985).
7. G. Donaldson, *Scotland; James V to James VII* (New York, 1965), pp. 343–57; R. Mitchison, *Lordship to Patronage; Scotland 1603–1745* (1983), pp. 62–7; F. D. Dow, *Cromwellian Scotland 1651–1660* (Edinburgh, 1979), esp. pp. 162–4; K. M. Brown, *Kingdom or Province? Scotland and the Regal Union, 1603–1715* (New York, 1992), pp. 138–41.
8. P. J. Corish, 'The Cromwellian Conquest, 1649–53' and 'The Cromwellian Regime, 1650–60', in T. W. Moody, F. X. Martin, and F. J. Byrne, eds, *A New History of Ireland*, 9 vols (Oxford, 1976–96), vol. 3, *Early Modern Ireland 1534–1691*, pp. 336–86; T. C. Barnard, 'The Protestant Interest, 1641–1660', in J. H. Ohlmeyer, ed., *Ireland from Independence to Occupation 1641–1660* (Cambridge, 1995),

pp. 218–40; R. F. Foster, *Modern Ireland, 1660–1972* (1988), pp. 79–116; D. Dickson, *New Foundations: Ireland 1660–1800*, 2nd. ed. (Dublin, 2000), pp. 1–3.

9. The following narrative about 1658–60 draws on Hutton, *Restoration*; A. Woolrych, 'Introduction' to *Complete Prose Works of John Milton*, D. M. Wolfe, gen. ed., 8 vols (New Haven, CT, 1958–82), vol. 7, *1659–60*, pp. 1–228; N. H. Keeble, *The Restoration: England in the 1660s* (Oxford, 2002), pp. 5–31; G. S. De Krey, *London and the Restoration, 1659–1683* (Cambridge, 2005), pp. 19–66.

10. Richard Baxter, *Reliquiae Baxteriane*, Matthew Sylvester, ed. (1696), vol. 1, p. 100.

11. *Clarke Papers*, Sir C. Firth, ed., 4 vols (Camden Society, 1891–1901), vol. 3, p. 210.

12. *A Free Parliament Proposed by the City to the Nation* (1660); *To his Excellency the Lord General Monck. The Unanimous Representation of the Apprentices* [1660].

13. *The Diurnal of Thomas Rugg 1659–1661*, W. L. Sachse, ed., Camden 3rd. ser., XCI (1961), p. 39.

14. *The Diary of Samuel Pepys*, R. Latham and W. Matthews, eds, 11 vols (Berkeley and Los Angeles, CA, 1970–83), vol. 1, p. 79.

15. *English Historical Documents*, D. C. Douglas, gen. ed., 12 vols (New York, 1955–77), vol. 8, pp. 57–8.

16. *The Diary of John Evelyn*, E. S. De Beer, 6 vols (Oxford, 1955), vol. 3, p. 246; B. D. Henning, *The House of Commons, 1660–1690,* The History of Parliament, 3 vols (1983), vol. 1, pp. 11–13, 31–2, 77.

17. Quoted in W. Matthews, ed., *Charles II's Escape from Worcester* (Berkeley, CA, 1966), p. 5; R. Ollard, *The Escape of Charles II after the Battle of Worcester* (1966), p. 21.

18. *By the Parliament. A Proclamation for the Discovery and Apprehending of Charles Stuart* (1651); Matthews, ed., *Escape*, pp. 53, 55, 97.

19. John Aubrey, *Aubrey's Brief Lives*, O. L. Dick, ed. (Ann Arbor, 1957), p. cii; *ODNB*, vol. 57, pp. 179–80.

20. Pepys, *Diary*, vol. 9, p. 410.

21. For Charles II's mistresses, see esp., E. Hamilton, *The Illustrious Lady: A Biography of Barbara Villiers, Countess of Castlemaine and Duchess of Cleveland* (Newton Abbot, 1981); D. Parker, *Nell Gwyn* (Stroud, 2001); C. MacLeod and J. M. Alexander, *Painted Ladies: Women at the Court of Charles II* (2001); G. Hopkins, *Nell Gwynne: a Passionate Life* (2002).

22. Sir Robert Filmer, *Patriarcha and Other Writings*, J. P. Sommerville, ed. (Cambridge, 1991), p. 12; James Ussher, *The Power Communicated by God to the Prince* (1661), p. 134.

23. [Richard Mocket], *God and the King* (1663), p. 2; Pepys, *Diary*, vol. 4, p. 136.

24. Quoted in T. Harris, *London Crowds in the Reign of Charles II* (Cambridge, 1987), p. 79.

25. J. Buckroyd, 'Bridging the Gap: Scotland, 1659–60', *SHR*, 66 (1987), 1–25; J. Buckroyd, *Church and State in Scotland, 1660–1681* (Edinburgh, 1980), pp. 22–40; Dow, *Cromwellian Scotland*,

pp. 268–70; Hutton, *Charles II, King of England, Scotland, and Ireland* (Oxford, 1989), pp. 136–7; Donaldson, *Scotland*, pp. 358–61; Mitchison, *Lordship*, pp. 68–70.

26. A. Clarke, *Prelude to Restoration in Ireland: the End of the Commonwealth, 1659–60* (Cambridge, 1999); Hutton, *Charles II*, pp. 137–9.

27. Hutton, *Charles II*, pp. 141–5.

28. Edward Hyde, Earl of Clarendon, *Selections from The History of the Rebellion and Civil Wars and The Life by Himself*, G. Huehns, ed. (1955), p. 391; P. Seaward, *The Cavalier Parliament and the Reconstruction of the Old Regime, 1661–1667* (Cambridge, 1988), pp. 15–22.

29. The Convention's status as a parliament was confirmed in June 1660. A. Swatland, *The House of Lords in the Reign of Charles II* (Cambridge, 1996), pp. 17–23.

30. *EHD*, vol. 8, p. 164.

31. J. Childs, *The Army of Charles II* (1976), pp. 7–20.

32. Hutton, *Restoration*, pp. 132–9, 148–9; Keeble, *Restoration*, pp. 70–80; J. Miller, *Charles II* (1991), pp. 45–50, 64–8.

33. Burnet, *History*, p. 39; J. Thirsk, *The Rural Economy of England* (1984), pp. 85–127; H. J. Habakkuk, 'The Land Settlement and the Restoration of Charles II', *TRHS*, 5th ser., 28 (1978), 201–22; Hutton, *Restoration*, pp. 139–42.

34. For the re-settlement of the Church of England, see esp. J. Spurr, *The Restoration Church of England, 1646–1689* (New Haven, 1991), pp. 29–42; R. S. Bosher, *The Making of the Restoration Settlement; the Influence of the Laudians, 1649–1662* (New York, 1951); G. R. Abernathy, *The English Presbyterians and the Stuart Restoration, 1648-1663*, TAPS, NS, 55, Pt 2 (Philadelphia, 1965); I. M. Green, *The Re-establishment of the Church of England 1660–1663* (Oxford, 1978); Hutton, *Restoration*, pp. 143–6; Keeble, *Restoration*, pp. 109–13; Miller, *Charles II*, pp. 50–62.

35. *The Poems and Letters of Andrew Marvell*, H. M. Margoliouth, 3rd ed., 2 vols. (Oxford, 1971), vol. 2, p. 6; Green, *Re-establishment*, chaps 3–4; Bosher, *Restoration Settlement*, chap. 4; Abernathy, *Presbyterians*, pp. 76–8; Keeble, *Restoration*, pp. 113–15.

36. Henning, *Commons*, vol. 3, pp. 10–13, 26–7, 44–5, 106.

37. I. M. Green, *Re-establishment*, chap. 9.

38. De Krey, *London and the Restoration*, pp. 71, 75–77.

39. Seaward, *Cavalier Parliament*, pp. 162–95; Hutton, *Restoration*, pp. 166–80; Abernathy, *Presbyterians*, pp. 79–91; Keeble, *Restoration*, pp. 115–20; De Krey, *London and the Restoration*, pp. 87–90.

40. Clarendon MS 73, f. 359.

41. [William Prynne], *Summary Reasons ... against the New Intended Bill for Governing and Reforming Corporations* [1661]; Hutton, *Restoration*, pp. 158–61; P. D. Halliday, *Dismembering the Body Politic; Partisan Politics in England's Towns, 1650–1730* (Cambridge, 1998), pp. 84–105.

42. A. Macfarlane, *The Family Life of Ralph Josselin* (Cambridge 1970), pp. 21–32; N. Key, 'Cromprehension and the Breakdown of Consensus in Restoration Herefordshire', in T. Harris *et al.*, eds, *The Politics of Religion in Restoration England* (Oxford, 1990), pp. 191–215; Spurr, *Restoration Church*.

43. Parliamentary act quoted in Buckroyd, *Church and State*, p. 34.

44. Burnet, *History*, p. 74.
45. Buckroyd, *Church and State*, pp. 22–56; E. H. Hyman, 'A Church Militant: Scotland, 1661–1690', *Sixteenth Century Journal*, 26 (Spring, 1995), 49–56; Dow, *Cromwellian Scotland*, pp. 270–6; Hutton, *Charles II*, pp. 149–50, 160–3, 171–2, 178–80; Mitchison, *Lordship*, pp. 70–3; Childs, *Army of Charles II*, pp. 196–8.
46. J. I. McGuire, 'The Dublin Convention, the Protestant Community and the emergence of an Ecclesiastical Settlement in 1660', in A. Cosgrove and J. I. McGuire, eds, *Parliament & Community* (Belfast, 1983), pp. 121–46; J. McGuire, 'Ormond and Presbyterian Nonconformity, 1660–63', in K. Herlihy, ed., *The Politics of Irish Dissent 1650–1800* (Dublin, 1997), pp. 40–51; J. McGuire, 'Policy and Patronage: the Appointment of Bishops, 1660–61', and R. L. Greaves, "That's no good religion that disturbs government": the Church of Ireland and the Nonconformist Challenge, 1660–1688', in A. Ford *et al.*, eds, *As by Law Established: the Church of Ireland since the Reformation* (Dublin, 1995), pp. 112–19, 120–135; J. G. Simms, 'The Restoration, 1660–85', in *Early Modern Ireland*, pp. 420–5; Dickson, *New Foundations*, pp. 4–7.
47. *Essex Papers*, ed. O. Airy, 2 vols (1890), vol. 1, p. 201; L. J. Arnold, 'The Irish Court of Claims of 1663', *IHS*, 24 (1984), 417–30; Simms, 'Restoration', pp. 426–7.
48. *EHD*, vol. 8, p. 465; [Mocket], *God and the King*.
49. Further discussion of the nonconformist population follows in chap. 2, section 3.
50. B. Reay, 'The Authorities and Early Restoration Quakerism', *JEcH*, 34 (1983), 72–3; C. W. Horle, *The Quakers and the English Legal System 1660–1688* (Philadelphia, 1988), p. 102.
51. A. Marshall, *Intelligence and Espionage in the Reign of Charles II, 1660–1685* (Cambridge, 1994); J. Todd, *The Secret Life of Aphra Behn* (New Brunswick, NJ, 1997).
52. Anthony á Wood, *The Life and Times of Anthony á Wood* (1961), p.130; Seaward, *Cavalier Parliament*, pp. 180–9, Hutton, *Charles II*, pp. 194–6, 202–04.
53. Marshall, *Intelligence*, pp. 186–223; R. Greaves, *Deliver us from Evil; the Radical Underground in Britain, 1660–1663* (New York, 1986), pp. 135–206.
54. A. Taylor, *American Colonies* (New York, 2001), p. 256.
55. S. C. A. Pincus, 'Popery, Trade and Universal Monarchy: the Ideological Context of the Outbreak of the Second Anglo-Dutch War', *EHR*, 422 (1992), 23, 25; S. C. A. Pincus, *Protestantism and Patriotism, Ideologies and the making of English Foreign Policy, 1650–1668* (Cambridge, 1996), pp. 289–342.
56. Clarendon, *Selections*, p. 445.
57. Pepys, *Diary*, vol. 6, pp. 86, 122–3.
58. Ibid., pp. 93, 120.

2 Court and Kingdoms, 1665–72

1. Anthony Hamilton, *Count Gramont at the Court of Charles II*, ed. and trans. N. Deakin (1965), p. 68.

2. For the three kingdoms issue, see esp.: J. G. A. Pocock, 'The Limits and Divisions of British History: in Search of the Unknown Subject", *AHR*, 87 (1982), 311–36; J. Morrill, 'The British Problem, *c.* 1534–1707', in B. Bradshaw and J. Morrill, eds, *The British Problem, c. 1534–1707: State Formation in the Atlantic Archipelago* (Basingstoke, 1996), pp. 1–38; M. Goldie, 'Divergence and Union: Scotland and England, 1660–1707' in Ibid., esp. pp. 220–30.

3. M. Bloch, *The Royal Touch: Sacred Monarchy and Scrofula in England and France* (1973), pp. 211–23; J. P. Montaño, *Courting the Moderates: Ideology, Propaganda, and the Emergence of Party, 1660–1678* (Newark, DE, 2002). For Charles's court, also see: R. O. Bucholz, *The Augustan Court: Queen Anne and the Decline of Court Culture* (Stanford, CA, 1993), pp. 12–22; A. Marshall, *The Age of Faction: Court Politics, 1660–1702* (Manchester, 1999), pp. 68–77.

4. *The Diary of Samuel Pepys*, R. Latham and W. Matthews, eds, 11 vols, (Berkeley and Los Angeles, CA, 1970–83) vol. 9, p. 342; Hamilton, *Gramont*, p. 18.

5. Pepys, *Diary*, vol. 4, pp. 37–8, 113, 134, 270–1; vol. 5, p. 21; vol. 9, p. 515; L. Stone, *The Family, Sex and Marriage in England 1500–1800* (1977), pp. 530, 553–7; J. Miller, *James II* (New Haven, CT, 2000), pp. 46–7; Arlington quoted in M. Lee, *The Cabal* (Urbana, IL, 1965), p. 77.

6. Pepys, *Diary*, vol. 3, p.197; vol. 8, pp. 70, 121; *The Diary of John Evelyn*, E. S. De Beer, 6 vols (Oxford, 1955), vol. 3, p. 347; vol. 4, p. 410.

7. Hamilton, *Gramont*, p. 66; Evelyn, *Diary*, vol. 3, p. 489; vol. 4, pp. 176–7; [Roger North], *Of Building: Roger North's Writings on Architecture*, ed. H. Colvin and J. Newman (Oxford, 1981), pp. 142–3; Bishop Gilbert Burnet, *History of His Own Time*, abr. Thomas Stackhouse, Everyman Classics (1979), p. 37; Lee, *Cabal*, p. 162; V. Barbour, *Henry Bennet, Earl of Arlington, Secretary of State to Charles II* (Baltimore, MD, 1913), pp. 102–3, 181–2; J. H. Wilson, *A Rake and his Times: George Villiers, 2nd Duke of Buckingham* (New York, 1954), pp. 188–91.

8. Burnet, *History*, p. 37; John Dryden, *Absalom and Achitophel* (1681), line 563, *Poems on Affairs of State: Augustan Satirical Verse, 1660–1714*, G. deF. Lord [*et al.*], eds, 7 vols (New Haven, CT, 1963–75), vol. 2, p. 476; V. de Sola Pinto, *Enthusiast in Wit: a Portrait of John Wilmot Earl of Rochester, 1647–1680* (1962), p. 74; G. Hopkins, *Nell Gwynne: a Passionate Life (2002)*, p. 120.

9. Pepys, *Diary*, vol. 4, p. 209; Anthony á Wood, *The Life and Times of Anthony á Wood* (1961), pp. 132–3, Hamilton, *Gramont*, pp. 120–1, 142; J. H. Wilson, *The Court Wits of the Restoration* (Princeton, NJ, 1948), pp. 40–2; Pinto, *Rochester*, pp. 81–2; V. de Sola Pinto, *Sir Charles Sedley, 1639–1701* (1927), pp. 61–3; A. Fraser, *The Weaker Vessel* (1994), pp. 425–6.

10. Pepys, *Diary*, vol. 2, pp. 32–3; vol. 7, pp. 343, 414–15; vol. 9, pp. 435, 451, 462–3; Pinto, *Rochester*, pp. 71–2; Pinto, *Sedley*, 111–12; Wilson, *Buckingham*, pp. 60–2, 112–19, 142–3.

11. Evelyn, *Diary*, vol. 3, pp. 465–6; E. Howe, *The First English Actresses: Women and Drama, 1660–1700* (Cambridge, 1992), pp. 32–6 and chapt. 6; Fraser, *Vessel*, chapt. 21.

12. Gilbert Burnet, *A Supplement to Burnet's History of My Own Time*, ed. H. C. Foxcroft (Oxford, 1902), p. 49, Pepys, *Diary*, vol. 3, p. 289; *POAS*, vol. 1, p. 424; S. Wynne, 'The Mistresses of Charles II and Restoration Court Politics', in E. Cruickshanks, ed., *The Stuart Courts*, (Stroud, Gloucestershire, 2000), pp. 171–90; Marshall, *The Age of Faction*, pp. 49–53.

13. Burnet, *History*, p. 98; J. Buckroyd, *Church and State in Scotland, 1660–1661* (New York, 1989), pp. 94, 103, 111, 114, 124; Fraser, *Vessel*, pp. 399–408; Pinto, *Sedley*, p. 238.

14. Pepys, *Diary*, vol. 6, pp. 204–5; Richard Baxter, *The Autobiography of Richard Baxter*, ed. N. H. Keeble (1974), p. 195; P. Slack, *The Impact of Plague in Tudor and Stuart England* (1985), pp. 106–8, 145–64, 167–8, 177, 183; A. L. Moote and D. C. Moote, *The Great Plague* (Baltimore, MD, 2004).

15. *English Historical Documents*, D. C. Douglas, gen. ed., 12 vols (New York, 1955–77), vol. 8, p. 383.

16. R. Hutton, *The Restoration: A Political and Religious History of England and Wales, 1658–1667* (Oxford, 1985), pp. 234–7; A. Swatland, *The House of Lords in the Reign of Charles II* (Cambridge, 1996), pp. 179–81.

17. Pepys, *Diary*, vol. 8, pp. 142, 145, 151, 216.

18. [T. B. Macaulay,] Lord Macaulay, *The History of England from the Accession of James the Second*, C. H. Firth, ed., 6 vols (1913–15), vol. 1, p. 174.

19. Historical Manuscripts Commission, *Hodgkin Manuscripts*, p. 306; Evelyn, *Diary*, vol. 3, pp. 453 and n3, 454, 460–2, 464; Baxter, *Autobiography*, pp. 198–9; S. Porter, *The Great Fire of London* (Stroud, 1996), esp. pp. 53–6; J. C. Sainty and R. O. Bucholz, *Officials of the Royal Household*, 2 vols (1997–98), vol. 2, p. 103.

20. P. Seaward, *The Cavalier Parliament and the Reconstruction of the Old Regime, 1661–1667* (Cambridge, 1988), pp. 250–99; S. C. A. Pincus, *Protestantism and Patriotism: Ideologies and the Making of English Foreign Policy, 1650–1668* (Cambridge, 1996), chapt. 23; Marshall, *Age of Faction*, pp. 41–4; Hutton, *Restoration*, pp. 252–6.

21. C. D. Chandaman, *The English Public Revenue, 1660–1688* (Oxford, 1975), p. 212.

22. *EHD*, vol. 8, p. 732; Seaward, *Cavalier Parliament*, p. 253; C. A. Edie, *The Irish Cattle Bills: A Study in Restoration Politics*, Transactions of the American Philosophical Society, NS, 60, Pt 2 (Philadelphia, 1970).

23. Burnet, *History*, p. 84; Buckroyd, *Church and State*, chapt. 5; R. Mitchison, *Lordship to Patronage; Scotland 1603–1745* (1983), pp. 74–6.

24. Buckroyd, *Church and State*, pp. 66–7, R. L. Greaves; *Enemies under his Feet: Radicals and Nonconformists in Britain, 1664–77* (Stanford, CA, 1990), pp. 64–84.

25. Bodleian Library, Oxford University, Carte MS 35, fo 240, as quoted by Seaward, *Cavalier Parliament*, p. 289; Pincus, *Protestantism and Patriotism*, p. 394.

26. R. F. Foster, *Modern Ireland, 1660–1972* (1988), pp. 128–9; D. Dickson, *New Foundations: Ireland 1660–1800*, 2nd. ed. (Dublin, 2000), p. 12; L. M. Cullen, 'Economic Trends, 1660–91', in

T. W. Moody, F. X. Martin, and F. J. Byrne, eds, *A New History of Ireland*, 9 vols (Oxford 1976–96), vol. 3, *Early Modern Ireland 1534–1691*, pp. 392–5.

27. Chandaman, *Revenue*, pp. 211–12; Hutton, *Restoration*, p. 261; Seaward, *Cavalier Parliament*, pp. 303–4; Pincus, *Protestantism and Patriotism*, pp. 381–3.

28. Pepys, *Diary*, vol. 1, pp. 268–70.

29. *POAS*, vol. 1, p. 158; Burnet, *History*, p. 92.

30. R. H. Tawney, *Religion and the Rise of Capitalism* (1926), chapt. 4; M. Weber, *The Protestant Ethic and the Spirit of Capitalism* (1930), chapt. 5. Some historians follow some contemporaries in distinguishing between 'nonconformists', who desired to be comprehended in the national church, and more sectarian 'dissenters'. As important as this distinction about attitudes towards comprehension is, a terminological distinction between words that have also been treated as synonyms is unhelpful.

31. Baxter, *Autobiography*, p. 190; B. D. Henning, *The House of Commons 1660–1690*, The History of Parliament, 3 vols (1983), vol. 2, p. 340; D. R. Lacey, *Dissent and Parliamentary Politics in England, 1661–1689* (New Brunswick, NJ, 1969), pp. 396–7, 466–7.

32. [John Hunfrey], *A Defence of the Proposition* (1668), pp. 57–8; *Letters of the Honourable Algernon Sydney, to the Honourable Henry Savile* (1742), p. 165; [William Popple], *Som Free Reflections upon Occasion of the Public Discourse about Liberty of Conscience* (1687), p. 7 [my attribution]; William Penn, *The Great and Popular Objection* (1687), p. 23; Anonymous, *A Letter to a Friend in the Country* [1680], p. 1; Montaño, *Moderates*, p. 234 (quotation). Historians have too readily followed the Compton 'census', a politically motivated religious enumeration of 1676. It was prepared by the bishops to prove to Charles that, since the dissenters were inconsiderable in number, he could safely hitch the wagon of state to an exclusively Episcopal team. *The Compton Census of 1676: A Critical Edition*, ed. A. Whiteman (1986); *EHD*, vol. 8, pp. 411–16.

33. R. Wodrow, *The History of the Sufferings of the Church of Scotland*, 4 vols (Glasgow, 1829–30), vol. 2, p. 116; Greaves, *Enemies*, pp. 55, 98; R. L. Greaves, "'That's No Good Religion that Disturbs Government": the Church of Ireland and the Nonconformist Challenge, 1660–1688', in A. Ford, J. I. McGuire, and K. Milne, eds, *As by Law Established: the Church of Ireland since the Reformation* (Dublin, 1995), p. 120; R. L. Greaves, *God's Other Children: Protestant Nonconformists and the Emergence of Denominational Churches in Ireland, 1660–1700* (Stanford, CA, 1997), pp. 97–8; P. Gauci, *Politics and Society in Great Yarmouth 1660–1722* (Oxford, 1996), pp. 133–4; P. Kilroy, *Protestant Dissent and Controversy in Ireland 1660–1714* (Cork, 1994), pp. 25–6, 42.

34. Anonymous, *An Expedient or a sure & easy way of reducing all dissenters* (1672), pp. 1–2; Slingsby Bethel, *The Present Interest of England Stated* (1671), p. 13; J. Spurr, *English Puritanism, 1603–1689* (New York, 1998), p. 144; G. S. De Krey, *A Fractured Society: the Politics of London in the First Age of Party, 1688–1715* (Oxford, 1985), pp. 101–6.

35. G. G. Crippen, 'Dr. Watts's Church-book', *Transactions of the Congregational Historical Society*, 1 (April, 1901), pp. 27–8; *Calendar of State Papers, Domestic, 1667–8*, p. 360; Lacey, *Dissent*, pp. 460, 464, R. L. Greaves, *Glimpses of Glory: John Bunyan and English Dissent* (Stanford, CA, 2002), pp. 469–70, 503–7; N. H. Keeble, *The Restoration: England in the 1660s* (Oxford, 2002), pp. 154–6; P. Crawford, *Women and Religion in England 1500–1720* (1993), p. 189; Fraser, *Vessel*, chapt. 18; *Oxford Dictionary of National Biography*, H. C. G. Matthew and B. H. Harrison, eds, 60 vols (Oxford, 2004), vol. 9, p. 581; vol. 28, pp. 1–2; vol. 51, p. 789; vol. 56, p. 591.

36. [Vincent Alsop], *Melius Inquirendum* (1681), pp. 34, 38; John Bunyan, *The Pilgrim's Progress* (Oxford, 1984), p. 65; Richard Baxter, *The Nonconformists Plea for Peace* (1679), p. 238.

37. [William Penn], *Letter from a Gentleman in the Country* (1687), p. 2; Andrew Marvell, 'A Short Historical Essay, touching General Councils', in *Mr. Smirke; or, the Divine in Mode* (1676), pp. 70–2; Richard Baxter, *Church-History of the Government of Bishops* (1680), p. 25; [Sir Charles Wolseley], *Liberty of Conscience upon its true and proper Grounds Asserted* (1668), p. 44; Anonymous, *A Discourse in Vindication of ... the Clergy of the Church of England* (1673), p. 12; G. S. De Krey, 'Rethinking the Restoration: Dissenting Cases for Conscience, 1667–1672', *Historical Journal*, 38 (1995), 53–83.

38. Greaves, *Bunyan*, pp. 47–8, 65, 108; [Sir Charles Wolseley], *Liberty of Conscience: the Magistrate's Interest* (1668), p. 10.

39. John Milton, *Samson Agonistes* (1668), line 1653; Bunyan, *Pilgrim's Progress*, pp. 77–8; Thomas Watson, *Heaven Taken by Storm* (1670), pp. 5–6, 10; Keeble, *Restoration*, pp. 144–8; T. Harris, 'The Bawdy House Riots of 1668', *Historical Journal*, 29 (1986), 537–56; G. S. De Krey, 'The First Restoration Crisis: Conscience and Coercion in London, 1667–73', *Albion*, 25 (1993), 565–80.

40. Seaward, *Cavalier Parliament*, pp. 318–19; Pincus, *Protestantism and Patriotism*, pp. 472–4; Lacey, *Dissent*, p. 56.

41. Hutton, *Charles II*, p. 254.

42. Pepys, *Diary*, vol. 9, p. 31; Richard Baxter, *Reliquiae Baxterianae*, Matthew Sylvester, ed. (1696), pp. 36–7.

43. Anchitell Grey, *Debates of the House of Commons from the Year 1667 to the Year 1694*, 10 vols (1763), vol. 1, pp. 129, 131; *The Diary of John Milward, Esq.*, ed. C. Robbins (Cambridge, 1938), p. 221; Lacey, *Dissent*, pp. 56–9; Lee, *Cabal*, pp. 175–7; Swatland, *House of Lords*, pp. 132–3.

44. *Miscellany of the Scottish Historical Society* (Edinburgh, 1893), vol. 1, p. 263.

45. Burnet, *History*, pp. 105–8; Wodrow, *Sufferings*, vol. 2, pp. 129–41, 146–59, 166–82, 197–211; [John Maitland, Duke of Lauderdale], *The Lauderdale Papers*, O. Airy, ed., Camden Society, Ser. 2 (3 vols, 1884–5), vol. 2, pp. 166–7, 175, 184–5, 187, 189–90, 193–5, 204–7, and Appendix A, pp. lxii–lxvii; Sir G. Mackenzie, *Memoirs of the Affairs of Scotland from the Restoration of King Charles II* (Edinburgh, 1821), pp. 158–60, 188–9; Buckroyd, *Church and State*, chapts

6–8; I. Cowan, *The Scottish Covenanters, 1660–1688* (1976), chapt. 5;
E. H. Hyman, 'A Church Militant: Scotland, 1661–1690', *Sixteenth
Century Journal*, 26 (Spring, 1995), 58–64; Greaves, *Enemies*, pp.
85–96; *ODNB*, vol. 8, p. 910.

46. Greaves, *Enemies*, pp. 112–20; Greaves, *God's Other Children*, pp.
95–107; Hutton, *Charles II*, pp. 260–2, 274, 281–2; Kilroy, *Dissent in
Ireland*, pp. 42, 69, 236 (quote); *ODNB*, vol. 5, p. 382; vol. 9, p. 610;
vol. 44, p. 630.

47. *The Poems and Letters of Andrew Marvell*, H. M. Margoliouth, ed., 3rd
ed., 2 vols (Oxford, 1971), vol. 2, p. 314; Anonymous, *The Englishman, or a Letter from a Universal Friend* (1670), pp. 9–10; [Thomas
Rudyerd], *The Peoples Antient and Just Liberties Asserted* (1670);
De Krey, 'First Restoration Crisis', pp. 565–80; Greaves, *Enemies*,
pp. 151–9; Lacey, *Dissent*, pp. 60–2; Lee, *Cabal*, pp. 180–1; Hutton,
Charles II, p. 270.

48. A. Marshall, *Intelligence and Espionage in the Reign of Charles II, 1660–
1685* (Cambridge, 1994), pp. 186–206; Greaves, *Enemies*, chapt. 6;
CSPD 1671, p. 554; De Krey, *London and the Restoration*, pp. 119–23.

49. *Lauderdale Papers*, vol. 2, p. 164; Gilbert Burnet, *Burnet's History of
My Own Time*, O. Airy, ed., 2 vols (Oxford, 1900), vol. 1, p. 505; Lee,
Cabal, pp. 43–69; Hutton, *Charles II*, pp. 267–9.

50. Hutton, *Charles II*, pp. 271–3; K. H. D.Haley, *The First Earl of Shaftesbury* (Oxford, 1968) pp. 281–6; Lee, *Cabal*, pp. 86–118.

51. Haley, *Shaftesbury*, pp. 287–91; Hutton, *Charles II*, pp. 276–7;
Chandaman, *Revenue*, pp. 221–2.

52. Haley, *Shaftesbury*, pp. 293–6; Lee, *Cabal*, pp. 150–5, Chandaman,
Revenue, pp. 227–8.

53. Hutton, *Charles II*, pp. 282–6; J. Spurr, *England in the 1670s: 'This
Masquerading Age'* (Oxford, 2000), pp. 25–8.

54. *Calendar of State Papers, Venetian*, vol. 37, p. 116.

3 Church and Country, 1672–8

1.   [Andrew Marvell], *An Account of the Growth of Popery and Arbitrary
Government in England (1677)*, in A. Patterson *et al.* eds, *The Prose
Works of Andrew Marvell*, 2 vols (New Haven, CT, 2003), vol. 2,
p. 225.

2.   Anchitell Grey, *Debates of the House of Commons from the Year 1667
to the Year 1694*, 10 vols (1763), vol. 3, p. 6; [Slingsby Bethel],
The Present Interest of England Stated (1671), p. 34; J. Scott, *England's
Troubles; Seventeenth-Century English Political Instability in European
Context* (Cambridge, 2000), chaps 4–7.

3.   R. Hutton, *Charles II, King of England, Scotland, and Ireland*
(Cambridge, 1989), pp. 296–7; K. H. D. Haley, *The First Earl of
Shaftesbury*, (Oxford, 1968), pp. 315–16.

4.   Grey, *Debates*, vol. 2, pp. 15, 26–7, 62; Edward Dering, *The Diaries
and Papers of Sir Edward Dering, Second Baronet, 1644 to 1684*, M.
F. Bond, ed. (1976), pp. 119–20, 122–6, 133–5; W. D. Christie, *A*

Life of Anthony Ashley Cooper; first Earl of Shaftesbury, 2 vols (1871), vol. 2, Appendices, lxiv–lxv; Haley, *Shaftesbury*, pp. 315–26; J. Spurr, *England in the 1670s; 'This Masquerading Age'* (Oxford, 2000), pp. 36–9.

5. N. Sykes, *From Sheldon to Secker; Aspects of English Church History, 1660–1765* (Cambridge, 1959), p. 78; *Letters to Sir Joseph Williamson*, W. D. Christie, ed., 2 vols, Camden Society, NS, 8–9 (1874), vol. 1, pp. 33–4; G. S. De Krey, *London and the Restoration, 1659–1683* (Cambridge, 2005), pp. 123–5; Hutton, *Charles II*, p. 306; Spurr, *1670s*, pp. 41–2.

6. [Peter Du Moulin], *England's Appeal from the Private Cabal at White-Hall to the Great Council of the Nation, the Lords and Commons in Parliament Assembled* (1673), pp. 18, 23, 34–6, 46–7; K. H. D. Haley, *William of Orange and the English Opposition 1672–4* (Oxford, 1953), pp. 97–105; S. C. A. Pincus, '"Coffee Politicians Does Create": Coffeehouses and Restoration Political Culture', *JMH*, 67 (1995), 807–34.

7. *The Diary of John Evelyn*, E. S. De Beer, ed., 6 vols (Oxford, 1955) vol. 4, p. 13; *Williamson Letters*, vol. 1, pp. 6, 51, 63, 162, 168–9, 174, 185–6; vol. 2, p. 9; J. R. Jones, *The Anglo-Dutch Wars of the Seventeenth Century* (1996), pp. 201–11.

8. *Williamson Letters*, vol. 1, pp. 88, 99, 108, 137–8, 143, 194; vol. 2, pp. 1–2, 4, 16, 24, 29, 36, 99; Bishop Gilbert Burnet, *History of His Own Time*, abr. Thomas Stackhouse, Everyman Classics (1979), p. 129; S. C. A. Pincus, 'From Butterboxes to Wooden Shoes: the Shift in English Popular Sentiment from Anti-Dutch to Anti-French in the 1670s', *Historical Journal*, 38 (June, 1995), 333–61; Haley, *Shaftesbury*, pp. 332–5.

9. Grey, *Debates*, vol. 2, pp. 182, 196–8, 203, 222–3; Dering, *Diary*, p. 160; *Williamson Letters*, vol. 2, pp. 49, 62; *Calendar of State Papers, Venetian, 1673–75*, p. 163; *Essex Papers*, [vol. 1] O. Airy, ed., Camden Society, NS, 47 (1890); [vol. 2] C. E. Pike, ed., Camden Society, 3rd Ser., 24 (1913), vol. 1, pp. 130–3.

10. [John Maitland, Duke of Lauderdale], *The Lauderdale Papers*, O. Airy, ed., Camden Society, 2nd Ser. (3 vols, 1884–5), vol. 2, pp. 241–7; Sir G. Mackenzie, *Memoirs of the Affairs of Scotland from the Restoration of King Charles II* (Edinburgh, 1821), p. 263; Burnet, *History*, p. 143; *Williamson Letters*, vol. 2, pp. 98, 100; J. Patrick, 'The Origins of Opposition to Lauderdale in the Scottish Parliament of 1673', *SHR*, 53 (April, 1974), 1–21; C. Jackson, *Restoration Scotland, 1660–1690: Royalist Politics, Religion and Ideas* (Woodbridge, Suffolk, 2003), pp. 92–5; Haley, *Shaftesbury*, pp. 340–1; Hutton, *Charles II*, pp. 309–11.

11. *Essex Papers*, vol. 1, pp. 17–18, 23–4, 36, 60–2, 64–5; Grey, *Debates*, vol. 2, p. 160; Hutton, *Charles II*, pp. 298–301, 312; *Oxford Dictionary of National Biography*, H. C. G. Matthew and B. H. Harrison, eds, 60 vols (Oxford, 2004), vol. 9, pp. 977–8.

12. Grey, *Debates*, vol. 2, pp. 236–70, 275–93, 303–29; *Essex Papers*, vol. 1, pp. 160–1, 162–3, 173–4; *Williamson Letters*, vol. 2, pp. 107, 114–16, 119–20, 128–30, 152.

13. Grey, *Debates*, vol. 2, pp. 390–1, 404–6, 413–17, *Williamson Letters*, vol. 2, pp. 142–4; Haley, *Shaftesbury*, pp. 354–61; Hutton, *Charles II*, pp. 315–18; Spurr, *1670s*, pp. 49–57; A. Swatland, *The House of Lords in the Reign of Charles II* (Cambridge, 1996), pp. 212–13.

14. Dering, *Diary*, pp. 109, 129; Grey, *Debates*, vol. 2, pp. 52, 60; *Essex Papers*, vol. 1, p. 168; *Williamson Letters*, vol. 2, pp. 55–6, 156; Mackenzie, *Memoirs*, p. 264; Haley, *Shaftesbury*, pp. 339, 357; Hutton, *Charles II*, p. 315; M. Kishlansky, *A Monarchy Transformed, Britain 1603–1714* (1996), p. 245; T. Harris, *Politics under the Later Stuarts: Party Conflict in a Divided Society 1660–1715* (1993), p. 61; Patrick, 'Opposition to Lauderdale', p. 1; Jackson, *Restoration Scotland*, p. 92; Swatland, *House of Lords*, pp. 211–12; De Krey, *London and the Restoration*, p. 137; A. Coleby, *Central Government and the Localities: Hampshire 1649–1689* (Cambridge, 1987), pp 151–5; J. M. Rosenheim, *The Townshends of Raynham* (Middletown, CT, 1989), pp. 35–46.

15. Marvell, *Prose Works*, vol. 2, pp. 256–7, 263, 273; Grey, *Debates*, vol. 2, pp. 78–9, 195, 203.

16. Grey, *Debates*, vol. 1, pp. 128, 412; vol. 2, pp. 43–4; Haley, *Shaftesbury*, p. 326.

17. Marvell, *Prose Works*, vol. 2, p. 225.

18. Grey, *Debates*, vol. 2, pp. 26, 62 (my italics); Dering, *Diary*, pp. 114–18; M. Lee, *The Cabal* (Urbana, IL, 1965), p. 27; Hutton, *Charles II*, pp. 318–19; C. C. Weston and J. R. Greenberg, *Subjects and Sovereigns: the Grand Controversy over Legal Sovereignty in Stuart England* (Cambridge, 1981), pp. 164–73.

19. Grey, *Debates*, vol. 2, pp. 2–8, 187; Dering, *Diary*, pp. 103–10; [Robert McWard], *The English Ballance* (1672), pp. 61–2; Haley, *Shaftesbury*, p. 318.

20. Grey, *Debates*, vol. 2, pp. 216, 218, 221, 260, 271; L. G. Schwoerer, *'No Standing Armies!' The Antiarmy Ideology in Seventeenth-Century England* (Baltimore, 1974), pp. 97–107.

21. Grey, *Debates*, vol. 2, pp. 52, 202, 205, 210–11, 234; Dering, *Diary*, p. 128; *Williamson Letters*, vol. 2, p. 62.

22. Grey, *Debates*, vol. 2, pp. 201–2, 211, 231; M. Priestley, 'London Merchants and Opposition Politics in Charles II's Reign', *BIHR*, 29 (Nov., 1956), 205–19.

23. My approach to Restoration Anglicanism is heavily influenced by Spurr, *Restoration Church*.

24. Sir Robert Filmer, *Patriarcha and Other Writings*, J. P. Sommerville, ed. (Cambridge, 1991), pp. 23, 28; John Dryden, *Annus Mirabilis: the Year of Wonders, 1666* (1667), line 1141; John Dryden, *Astrea Redux. A Poem* (1660), line 46; [Richard Mocket], *God and the King* (1663), pp. 14–16; John Nalson, *The Common Interest of King and People* (1677), pp. 140, 143; H. W. Randall, 'The Rise and Fall of a Martyrology: Sermons on Charles I', *Huntington Library Quarterly*, 10 (Feb., 1947), 151.

25. Nalson, *Common Interest*, p. 140; Filmer, *Patriarcha*, pp. 31–2, 35, 52–5; Weston and Greenberg, *Subjects and Sovereigns*, pp. 152–61; M. Goldie, 'John Locke and Anglican Royalism', *Political Studies*, 31 (1983), 69–71.

26. Jackson, *Restoration Scotland*, pp. 45–64, with quotations at pp. 54, 61; T. Harris, *Restoration; Charles II and his Kingdoms* (2005), pp. 375–7, 402–3.

27. John Dryden, *To his Sacred Majesty, a Panegyrick on his Coronation* (1661), line 94; Jeremy Taylor, *Holy Living and Holy Dying*, P. G. Stanwood, ed. (Oxford, 1989), vol. 1, pp. 146–7; Jackson, *Restoration Scotland*, pp. 54–5.

28. A. Fletcher, 'The Enforcement of the Conventicle Acts 1664–1679', in *Persecution and Toleration*, W. J. Sheils, ed. (Oxford, 1984), pp. 235–46; Coleby, *Hampshire*, p. 98; P. D. Halliday, *Dismembering the Body Politic; Partisan Politics in England's Towns, 1650–1730* (Cambridge, 1998), pp. 106–117; P. Gauci, *Politics and Society in Great Yarmouth 1660–1722* (Oxford, 1996), pp. 103–5.

29. *Williamson Letters*, vol. 2, p. 68; [William Lloyd], *The Late Apology in behalf of the Papists Re-printed and Answered* (1667), p. 46; G. S. De Krey, 'Rethinking the Restoration: Dissenting Cases for Conscience, 1667–1672', *HJ*, 38 (1995), 53–83; Pincus, 'Coffeehouses'.

30. [Samuel Parker], *A Discourse of Ecclesiastical Politie*, 3rd. ed. (1671), pp. 7, 22, 91, 212; [Sir Roger L'Estrange], *Toleration Discuss'd, in two Dialogues* (1670), pp. 7–8, 11, 19, 40–1; M. Goldie, 'The Theory of Religious Intolerance in Restoration England', in *From Persecution to Toleration; the Glorious Revolution and Religion in England*, O. P. Grell *et al.*, eds (Oxford, 1991), pp. 331–68.

31. John Tillotson, *A Sermon lately preached on I Corinthians 3:15* (1673) in the *Works of ... Dr. John Tillotson*, 12 vols (1742–4), vol. 1, p. 277; Parker, *Ecclesiastical Politie*, pp. 209–10; [Samuel Parker], *A Discourse in Vindication of Bp. Bramhall and the Clergy of the Church of England* (1673), p. 48; *The Religion of the Church of England, the Surest Establishment* (1673), p. 33; J. P. Montaño, *Courting the Moderates: Ideology, Propaganda, and the Emergence of Party, 1660–1678* (Newark, DE, 2002), pp. 154–7; Goldie, 'Locke and Anglican Royalism', pp. 71–5.

32. J. Spurr, "Latitudinarianism" and the Restoration Church', *HJ*, 31 (March, 1988), 61–82; I. Rivers, *Reason, Grace, and Sentiment: a Study of the Language of Religion and Ethics in England, 1660–1730* (Cambridge, 1991), pp. 31–7; J. Marshall, *John Locke: Resistance, Religion and Responsibility* (Cambridge, 1994), pp 78–80; *ODNB*, vol. 13, pp. 42–3; vol. 54, pp. 793–4; *Cambridge Platonist Spirituality*, C. Taliaferro and A. J. Teply, eds (New York, 2004).

33. *Williamson Letters*, vol. 2, pp. 94, 105, 129; *Essex Papers*, vol. 2, p. 1; A. Browning, *Thomas Osborne, Earl of Danby and Duke of Leeds, 1632–1712*, 3 vols (Glasgow, 1944–51), vol. 1, pp. 146–52; R. A. Beddard, 'Wren's Mausoleum for Charles I and the Cult of the Royal Martyr', *Architectural History*, 27 (1984), 36–49; Spurr, *1670s*, pp. 58–63; Spurr, *Restoration Church*, pp. 67–9; Coleby, *Hampshire*, pp. 98–9.

34. Evelyn, *Diary*, vol. 4, p. 20.

35. Grey, *Debates*, vol. 3, pp. 3, 29, 41, 49–50, 56, 128–9; *Essex Papers*, vol. 2, pp. 9, 11; *The Bulstrode Papers*, The Collection of Autograph Letters and Historical Documents formed by Alfred Morrison, 2nd Ser. (1897), vol. 1, pp. 284–8; Browning, *Danby*, vol. 1, p. 154.

36. *Bulstrode Papers*, vol. 1, pp. 286–9; Gilbert Burnet, *Burnet's History of My Own Time*, O. Airy, ed., 2 vols (Oxford, 1900), vol. 2, pp. 81–4; Dering, *The Diaries and Papers of Sir Edward Dering, Second Baronet, 1644 to 1684*, M. F. Bond, ed. (1976), pp. 60–1, 63, 65, 68, 70–4, 81–3, 90, 96; Swatland, *House of Lords*, pp. 213–15; Spurr, *1670s*, pp. 63–9; Haley, *Shaftesbury*, pp. 374–80.

37. Grey, *Debates*, vol. 3, pp. 341, 367–8; *Bulstrode Papers*, vol. 1, pp. 316–24; Dering, *Diaries and Papers*, p. 92; Browning, *Danby*, vol. 1, pp. 165–84; Haley, *Shaftesbury*, pp. 393–402; Spurr, *1670s*, pp. 72–6.

38. John Locke was probably also involved in the authorship of the *Letter*. [Anthony Ashley Cooper, Earl of Shaftesbury], *A Letter from a Person of Quality to his Friend in the Country* (1675), pp.1–2, 6, 8, 24–5, 34; [Anthony Ashley Cooper, Earl of Shaftesbury], *A Letter from a Parliament Man to his Friend* (1675); Anthony Ashley Cooper, Earl of Shaftesbury, *Two Speeches* (Amsterdam, 1675); [Holles, Denzil, Baron Holles], *The Long Parliament Dissolved* (1676), esp. pp. 4, 25; Historical Manuscripts Commission, *Verney Manuscripts* (7th Report, Part 1, Appendix), p. 467; Haley, *Shaftesbury*, pp. 390–3; Spurr, *1670s*, pp. 77–81; Montaño, *Moderates*, pp. 197–9; De Krey, *London and the Restoration*, pp. 140–57.

39. Nalson, *Common Interest*, p. 201; [Marchamont Nedham], *A Pacquet of Advices and Animadversions* (1676), pp. 3, 30; *English Historical Documents*, D. C. Douglas, gen. ed., 12 vols (New York, 1955–77), vol. 8, pp. 482–3; *Poems on Affairs of State; Augustan Satirical Verse, 1660–1714*, G. deF. Lord [*et al.*], eds, 7 vols (New Haven, CT, 1963–75), vol. 1, p. 283; Pincus, 'Coffeehouses', pp. 822–34; Browning, *Danby*, vol. 1, pp. 194–5; Montaño, *Moderates*, pp. 214–22, 321–3.

40. Grey, *Debates*, vol. 4, pp. 223, 255, 375, 390–1; *Essex Papers*, vol. 2, pp. 101, 105, 110, 118, 121, 141–3; *Memoirs of Sir John Reresby*, A. Browning *et al.*, eds, 2nd ed. (1991), pp. 111, 115–16, 123–4; HMC *Verney*, pp. 468, 469; Spurr, *1670s*, pp. 241–8; Haley, *Shaftesbury*, pp. 417–19, 422–8.

41. Burnet, *History*, p. 147; Browning, *Danby*, pp. 234–44, 247–58; *ODNB*, vol. 42, pp. 28–9; Hutton, *Charles II*, pp. 344–7; Spurr, *1670s*, pp. 249–50.

42. *The Poems and Letters of Andrew Marvell*, H. M. Margoliouth, 3rd ed., 2 vols (Oxford, 1971), vol. 2, pp. 224–6; Grey, *Debates*, vol. 5, p. 226; Reresby, *Memoirs*, pp. 134, 136–7; Browning, *Danby*, pp. 261–70; Spurr, *1670s*, pp. 251–7; Haley, *Shaftesbury*, pp. 442–8; Schwoerer, *Armies*, pp. 118–21.

43. Grey, *Debates*, vol. 5, p. 287; vol. 6, pp. 79–86, 96–100; Marvell, *Poems and Letters*, vol. 2, pp. 231, 233, 237, 242, 245; Reresby, *Memoirs*, pp. 143–4, 147; Browning, *Danby*, pp. 270–83; Spurr, *1670s*, pp. 257–60; Haley, *Shaftesbury*, pp. 448–51.

44. Grey, *Debates*, vol. 3, p. 136.

45. J. Bossy, *The English Catholic Community 1570–1850* (New York, 1976), pp. 188–9, 408; J. Miller, *Popery & Politics in England 1660–1688* (Cambridge, 1973), pp. 11–27; Swatland, *House of Lords*, pp. 146–8, 266–71.

46. D. Maclean, 'Roman Catholicism in Scotland during the Reign of Charles II', *Records of the Scottish Church History Society*, 3 (1929), 43–54; P. Hopkins, *Glencoe and the End of the Highland War* (Edinburgh, 1986), p. 25.

47. Bossy, pp. 216–18, 225.

48. Evelyn, *Diary*, vol. 4, p. 26; *Williamson Letters*, vol. 2, pp. 63, 67; *Calendar of State Papers, Domestic 1676–77*, pp. 253–5; O. W. Furley, 'The Pope-burning Processions of the Late Seventeenth Century', *History*, 44 (Feb., 1959), 16–23; Miller, *Popery*, pp. 124, 131–2, 134, 140–1, 143, 183–4.

49. Grey, *Debates*, vol. 4, pp. 284–96, 318–26, 334–40; M. Goldie, 'Danby, the Bishops and the Whigs', in *The Politics of Religion in Restoration England*, T. Harris *et al.*, eds (Oxford, 1990), pp. 83–6; Spurr, *1670s*, p. 244; Miller, *Popery*, pp. 144–6.

50. Marvell, *Prose Works*, p. 238; Grey, *Debates*, vol. 5, pp. 154, 224, 241–2, 275–6, 281–7 (quote at p. 286); vol. 6, 41–2, 86–9; Marvell, *Poems and Letters*, vol. 2, pp. 217, 222, 225–7, 230, 244; Haley, *Shaftesbury*, pp. 445–6, 448, 451; Spurr, *1670s*, pp. 254–8.

51. Greaves, *God's Other Children*, pp. 110–13; Hutton, *Charles II*, pp. 338–40, 349, 358.

52. The Scottish estates met as a convention when the king summonned them for supply only, without the consideration of legislation. [Alexander Shields], *A Hind let Loose* (1687), p.190, as quoted by J. R. Elder, *The Highland Host of 1678* (Glasgow, 1914), p. 134; Burnet, *History*, pp. 148; Buckroyd, *Church and State*, pp. 106–31(quotation from Sharpe, p. 114); J. Buckroyd, *The Life of James Sharp Archbishop of St Andrews 1618–1679* (Edinburgh, 1987), pp. 98–105; R. L. Greaves, *Enemies under his Feet: Radicals and Nonconformists in Britain, 1664–77* (Stanford, CA, 1990), pp. 235–41; I. Cowan, *The Scottish Covenanters, 1660–1688* (1976), pp. 84–91; Hutton, *Charles II*, pp. 349–52, 352; R. Mitchison, *Lordship to Patronage; Scotland 1603–1745* (1983), *Lordship to Patronage*, pp. 76–7; R. Greaves, *Secrets of the Kingdom: British Radicals from the Popish Plot to the Revolution of 1688–89* (Stanford, CA, 1992), pp. 53–4.

53. Grey, *Debates*, vol. 5, pp. 233, 283 (quoted), 331–2 (2nd numbering), 358–66 (quotes at 359, 361), 381; Reresby, *Memoirs*, p. 142.

54. *EHD*, vol. 8, pp. 109–12; Reresby, *Memoirs*, pp. 152–4; HMC *Verney*, p. 471; J. Kenyon, *The Popish Plot* (New York, 1972), chapts 2–4; Miller, *Popery*, pp. 155–60; Haley, *Shaftesbury*, pp. 453–9; *ODNB*, vol. 22, pp. 565–8; vol. 41, pp. 335–8; vol. 54, pp. 966–9; A. Bakshian, 'Historical Reference', *New York Times*, 122 (June 12, 1973), 45; M. Barone, 'Our Titus Oates', http://www.townhall.com/opinion/columns/michaelbarone/2005/07/18/154939.html, originally posted at http://www.realclearpolitics.com.

4 The Restoration Crisis, 1678–83

1. Charles II, *His Majesty's Declaration to All His Loving Subjects* (1681) in *English Historical Documents*, D. C. Douglas, gen. ed., 12 vols (New York, 1955–77), vol. 8, pp. 185–6.

2. T. Harris provides a new standard for historical treatment of Scotland in the crisis in *Restoration; Charles II and His Kingdoms* (2005), chapt. 6.

3. T. Harris, *London Crowds in the Reign of Charles II* (Cambridge, 1987), p.193 n. 24; T. Harris, 'The Parties and the People: the Press, the Crowd and Politics "Out-of-doors" in Restoration England', in L. K. J. Glassey, ed., *The Reigns of Charles II and James VII & II* (New York, 1997), pp. 125–51.

4. W. G. Mason, 'The Annual Output of Wing-listed Titles 1649–1684', *The Library*, 39 (1974), 219–20; M. Knights, *Politics and Opinion in Crisis, 1678–81* (Cambridge, 1994), pp. 157, 168–70; D. Cressy, *Literacy and the Social Order: Reading and Writing in Tudor and Stuart England* (Cambridge, 1980), pp. 129, 146–7, 154, 177; M. Knights, *Representation and Misrepresentation in Later Stuart Britain: Partisanship and Political Culture* (Oxford, 2005), pp. 16–17.

5. For further discussion, see: J. Scott, *Algernon Sidney and the Restoration Crisis, 1677–1683* (Cambridge, 1991), esp. pp. 3–82.

6. Anchitell Grey, *Debates of the House of Commons from the year 1667 to the year 1694*, 10 vols (1763), vol. 6, pp. 132–49, 172; *Memoirs of Sir John Reresby*, A. Browning *et al.*, eds, 2nd ed. (1991), p. 157; Historical Manuscripts Commission, *Ormonde*, NS, vol. 4, pp. 467–8, 478–9; Knights, *Politics and Opinion*, pp. 29–33; J. Kenyon, *The Popish Plot* (New York, 1972), pp. 88–104; A. Browning, *Thomas Osborne, Earl of Danby and Duke of Leeds, 1632–1712*, 3 vols. (Glasgow, 1944–51), pp. 297–9; K. H. D. Haley, *The First Earl of Shaftesbury* (Oxford, 1968), pp. 468–73, 480–2.

7. Grey, *Debates*, vol. 6, pp. 387–400; Historical Manuscripts Commission, *House of Lords, 1678–88*, pp. 46–53; HMC *Ormonde*, NS, vol. 4, pp. 463–6, 468–9, 471, 475, 480–5; Kenyon, *Popish Plot*, pp. 106–110, 126–31; Haley, *Shaftesbury*, pp. 477–9, 483–5.

8. *Oxford Dictionary of National Biography*, H. C. G. Matthew and B. H. Harrison, eds, 60 vols (Oxford, 2004), vol. 38, pp. 760–3; Browning, *Danby*, pp. 284–8; Knights, *Politics and Opinion*, pp. 25–8; Haley, *Shaftesbury*, pp. 487–90; J. Spurr, *England in the 1670s: 'This Masquerading Age'* (Oxford, 2000), pp. 268–9.

9. Grey, *Debates*, vol. 6, pp. 346–50; HMC *Ormonde*, NS, vol. 4, pp. 486, 488, 492–3; HMC *Lords 1678–88*, p. 85; Reresby, *Memoirs*, pp. 162–7; Haley, *Shaftesbury*, pp. 490–7; Browning, *Danby*, pp. 301–13; R. Hutton, *Charles II, King of England, Scotland, and Ireland* (Cambridge, 1989), pp. 365–6.

10. *Calendar of State Papers, Domestic 1679–80*, p. 21; Narcissus Luttrell, *A Brief Historical Relation of State Affairs*, 6 vols (Oxford, 1857), vol. 1, pp. 6–9; *The Diary of Ralph Josselin 1616–1683*, ed. A. Macfarlane (1976), p. 618; M. Knights, 'London Petitions and Parliamentary Politics in 1679', *Parliamentary History*, 12 (1993), 30–1; De Krey, *London and the Restoration, 1659–1683* (Cambridge, 2005), pp. 160–1; Haley, *Shaftesbury*, pp. 495, 502 (quote).

11. *Josselin Diary*, p. 619; HMC, *Ormonde*, NS, vol. 4, p. 340; Knights, *Politics and Opinion*, pp. 194–7; B. D. Henning, *The House of Commons*

1660–1690, The History of Parliament, 3 vols (1983), vol. 1, pp. 10, 27, 65, 106; Harris, *Later Stuarts*, p. 103; G. S. De Krey, *London and the Restoration*, p. 160; Spurr, *1670s*, p. 271; Haley, *Shaftesbury*, p. 500.

12. Reresby *Memoirs*, pp. 171, 173; Knights, *Politics and Opinion*, pp. 43–5; Hutton, *Charles II*, 368–71; Browning, *Danby*, pp. 317–20; Haley, *Shaftesbury*, pp. 503–10.

13. Anonymous, *A Proposal of Union amongst Protestants* (1679); [William Penn], *One Project for the Good of England* [1679]; Anthony á Wood, *The Life and Times of Anthony á Wood* (1961), p. 236; Grey, *Debates*, vol. 7, pp. 9–19; HMC *Ormonde*, NS, vol. 4, p. xx; Knights, *Politics and Opinion*, pp. 37, 197; Kenyon, *Popish Plot*, pp. 172–6; H. Horwitz, 'Protestant Reconciliation in the Exclusion Crisis', *Journal of Ecclesiastical History*, 15 (Oct. 1964), p. 203; Spurr, *1670s*, p. 278; Haley, *Shaftesbury*, pp. 510–11.

14. Grey, *Debates*, vol. 7, pp. 137–52, 158–64; HMC *Ormonde*, NS, vol. 4, pp. xviii, 504–5, 506–7 (quote), 508; Reresby, *Memoirs*, p. 178; Knights, *Politics and Opinion*, pp. 45–8; Haley, *Shaftesbury*, pp. 512–14, 516–17; Spurr, *1670s*, pp. 278–9.

15. Grey, *Debates*, vol. 7, pp. 159–60, 237–60 (quotes at pp. 159, 240); HMC *Ormonde*, NS, vol. 4, pp. 511–14, 516–17; vol. 5, p. 102; De Krey, *London and the Restoration*, pp. 144–51, 162–4; Knights, 'London Petitions', pp. 32–5; Haley, *Shaftesbury*, pp. 519–20; Knights, *Politics and Opinion*, pp. 51–2; Spurr, *1670s*, pp. 280–1.

16. Grey, *Debates*, vol. 7, pp. 279–85, 313–14 (quote at p. 314), Bishop Gilbert Burnet, *History of His Own Time*, abr. Thomas Stackhouse, Everyman Classics (1979), p. 167; HMC *Ormonde*, NS, vol. 4, pp. 516–17, vol. 5, pp. 84–6, 98–9, 102–03, 106–8; Reresby, *Memoirs*, pp. 180, 182; M. Goldie, 'Danby, the Bishops and the Whigs', in *The Politics of Religion in Restoration England*, T. Harris *et al.*, eds (Oxford, 1990), pp. 90–2; Haley, *Shaftesbury*, pp. 520–5.

17. Reresby, *Memoirs*, p. 183; HMC *Ormonde*, NS, vol. 5, p. 116.

18. HMC *Ormonde*, NS, vol. 4, p. 463; vol. 5, pp. 1, 3, 24–9, 46, 313; D. Dickson, *New Foundations: Ireland 1660–1800*, 2nd ed. (Dublin, 2000), pp. 17–20; S. J. Connolly, *Religion, Law, and Power: the Making of Protestant Ireland 1660–1760* (Oxford, 1992), pp. 29–32; *ODNB*, vol. 9, p. 161; vol. 44, p. 631.

19. R. Wodrow, *The History of the Sufferings of the Church of Scotland*, 4 vols (Glasgow, 1829–30), vol. 3, p. 43; Andrew Crichton, *Memoirs of John Blackader* (Edinburgh, 1823), pp. 224–5, 228–32; Burnet, *History*, p. 170; Grey, *Debates*, vol. 7, pp. 188–9, 192–3; R. Greaves, *Secrets of the Kingdom: British Radicals from the Popish Plot to the Revolution of 1688–89* (Stanford, 1992), pp. 53–60; R. L. Greaves, *God's Other Children: Protestant Nonconformists and the Emergence of Denominational Churches in Ireland, 1660–1700* (Stanford, CA, 1997), pp. 115–16; I. Cowan, *The Scottish Covenanters, 1660–1688* (1976), pp. 91–4; J. Buckroyd, *Church and State in Scotland, 1660–1681* (Edinburgh, 1980), pp. 129–30; J. Buckroyd, *The Life of James Sharp Archbishop of St Andrews 1618–1679* (Edinburgh, 1987), pp. 106–9; P. Kilroy, *Protestant Dissent and Controversy in Ireland 1660–1714* (Cork, 1994), pp. 236–7.

20. Wodrow, *Sufferings*, vol. 3, pp. 49–111 (with quotes from sources at 66–7, 94–5); *Blackader Memoirs*, pp. 239–49; HMC *Verney*, pp. 472–3; Greaves, *Secrets*, pp. 60–6, Cowan, *Covenanters*, pp. 94–9.

21. Wodrow, *Sufferings*, vol. 3, pp. 147–52; Greaves, *Secrets*, pp. 66–9; Cowan, *Covenanters*, pp. 98–102; Hutton, *Charles II*, p. 376; Haley, *Shaftesbury*, pp. 534–6.

22. HMC *Ormonde*, NS, vol. 5, pp. 128–9, 208; Greaves, *God's Other Children*, p. 117; Dickson, *New Foundations*, pp. 20–1.

23. HMC *Ormonde*, NS, vol. 4, p. 470; HMC *Verney*, p. 475; *ODNB*, vol. 49, pp. 395–404.

24. HMC *Verney*, pp. 474, 476; HMC *Ormonde*, NS, vol. 5, p. 204; *ODNB*, vol. 13, pp. 199–217; vol. 49, p. 399, Knights, *Politics and Opinion*, pp. 56–61; Haley, *Shaftesbury*, pp. 529–61.

25. Henning, *Commons*, vol. 1, pp. 65, 106ff., 229, 428; T. Harris, *Politics under the Later Stuarts: Party Conflict in a Divided Society 1660–1715* (1993), pp. 103–4; J. R. Jones, *The First Whigs: the Politics of the Exclusion Crisis 1678–83*, rev. ed. (1970), pp. 92–106, esp. 97–8, 102.

26. HMC *Ormonde*, vol. 4, pp. 528, 535–6; [Charles Blount], *An Appeal from the Country to the City* (1679), pp. 1–2; *The Freeholders Choice* (1679), p. 3; [William Penn], *England's Great Interest in the Choice of this New Parliament* (1679), pp. 3–4; *The Character of Popery and Arbitrary Government* (1679), p.4; *The Moderate Parliament* (1679), p.2; D. R. Lacey, *Dissent and Parliamentary Politics in England, 1661–1689* (New Brunswick, NJ, 1969), pp. 134–5; Knights, *Politics and Opinion*, pp. 206–19.

27. HMC *Verney*, p. 477; HMC *Ormonde*, NS, vol. 4, p. 561; De Krey, *London and the Restoration*, pp. 181–2; Harris, *London Crowds*, pp. 103–6.

28. *The Correspondence of the Hatton Family*, E. M. Thompson, ed., 2 vols (1978), vol. 1, pp. 203–7 (with quote at p. 203); Roger North, *Examen* (1740), p. 542; HMC *Ormonde*, NS, vol. 4, pp. 560, 565–6, 568–9, 574, 576; Reresby, *Memoirs*, pp. 198–9; M. Knights, 'London's "Monster" Petition of 1680', *Historical Journal*, 36, 1 (1993), 39–66; Knights, *Politics and Opinion*, pp. 227–42, 258–68 (with quotations from Charles and Burnet at pp. 236, 241); De Krey, *London and the Restoration*, pp. 183–7; Haley, *Shaftesbury*, pp. 557–65.

29. *Newdigate Newsletters*, Folger Shakespeare Library, L.c. 906–7, 916–18 (28 Feb. and 1, 25, 27, 29 Mar. 1680); HMC *Ormonde*, NS, vol. 4, p. 580, vol. 5, pp. 271, 288, 293, 296, 312; Reresby, *Memoirs*, p. 193; *Protestant (Domestick) Intelligence* 76–7 (26, 30 Mar. 1680); Henning, *Commons*, vol. 1, pp. 420–1; De Krey, *London and the Restoration*, p. 189; Harris, *London Crowds*, pp. 166–7; Knights, *Politics and Opinion*, p. 264. Also see N. E. Key, '"High Feeding and Smart Drinking": Associating Hedge-Lane Lords in Exclusion Crisis London', in *Fear, Exclusion and Revolution: Roger Morrice and Britain in the 1680s*, J. McElligott, ed. (Ashgate, 2006), pp. 154–73.

30. Newdigate L.c. 940, 955–6, 963–4 (29 May and 1, 3, 20, 22 July 1680); LC MS 18,124, vol. 7, p. 101 (16 Sept. 1680); *A True Narrative of the Duke of Monmouth's Late Journey into the West* (1680), p. 2; HMC *Verney*, p. 479; *Poems on Affairs of State: Augustan Satirical*

Verse, 1660–1714, G. deF. Lord [*et al.*], eds, 7 vols (New Haven, CT, 1963–75), vol. 2, p. 261; Haley, *Shaftesbury*, pp. 574–87; *ODNB*, vol. 49, pp. 399–400; De Krey, *London and the Restoration*, p. 199.

31. The *Domestick Intelligence* soon became the *Protestant (Domestick) Intelligence*. HMC *Ormonde*, vol. 4, p. 546; L. G. Schwoerer, *The Ingenious Mr. Henry Care, Restoration Publicist* (Baltimore, 2001); *ODNB*, vol. 12, pp. 616–18, vol. 54; pp. 459–60; A. Griffiths, *The Print in Stuart Britain, 1603–1689* (1998), pp. 283–4. For print and the crisis, generally, see Knights, *Politics and Opinion*, chapt. 6; Harris, *London Crowds*, chaps 5–6; Harris, *Restoration*, chaps 3–4.

32. *The Present Great Interest Both of King and People* (1679), p. 2; Edward Stillingfleet, *Unreasonableness of Separation* (1681), p. lv; Sir Roger L'Estrange, *Observator*, vol. 1, 1 (13 April 1681); Knights, *Politics and Opinion*, pp. 165–7, 245–50; Harris, *Restoration*, pp. 214–20.

33. [Sir Roger L'Estrange], *Citt and Bumpkin. In a Dialogue over a Pot of Ale, Concerning Matters of Religion and Government* (1680), reprinted by the Augustan Reprint Society, 117 (Los Angeles, CA, 1965); [Sir Roger L'Estrange], *The Committee; or Popery in Masquerade* (1680); British Museum, Dept. of Prints and Drawings, *Catalogue of Prints and Drawings in the British Museum*, 11 vols. (1870–1954), vol. 1, pp. 623–7; Schwoerer, *Henry Care*, pp. 112–18; Griffiths, *Print*, pp. 286–7; Harris, *Restoration*, pp. 237–52.

34. Scott, *Restoration Crisis*, pp. 9–17, 21–5.

35. Newdigate L.c. 997 (21 Oct. 1680); Grey, *Debates*, vol. 7, p. 348; Knights, *Politics and Opinion*, pp. 71–6; Haley, *Shaftesbury*, pp. 588–93.

36. Grey, *Debates*, vol. 7, pp. 395–413 (quotes at pp. 396, 406), 418–21 (quote at p. 419), 425–30, 433, 439–59 (quote at p. 448); HMC *Lords 1678–1688*, p. 197; HMC *Verney*, p. 479; HMC *Ormonde*, NS, vol. 5, p. 488; Reresby, *Memoirs*, p. 203; *The Solemn Mock Procession: or the Trial and Execution of the Pope and His Ministers, on the 17. of Nov. at Temple Bar* (1680); Newdigate L.c. 1009 (18 Nov. 1680); Haley, *Shaftesbury*, pp. 593–602; De Krey, *London and the Restoration*, pp. 174–205; Knights, *Politics and Opinion*, pp. 78–82.

37. Grey, *Debates*, vol. 7, pp. 370, 372, 414; vol. 8, pp. 203, 226–29; HMC *Ormonde*, NS, vol. 5, p. 530; Edward Dering, *The Diaries and Papers of Sir Edward Dering, Second Baronet, 1644 to 1684*, M. F. Bond, ed. (1976), pp. 194–6; Reresby, *Memoirs*, p. 207; Horwitz, 'Protestant Reconciliation', pp. 204–14; Lacey, *Dissent*, pp. 143–6.

38. Grey, *Debates*, vol. 8, pp. 13, 21, 31, 168, 171, 188, 289–90; *Votes of the House of Commons* 58 (10 Jan. 1681); Newdigate L.c. 1019 (14. Dec. 1680); Library of Congress, MS 18,124, vol. 8, p. 145 (10 Jan. 1681); HMC *Ormonde*, NS, vol. 5, pp. 530, 549; Knights, *Politics and Opinion*, pp. 80–94; Haley, *Shaftesbury*, pp. 603–19.

39. Wood, *Life*, pp. 253–4; Grey, *Debates*, vol. 8, pp. 291–2, 309–10; Reresby, *Memoirs*, pp. 219–22; *POAS*, vol. 2, pp. 425–31; Henning, *Commons*, vol. 1, pp. 65, 106 239, 317, 360, 416; vol. 3, p. 695; Knights, *Politics and Opinion*, pp. 94–103, 280–303; Jones, *First Whigs*, pp. 163–73; De Krey, *London and the Restoration*, pp. 210–19; *ODNB*, vol. 12, p. 617; vol. 49, p. 400; Haley, *Shaftesbury*, pp. 626–38.

40. *EHD*, vol. 8, pp. 185–8; Knights, *Politics and Opinion*, pp. 306–29.
41. Reresby, *Memoirs*, pp. 230, 246; Knights, *Politics and Opinion*, pp. 329–45; Harris, *Restoration*, pp. 268–77, 390–95.
42. C. D. Chandaman, *The English Public Revenue, 1660–1688* (Oxford, 1975), pp. 247–53.
43. *A Source Book of Scottish History*, W. C. Dickinson, G. Donaldson, and I. A. Milne, eds, 3 vols, 2nd ed. (1958), vol. 3, pp. 174–9; Burnet, *History*, pp. 185–6; Wodrow, *Sufferings*, vol. 3, pp. 202–23; Cowan, *Covenanters*, pp. 103–06; Greaves, *Secrets*, pp. 69–75.
44. Officially adopted in 1567, this Reformation confession was written in 1560. *Scottish Sourcebook*, vol. 3, pp. 185–9; Wodrow, *Sufferings*, vol. 3, pp. 181–88, 291–7; Harris, *Restoration*, pp. 341–9; Buckroyd, *Church and State*, pp. 131–5; Greaves, *Secrets*, pp. 75–81.
45. Burnet, *History*, pp. 187–91; Reresby, *Memoirs*, p. 241; Wodrow, *Sufferings*, vol. 3, pp. 303–09, 312–44, 369–91, 475–82; Harris, *Restoration*, pp. 349–64; Greaves, *Secrets*, pp. 81–9; C. Jackson, *Restoration Scotland, 1660–1690: Royalist Politics, Religion and Ideas* (Woodbridge, Suffolk, 2003), pp. 149–52; *ODNB*, vol. 9, pp. 716—24; vol. 14, pp. 988–95; Cowan, *Covenanters*, pp. 108–19.
46. HMC *Ormonde*, NS, vol. 5, p. 368; Greaves, *God's Other Children*, pp. 119–21, 128–9; Kilroy, *Dissent in Ireland*, pp. 238–41; Harris, *Restoration*, p. 389.
47. *ODNB*, vol. 12, pp. 617–18.
48. Reresby, *Memoirs*, p. 237; Haley, *Shaftesbury*, pp. 655–61; De Krey, *London and the Restoration*, pp. 233–6; Harris, *London Crowds*, pp. 169, 180.
49. Schwoerer, *Henry Care*, pp. 180–3; Greaves, *Secrets*, pp. 17–19, 40–9; Harris, *London Crowds*, pp. 130–1, 145–8; *ODNB*, vol. 25, pp. 407–10.
50. Richard Baxter, *Reliquiae Baxteriane*, Matthew Sylvester, ed. (1696), part 3, p.191; Reresby, *Memoirs*, p. 240; Greaves, *Bunyan*, pp. 404–14, 439–58, 485–6; De Krey, *London and the Restoration*, pp. 242–6, 353–4; C. W. Horle, *The Quakers and the English Legal System 1660–1688* (Philadelphia, 1988), p. 284; M. Goldie, 'The Hilton Gang and the Purge of London in the 1680s', in *Politics and the Political Imagination in Later Stuart Britain*, H. Nenner, ed. (Rochester, NY, 1997), pp. 44–73; Harris, *Restoration*, pp. 300–9.
51. Burnet, *History*, p. 194; Evelyn, *Diary*, vol. 4, pp. 342–3; Reresby, *Memoirs*, p. 244; De Krey, *London and the Restoration*, pp. 246–71, 341–58, 362, 370–2, 382–6; Haley, *Shaftesbury*, pp. 684–704; Harris, *London Crowds*, pp. 139–55, 180–8.
52. A. Coleby, *Central Government and the Localities: Hampshire 1649–1689* (Cambridge, 1987), pp. 162–6; P. D. Halliday, *Dismembering the Body Politic: Partisan Politics in England's Towns, 1650–1730* (Cambridge, 1998), pp. 124–31, 192–236; J. Miller, 'The Crown and the Borough Charters in the Reign of Charles II', *English Historical Review*, 100 (1985), 53–84; L. K. J. Glassey, *Politics and the Appointment of Justices of the Peace 1675–1720* (Oxford, 1979), pp. 45–55; P. Gauci, *Politics and Society in Great Yarmouth 1660–1722* (Oxford, 1996), pp. 151–7; Harris, *Restoration*, pp. 293–300.

53. De Krey, *London and the Restoration*, pp. 263–4, 345–52; Greaves, *Secrets*, pp. 109–32; Haley, *Shaftesbury*, pp. 707–24; *ODNB*, vol. 9, p. 721, vol. 49, pp. 400–1.

54. John Owen, *A Brief and Impartial Account of the Nature of the Protestant Religion* (1682) in *The Works of John Owen*, W. H. Goold, ed., 16 vols. (1850–53), vol. 14, p. 537; Robert Ferguson, *An Impartial Enquiry* (1683), pp. 3–4, 7, 26–8; George Buchanan, *De jure regni apud Scotos, or, a Dialogue, Concerning the Due Priviledge of Government* (1680); John Locke, *Second Treatise of Government*, Paragraphs 210 (quote), 214–16, 218, 222; Algernon Sidney, *Discourses Concerning Government*, Chapter II, section 32 (quote) and Chapter III, sections 19, 26, 38; De Krey, *London and the Restoration*, pp. 307–8, 392–6; Scott, *Restoration Crisis*, pp. 201–64; Jackson, *Restoration Scotland*, p. 198.

5 Resettlement and Unsettlement, 1683–8

1. [James II], *His Majesties Gracious Declaration to All His Loving Subjects for Liberty of Conscience* (1687) in *English Historical Documents*, D. C. Douglas, gen. ed., 12 vols (New York, 1955–77), vol. 8, pp. 395–6.

2. *EHD*, vol. 8, p. 122; J. P. Kenyon, *Robert Spencer, Earl of Sunderland, 1641–1702* (1958), pp. 90–1; G. M. Trevelyan, *The English Revolution 1688–1689* (Oxford, 1974, first issued 1938), p. 130. Strong restatements of the argument include G. Holmes, The Making of a *Great Power: Late Stuart and early Georgian Britain, 1660-1722* (Longman, 1993), pp. 160–74; and W. A. Speck, *Reluctant Revolutionaries: Englishmen and the Revolution of 1688* (Oxford, 1989), pp. 153–62.

3. J. Miller, 'The Potential for "Absolutism" in Later Stuart England', *History*, 69 (June, 1984), 187–207; T. Harris, 'Tories and the Rule of Law in the Reign of Charles II', *The Seventeenth Century*, 8 (Spring, 1993), 9–27, esp. 20-4.

4. See Introduction to chapt. 1 above.

5. For the destabilizing impact of ideas and fears, see J. Scott, *England's Troubles: Seventeenth-Century English Political Instability in European Context* (Cambridge, 2000), esp. pp. 43–65; and the essays in *Fear, Exclusion and Revolution: Roger Morrice and Britain in the 1680s*, J. McElligott, ed. (Ashgate, 2006).

6. See P. Harth, *Pen for a Party: Dryden's Tory Propaganda in its Contexts* (Princeton, NJ, 1993), chapt. 5 for the idea of a 'second Restoration'.

7. *Observator*, vol. 1, 3 July, 14 August 1683; *The Speeches of Captain Walcot, Jo. Rouse, and Will. Hone* (1683); *His Majesties Declaration to All His Loving Subjects* (1683); Harth, *Pen*, pp. 213–14, 219–28; T. Harris, *Restoration; Charles II and His Kingdoms* (2005), pp. 317–23.

8. *The Diary of John Evelyn*, E. S. De Beer, ed., 6 vols (Oxford, 1955), vol. 4, p. 326; M. MacDonald, 'The Strange Death of the Earl of Essex, 1683', *History Today*, 41 (November, 1991), 13–18; R. Greaves, *Secrets of the Kingdom: British Radicals from the Popish Plot to the Revolution of 1688–89* (Stanford, 1992), pp. 206–41; L. G. Schwoerer, 'The Trial of Lord William Russell (1683): Judicial Murder?'

Journal of Legal History, 9 (1988), 142–68; M. Zook, *Radical Whigs and Conspiratorial Politics in Late Stuart England* (University Park, PA, 1999), pp. 116–26; *Oxford Dictionary of National Biography*, H. C. G. Matthew and B. H. Harrison, eds, 60 vols (Oxford, 2004), vol. 9, pp. 981–2.

9. Recent treatments of the Rye House Plot are found in Greaves, *Secrets*, pp. 133–60, 171–205; Zook, *Whigs*, pp. 87–113; G. S. De Krey, *London and the Restoration, 1659–1683* (Cambridge, 2005), pp. 358–70, 373–82. J. Scott has argued for a more pervasive republican influence in *Algernon Sidney and the Restoration Crisis, 1677–1683* (Cambridge, 1991), pp. 105–6, 125, 162–9.

10. *The Judgment and Decree of the University of Oxford* (1683); [Sir Robert Filmer], *Patriarcha: or, the Natural Power of Kings*, 2nd ed. (1685); [Thomas Sprat], *A True Account and Declaration of the Horrid Conspiracy* (1685); *The Stuart Constitution*, J. P. Kenyon, ed. (Cambridge, 1966), pp. 471–4; P. Laslett, 'Introduction', to John Locke, *Two Treatises of Government*, 2nd ed. (Cambridge, 1967), p. 24; Harth, *Pen*, pp. 254–68; R. Beddard, 'Tory Oxford', in *Seventeenth-Century Oxford*, N. Tyacke, ed., *History of the University of Oxford* (Oxford, 1997), pp. 891–98; R. Beddard, 'The Commission for Ecclesiastical Promotions, 1681–4: An instrument of Tory Reaction', *Historical Journal*, 10, 1 (1967), 11–40; J. Spurr, *The Restoration Church of England, 1646–1689* (New Haven, 1991), pp. 82–5.

11. Anthony á Wood, *The Life and Times of Anthony á Wood* (1961), p. 271; De Krey, *London and the Restoration*, pp. 336, 352, 371, 383.

12. D. C. Coleman, *The Economy of England 1450–1750* (Oxford, 1977), pp. 133–45; C. D. Chandaman, *The English Public Revenue, 1660–1688* (Oxford, 1975), p. 254; Holmes, *Great Power*, pp. 61–6; *ODNB*, vol. 3, pp. 966–7.

13. Newdigate L.c. 1497 (14 Feb 1684); B. Weiser, *Charles II and the Politics of Access* (Woodbridge, Suffolk, 2003), pp. 46–53; R. Hutton, *Charles II, King of England, Scotland, and Ireland* (Cambridge, 1989), p. 429; *ODNB*, vol. 60, p. 415.

14. Newdigate L.c. 1535 (13 May 1684); Kenyon, *Sunderland*, pp. 83–100, 107–9; Hutton, *Charles II*, pp. 425–34; J. R. Jones, *Charles II*, pp. 175–7, 180, 183–5; J. Miller, *Popery & Politics in England 1660–1688* (Cambridge, 1973), p. 194; *ODNB*, vol. 29, pp. 149–50, vol. 49, pp. 102–3.

15. Newdigate L. c. 1489, 1513, 1515, 1520, 1542, 1569, 1623 (31 Jan., 22 and 27 March, 8 April, 29 May, 31 July, 6 Dec. 1684); Harris, *Later Stuarts*, pp. 119–23; Harris, *Restoration*, p. 407.

16. Newdigate L.c. 1491, 1497, 1522, 1532, 1543, 1554, 1558, 1561; P. D. Halliday, *Dismembering the Body Politic: Partisan Politics in England's Towns, 1650–1730* (Cambridge, 1998), pp. 229–32; De Krey, *London and the Restoration*, pp. 388–92; Harris, *Restoration*, pp. 261–2, 321, 323–4, 414–17; Greaves, *Secrets*, p. 251.

17. Kenyon, *Sunderland*, p. 90.

18. *Memoirs of Sir John Reresby*, A. Browning, *et al.*, eds, 2nd ed. (1991), pp. 352–3, F. C. Turner, *James II* (1948), p. 240; T. Harris, *Revolution: The Great Crisis of the British Monarchy, 1685–1720* (2006), pp. 46–54.

19. J. Miller, *James II* (New Haven, CT, 2000, pp. 120–8; Kenyon, *Sunderland*, pp. 111–16.

20. R. H. George, 'Parliamentary Elections and Electioneering in 1685', *Transactions of the Royal Historical Society*, 4th Ser., 19 (1936), 167–95; B. D. Henning, *The House of Commons 1660–1690*, The History of Parliament, 3 vols (1983), vol. 1, pp. 13, 106, 126, 136, 141, 145, 152, 373–4, 379, 421; Speck, *Revolutionaries*, pp. 44–6; J. Miller, *After the Civil Wars; English Politics and Government in the Reign of Charles II* (Harlow, Essex, 2000), pp. 288–90; J. R. Western, *Monarchy and Revolution; The English State in the 1680s* (1972), pp. 78–81.

21. Bishop Gilbert Burnet, *History of His Own Time*, abr. Thomas Stackhouse, Everyman Classics (1979), p. 224; George, 'Elections', p. 195 (quote from ambassador); Reresby, *Memoirs*, pp. 360, 362; Evelyn, *Diary*, vol. 4, p. 437; Wood, *Life*, p. 279; Henning, *Commons*, vol. 1, p. 27; Miller, *James II*, p. 136; Miller, *Popery*, p. 204; R. A. Beddard, 'James II and the Catholic Challenge', in *Seventeenth-Century Oxford*, pp. 909–11.

22. Anchitell Grey, *Debates of the House of Commons from the year 1667 to the year 1694*, 10 vols (1763), vol. 8, pp. 343–52; Reresby, *Memoirs*, pp. 366–71; Speck, *Revolutionaries*, pp. 47–50; Miller, *James II*, pp. 136–7; Western, *Monarchy*, p. 195.

23. BL Harleian MS 6845, fols 256–9; Reresby, *Memoirs*, 374–5, 377, 380–1, 384–5 (quote with my italics); Speck, *Revolutionaries*, pp. 151–3; Zook, *Whigs*, pp. 129–37; Greaves, *Secrets*, pp. 284–92; R. Clifton, *The Last Popular Rebellion: the Western Rising of 1685* (1984), esp. pp. 158–71, 180–9, 203ff., 249–76.

24. P. Earl, *Monmouth's Rebels; The Road to Sedgemoor 1685* (New York, 1977), pp. 161–87; Speck, *Revolutionaries*, pp. 53–5; [T. B. Macaulay,] Lord Macaulay, *The History of England from the Accession of James the Second*, C. H. Firth, ed., 6 vols (1913–15), vol. 2, pp. 629–45; *ODNB*: vol. 21, pp. 650–1, vol. 29, pp. 887—8; vol. 33, pp. 960–1.

25. Grey, *Debates*, vol. 1, pp. 353–72; Reresby, *Memoirs*, pp. 394–9; C. J. Fox, *A History of the Early Part of the Reign of James the Second* (1808), Appendix, cxxix–cxli; H. C. Foxcroft, *The Life and Letters of Sir George Savile, Bart., First Marquis of Halifax*, 2 vols (1898), vol. 1, pp. 449–50; *The Works of George Savile Marquis of Halifax*, ed. M. N. Brown, 3 vols (Oxford, 1989), vol. 1, p. 71; L. G. Schwoerer, *'No Standing Armies!' The Antiarmy Ideology in Seventeenth-Century England* (Baltimore, 1974), pp. 140–5; J. Childs, *The Army, James II, and the Glorious Revolution* (New York, 1980), pp. 1–2, 7–8, 11–14, 19–22; Speck, *Revolutionaries*, pp. 56–62, Miller, *James II*, 142–3, 146–7.

26. C. D. Chandaman, 'The Financial Settlement in the Parliament of 1685', in *British Government and Administration; Studies Presented to S. B. Chrimes*, ed. H. Hearder and H. R. Loyn (Cardiff, 1974), p. 152.

27. These 3000 English and Scots soldiers and officers traced their origins as a brigade to Elizabeth I's military commitments to the Netherlands against Philip II of Spain. They returned to the Netherlands after Monmouth's defeat. Childs, *Army, James II*, pp. 119–35.

28. Evelyn, *Diary*, vol. 4, p. 524; Reresby, *Memoirs*, pp. 404–5, 420–2, 429, 444–5, 447–8; Miller, *James II*, pp. 148–66; Miller, *Popery*, pp. 269–72; Kenyon, *Sunderland*, pp. 115–18, 125–7, 132–6, 139–40; Harris, *Revolution*, pp. 202–5; J. P. Kenyon, 'The Commission for Ecclesiastical Causes 1686–1688: A Reconsideration', *HJ*, 34 (Sept., 1991), 727–36; Speck, *Revolutionaries*, pp. 62–4; Edward Carpenter, *The Protestant Bishop* (1956), pp. 84–103; L. K. J. Glassey, *Politics and the Appointment of Justices of the Peace 1675–1720* (Oxford, 1979), pp. 70–7; Turner, *James II*, p. 295; *ODNB*, vol. 29, pp. 149–50.

29. *The Correspondence of Henry Hyde, Earl of Clarendon*, S. W. Singer, ed., 2 vols (1828), vol. 1, p. 357; Burnet, *History*, p. 248; Harris, R*evolution*, pp. 101–18.

30. P. Melvin, 'Sir Paul Rycaut's Memoranda and Letters from Ireland', *Analecta Hibernica*, 27 (1972), 157; Harris, *Revolution*, pp. 119–25, 129–31, 137–9.

31. Evelyn, *Diary*, vol. 4, pp. 535–6.

32. Melvin, 'Rycaut's Memorandum', p. 157; Burnet, *History*, p. 248; J. G. Simms, *Jacobite Ireland, 1685–91* (Dublin, 2000), p. 34 (Gaelic quote); W. A. Speck, *James II* (2002), p.106 ('Turk-conel'); Greaves, *God's Other Children*, pp. 139–41; Kilroy, *Protestant Dissent*, pp. 242–3.

33. *Clarendon Correspondence*, vol. 1, pp. 217, 276, 294, 296–7, 299, 313, 342–3, 349, 376, 414, 431–3 (quote at p. 432), 447, 461–2, 464, 476, 514, 521–2, 534–6, 560, 581–2; HMC *Ormonde*, NS, vol. 7, pp. 374, 395–6, 400, 448–9, 464–7 (quote at p. 464), 483—4; vol. 8, pp. 344–52; HMC *Egmont*, vol. 2, pp. 158, 161; Melvin, 'Rycaut's Memorandum', pp. 153, 155, 166, 175; [William King], *The State of the Protestants of Ireland under the late King James*, 4th ed. (1692), pp. 29, 84–93, 223–8; Simms, *Jacobite Ireland*, pp. 19–40; J. Miller, 'The Earl of Tyrconnell and James II's Irish Policy, 1685–1688', *HJ*, 20 (Dec. 1977), 803–23; Childs, *Army, James II*, pp. 56–82; Miller, *James II*, pp. 210–13, 216–19; *ODNB*, vol. 53, p. 719; Harris, *Revolution*, pp. 125–8, 132–6; Kenyon, *Sunderland*, pp. 136–7, 141–4, 162–3; Dickson, *New Foundations*, pp. 23–7; Connolly, *Protestant Ireland*, pp. 33–40; Speck, *James II*, pp. 101–7.

34. I. Cowan, *The Scottish Covenanters, 1660–1688* (1976), 128–9; R. Wodrow, *The History of the Sufferings of the Church of Scotland*, 4 vols (Glasgow, 1829–30), vol. 4, pp. 248–9; Harris, *Restoration*, pp. 368–74; *ODNB* vol. 59, p. 615.

35. HMC *Buccleuch and Queensberry*, vol. 1, p. 91; *A Source Book of Scottish History*, 3 vols, 2nd ed. (1961), vol. 3, pp. 190–1; Woodrow, *Sufferings*, vol. 4, pp. 259–74, 282–90; Harris, *Revolution*, pp. 69–70, 76–8; Speck, *James II*, pp. 85–8; Greaves, *Secrets*, pp. 278–84; P. Hopkins, *Glencoe and the End of the Highland War* (Edinburgh, 1986), pp. 95–103; C. Jackson, *Restoration Scotland, 1660–1690: Royalist Politics, Religion and Ideas* (Woodbridge, Suffolk, 2003), pp. 155–7.

36. D. Maclean, 'Roman Catholicism in Scotland during the Reign of Charles II', *Records of the Scottish Church History Society*, 3 (1929), p. 47; Sir John Lauder of Fountainhall, *Historical Notices of Scottish*

Affairs, 2 vols (Edinburgh, 1848), vol. 2, pp. 700–2; *Register of the Privy Council of Scotland*, vol. 12, pp. 7–16, 30–4, 41–4, 69–71, 92–7; Harris, *Restoration*, p. 29; Harris, *Revolution*, pp. 149–53; Speck, *James II*, pp. 88–91.

37. Fountainhall, *Historical Notices*, vol. 2, p. 717 (quote), 732–9 (quote at 737); [Alexander Shields], *A Hind let Loose* (1687), pp. 152–3; *Scottish Source Book,*, vol. 3, pp. 192–7; Harris, *Revolution*, pp. 153–73 (esp. 166), 179–81; Cowan, *Covenanters*, pp. 130–1; Speck, *James II*, pp. 91–4; Jackson, *Restoration Scotland*, pp. 157–61; I. B. Cowan, 'The Reluctant Revolutionaries: Scotland in 1688', in *By Force or by Default? The Revolution of 1688–1689*, E. Cruickshanks, ed. (Edinburgh, 1989), pp. 68–9, 72.

38. Evelyn, *Diary*, vol. 3, p. 581; A. Taylor, *American Colonies* (New York, 2001), pp. 137, 170–8, 203, 255–72, 281; R. R. Johnson, *Adjustment to Empire; the New England Colonies, 1675–1715* (New Brunswick, NJ, 1981), pp. 3–36; R. C. Ritchie, *The Duke's Province; a Study of New York Politics and Society, 1664–1691* (Chapel Hill, NC, 1977), pp. 31–42, 92–117, 167–79; Speck, *James II*, pp. 120–2; M. K. Geiter, 'The Restoration Crisis and the Launching of Pennsylvania', *EHR*, 112 (April, 1997), 300–18.

39. *The Diary of Samuel Sewall, 1674–1720*, ed. M. H. Thomas, 2 vols (New York, 1973), vol. 1, pp. 132, 140–1, 143, 159, 163; Essex Institute, *Historical Collections*, 43 (1907), p. 182; Johnson, *Adjustment to Empire*, pp. 63–83; D. S. Lovejoy, *The Glorious Revolution in America* (New York, 1972), pp. 179–95; Speck, *James II*, pp. 122–6; *ODNB* vol. 2, pp. 138–9.

40. *EHD*, vol. 8, pp. 395–7; Reresby, *Memoirs*, pp. 450, 452 (quote); Evelyn, *Diary*, vol. 4, p. 546; *ODNB*, vol. 43, p. 563; vol. 51, p. 887.

41. Kenyon, *Sunderland*, pp. 145–66.

42. *Scottish Source Book*, vol. 3, p. 197; G. S. De Krey, 'Reformation and "Arbitrary Government": London Dissenters and James II's Polity of Toleration, 1687–8', in *Fear, Exclusion and Revolution*, pp. 13–17; R. L. Greaves, *Glimpses of Glory: John Bunyan and English Dissent* (Stanford, 2002), p. 573; P. Gauci, *Politics and Society in Great Yarmouth 1660–1722* (Oxford, 1996), p. 166; Wodrow, *Sufferings*, vol. 4, pp. 426–34; Cowan, *Covenanters*, pp. 130–2; Harris, *Revolution*, pp. 173–6; Lovejoy, *Glorious Revolution*, pp. 194–5; Greaves, *God's Other Children*, p. 139.

43. *A Letter to a Dissenter* (1687) in Halifax, *Works*, vol. 1, pp. 251–2, 257, 259; Spurr, *Restoration Church*, pp. 90–2; Speck, *Reluctant Revolutionaries*, pp. 176–82; Harris, *Revolution*, pp. 177–8; M. Knights, '"Meer religion" and the "church-state" of Restoration England: the Impact and Ideology of James II's Declarations of Indulgence', in *A Nation Transformed: England after the Restoration*, A. Houston and S. Pincus, eds (Cambridge, 2001), pp. 56–60.

44. Reresby, *Memoirs*, p. 469; R. A. Beddard, 'James II and the Catholic Challenge', in *Seventeenth-Century Oxford*, pp. 921–47; J. Twigg, *The University of Cambridge and the English Revolution, 1625–1688* (Woodbridge, Suffolk, 1990), pp. 279–84; Miller, *James II*, p. 170 (quote from James); *ODNB*, vol. 19, p. 58, vol. 28, pp. 271–2.

45. S. B. Baxter, *William III* (1966), pp. 218–21; Kenyon, *Sunderland*, pp. 150–3, 157–8; Miller, *James II*, pp. 175–7, A. Browning, *Thomas Osborne, Earl of Danby and Duke of Leeds, 1632–1712*, 3 vols (Glasgow, 1944-51), vol. 1, pp. 378–80, vol. 2, pp.116–22; H. Horwitz, *Revolution Politicks: the Career of Daniel Finch, second Earl of Nottingham, 1647–1730* (Cambridge, 1968), pp. 44–9.

46. P. D. Halliday, *Body Politic*, pp. 243–50; Glassey, *Justices*, pp. 77–92 (Bishop of Norwich quote, p. 87); J. R. Jones, *The Revolution of 1688 in England* (1972), pp. 138–52; Miller, *Popery*, pp. 217–22; Miller, *James II*, pp. 178–80; Kenyon, *Sunderland*, pp. 171–4, De Krey, 'Reformation and "Arbitrary Government"', pp. 18–20; L. G. Schwoerer, *The Ingenious Mr. Henry Care, Restoration Publicist* (Baltimore, 2001), pp. 189–219; M. Knights, 'A City Revolution: the Remodelling of the London Livery Companies in the 1680s', *EHR*, 112 (Nov., 1997), 1157–63; M. Goldie, 'John Locke's Circle and James II', *HJ*, 35 (Sept., 1992), pp. 570–3; Western, *Monarchy*, pp. 210–24; A. Coleby, *Central Government and the Localities: Hampshire 1649–1689* (Cambridge, 1987), pp. 171–8; Gauci, *Yarmouth*, p. 167.

47. Miller, *Popery*, pp. 239–49; Miller, 'Tyrconnel', p. 820; P. F. Anson, *Underground Catholicism in Scotland 1622–1878* (Montrose, 1970), pp. 78–87; M. Glozier, 'The Earl of Melfort, the Court Catholic Party and the Foundation of the Order of the Thistle, 1687', *SHR*, 79 (October, 2000), 233–8; Simms, *Jacobite Ireland*, pp. 39–42.

48. *ODNB*, vol. 37, pp. 98–9.

49. Kenyon, *Sunderland*, pp. 186, 201; De Krey, 'Reformation and "Arbitrary Government"', p. 22.

50. [H]enry [C]are, *Animadversions on a Late Paper* (1687), pp. 36–7; [William Penn], *The Great and Popular Objection* (1688), p. 6; [G]iles [S]hute], *A New Test in Lieu of the Old One* (1688), p. 30; Halifax, *Works*, vol. 1, pp. 90–7; Schwoerer, *Henry Care*, pp. 202–07; De Krey, 'Reformation and "Arbitrary Government"', pp. 26–7.

51. Doctor Williams's Library: Roger Morrice, Ent'ring Book, MS 31, Q. 84, 237; De Krey, 'Reformation and "Arbitrary Government"', pp. 25, 27–9; D. N. Marshall, 'Protestant Dissent in England in the Reign of James II' (Unpublished PhD thesis, Hull University, 1976), pp. 411–17; Gauci, *Yarmouth*, p. 169; D. R. Lacey, *Dissent and Parliamentary Politics in England, 1661–1689* (New Brunswick, NJ, 1969), pp. 191–8, 203–5; P. D. Halliday, *Body Politic*, pp. 247–8; Knights, 'City Revolution', p. 1166.

52. Reresby, *Memoirs*, pp. 500–1; *Clarendon Correspondence*, vol. 2, p. 171; Morrice, Q. 259; R. Thomas, 'The Seven Bishops and their Petition, 18 May 1688', *JEcH*, 12 (April, 1961), 56–70; G. V. Bennett, 'The Seven Bishops: a Reconsideration', *Religious Motivation*, ed. D. Baker (Oxford, 1978), pp. 267–87; Spurr, *Restoration Church*, pp. 93–7; Lacey, *Dissent*, pp. 209–13; Speck, *Reluctant Revolutionaries*, pp. 221–3; Kenyon, *Sunderland*, pp. 194–200; R. Weil, *Political Passions: Gender, the Family and Political Argument in England 1680–1714* (Manchester, 1999), pp. 87–8.

53. *EHD*, vol. 8, pp. 120–1; W. A. Speck, 'The Orangist Conspiracy against James II', *HJ*, 30 (June, 1987), 453–62; Childs, *Army, James II*, pp. 138–67; Lacey, *Dissent*, p. 215; Horwitz, *Revolution Politics*, pp. 51–4.

54. Jones, *Revolution*, pp. 164–75; De Krey, 'Reformation and "Arbitrary Government"'; P. D. Halliday, *Body Politic*, pp. 254–6; Knights, 'City Revolution', p. 1167; Lacey, *Dissent*, pp. 203, 218, 296ff.; Western, *Monarchy*, p. 225; Coleby, *Hampshire*, p. 177; Gauci, *Yarmouth*, p. 172.

55. *The Eighteenth-Century Constitution*, E. N. Williams, ed. (Cambridge, 1960), pp. 15–16; Wodrow, *Sufferings*, vol. 4, pp. 470–2; Kenyon, *Sunderland*, pp. 202–23; Miller, *James II*, pp. 188–99; Jones, *Revolution*, pp. 254–87; Glassey, *Justices*, pp. 94–9; Horwitz, *Revolution Politicks*, p. 55; Simms, *Jacobite Ireland*, pp. 46–7, Spurr, *Church of England*, p. 99.

6 The Glorious Revolution and Its Aftermath

1. John Locke, *Second Treatise of Government* (1689), paragraph 232.

2. S. B. Baxter, *William III* (1966), pp. 223–33.

3. J. Childs, *The Army, James II, and the Glorious Revolution* (New York, 1980), pp. 168–84; Baxter, *William III*, pp. 233–38; W. A. Speck, *Reluctant Revolutionaries: Englishmen and the Revolution of 1688* (Oxford, 1989), pp. 76–86; J. R. Jones, *The Revolution of 1688 in England* (1972), pp. 288–94.

4. *Memoirs of Sir John Reresby*, A. Browning, M. K. Geiter, and W. A. Speck, eds, 2nd ed. (1991), pp. 526–33 (quote at p. 529).

5. Childs, *Army, James II*, pp. 184–92; Jones, *Revolution*, pp. 294–301; A. Browning, *Thomas Osborne, Earl of Danby and Duke of Leeds, 1632–1712*, 3 vols. (Glasgow, 1944–51), vol. 1, pp. 386–411; D. H. Hosford, *Nottingham, Nobles, and the North* (Hamden, CT, 1976), pp. 84–125; *Oxford Dictionary of National Biography*, H. C. G. Matthew and B. H. Harrison, eds, 60 vols (Oxford, 2004), vol. 23, p. 733.

6. Narcissus Luttrell, *A Brief Historical Relation of State Affairs*, 6 vols (Oxford, 1857), vol. 1, pp. 467, 474, 477, 486–88; Doctor Williams's Library, Roger Morrice, Ent'ring Book, Q. 317, 323, 348, 351; R. Wodrow, *The History of the Sufferings of the Church of Scotland*, 4 vols (Glasgow, 1829–30), vol. 4, pp. 472–5; T. Harris, *Revolution: The Great Crisis of the British Monarchy, 1685–1720* (2006), pp. 290–32, 372–78.

7. L. Schwoerer, *The Declaration of Rights, 1689* (1981), pp. 126–37; R. Beddard, 'The Unexpected Whig Revolution of 1688', in *The Revolutions of 1688*, R. Beddard, ed. (Oxford, 1991), pp. 11–47; R. Beddard, *A Kingdom without a King* (Oxford, 1988), esp. pp. 37–45, 51–4, 66ff; Jones, *Revolution*, pp. 301–13.

8. Schwoerer, *Declaration of Rights*, pp. 138–52; B. D. Henning, *The House of Commons 1660–1690*, The History of Parliament, 3 vols (1983), vol. 1, pp. 13, 27, 106–7; Speck, *Reluctant Revolutionaries*,

pp. 92–4; H. Horwitz, *Revolution Politicks: the Career of Daniel Finch, second Earl of Nottingham, 1647–1730* (Cambridge, 1968), pp. 68–73; H. Horwitz, *Parliament, Policy and Politics in the Reign of William III* (Manchester, 1977), pp. 8–9; *ODNB*, vol. 45, pp. 152–3.

9. Anchitell Grey, *Debates of the House of Commons from the year 1667 to the year 1694*, 10 vols (1763), vol. 9, pp. 6–25 (quotes at pp. 7, 20, 25); *The Correspondence of Henry Hyde, Earl of Clarendon*, S. W. Singer, ed., 2 vols (1828), vol. 2, pp. 255–6; Reresby, *Memoirs*, pp. 545–6; Bishop Gilbert Burnet, *History of His Own Time*, abr. Thomas Stackhouse, Everyman Classics (1979)., pp. 292–4; Speck, *Reluctant Revolutionaries*, pp. 96–101; Horwitz, *Nottingham*, pp.74–8; Schwoerer, *Declaration of Rights*, pp. 184–98, 203–8.

10. Grey, *Debates*, vol. 9, pp. 26–32, 46–50, 53–65 (quotes at pp. 62, 64); *Clarendon Correspondence*, vol. 2, pp. 257–62 (quote at p. 261–2); Burnet, *History*, 295–6 (quote at p. 296); Reresby, *Memoirs*, pp. 547–9, 551–2, 553; Speck, *Reluctant Revolutionaries*, pp. 101–10; Schwoerer, *Declaration of Rights*, pp. 208–20; Horwitz, *Nottingham*, pp. 78–82; Horwitz, *Parliament*, pp. 10–11; R. Weil, *Political Passions: Gender, the family and political argument in England 1680–1714* (Manchester, 1999), pp. 105–7 with quote from *Reasons for Crowning the Prince and Princess of Orange* (1689) at p. 106.

11. Grey, *Debates*, vol. 9, p. 29 (quote), 42–4, 70–83; Schwoerer, *Declaration of Rights*, pp. 199–203, 220–63, 281–300; M. Goldie, 'The Revolution of 1689 and the Structure of Political Argument', *Bulletin of Research in the Humanities*, 83 (1980), 473–564; Speck, *Reluctant Revolutionaries*, pp. 110–14; Holmes, *Great Power*, pp. 215–18; Harris, *Revolution*, pp. 329–54 presents a different interpretation.

12. *The Correspondence of the Hatton Family*, E. M. Thompson, ed., 2 vols (1978), vol. 2, p. 128; Reresby, *Memoirs*, pp. 567, 569, 570; Schwoerer, *Declaration of Rights*, pp. 299–300; J. Israel, 'William III and Toleration', in *From Persecution to Toleration: The Glorious Revolution and Religion in England*, O. P. Grell, J. I. Israel, and N. Tyacke., eds. (Oxford, 1991), pp. 151–4; D. R. Lacey, *Dissent and Parliamentary Politics in England, 1661-1689* (New Brunswick, New Jersey, 1969), pp. 232–8; Horwitz, *Nottingham*, pp. 86–95; Horwitz, *Parliament*, pp. 21–9; J. Spurr, *The Restoration Church of England, 1646-1689* (New Haven, CT, 1991), pp. 103–4; Speck, *Reluctant Revolutionaries*, pp. 185–7; C. Rose, *England in the 1690s: Revolution, Religion and War* (Oxford, 1999), pp. 161–71.

13. For the party political culture of these years, see Horwitz, *Parliament*; T. Harris, *Politics under the Later Stuarts: Party Conflict in a Divided Society 1660–1715* (1993), pp. 147–75; Rose, *1690s*, pp. 63–77; G. Holmes, *British Politics in the Age of Anne* (1967).

14. Horwitz, *Parliament*, pp. 27, 37, 53, 62; P. G. M. Dickson, *The Financial Revolution in England* (1967), p. 10; J. Brewer, *The Sinews of Power: War, Money and the English State, 1688–1783* (New York, 1989), pp. 40, 95–101.

15. Harris, *Politics*, pp. 161–9; J. H. Plumb, *The Growth of Political Stability in England, 1675–1725* (1967), pp. 136–60 (quote at p. 138); Horwitz,

Parliament, pp. 138–9, 211–12, 248–54, 265, 283–7; Brewer, *Sinews*, pp. 30, 66, 155–61; Rose, *1690s*, pp. 82–104. For the eighteenth-century state, also see especially L. Stone, 'Introduction' and J. Brewer, 'The Eighteenth-Century State' in *An Imperial Sate at War: Britain from 1689 to 1715*, L. Stone, ed. (1994), pp. 1–32, 52–71. Some 'old' or Country Whigs also remained hostile to a large standing army: L. G. Schwoerer, *'No Standing Armies!' The Antiarmy Ideology in Seventeenth-Century England* (Baltimore, MD, 1974), pp. 155–87.

16. Historical Manuscripts Commission, *Egmont*, p. 190; J. G. Simms, *Jacobite Ireland, 1685–91* (Dublin, 2000), pp. 48–57, 69–94; J. G. Simms, *War and Politics in Ireland, 1649–1730*, D. W. Hayton and G. O'Brien, eds (1986), pp. 65–90; Harris, *Revolution*, pp. 422–45; *ODNB*, vol. 53, pp. 719–20.

17. H. Murtagh, 'The War in Ireland, 1689–91', in *Kings in Conflict: the Revolutionary War in Ireland and its Aftermath*, W. A. Maguire, ed. (Belfast, 1990), pp. 61–91; D. W. Hayton, 'The Williamite Revolution in Ireland, 1688–1691', in *The Anglo-Dutch Moment*, ed. J. I. Israel (Cambridge, 1991), pp. 195-208; D. Dickson, *New Foundations; Ireland 1660–1800*, 2nd. ed. (Dublin, 2000), pp. 31–42; Simms, *War and Politics*, pp. 213–24; Simms, *Jacobite Ireland*; R. Doherty, *The Williamite War in Ireland, 1688–1691* (Dublin, 1998).

18. J. I. McGuire, 'The Irish Parliament of 1692', in *Penal Era and Golden Age: Essays in Irish History, 1690–1800*, T. Bartlett and D. W. Hayton, eds (Belfast, 1979), pp. 1–31; S. J. Connolly, 'The Penal Laws', in *Kings in Conflict*, W. A. Maguire, ed., pp. 160–5; S. J. Connolly, *Religion, Law, and Power: the Making of Protestant Ireland 1660–1760* (Oxford, 1992), pp. 149–59; Simms, *War and Politics*, pp. 225–50, 263–76; P. Kelly, 'Ireland and the Glorious Revolution: From Kingdom to Colony', in *Revolutions of 1688*, R. Beddard, ed., pp. 175–86; C. I. McGrath, 'Securing the Protestant Interest: the Origins and Purpose of the Penal Laws of 1695', *IHS*, 30 (1996), 25–46; D. W. Hayton, *Ruling Ireland, 1685–1742; Politics, Politicians and Parties* (Woodbridge, Suffolk, 2004), pp. 40–62; Rose, *1690s*, pp. 218–26; Dickson, *New Foundations*, pp. 42–6.

19. J. C. Beckett, *Protestant Dissent in Ireland 1687–1780* (1948), pp. 27–39; R. L. Greaves, *God's Other Children: Protestant Nonconformists and the Emergence of Denominational Churches in Ireland, 1660–1700* (Stanford, CA, 1997), pp. 141–58; Connolly, *Religion, Law, and Power*, pp. 159–71, 307–13; Rose, *1690s*, pp. 226–33; P. Kilroy, *Protestant Dissent and Controversy in Ireland 1660–1714* (Cork, 1994), pp. 26, 188–93.

20. Connolly, 'Penal Laws', pp. 162, 169–72; W. A. Maguire, 'The Land Settlement', in *Kings in Conflict*, W. A. Maguire, ed., pp. 142–6.

21. William Molyneux, *The Case for Ireland's being bound by Acts of Parliament in England Stated* (Dublin, 1698); *Journals of the House of Commons*, vol. 12, p. 331; Rose, *1690s*, pp. 248–57; Hayton, *Ruling Ireland*, esp. chapts 2–3, 5, 7–8; Connolly, *Religion, Law, and Power*, pp. 74–97, 105–9; Simms, *War and Politics*, pp. 251–61; Kelly, 'Glorious Revolution', pp. 186–90; D. Dickson, *New Foundations*, pp. 48–106.

22. Wodrow, *Sufferings*, vol. 4, pp. 481–2; Harris, *Revolution*, pp. 376–8, 382, 412; I. Cowan, *The Scottish Covenanters, 1660–1688* (1976), p. 134; I. B. Cowan, 'The Reluctant Revolutionaries: Scotland in 1688', in *By Force or by Default? The Revolution of 1688–1689*, E. Cruickshanks, ed. (Edinburgh, 1989), p. 74.

23. *A Source Book of Scottish History*, 3 vols, 2nd ed. (1961), vol. 3, pp. 203–7; J. Halliday, 'The Club and the Revolution in Scotland, 1689–90', *Scottish Historical Review*, 45 (1966), 143–5; I. B. Cowan, 'Church and State Reformed? The Revolution of 1688–89 in Scotland', in *The Anglo-Dutch Moment*, J. I. Israel, ed., pp. 164–6; J. R. Young, 'The Scottish Parliament and the Covenanting herit-age of Constitutional Reform' in *The Stuart Kingdoms in the Seven-teenth Century*, A. I. Macinnes and J. Ohlmeyer, eds (Dublin, 2002), pp. 230–4; Harris, *Revolution*, pp. 390–406; W. Ferguson, *Scotland, 1689 to the Present* (Edinburgh, 1968), pp. 2–6. But see C. Jackson, *Restoration Scotland, 1660–1690: Royalist Politics, Religion and Ideas* (Woodbridge, Suffolk, 2003), pp. 191–203, for important qualifica-tions to the idea that Scots revolutionaries understood their revolu-tion in contractual terms.

24. J. Halliday, 'Club', pp. 145–59; Cowan, 'Church and State Reformed', pp. 166–74; Young, 'Scottish Parliament', pp. 235–42. Some Club members turned Jacobite in frustration with William's moderation.

25. P. W. J. Riley, *King William and the Scottish Politicians* (Edinburgh, 1979).

26. *ODNB*, vol. 23, pp. 218–20; P. Hopkins, *Glencoe and the End of the Highland War* (Edinburgh, 1986), esp. chapts 4–5, 7, 10.

27. *Scottish Source Book*, vol. 3, pp. 213–19; Cowan, 'Church and State', pp. 174–83; Cowan, *Covenanters*, pp. 135–47; Rose, *1690s*, pp. 212–18; T. Clarke, 'The Williamite Episcopalians and the Glorious Revolution in Scotland', *Records of the Scottish Church History Society*, 24 (1990), 33–51.

28. Rose, *1690s*, pp. 233–48; Ferguson, *Scotland*, pp. 27–39; G. P. Insh, *The Company of Scotland Trading to Africa and the Indies* (1932); Riley, *Scottish Politicians*, pp. 125–64; *ODNB*, vol. 43, p. 28.

29. Ferguson, *Scotland*, pp. 28–53, 59; P. W. J. Riley, *The Union of England and Scotland* (Manchester, 1978).

30. *The Glorious Revolution in America*, M. G. Hall, L. H. Leder, and M. G. Kammen, eds (Chapel Hill, NC, 1964), pp. 39–40, 42–6, 109–10, 171–5; *Narratives of the Insurrections, 1675–1690*, C. M. Andrews, ed. (New York, 1915), pp. 186–90, 305–14; A. Taylor, *American Colonies* (New York, 2001), pp. 278–300; D. S. Lovejoy, *The Glorious Revolution in America* (New York, 1972), pp. 235–311; R. R. Johnson, 'The Revolution of 1688–89 in the American Colonies', in *The Anglo-Dutch Moment*, J. I. Israel, ed., pp. 215–40; K. G. Davies, 'The Revolutions in America' in *The Revolutions of 1688*, R. Beddard, ed. (Oxford, 1991), pp. 246–70.

31. D. C. Coleman, *The Economy of England, 1540–1750* (Oxford, 1977), p. 133; Holmes, *Great Power*, pp. 295–9; D. W. Jones, 'Sequel to

Revolution: the Economics of England's Emergence as a Great Power, 1688–1712', and K. N. Chaudhuri and J. I. Israel, 'The English and Dutch East India Companies and the Glorious Revolution of 1688-89', in *The Anglo-Dutch Moment*, J. I. Israel, ed., pp. 389–438; D. W. Jones, *War and Economy in the Age of William III and Marlborough* (Oxford, 1988); L. Colley, *Britons: Forging the Nation 1707–1837* (New Haven, CT, 1992), pp. 117–32.

32. Brewer, *Sinews*, pp. 95–9; P. G. M. Dickson, *Financial Revolution*, pp. 10, 39–75, 262, 271; G. S. De Krey, *A Fractured Society: the Politics of London in the First Age of Party, 1688–1715* (Oxford, 1985), pp. 121–65.

33. Horwitz, *Parliament*, pp. 280, 282; P. Gauci, *The Politics of Trade: the Overseas Merchant in State and Society, 1660–1720* (Oxford, 2001), pp. 198–200; The History of Parliament, *The House of Commons 1690–1715*, D. W. Hayton, ed., 5 vols (Cambridge, 2002), vol. 1, pp. 300–11; De Krey, *Fractured Society*, pp. 101–12; H. J. Habakkuk, 'English Landownership, 1680–1740', *Economic History Review*, 10 (Feb. 1940), 2–17; C. Clay, 'Marriage, Inheritance, and the Rise of Large Estates in England, 1660–1815', *EcHR*, NS, 21 (Dec. 1968), 503–18; L. Stone and J. C. F. Stone, *An Open Elite? England 1640–1880* (Oxford, 1984), pp. 211–21; N. Rogers, 'Money, Land and Lineage: the Big Bourgeoisie of Hanoverian London', *Social History*, 4 (1979), 437–54; Holmes, *Great Power*, pp. 280–6.

34. G. C. Gibbs, 'The Revolution in Foreign Policy', in *Britain after the Glorious Revolution 1689–1714*, ed. G. Holmes (1969), pp. 59–79.

35. Horwitz, *Parliament*, pp. 113–14, 152–3; M. Knights, *Representation and Misrepresentation in Later Stuart Britain: Partisanship and Political Culture* (Oxford, 2005), p. 16.

36. Holmes, *British Politics*, pp. 30–3; De Krey, *Fractured Society*, pp. 213–22; Knights, *Representation*, pp. 220–71.

37. Henry Sacheverell, *The Political Union* (Oxford, 1702), quoted in G. Holmes, *The Trial of Doctor Sacheverell* (1973), p. 17; Hayton, *Commons*, vol. 1, pp. 311–16; M. Watts, *The Dissenters from the Reformation to the French Revolution* (Oxford, 1978), pp. 262–303, 371–93; Rose, *1690s*, pp. 171–8.

38. G. V. Bennett, 'King William III and the Episcopate', in *Essays in Modern English Church History*, G. V. Bennett and J. D. Walsh, eds (Oxford, 1966), pp. 104–31; Rose, *1690s*, pp. 152–60, 182–3, 190–4; Holmes, *Sacheverell*, pp. 21–41; J. Marshall, *John Locke: Resistance, Religion and Responsibility* (Cambridge, 1994), pp. 373–4.

39. J. A. I. Champion, *The Pillars of Priestcraft Shaken: the Church of England and its Enemies, 1660–1730* (Cambridge, 1992), esp. pp. 125–6, 176–7; *ODNB*, vol. 54, pp. 894–6; R. H. Popkin, 'The Deist Challenge', in *From Persecution to Toleration*, O. P. Grell, J. I. Israel, and N. Tyacke, eds, pp. 195–215; B. Worden, 'The Revolution of 1688–89 and the English Republican Tradition', in *Anglo-Dutch Moment*, ed. J. I. Israel, pp. 241–77; M. Goldie, 'Priestcraft and the Birth of Whiggism', in *Political Discourse in Early Modern Britain*, N. Phillipson and Q. Skinner, eds (Cambridge, 1993), pp. 209–31; Rose, *1690s*, pp. 175–82.

40.	T. Claydon, *William III and the Godly Revolution* (Cambridge, 1996), esp. pp. 28–63, 90–121; T. C. Curtis and W. A. Speck, 'The Societies for Reformation of Manners: a Case Study in the Theory and Practice of Moral Reform', *Literature and History*, 3 (1976), 45–64; M.C. Jacob, *The Newtonians and the English Revolution 1689–1720* (Ithaca, NY, 1976), pp. 137, 178–200; Rose, *1690s*, pp. 18–28, 182–9, 195–209.

41.	R. Ashcraft, and M. M. Goldsmith, 'Revolution Principles and the Formation of Whig Ideology, '*HJ*, 26, 4 (1983), pp. 773–800; J. C. D. Clark, *English Society 1688–1832: Ideology, Social Structure and Political Practice during the Ancien Regime* (Cambridge, 1985), pp. 119–61; *The Reception of Locke's Politics*, ed. M. Goldie, 6 vols (1999), esp. vols 1–2.

Select Bibliography

The place of publication of books is London, unless otherwise noted.

The Anglo-Dutch Moment, ed. J. I. Israel (Cambridge, 1991).

Baxter, S. B. *William III* (1966).

Brewer, J. *The Sinews of Power: War, Money and the English State, 1688–1783* (New York, 1989).

Buckroyd, J. *Church and State in Scotland, 1660–1681* (Edinburgh, 1980).

Champion, J. A. I. *The Pillars of Priestcraft Shaken: the Church of England and its Enemies, 1660–1730* (Cambridge, 1992).

Claydon, T. *William III and the Godly Revolution* (Cambridge, 1996).

Connolly, S. J. *Religion, Law, and Power: the Making of Protestant Ireland 1660–1760* (Oxford, 1992).

Cowan, I. *The Scottish Covenanters, 1660–1688* (1976).

De Krey, G. S. *A Fractured Society: the Politics of London in the First Age of Party, 1688–1715* (Oxford, 1985).

———. *London and the Restoration, 1659–1683* (Cambridge, 2005).

———. 'Rethinking the Restoration: Dissenting Cases for Conscience, 1667–1672', *Historical Journal*, 38 (1995), 53–83.

Dickson, P. G. M. *The Financial Revolution in England* (1967).

Fear, Exclusion and Revolution: Roger Morrice and Britain in the 1680s, J. McElligott, ed. (Ashgate, 2006).

From Persecution to Toleration: the Glorious Revolution and Religion in England, O. P. Grell, J. I. Israel, and N. Tyacke, eds (Oxford, 1991).

Gauci, P. *Politics and Society in Great Yarmouth 1660–1722* (Oxford, 1996).

———. *The Politics of Trade: the Overseas Merchant in State and Society, 1660–1720* (Oxford, 2001).

Goldie, M. 'John Locke and Anglican Royalism', *Political Studies*, 31 (1983), 61–85.

———. 'John Locke's Circle and James II', *Historical Journal*, 35 (Sept., 1992), 557–86.

———. 'The Revolution of 1689 and the Structure of Political Argument', *Bulletin of Research in the Humanities*, 83 (1980), 473–564.

Greaves, R. L. *God's Other Children: Protestant Nonconformists and the Emergence of Denominational Churches in Ireland, 1660–1700* (Stanford, CA, 1997).

———. *Secrets of the Kingdom: British Radicals from the Popish Plot to the Revolution of 1688–89* (Stanford, 1992).

Haley, K. H. D. *The First Earl of Shaftesbury* (Oxford, 1968).

337

Halliday, J. 'The Club and the Revolution in Scotland, 1689–90', *Scottish Historical Review*, 45 (1966), 143–59.

Halliday, P. D. *Dismembering the Body Politic: Partisan Politics in England's Towns, 1650–1730* (Cambridge, 1998).

Harris, T. *London Crowds in the Reign of Charles II* (Cambridge, 1987).

———. *Restoration: Charles II and his Kingdoms* (2005).

———. *Revolution: The Great Crisis of the British Monarchy, 1685–1720* (2006).

Hayton, D. W. *Ruling Ireland, 1685–1742: Politics, Politicians and Parties* (Woodbridge, Suffolk, 2004).

Horwitz, H. *Parliament, Policy and Politics in the Reign of William III* (Manchester, 1977).

———. *Revolution Politicks: the Career of Daniel Finch, second Earl of Nottingham, 1647–1730* (Cambridge, 1968).

Hutton, R. *Charles II, King of England, Scotland, and Ireland* (Cambridge, 1989).

———. *The Restoration: A Political and Religious History of England and Wales, 1658–1667* (Oxford, 1985).

Jackson, C. *Restoration Scotland, 1660–1690: Royalist Politics, Religion and Ideas* (Woodbridge, Suffolk, 2003).

Johnson, R. R. *Adjustment to Empire: the New England Colonies, 1675–1715* (New Brunswick, NJ, 1981).

Jones, J. R. *The First Whigs: the Politics of the Exclusion Crisis, 1678–83*, rev. ed. (1970).

———. *The Revolution of 1688 in England* (1972).

Keeble, N. H. *The Restoration: England in the 1660s* (Oxford, 2002).

Kenyon, J. P. *Robert Spencer, Earl of Sunderland, 1641–1702* (1958).

Kilroy, P. *Protestant Dissent and Controversy in Ireland, 1660–1714* (Cork, 1994).

Knights, M. *Politics and Opinion in Crisis, 1678–81* (Cambridge, 1994).

———. *Representation and Misrepresentation in Later Stuart Britain: Partisanship and Political Culture* (Oxford, 2005).

Lovejoy, D. S. *The Glorious Revolution in America* (New York, 1972).

Marshall, A. *The Age of Faction; Court Politics, 1660–1702* (Manchester, 1999).

———. *Intelligence and Espionage in the Reign of Charles II, 1660–1685* (Cambridge, 1994).

Marshall, J. *John Locke: Resistance, Religion and Responsibility* (Cambridge, 1994).

McGuire, J. I. 'The Dublin Convention, the Protestant Community and the emergence of an Ecclesiastical Settlement in 1660', in *Parliament & Community*, A. Cosgrove and J. I. McGuire, eds, (Belfast, 1983), pp. 121–46.

Miller, J. 'The Crown and the Borough Charters in the Reign, of Charles II', *English Historical Review*, 100 (1985), 53–84.

———. 'The Potential for "Absolutism" in Later Stuart England,' *History*, 69 (June, 1984), 187–207.

———. *Popery & Politics in England 1660–1688* (Cambridge, 1973).

Morrill, J. 'The British Problem, *c.* 1534–1707', in *The British Problem, c. 1534–1707: State Formation in the Atlantic Archipelago*, B. Bradshaw and J. Morrill, eds (Basingstoke, 1996), pp. 1–38.

A Nation Transformed: England after the Restoration, A. Houston and S. Pincus, eds (Cambridge, 2001).

A New History of Ireland, T. W. Moody, F. X. Martin, and F. J. Byrne, eds, vol. 3, *Early Modern Ireland 1534–1691* (Oxford, 1976).

Pincus, S. C. A. '"Coffee Politicians Does Create": Coffeehouses and Restoration Political Culture', *Journal of Modern History*, 67 (1995), 807–34.

———. *Protestantism and Patriotism: Ideologies and the making of English Foreign Policy, 1650–1668* (Cambridge, 1996).

Plumb, J. H. *The Growth of Political Stability in England, 1675–1725* (1967).

Politics and the Political Imagination in Later Stuart Britain, H. Nenner, ed. (Rochester, NY, 1997).

The Politics of Religion in Restoration England, T. Harris, P. Seaward, and M. Goldie, eds (Oxford, 1990).

The Revolutions of 1688, R. Beddard, ed (Oxford, 1991).

Riley, P. W. J. *King William and the Scottish Politicians* (Edinburgh, 1979).

Rose, C. *England in the 1690s: Revolution, Religion and War* (Oxford, 1999).

Schwoerer, L. G. *The Declaration of Rights, 1689* (1981).

———. *The Ingenious Mr. Henry Care, Restoration Publicist* (Baltimore, 2001).

———. *'No Standing Armies!' The Antiarmy Ideology in Seventeenth-Century England* (Baltimore, 1974).

Scott, J. *Algernon Sidney and the Restoration Crisis, 1677–1683* (Cambridge, 1991).

Seaward, P. *The Cavalier Parliament and the Reconstruction of the Old Regime, 1661–1667* (Cambridge, 1988).

Simms, J. G. *Jacobite Ireland, 1685–91* (Dublin, 2000).

———. *War and Politics in Ireland, 1649–1730*, D. W. Hayton and G. O'Brien, eds (1986).

Speck, W. A. *James II* (2002).

———. *Reluctant Revolutionaries: Englishmen and the Revolution of 1688* (Oxford, 1989).

Spurr, J. *England in the 1670s: 'This Masquerading Age'* (Oxford, 2000).

———. '"Latitudinarianism" and the Restoration Church', *HJ*, 31 (March, 1988), 61–82.

———. *The Restoration Church of England, 1646–1689* (New Haven, CT, 1991).

Swatland, A. *The House of Lords in the Reign of Charles II* (Cambridge, 1996).

Weil, R. *Political Passions: Gender, the Family and Political Argument in England, 1680–1714* (Manchester, 1999).

Young, J. R. 'The Scottish Parliament and the Covenanting heritage of Constitutional Reform' in *The Stuart Kingdoms in the Seventeenth Century*, A. I. Macinnes and J. Ohlmeyer, eds (Dublin, 2002), pp. 226-50.

Zook, M. *Radical Whigs and Conspiratorial Politics in Late Stuart England* (University Park, PA, 1999).

Index